Relational Justice

Hanoch Dagan is the Elizabeth J. Boalt Distinguished Professor of Law and the founding Director of the Berkeley Center for Private Law Theory. Dagan has written eight books, including *The Choice Theory of Contracts* (2017), *A Liberal Theory of Property* (2021), and *Advanced Introduction to Private Law Theory* (2026), and has published over 140 articles in major law reviews and journals. He edited six books, including *Research Handbook on Private Law Theory* (2020) (with Benjamin Zipursky). Before joining Berkeley, Dagan was the Stewart and Judy Colton Professor of Legal Theory and Innovation and the Director of the Edmond J. Safra Center for Ethics at Tel-Aviv University. He has been a visiting professor at Yale, Columbia, Michigan, Cornell, UCLA, and Toronto, and delivered keynote speeches and endowed lectures in Singapore, Alabama, Toronto, Queensland, Cape Town, Monash, and Oxford.

Avihay Dorfman is "The Friends of Joe Jamail" Regents Chair in Law and Founding Academic Director of the Private Law Theory Program at the University of Texas at Austin School of Law. Dorfman is the author of *Reclaiming the Public* (2024) and, most recently, *Conflict between Equals: Tort Law beyond Wrong, Harm, and Cost* (2026). His work focuses on the conceptual and normative foundations of law. He has written on fundamental questions in private law theory and doctrine as well as on the morality of public ordering, including privatization, public property, institutional pluralism, and political authority. Before joining Texas, Dorfman was a law professor at Tel Aviv University. Dorfman is a graduate of Yale Law School and a former law clerk to the (then) Chief Justice Aharon Barak. He has been a visiting professor at Harvard and Cornell.

OXFORD PRIVATE LAW THEORY

Oxford Private Law Theory publishes leading work in private law theory. It commissions and solicits monographs and edited collections in general private law theory as well as specific fields, including the theoretical analysis of tort law, property law, contract law, fiduciary law, trust law, remedies and restitution, and the law of equity. The series is open to diverse theoretical approaches, including those informed by philosophy, economics, history, and political theory. Oxford Private Law Theory sets the standard for rigorous and original work in private law theory.

ALSO PUBLISHED IN THIS SERIES

Rights, Wrongs, and Injustices
The Structure of Remedial Law
Stephen A Smith

Civil Wrongs and Justice in Private Law
Edited by Paul B Miller and John Oberdiek

Private Law and Practical Reason
Essays on John Gardner's Private Law Theory
Edited by Haris Psarras and Sandy Steel

Standing in Private Law
Powers of Enforcement in the Law of Obligations and Trusts
Edited by Timothy Liau

Relational Justice

A Theory of Private Law

HANOCH DAGAN
The Elizabeth J. Boalt Distinguished Professor of Law and founding Director of the Berkeley Center for Private Law Theory, University of California, Berkeley, School of Law

AVIHAY DORFMAN
"The Friends of Joe Jamail" Regents Chair in Law and Founding Academic Director of the Private Law Theory Program at the University of Texas at Austin School of Law

OXFORD
UNIVERSITY PRESS

OXFORD
UNIVERSITY PRESS

Great Clarendon Street, Oxford, OX2 6DP,
United Kingdom

Oxford University Press is a department of the University of Oxford.
It furthers the University's objective of excellence in research, scholarship,
and education by publishing worldwide. Oxford is a registered trade mark of
Oxford University Press in the UK and in certain other countries.

First Edition published in 2024

First published in paperback in 2026

Published in the United States of America by Oxford University Press
546 Fifth Avenue, New York, NY 10036, United States of America

British Library Cataloguing in Publication Data
Data available

Library of Congress Control Number: 2024934052

ISBN 9780198876229 (hbk.)
ISBN 9780197921425 (pbk.)

DOI: 10.1093/ 9780191987762.001.0001

The manufacturer's authorized representative in the EU for product safety is
Oxford University Press España S.A. of Parque Empresarial San Fernando de Henares,
Avenida de Castilla, 2 – 28830 Madrid (www.oup.es/en or product.safety@oup.com).
OUP España S.A. also acts as importer into Spain of products made by the manufacturer.

Advance Praise

Relational Justice delivers on its sweeping promise to offer a unifying theory of private law. It does so by examining fundamental questions about how citizens in a liberal state should treat one another, and then linking its theoretical conclusions with concrete examples of how the state can provide the legal framework for just interpersonal relationships. The project is animated by a sense of deep moral urgency, and the theory that Dagan and Dorfman offer should indeed help advance the moral imperatives to which they respond.

—Aditi Bagchi, Wilkinson Professor of Law, Fordham University

Dagan and Dorfman present a conceptually coherent vision of private law arguing that it should, and to a significant degree already does, abide by the fundamental maxim of reciprocal respect for self-determination and substantive equality. This is the best book we have, not just on the distinctive significance and core intellectual principles of private law, but also on its heart and soul.

—Thomas Gutmann, Chair for Private Law and Legal Philosophy,
University of Muenster

Going against the grain of fragmentation and relativism in contemporary private law and its theory, Dagan and Dorfman offer a comprehensive account with universal vocation of how the law should contribute to just interpersonal relations. This is grand theory at its best.

—Martijn Hesselink, Professor of Transnational Law and Theory,
European University Institute

Relational Justice makes a fundamental contribution toward shifting the dominant theory of private law scholarship away from the view that private law is all about wealth and consequences, and toward the view that private law is about what we owe to one another in some of our most important and pervasive interpersonal relationships. *Relational Justice* bills itself as a theory of private law but, in a tribute to the fertility of the conception it advances, the book ranges beyond private law to illuminate legal domains as diverse as discrimination and workplace safety. By synthesizing and extending a decade's worth of influential scholarship, *Relational Justice* makes clear the richness, the range, the perceptiveness—and the importance—of Hanoch Dagan's and Avihay Dorfman's theory of private law.

—Gregory C. Keating, William T. Dalessi Professor of Law and
Philosophy, USC Gould School of Law

Relational Justice proposes a wholesale renovation of private law. Familiar theories remain caught between two equal but opposite vices: a quietist commitment to restoring the status quo and flat-footed reduction of private law into a tool of public justice. Now Dagan and Dorfman argue that law should help people to establish reciprocal respect for self-determination and substantive equality, one private relationship at a time. They then apply this overarching insight to reconstruct all of private law doctrine, across both conventional topics—including remedies, negligence, and good faith—and unconventional ones—including poverty, discrimination, and even workplace safety. This is a hugely creative and ambitious book.

—Daniel Markovits, Guido Calabresi Professor of Law, Yale Law School

The limelight of legal scholarship seems to be focusing once again on the significance of private law within a wider political economy, drawing as much on ethical-relational exploration of care or human rights as on recent moves in the opposite direction of neo-formalism. Dagan and Dorfman's ambitious and fascinating book joins forces with the former, standing out however by its unusual plea for the responsibility of private law theory to make explicit private law's core normative commitments in respect of pre-distributional, structural justice toward the poor, the marginalized, and the foreign. Interestingly in this latter respect, their argument also resonates with current attempts on the private international scene to engage responsibly with natural and cultural alterity in legal terms.

—Horatia Muir Watt, Professor of Law, Sciences Po Law School (Paris)

In this important book, Dagan and Dorfman argue that private law, at its core, is not about markets or power, but about relational justice. Private law in theory and practice enables individuals to organize their horizontal relations with one another, unburdened by the demands of collective politics. The book is a must read for anybody who wishes to construct a just order from the deeply fractured order of capitalism.

—Katharina Pistor, Edwin B. Parker Professor of Comparative Law,
Columbia Law School

If you think that the ideas of self-determination and substantive equality are too abstract or malleable to support a unifying account of private law, *Relational Justice* is the best attempt to convince you otherwise. No other work in private law theory treats those ideas in so deep, insightful, and carefully balanced manner, or derives more practical mileage from them. As the culmination of Dagan and Dorfman's pioneering research, this book is both a major reference point and the seed for fruitful new lines of thought.

—Emmanuel Voyiakis, Professor of Law, LSE Law School

In this remarkable book, Professors Dagan and Dorfman provide a compelling case for strengthening the presently threadbare theory of justice that underlies private law. *Relational Justice*, they argue—meaning, the justice required of and for people in relation with each other—is the conception of justice served, although incompletely and imperfectly, by vast swaths of private law. The authors show that this conception of relational justice provides a far stronger rationale than either efficiency or distributive justice for many of our current legal doctrines that originate in public law but that most impact and limit contracting behavior, such as, for example, minimum wage and workplace safety laws in the workplace, warranties of habitability in landlord-tenant law, and anti-discrimination laws at work and school. A full understanding of the demands of relational justice, however, the authors argue, also requires a thorough remaking of the obligations of market actors to accommodate the autonomy and substantive equality of the poor.

The book is a breakthrough achievement, first for showing the sheer need for some sort of theory of justice that might make our private law intelligible, and then for proposing one. The theory of relational justice the authors propose is morally attractive, and the proposed reforms they claim it requires are provocative, well-reasoned, and attainable. Their account will convince many, and will move others who may not be convinced by the theory's particulars to propose alternatives. The result will be a conversation which is long overdue.

—Robin West, Professor of Law, Emerita, Georgetown University Law Center

To the Memory of My Parents
H.D.

To Einat, my love, for everything
A.D.

Acknowledgments

This book is the culmination of our extensive co-authorship. Hopefully, it presents a systematic and cohesive statement of a distinctive account of private law we have developed for over a decade. So, while it includes a substantial amount of new writing, some of its sections draw on our prior work, though at times with significant revisions. We thus gratefully acknowledge permission to include materials from *Just Relationships*, 116 Colum. L. Rev. 1395 (2016); *Negligence and Accommodation*, 22 Legal Theory 77 (2016); *Postscript to* Just Relationships*: Reply to Gardner, West, and Zipursky*, 117 Colum. L. Rev. Online 261 (2017); *Against Private Law Escapism: Comment on Arthur Ripstein,* Private Wrongs, 14 Jerusalem Rev. Legal Stud. 37 (2017); *Justice in Private: Beyond the Rawlsian Framework*, 37 L. & Phil. 171 (2018); *Interpersonal Human Rights*, 51 Cornell Int'l L.J. 361 (2018); *Justice, Politics, and Interpersonal Human Rights*, 51 Cornell Int'l L.J. Online 139 (2018); *Reply to Commentators: Relational Justice—On Legal, Political, and Critical Theory*, 41 Tel-Aviv U.L. Rev. 439 (2019) [in Hebrew]; *Substantive Remedies*, 96 Notre Dame L. Rev. (2020); *Autonomy, Relational Justice, and Restitution, in* Research Handbook on Unjust Enrichment and Restitution 219 (Elise Bant et al. eds., 2020); *Relational Justice and Torts, in* Research Handbook on Private Law Theory (Hanoch Dagan & Benjamin Zipursky eds., 2020); *The Domain of Private Law*, 71 U. Toronto L.J. 207 (2021); *Justice in Contracts*, 67 Am. J. Jurisprudence 1 (2022); *Precontractual Justice*, 28 Legal Theory 89 (2022); *Public Nuisance for Private Law*, 73 U. Toronto L.J. 198 (2024); *Poverty and Private Law: Beyond Distributive Justice*, 68 Am. J. Jurisprudence 229 (2023); *The Tort of Discrimination*, 16(2) J. Tort L. 393 (2023); *From Civil Recourse to Class Actions: Comments on John Goldberg & Benjamin Zipursky's* Recognizing Wrongs, 57 Jerusalem Rev. Legal Stud. 27 (2023); and *Private Law and the Embedded Person, in* The Future of The Person (Hans-Wolfgang Micklitz & Giuseppe Vettori eds., 2024).

These papers benefited from comments by many colleagues as well as by workshop and conference participants in Amsterdam, Bar-Ilan, Columbia, Cornell, Duke, Firenze, EUI, Hebrew, IDC, Georgetown, Maryland, NYU, Oxford, Tel-Aviv, Texas, Toronto, Western, Wharton, and Yale. Particular gratitude goes to Roxana Banu, Yitzhak Benbaji, Evan Fox-Decent, John Gardner, Mitchel Lasser, Sarah Hamill, Ralf Michaels, Ariel Porat, Manal Totry-Jubran, Horatia Muir Watt, Robin West, and Ben Zipursky for their published critical responses.

For very helpful comments on this manuscript or parts of it we are deeply grateful to Ron Aboodi, Marietta Auer, Lisa Austin, Ronen Avraham, Aditi Bagchi,

Roderick Bagshaw, Marija Bartl, Debadatta Bose, Andrew Botterell, Sue Bright, Alan Brudner, Alex Bryan, Erwin Chemerinsky, Mindy Chen-Wishart, Tom Christiano, Hugh Collins, Nico Cornell, Yaron Covo, Natalie Davidson, Seth Davis, Matt Dyson, Erik Encarnacion, David Enoch, Rachel Friedman, Victoria Garin, Mark Geistfeld, Adi Goldiner, James Goudkamp, Jon Gould, Thomas Gutmann, Daphna Hacker, Andrew Halpin, Sarah Hamill, Alon Harel, Lisa Herzog, Martijn Hesselink, Nien-hê Hsieh, Felipe Jiménez, Mirthe Jiwa, Julian Jonker, Yotam Kaplan, Lorenz Kähler, Ciara Kennefick, David Kershaw, Tom Kohavi, Roy Kreitner, Tamar Kricheli-Katz, Chris Kutz, Tim Liau, Nethanel Lipshitz, Bertram Lomfeld, Paul MacMahon, Daniel Markovits, Colin Mayer, Chris Mills, Jennifer Nadler, Donal Nolan, Szymon Osmola, Katharina Pistor, Yaniv Ron-El, Florian Rödl, Arie Rosen, Luke Rostill, Nick Sage, Irit Samet, Amy Sepinwall, Assaf Sharon, Igor Shoikhedbrod, Sandy Steel, Batya Stein, Rob Stevens, Rebecca Stone, Talha Syed, Emmanuel Voyiakis, Charlie Webb, Brad Wendel, Thomas Wilhelmsson, Ben Zipursky, and participants at the Safra-Wharton Conference on the Normative Foundations of the Market as well as workshops and pre-book colloquia at Berkeley Law School, the European University Institute, London School of Economics, Max Planck Institute for Legal History and Legal Theory, Oxford Law School, and Tel-Aviv University Faculty of Law.

Contents

PART III THE FAMILIAR TERRAIN

PART IV BEYOND THE FAMILIAR

PART V CONCLUSION

Part I

Introduction

1
The Law of Just Relationships

Relational Justice

Private law is the law of interpersonal relationships. It structures (a significant subset of) the horizontal interactions of people in their personal capacity, as opposed to their capacity as citizens, as members of a given political community, or as holders of political authority. Whether judge-made or statutory, private law sets up the terms of these interactions rather than merely responding ex post facto to instances of wrongdoing by adjudicating the disputing claims of parties in a particular interaction. Its ambition, then, is both constructive and prospective. Instead of merely addressing wrongful encounters, say, between a driver and a pedestrian, private law constructs edifices of human relationships. The terms of the interactions it prescribes are thus typically prospective: they often set the preconditions for just horizontal interactions.

Private law doctrines also affect public concerns, such as distributive justice, democratic equality, or aggregate welfare. But private law's distinctive role, its core responsibility, is the structuring of our private, social, and economic life as opposed to our life as members of a political community, and its doctrines touch on the ways we live and interact in the world as private persons instead of as citizens. Rather than the outgrowth of the state, this role of private law is manifest in the trans-national interactions increasingly typical of our lives and no less apparent in the relationships within states—in the market, the workplace, the great outdoors, the neighborhood, and the road (to mention but a few obvious loci).

The implication is that our understanding of the nature of private law, its proper domain, and the values it should vindicate or promote is critical. Whether explicitly articulated or implicitly assumed, this understanding underlies the "specific language" that legislators, judges, lawyers, and academics draw on when making claims about what the law is and how it should be reformed. The language is specific in being typical of (and in some theories exclusive to) its domain of application and, by implication, less typical outside of it. Thus, its effect on how rules are set, interpreted, applied, and reformed is substantive rather than merely semantic. In short, the specific language of private law forms a normative web of ideas and ideals about the powers and responsibilities that inform vast swaths of our everyday lives.[1]

Consider a gathering at someone's home. The host serves the guests alcoholic beverages and maintains the supply of drinks even though some of them are visibly

Relational Justice. Hanoch Dagan and Avihay Dorfman, Oxford University Press. © Hanoch Dagan and Avihay Dorfman 2024.
DOI: 10.1093/9780191987762.003.0001

intoxicated. One of these guests, when driving home, accidentally crashes into another driver. Current law says that the host does not owe a duty of reasonable care to the injured person. We argue that they should.

Or think about prenuptial agreements that opt out of default rules governing marital property in a highly prejudicial way to women. Currently, most courts do not use the duress doctrine to invalidate such a prenup, even if it was signed closely before the marriage or when a spouse cannot afford independent legal counsel. Again, we contend that, in proper cases, duress can and should be invoked as a vitiating factor.

Our discussion of these examples in Chapters 6 and 9—and of many others we address below—draws on the theory of private law we develop and defend in this book. We argue that private law should, and to a significant degree already does, abide by the fundamental maxim of reciprocal respect for self-determination and substantive equality we refer to as relational justice.

This maxim concerns the two basic commitments (or organizing values) of any liberal legal order.[2] At this point, it seems fit to clarify how we understand these commitments in this book. When we write that people are entitled to a private law supportive of their self-determination, we mean that law should go beyond respecting their capacity for uncoerced choice to proactively support their ability to shape a life they can view as their own. Hence, it is legitimate for private law, and at times even required, to impose on others (such as the host in our first example) certain—limited—affirmative obligations.

Substantive equality, in turn, stands for the egalitarian ideal of relating to other persons as equals. It thus requires that private law's terms of interaction reflect, rather than disregard, certain differences between the parties. Two types of differences closely related to self-determination are particularly significant. One concerns the qualitative distinction between sheer preferences as opposed to the features and choices that make us who we are. Another touches on imbalances of power and vulnerability (as in our prenup example).

We argue that these two commitments—to self-determination and to substantive equality—ground the basic rights and powers that make up the domain of private law and, further, help to assess what counts as just terms of interactions. We do not suggest that collectivist goals like distributive justice, democratic citizenship, or aggregate welfare must be excluded from the domain of private law. As citizens, people are justifiably required to support just legal institutions at the national level. But this obligation must not overshadow the distinctive significance of private law that, more than any other legal realm, underpins our quotidian interactions in a range of social and economic spheres such as family, work, community, commerce, and the great outdoors. These interactions play a crucial role in people's lives, and private law brings a unique set of considerations to bear on this social and economic reality.

To see why these considerations must rely on self-determination and substantive equality, we need to zoom in on the circumstances of justice, namely, the circumstances wherein the question of justice first arises in private law contexts. Two facts about the human condition stand out. The first is that our practical affairs are interdependent and replete with interactions, some voluntary and others involuntary, some transformative and others trivial. The ability to lead one's life is influenced at almost every turn by these interactions, a truism that highlights the second fact: personal differences between individuals inevitably affect their relative standing in these interactions.

Given the implications of these two facts, if private law is meant to vindicate people's freedom and equality, meeting the requirement to respect one another as independent and formally equal individuals is not enough. Instead, private law must be guided by the maxim of reciprocal respect for self-determination and substantive equality. Only by vindicating self-determination can private law forge and sustain the variety of interaction frameworks so crucial to our ability to form and implement a conception of the good life. Furthermore, only by structuring these interactions in terms requiring parties to respect one another for the persons they are can private law truly cast them as interactions between equals.

Thus, although relational justice is concerned with fixing *just* terms of interactions, one aspect of the grand question of what makes people's lives go well remains in its focus. Like (the early) Rawls, relational justice presupposes a "thin theory of the good" that, in our case, is framed by the basic liberal commitments to self-determination and substantive equality.[3] But this foundation does not render our thesis parochial. Given that the law *qua* law claims legitimate authority, its prescriptions must appeal to acceptable reasons.[4] Therefore, legal theories—at least humanist ones—rightly assume that to be legitimate, law's claim to authority should reflect these core commitments to self-determination and substantive equality.

Rejecting Private Law's Dominant Languages

Implicit in this sketch of our thesis is our opposition to the dominant schools of private law theory, whether they take the private law category seriously or marginalize its significance. We employ these contrasts throughout the book because they help to refine the distinctiveness of relational justice theory. At this stage, a brief preview will suffice.

The former schools, often subsumed here under the "traditional account of private law" category, include many variants. The most familiar ones rely on one of two features, either institutional or substantive, while some rely on both.

Institutionally, private law is often identified (usually implicitly) with adjudication, suggesting that its core commitments revolve around the standing it secures to individuals seeking civil recourse and accountability.

Substantively, private law is typically associated with a regime that enforces people's independence and formal equality, relegating responsibility for their self-determination and substantive equality to public law. This approach may allow this responsibility to slip partly to private law (mainly due to people's civic obligation to support just institutions) but still denies any primary and freestanding interpersonal responsibility for self-determination and substantive equality.

This book unapologetically discards both prongs of the traditional account. Private law, we argue, is not just common law (our civil law readers would, of course, wonder who could think otherwise). While judges have contributed, and still do, to the life of our private law, legislators and regulators can and increasingly do, as they should, play a significant part in its design and maintenance.

We likewise reject the traditional vision of private law as a bastion of strictly negative duties of non-interference. Traditionalists warn that allowing—let alone inviting, as we do—affirmative interpersonal obligations to be part of private law necessarily implies that everyone has a standing duty to promote the self-determination of others. But this book shows that their worry is misplaced. Relational justice theory includes principled guidelines for safeguarding people's independence while keeping in mind that it is self-determination and substantive equality that justify and require respect for independence.[5] The most fundamental guideline derives from the liberal maxim of *reciprocal* respect for self-determination and substantive equality. This maxim contains an inherent limitation: the duties it entails can neither undermine the self-determination of the duty-ower nor subordinate her to another person.

The traditional approach is thus normatively disappointing and, as we will show, also misrepresents the function of private law and fails to account for some of its key doctrines. The failures of traditionalism, however, do not justify many of its critics' views of private law. One influential approach—or rather a set of approaches—insists that the doctrines of private law are neither conceptually nor normatively different from other legal doctrines. Therefore, torts, contracts, property, and other branches of private law should promote goals such as aggregate efficiency and sustain values such as distributive justice or democratic egalitarianism. These approaches do not necessarily deny that certain features of private law may affect its doctrines' potential contribution to these public goals. Yet, they all claim (or assume) that private law doctrines merely add a set of distinctive *tools* to the arsenal of legal techniques that, in principle, are all interchangeable.

The various schools that reject private law's distinctiveness—notably the dominant voices within both the economic analysis of law and critical legal studies—thereby fail to grasp the value of private law and miss out on its promise. The value of private law is not exhausted by its contribution to goals pertaining to the state (or some other political community) as a whole. Rather, a private law that adheres to relational justice is intrinsically valuable. Private law's core function is to prescribe the terms of interaction that structure how we live and interact as private persons, quite apart from these terms' aggregate effects on the polity as a whole. By focusing on these dimensions, relational justice theory seeks to ensure the justness of our interactions in both the sub-statist and trans-statist frameworks that structure our social and economic life. Therefore, besides cases such as the irresponsible hosts and abusive partners that we began with, relational justice theory addresses discrimination, poverty, and other forms of structural injustice on the one hand while calling for the recognition of a core set of interpersonal human rights on the other.

Consider private discrimination. Prohibitions on discrimination in the workplace or in housing are generally justified by reference to our public commitments to equal opportunity and social integration qua citizens in a democracy. Thus, they are widely perceived as external limitations on the core commitment of private law to vindicate the employers' and owners' independence and the formal equality of their possible interactions with all others. At other times, the justification of nondiscrimination relies on the discriminator's unusual market power or on the "public" nature of their calling. Either way, this public law perspective on what is essentially a case of discrimination among private persons is often accompanied by the view that duties of anti-discrimination are, and perhaps must be, imposed only by statutes.

By contrast, relational justice provides normative resources for treating instances of private discrimination as a private wrong. We argue that tort duties against private discrimination, be they judge-made or legislated, are entailments of private law's own endogenous commitments. These commitments imply that people to whom the law grants normative powers over others—such as private proprietors, employers, commercial providers, and landlords—cannot be allowed to use these powers in defiance of others' right to be treated as equals. Other things being equal, any attempt to do so must count as an instance of power overreach and, further, as a legally cognizable injury to the person of the plaintiff, regardless of whether the state or market competition generates generous work opportunities and creates integrative fora.

Treating private discrimination as a tort along these lines carries, as we show in Chapter 13, significant implications. Two of them stand out. First, this private law duty does not distinguish between deliberate and careless instances of discrimination, making both disparate treatment and disparate impact potential wrongs. Second, a general tort of private discrimination can potentially capture the all too many instances of impermissible discrimination now falling through the many statutory cracks, avoiding the many shortcomings of the current scheme of anti-discrimination laws.

Interpretation and Reconstruction

When proposing relational justice as the normative foundation of private law, we are not ignoring that many (perhaps most) private law systems do not fully comply with its requirements or imply that these systems were designed to do so in the first place. These facts are orthogonal to our mission, which is neither descriptive nor genealogical. Rather than pretend to divine the intentions of the judges and lawmakers who developed the doctrine, we seek to provide an interpretive theory of private law in a liberal legal order. Our focus—mainly for purposes of elaboration and exposition but also because it is such an unusually rich and diverse body of law—is largely on American private law.

Like other sympathetic reconstruction exercises, our theory builds on existing practices while suggesting a new perspective on the law that both reaffirms core aspects of existing law and proposes justified reforms. Interpretive legal theories do not aim to supplant existing practices with wholly innovative ways of organizing society or even law itself. They are necessarily reconstructive, however, because they inevitably rely on a normative judgment about which doctrinal facts count as core and which as marginal.[6]

Many of the existing rules cannot be justified by reliance on the core commitments of self-determination and substantive equality. However, this pitfall is not exclusive to the relational justice theory of private law, and merely implies that this theory (like the competing ones) offers a compass, an evaluative benchmark for law's pedigreed rules. In this book, we defend this compass, which affords internal resources of critique for prompting the law to comply more successfully with its commitment to justice.

Reflective Equilibrium and its Limits

Given that the compliance of existing law with relational justice is indeed, as will be shown, partial and stunted, why make existing law the object of our inquiry?[7] Partly due to respect for law's architects and the pragmatic advantage of speaking their current lingo, but mainly because private law's rich body of cases provides fruitful ground for identifying and illuminating the normative foundations of the frameworks that structure our human and social interactions.

Our approach when constructing the theory presented in these pages is a variation on the reflective equilibrium theme.[8] This method provides a justificatory procedure whereby drawing inductive inferences (as represented by considered judgments about specific cases) can constrain deductive inferences and vice-versa.[9] It identifies a set of considered judgments concerning categories of cases in a general domain of human action where a basic principle (or principles) of justice applies. These considered judgments express our moral intuitions about what the relevant demands of justice appear to require.

Presenting our thesis in that way would have made the book unreadable, but we do view Part II, where we flesh out the theory, and Parts III and IV, where we work out its implications in specific settings, as mutually supportive precisely along these lines. In Parts III and IV, we show that the maxim of reciprocal respect for self-determination and substantive equality matches our considered judgments about a list of legal rules that we take as fixed points.[10] We hold that these rules are self-evident and thus virtually unrevisable due to the fundamental value they express, not because they transcend critical reflection.[11]

The litmus test of interpretive success is thus qualitative rather than quantitative: interpretive theories are examined for their ability to persuasively and coherently identify and account for the core features of the object of their investigation. The decision on core features necessarily involves, as noted, marginalization and demarginalization of rules and is thus necessarily normative.

For relational justice theory to prevail on the interpretive front, then, we need to show enough fixed points that fit existing law. We also need to demonstrate that the theory outperforms its two main rivals, namely, the conception of private law as the bastion of independence and as a regulatory tool serving the public good. Should it pass this test, rules that offend relational justice can then be rightly seen as blemishes—cases showing that the ideals of private law are not sufficiently developed or that their scope of application is unjustifiably partial. Law's internal point of view should not reaffirm these rules or cases but point instead to the need to reform them.

There is no reason to assume that such morally appealing fixed points can be found in contemporary private law. If they are not, the critique of law should come from outside. We see no reason why, invariably, only the internal critique of law should count. Indeed, the normative prong of relational justice theory (as articulated in Chapter 3) can—and if this turns out to be the case, should—serve as one external source of criticism.

But the option of resorting to abstract moral analysis as an external source of legal criticism does not render the interpretive endeavor redundant. Interpretive private law theory requires us to justify the prevailing rules that currently govern our interpersonal relationships. The justification requirement, as we hope to show, is always potentially challenging to some of our legal practices: it entails an idealized picture setting standards that our current doctrines do not necessarily live up to and can thus be, and often is, a fruitful source of internal critique and reform. The idealism of our social and economic world, even if partial and limited, is often an important source of critical engagement.[12]

This approach to interpretation should be contrasted with two other methods. On the one hand, the reflective equilibrium method we employ rejects the appeal of common-denominator interpretive theories because they necessarily fail to distinguish between important and technical legal rules.[13] On the other, we also reject the opposite interpretive approach aiming to offer a theory of everything, or at least of everything that is associated with private law.[14] One implication of our method of reflective equilibrium is that private law rules and doctrines can, and sometimes should, serve compelling demands that do not emanate from relational justice.

From Theory to Doctrine

Relational justice theory, we claim, provides lawyers an indispensable framework for navigating and arguing about private law's rules and doctrines but does not fully determine the specific details of any legal doctrine. The gap between normative foundations and doctrinal details derives partly from the substantial role that democratic and bureaucratic institutions play in lawmaking, into which they (often) bring to bear circumstances, traditions, needs, and aspirations. But the gap is also partly an upshot of the distinction between justice and legality. Indeed, the translation of justice's abstract maxim of reciprocal respect for self-determination and substantive equality into legality's demand for formalistic and specific prescriptions is (almost) never seamless.

A theory of private law can bracket the impact of the institutional inputs (concerning "local" effects) and should indeed do so if it aspires to apply beyond the scope of specific jurisdictions. But private law theory must also pay close attention to the structural features behind the gap between theory and doctrine. This task is especially urgent in this book, which aims to formulate a *general* theory of private law for a liberal legal order across the broad range of private law subjects.

Partly for this reason, we explore various doctrines of private law at length. Analyzing this vast array of rules bolsters the interpretive ambitions of our account by demonstrating the significant fit of its prescriptions to existing law as well as its performance as a source of internal critique. This broad sweep is also important for demonstrating the complex (though tractable) interaction between the abstract commitment to reciprocal respect for self-determination and substantive equality on the one hand and the structural features of private law involved in its translation into legal prescriptions on the other.

A liberal legal order cannot (or at least should not) extend to our inner selves and should abide by rule of law concerns. Moreover, where law seeks to affect (and not merely respond to) human affairs, it must carefully examine the likely consequences of its prescriptions given the expected responses of pertinent actors.

Further complications arise when the focus is on private law. Private law is part of the larger fabric of law, meaning it is in a relationship of mutual dependence with public law that may require some modifications. Additional refinements may emerge within private law, given the heterogeneous contexts of its relationships and the various actors it governs, not all of them natural persons.

Finally, since the connection between private law and adjudication is often contingent, when turning its normative prescriptions into legal language, relational justice must pay heed to the institutional and procedural possibilities at hand.

Although these institutional features constrain the translation of its normative maxim into law, they also suggest informative guidelines for this crucial process.

The Task

This book explains why private law matters. It does so by defending a normatively attractive, conceptually coherent vision of private law and demonstrating its explanatory power and reformist potential, stressing its role as a crucial and distinctive legal category in any liberal legal order. In the process, as noted, it disavows some of its outdated or normatively unacceptable incarnations. In an increasingly complex and globalized environment, private law—the law of our interpersonal relationships—need not limit itself to traditional means of one-to-one adjudication nor confine its aspirations to the borders of one state. Even more fundamentally, private law need not—and indeed should not—subscribe to the normatively dubious vision of personal interactions structured around absolutist protection of independence and formal equality.

Freed from this laissez-faire conception of rights, private law theory should openly discard the misleading view associating liberalism with an essentially hands-off stance vis-à-vis private law. This book demonstrates law's inescapable role in shaping the frameworks through which people interact, enabling them to treat one another as self-determining and substantively equal individuals.

Although endorsing this genuinely liberal vision in both domestic and transnational settings admittedly poses a formidable challenge, it is one worth pursuing. This book points to several legal techniques available to private law, beyond judge-made law, potentially conducive to the attainment of this aim. It also invites substantive reforms by highlighting unappealing pockets in private law that have proved disturbingly resistant to other-regarding concerns, and thus inconsistent with its inspiring (albeit sometimes only latent) humanist promise.

Some of these reforms are specific to a particular doctrine that may have gone astray, but many share an important common denominator that points to relational justice's dramatic potential. Relational justice theory is sensitive to systematic patterns of disadvantage so ingrained in the ways our everyday life is structured that, too often, they become invisible. It thus highlights burdens impinging on the ability of members of disadvantaged groups to pursue their life plans and treat others as equals.

A Roadmap

Part II lays out the theoretical foundations of the book in three steps: elaborating our conception of private law, spelling out its normative underpinnings, and assessing the challenges of its translation into law. Though distinctive, these three tasks are complementary and largely interconnected. Nonetheless, we hope that the preview of the thesis as a whole presented in this chapter will facilitate their separate treatment.

Chapter 2 argues that civil recourse, though often instrumental to private law and at times even intrinsically valuable, must not serve as its defining characteristic. Private law, we claim, is the law governing our horizontal, interpersonal interactions—we use these adjectives interchangeably—in a variety of social and economic settings; it is, in short, the law of human relations. Private law meets people in their various interaction settings, implying they must not be viewed as dissociated individuals. By the same token, private law neither treats individuals as executive agents nor derives their mutual obligations from any civic duties they owe (when they do) to other members of their political communities.

People participate in these interpersonal interactions as real individuals with specific life-plans, distinctive personhoods, and special circumstances, not as abstract beings. The human condition of interdependence means that many of our valuable projects are *joint* projects. It also implies that, in pursuing their plans, people may often render themselves vulnerable to or interfere with the legitimate interests of others, both within and without the privity of the joint enterprise.

Chapter 3 aims to develop a conception of interpersonal justice that duly addresses these basic features of private law. Beyond merely safeguarding people's independence, the justice of private law must also attend to its responsibility for facilitating these interactions, lest it jeopardizes the significance of self-determination for people's mutual relationships. Likewise, beyond vindicating formal equality, the justice of private law should ensure that the relationships it oversees (and those it at times constructs) are interactions between substantively equal individuals. To fulfill this purpose, private law must ensure that people's mutual interactions pay heed to their circumstances as well as to constitutive choices pertaining to their ground projects (as opposed to mere preferences) insofar as these are crucial to their ability to act as self-determining agents and relate to one another as substantively equal.

Chapter 4 undertakes the task of translating this maxim of relational justice into the currency of law by articulating the systemic constraints on—and thus the guidelines for—this endeavor.

Whereas Part II articulates and defends the relational justice theory of private law, the task of Parts III and IV is to put it into action. In Part III, we analyze diverse doctrines of torts, contracts, and restitution, all casting interpersonal interactions as frameworks for relationships between self-determining individuals who respect one another as substantively equal.[15] Although the demands that this vast domain of private law places on people's conduct may frequently exceed respect for the independence of others, they are not overwhelming. Often, these doctrines cannot be justified by reference to people's civic duties or by attributing to them the status of state delegates, but they can be fully explained once the freestanding requirements of relational justice are acknowledged.

Appreciating the prevalence of compliance with the maxim of reciprocal respect for self-determination and substantive equality vindicates the interpretive credentials of relational justice theory. Studying the subtleties of this maxim's implementation in private law and the contribution to this endeavor of the guidelines formulated in Chapter 4 helps to identify some of the existing law's failings, suggesting a critical direction for their possible reform. We do not purport to offer a conceptual account of each of the various branches of private law we discuss in Part III (say, torts). Rather, our analysis of these divergent doctrines aims to flesh out the core features and animating principles that underlie private law in a genuinely liberal legal regime.

Thus, wherever we refer to the interpretive credentials of relational justice, we do not imply that it offers the only plausible explanation or justification of the pertinent rule. We do not deny that there may be other, at times even more specific, justifications for some of the rules and doctrines we deal with in Part III. However, the fact that these rules may be overdetermined does not impinge on the significance of our conclusion regarding the coherent normative voice common to this broad range of doctrinal sources.[16]

We begin Part III with the tort law standard of the reasonable person. Chapter 5 focuses on a prominent (though rarely acknowledged) doctrinal trend featuring a double asymmetry of due care between defendants and plaintiffs and between under- and over-skilled defendants. This asymmetry, inexplicable in the dominant tort theories of economic efficiency and corrective justice, is clearly called for as essential for addressing the vulnerability imbalances at hand when private law is grounded in relational justice.

In Chapter 6, we turn to the doctrine of nonfeasance liability, which sheds light on the interaction between the normative and institutional aspects of private law. We argue that the rule of nonfeasance liability is best explained as reflecting institutional rather than moral considerations. Fundamentally, tort law is—and should be—hostile to relieving private persons of easy rescue duties. The reason this hostility does not surface in many situations—the rule—is explained by reference to certain institutional limitations. It does surface, however, in the form of exceptions to the rule whenever these limitations are eliminated or satisfactorily contained. Chapter 6 shows that this account explains the existing doctrine more accurately than its rivals and provides lawmakers normative resources enabling them to develop the doctrine by recognizing additional exceptions to the rule.

Chapter 7 addresses a hitherto obscure dimension of tort remedies spelled out in relational justice theory. We call them "substantive remedies"—remedies that do not aim to enforce or vindicate underlying rights but to ensure *post*-wrong justice instead. In some cases, the focus on the parties' post-wrong situation affects the type of remedy awarded (damages in lieu of injunctive relief). In contrast, in others—for instance, the tort doctrine of crushing liability—it imposes a ceiling on the plaintiff's compensation. In yet other cases, dealing with the loss of earning capacity or with the thin skull rule, it entails a compensatory floor below which compensation should not go. Chapter 7 shows that these seemingly disparate rules are not embarrassing deviations from the traditional make-whole principle but manifestations of relational justice in the private law context of remedies law.

Before shifting from torts to contract, we offer (in Chapter 8) a reconstruction of the poorly understood tort of public nuisance. Contrary to the view that the underlying rights protected by this tort contrast with private rights, we claim they are private rights like any other in the law of torts since they protect private persons, taken severally. And yet, these private rights are also distinctively public in the sense that they protect the interests of private persons to use and enjoy the public space. Thereby, public nuisance does not merely impose ex post liability for undermining these interests but chiefly constructs a liberal public space. This analysis shows that private law extends beyond the private sphere to capture entitlements and responsibilities that do not arise from or attach to ownership of land. It also refines the potentially significant role of the public nuisance tort in addressing the urgent threat posed by climate change.

Chapter 9 begins our discussion of contract by briefly tracing the elusive quest for the justice of contract through a critical analysis of three notions: just exchange, transfer theory, and distributive justice. Yet, Chapter 9, which discusses precontractual justice, and Chapter 10, which turns to the governance of contractual performance, focus on demonstrating in some detail how relational justice theory solves this persistent puzzle.

The maxim of reciprocal respect for self-determination and substantive equality, we argue, is vital to liberal contract law because it justifies contracts enforcement and prescribes a mandatory floor for contractual justice. In modern contract law, this floor deviates from the traditional laissez-faire mode of regulating the parties' bargaining process, which only prohibits one party's *active* interference with the other's free will. And yet, discarding the contractual vision of interpersonal independence through close adherence to relational justice does not create unacceptable interpersonal subordination (as champions of the *ancien régime* would want us to believe).

Chapter 9 analyzes in these terms the affirmative interpersonal obligations that typify many of contract's invalidating factors, celebrating the expansion of the law of fraud beyond the traditional categories of misrepresentation and concealment to include affirmative disclosure duties. It also shows that the same conceptual expansion underlies doctrines as diverse as unilateral mistake, duress in cases of wrongful threats that do not violate others' rights, anti-price-gouging laws, and admiralty rules of salvage. Likewise, it explains why concern for relational justice offers the most charitable explanation of the unconscionability doctrine and some of its modern regulatory cognates.

The case of pre-contractual relational justice helpfully engages the discussion in Chapter 4 about the constraints affecting the translation of relational justice into private law. Two challenges to this translation stand out: the need for detail and line-drawing in order to comply with the rule of law, and the likely responses of legally informed potential promisees in ways that might render law's prescriptions counterproductive. Both challenges imply that, at times, courts are not equipped for the task, at least not all of it. Once the critical stance of relational justice toward the difference between law-making institutions is appreciated, however, we can see why neither of these challenges necessarily affects the substance of the law. As Chapter 9 demonstrates, some of law's pre-contractual rules are products of adjudication. Others, however, were enacted by legislatures and regulatory agencies, often after common law had set a vague standard that legislators and regulators are better suited to implement.

Similarly, contract doctrines on performance and remedies have expressed concern with relational justice. The sequential nature typical of contract performance implies that contractual parties are particularly exposed to opportunistic behavior, and relational justice requires contract law to respond to this heightened, contract-specific type of vulnerability. If law is to ensure substantive equality and facilitate contract (as it should, given contract's assistance to self-determination), it must offer a cooperative conception of contract performance extending beyond the mandatory floor of relational justice.

At the core of this web of doctrines, discussed in Chapter 10, is the duty of good faith and fair dealing that sets up the contractual rules of the game. The doctrine of substantial performance in service contracts and the principle against forfeiture in applying the condition/promise distinction can likewise be interpreted as belonging to this cooperative framework, as can the burden to mitigate and the choice of the expectation interest as the default measure of recovery. All these doctrines require the contractual parties to assist one another up to a point.

Because, in this context, relational justice goes beyond the requirements of private law as they apply to people generally, liberal law does not force contractual parties to follow its specific anti-opportunistic prescriptions. While the general duty of good faith is immutable, the specific obligations understood to derive from that duty function as *normative defaults*. The status of these rules does not depend on their correspondence with the preferences of most parties (these defaults are *not* majoritarian); instead, they are endorsed due to their freestanding value—in this case, relational justice. And yet, although the parties' preferences do not justify these rules, they can still constrain their scope of application. Contract law's normative defaults are typically sticky, even though they are offered to the parties as defaults they are free to reject.

We conclude Part III with a short chapter on the law of restitution that, purportedly, is governed by the principle of preventing unjust enrichment. The distinction between just and unjust enrichment, however, has puzzled generations of judges, lawyers, and scholars. We argue in Chapter 11 that private law's commitment to relational justice offers an answer and demonstrate this claim through the study of two paradigmatic categories of the law of restitution: the law of mistaken payments and the doctrines governing self-interested conferral of benefits.

Part IV transcends private law's familiar terrain, proving that the combination of understanding private law as the law governing our interpersonal interactions and elaborating its commitment to *substantive* freedom and equality yields important insights—both explanatory or transformative—across a wide range of social and economic contexts.

We begin with a short chapter on workplace safety. Chapter 12 analyzes two legal arrangements designed to vindicate people's right to bodily integrity: workers' compensation schemes and regulatory safety agencies. Seemingly confusing if understood as attending solely to the public good, these arrangements make perfect sense when the focus is on their private law task of vindicating relational justice. The coherence and normative strength of these arrangements help to defend some of their basic features, currently under attack mainly on collectivist (notably economic) grounds. A singular focus on one-to-one adjudication thus emerges as unduly limiting the procedural and institutional imagination of the law of horizontal relationships, that is, private law.

Chapters 13 and 14 shift to the two major challenges to the just society: discrimination and poverty. Whereas the proposition that private discrimination can constitute a tort should come as no surprise now and is defended in Chapter 13, the focus of Chapter 14 on poverty may seem out of place in a book on private law theory. Yet, we insist that it is not. Chapters 9–10 and 13 imply that poverty is currently the major challenge to the justice of private law by showing, respectively, that contracts can be relationally just for the contractors and that non-discrimination rules make an indispensable contribution to the universalization of this justice. They thereby leave poverty as a seemingly obvious but dramatically disappointing limitation.

Poverty, however, is widely perceived as only a matter of distributive justice and thus beyond the scope of interpersonal interactions. Given that poverty is surely a major instance of injustice, this widely shared intuition seems to challenge our case against the strict division of moral labor between public law and private law and, thus, the thesis that relational justice occupies the moral center of private law in a liberal legal order. This verdict is premature, however, and will indeed ultimately prove mistaken.

Poverty is certainly a collectivist problem of justice in holdings, but it also has an irreducible relational dimension due to its effects on people's ability to interact as self-determining and substantively equal persons. Like other social conditions and personal traits that make private discrimination unacceptable, poverty severely limits the options available to individuals, impairing their autonomous functioning and preventing them from relating to others as equals. As in other cases of private discrimination, a person's market counterparts are not causally responsible for his or her predicament. But this fact does not justify reading private law as empowering individuals to exercise their transactional Hohfeldian powers in violation of the self-determination and substantive equality of others.

Accommodating the poor is challenging, *not* as a matter of principle but due to significant *operational* difficulties in implementing private responsibility for poverty alleviation. The challenge, as Chapter 14 explains, lies in the difficulty of ascertaining a person's economic circumstances, a situation that can be epistemically demanding, overly intrusive, and at times even demeaning. As we show, however, private law can devise appropriate strategies for addressing this operational challenge and has, to some extent, done so. A particularly attractive strategy animates doctrines like minimum wage and the implied warranty of habitability, where accommodating the poor is built into the terms of the interaction. These doctrines target major spheres of interpersonal interaction—the workplace and the housing market—where poverty jeopardizes private law's compliance with relational justice. By setting the appropriate floors (which vary from one society to another), these doctrines manifest the concern of private law with relevant differences between the parties' economic conditions.

These doctrines may be inefficient and, at times, even regressive, making them suspicious from the public law perspective they are (too) often associated with. Like other regulatory cases discussed in this book, however, they are not normatively unintelligible and, indeed, show commitment to relational justice that, especially in transactions affecting the person or the ground projects of a contracting party, requires an immutable floor of interpersonal decency.

The last doctrinal application we discuss is not yet in the books but should be. Existing private law theory is largely confined to a statist conception that limits its scope to interactions among the citizens and fails to appreciate potential implications beyond borders. This failure is particularly critical when the grievances at stake affect victims of dire transnational wrongs, which is the focus of Chapter 15.

Strategies in both public and private international law face significant difficulties when addressing these wrongs partly due to what we call "the missing link of privity," namely, the reason for imposing the burden of plaintiffs' vertical rights on putative defendants. Acknowledgment of private law's cosmopolitan dimension as the law of interpersonal interactions is a promising response to this predicament. The key to the missing link, then, is to identify the normatively acceptable common denominator underlying private law in divergent legal systems—the *jus gentium privatum*—that can and should serve as the premise of *interpersonal human rights*. The *jus gentium privatum* functions as the basis for critiques of domestic private law rules and the standing of aggrieved parties vis-à-vis those who wronged them.

This task requires a normatively charitable reading of the diverse systems of private law that govern (and have governed) interpersonal interactions in different places at different times. Chapter 15 argues that the common denominator is the commitment of private law to relational justice while stressing the difference between using relational justice as an aspirational idea and prescribing a global floor that all private law systems *must* comply with to be legitimate. Relational justice theory acknowledges that states enjoy significant advantages—in terms of both legitimacy and competence—when performing the necessary tasks of elaborating, implementing, and enforcing interpersonal rights and obligations. We only emphasize that private law's *minimal* requirements of relational justice are ones that *every* humanist polity has a compelling reason to acknowledge. As with certain traditional human rights, core interpersonal human rights are so crucial to law's legitimacy that nothing could offset their absence.

Unlike in traditional human rights, in interpersonal human rights the focus is horizontal, not vertical, and unlike traditional private law, interpersonal human rights prescribe global mandatory minimum standards and do not aim to set up a full-blown system of rules for interpersonal conduct and coordination. Just as the traditional understanding of human rights implies a floor that cannot be transgressed by state law (not even for the sake of promoting distributive justice, democratic equality, or aggregate welfare), a humanist framework must acknowledge a core set of interpersonal human rights that are beyond the state's discretionary power to abrogate. These interpersonal human rights can thus supply a normative foundation for legal liability that current efforts to address grave transnational wrongs so urgently require.

* * *

Our liberal theory of private law does not provide a set of blueprints or a detailed description of prevailing doctrines in a specific jurisdiction. It aims to offer a framework for the critical study of private law that can guide its interpretation, development, and reform, a significant undertaking given that private law is indispensable and public law, even in its most generous and liberal version, does not suffice. Only private law can establish interpersonal frameworks of interaction among individuals who respect each other's self-determination and substantive equality. For a state to respect its citizens as genuinely free and equal persons is one thing. It is quite another to live in a society that expects *individuals* to comply with the ideal of just relationships between free and equal persons.

Part II

Foundations

2
Private Law

Simple but Significant

It is no wonder that the distinction between private law and public law fascinates legal theorists and lawyers. Private law is a significant legal category, and legal categories frame our thinking, inviting or marginalizing certain concerns. Our understanding of private law not only guides the default thematic division of legal scholarship and law school curriculum but also affects the reasoning of lawyers and reformers. Potentially, therefore, it also informs how judges and regulators reach legal decisions and, thus, how rules are set, interpreted, and applied.

Even if the focus is limited to the last century, the intellectual history of the academic debate on the public/private distinction is rich and often convoluted.[1] In this chapter, we concentrate the discussion only on its current instantiation and specifically on refining the conception of private law that guides us in this book, ignoring what is "public" and, more importantly, why it matters.[2] We do not pretend to offer a robust, let alone comprehensive, picture of other theories. In all fairness, our accounts of other theories (themselves diverse and contested) are somewhat stylized, and we use them here mainly to elucidate the distinctive features of our own.

This chapter focuses on our answer to the question, "What is private law?" The task of this chapter is not fully independent from that of the next two, notably from the defense of reciprocal respect for self-determination and substantive equality as private law's normative foundation in Chapter 3. But while the conceptual and normative tasks are, unsurprisingly, intertwined, there is enough to be said on the former to justify separate treatment.

Our understanding of private law is simple, indeed straightforward. Private law is the law that governs our horizontal interactions in a variety of settings where we encounter other persons in our capacity as persons rather than as citizens or, more generally, as members of a political community. It thus participates in constructing the economic and social, as opposed to the political, spheres of our lives. The implication is that private law is not reducible to judge-made law, and identifying the conception of the person that underlies—or should underlie—its prescriptions is key to any viable account of private law, be it explanatory, justificatory, or reformist.

Relational Justice. Hanoch Dagan and Avihay Dorfman, Oxford University Press. © Hanoch Dagan and Avihay Dorfman 2024.
DOI: 10.1093/9780191987762.003.0002

Private Law as the Law of Human Relations

Relational justice theory conceptualizes the public/private distinction by zooming in on those capacities of law's subjects (persons) at the focus of the pertinent legal prescription: as members of a political community *or* as individuals. The premise of this view is that law's orientation toward us is qualitatively salient: it makes a difference whether we are addressed as parts of a comprehensive unit of joint responsibility—a polity—or as persons with projects. We are surely both, and the relations between these two capacities are complicated, but they are not equally salient throughout the various contexts of our lives. Correspondingly, public law and private law are meaningful legal categories because the types of considerations that justify their norms are informed by these respective capacities.

Public law deals primarily with our interactions as subjects of the state or as members of a political community. It constructs our form of government—our collective institutions and their interrelationships—and regulates various interactions with our fellow citizens as well as with the public authorities, which are supposed to act on our behalf as a collectivity. As such, public law (at its best) vindicates our rights vis-à-vis the collectivity and is guided by our collective goals, such as distributive justice (which focuses on justice in holdings and opportunities), democratic citizenship (which seeks to eradicate hierarchies in our relationships *qua* members of a political community), and social welfare (which is concerned with improving living standards overall).

Private law is an important legal category because it specifically governs our interpersonal horizontal interactions and focuses on their proper legal construction.

Studying the distinctive features of private law must not be confused with a separation exercise looking for necessary and sufficient differences between private and public law that would make them mutually exclusive. There neither is nor should there be a strict division of labor between public and private law. Since public law affects our horizontal interactions too, it should not ignore its own interpersonal implications, just as private law takes note, as it should, of its own collectivist effects. But while public purposes like social welfare, democratic citizenship, and distributive justice are always potentially relevant, they do not exhaust private law's normative concerns.[3] The distinctive moral center of private law lies in the irreducible significance of relational justice. Relational justice, in other words, is private law's deontic element.

Private law both protects us from others' encroachments and empowers us in our cooperative endeavors. It sets the conditions of legitimate interaction among individuals and delineates what people owe each other in varied interactional frameworks—the neighborhood, the workplace, the market, or the road. While at the core of public law's outlook is the state (or some other political community), private law generally focuses on the sub-statist—and, as we discuss in

Chapter 15, the trans-statist—frameworks that structure our everyday social and economic life.[4]

Private law rules derive from a range of sources, including judge-made law (common law or equity), regulation, statutes, and constitutional provisions. Indeed, the entitlements relevant to interpersonal relations comprise norms with different institutional pedigrees. Some are doctrines familiar from casebooks in first-year courses on private law: negligence, nuisance, the duty to pay damages upon breach of contract and the limitation of that duty by doctrines of foreseeability and mitigation, the requirement to return mistaken payments, and so forth. Many others are the products of regulatory agencies. The rules of the Occupational Safety and Health Administration, for example, define the duties of employers to provide safe workplaces, and those of the Consumer Financial Protection Bureau determine which lending practices are unfair, deceptive, or abusive. Other private law entitlements are granted in statutes, such as the right to equal treatment that underlies statutory prohibitions on discrimination in housing, commerce, employment, education, and more. Constitutional provisions can also provide the legal grounding for private law entitlements. For instance, the 13th Amendment of the US Constitution recognizes our right not to be enslaved by private persons, not only by the government, and many liberal democracies treat certain constitutional rights as bearing directly or indirectly on the terms of interactions between private persons.

Work law, consumer law, anti-discrimination law, and horizontal constitutional rights are often described as specific interventions that override private law.[5] This conventional description, however, is deeply misleading. These doctrines set up the rules of the game in a specific setting, but so do the specific rules that govern, for example, the tort responsibilities of land or car owners, sellers of goods, or providers of services. Both tort law and contract law prescribe—beside the residual rules that apply outside our more familiar categories of interaction—more particularized sets of rules that apply and, indeed, regulate these categories. The residual rules are particularly important in liberal polities, both as means that the law relies on to develop new categories and as freestanding frameworks for interaction that do not neatly fit social conventions. But *both* settings—the socially familiar and the more idiosyncratic—necessarily rely on a robust legal infrastructure.[6]

Beyond Judge-Made Law

1. Adjudication and Other Venues. Compare this understanding of private law with its court-centric counterpart, which is particularly prevalent in common law jurisdictions. Private law, claimed Peter Birks, is defined as concerned with "the rights which, one against another, people are able to realise in courts."[7] This conventional view implies, for example, that workers' compensation schemes, which substitute administration for adjudication, should not be deemed to be extensions of tort law. The shift from the domain of one-to-one litigation before a judge to the administrative apparatus implies, in other words, a jurisdictional transfer of authority from private law to public law.[8]

It may make sense to begin thinking about private law through judge-made law. Historically, at least in common law jurisdictions, judges carried much of the burden of developing and implementing private law. At its best, adjudication may indeed be a hospitable setting for the complex task of elucidating and even creating the legal infrastructure of interpersonal relations. Its typical piecemeal, gradual mode of operation encourages judges to shape and reshape law "close and contemporary" to the human problems they deal with[9] in an "endless process of testing and retesting,"[10] which mediates "the seeming commands of the authorities and the felt demands of justice."[11]

Court proceedings are sensibly perceived as an obvious setting for private law since adjudication is designed to assess the parties' behavior vis-à-vis their interpersonal rights and obligations and refine the rules that delineate these rights and obligations to begin with. The normative significance of granting individual rights-holders the power to decide how to respond to the infringement of their rights and the standing to instigate a complaint explain the association of private law with adjudication and, more generally, the importance of personal rights of action.[12]

The traditional role of (common law) judges as lawmakers of private law and responsible for its normative development accounts for their contribution to areas currently governed mostly by regulation, such as the nondisclosure rules discussed in Chapter 9. It also explains why—once we defend relational justice as private law's normative core—judges should recognize private discrimination as a private wrong that must, prima facie, be treated as a tort, as we argue in Chapter 13.

Adjudication took, and at times still takes, center stage in the life of private law.[13] What makes private law a meaningful legal category is not the venue for the prescription and vindication of our interpersonal rights. Rules about litigation and remedies only represent law's fallback plan, which comes into effect when we fail to conform to the demands of duty. The distinctive core of private law is the types of considerations that supply the justifications—the grounds—of its substantive norms, dealing with our interpersonal interactions. None of the mentioned advantages of adjudication implies that private law only appears, thrives, or survives when run by judges or that, when operationalized by judges, it should necessarily assume the traditional form of one-to-one litigation.

At times, then, private law cannot perform its role in the structuring of our interpersonal affairs solely through adjudication. A further implication—and this is the flip side of the same coin—is that some of the existing regulatory apparatuses are best understood through the interpersonal prism of private law and its normative commitment to relational justice. We elaborate on this issue in Chapter 4 and demonstrate it throughout the remainder of the book, but the former, more principled one, needs to be addressed now.

2. The Value of Civil Recourse. Consider the significance of rights of action, whose role is to enforce secondary rights to the redress of injuries caused by the violation of primary rights. Civil recourse theory perceives the victim's personal right of action as a key—indeed, definitional—value of private law.[14]

We agree that, *sometimes*, personal rights of action are intrinsically valuable. Relational justice theory points to two (at times overlapping) categories in which a personal right of action is not merely instrumentally valuable for attaining a desirable outcome—recovery from the wrongdoer—but essential to what enforcing or vindicating one's rights might mean.

First, occupying the special position of plaintiff enables a public reassertion of agency vis-à-vis the defendant-wrongdoer. For a victim of deliberate wrongdoing, the right to pursue the wrongdoer is no less crucial for her ability to restore her autonomous life than securing a damages award. For sexual abuse victims, for instance, it is intrinsically important to personally vindicate their rights to bodily integrity by assuming the role of plaintiff.

Second, the right to sue may be required to repair a setback in an ongoing, special relationship between plaintiff and defendant. Not only does suing enable the plaintiff to obtain material redress, but it also reasserts her agency vis-à-vis the defendant with whom she is in a dependency relationship critical in her life (such as employment, landlord/tenant, and parent/child relationships).

But many other cases are different. Consider poor, unusually vulnerable, severely traumatized, or uninformed victims on the one hand and victims whose expected recovery falls below litigation costs on the other. In these types of cases, insisting on a one-to-one adjudication model might undermine, rather than advance, the possibility of enforcing or vindicating the secondary rights of repair of victims of wrongdoing.[15] In these categories of private law cases, overemphasizing the significance of (private) civil recourse unjustifiably denigrates other devices that may be innocuous, even laudable. A fitting response to the victims' condition in these cases—one that takes seriously their self-determination and substantive equality—may require going beyond civil recourse and, at times, even abandoning the traditional common law model.

The former alternative refers to our earlier point regarding the significance of supportive regulatory infrastructures. The latter, more radical alternative, applies to cases where a personal right of action has no freestanding value. Typical of this category are various consumer grievances but also many other private law cases where the plaintiff's complaint focuses on the harm she incidentally incurred without implicating autonomy, equality, or dignity in any significant way. The value of personal rights of action in these categories of cases is purely instrumental: they are means to the end of securing secondary rights to remedies. Why instrumental? Mainly due to the epistemic advantages of the immediate parties in presenting evidence or to the "invisible hand" of the private motivation to pursue rights infringers. While these concerns justify a reliable presumption for affording such rights of action, that presumption is, by definition, rebuttable. This other-things-being-equal presumption should be rebutted where things are not equal. When personal rights of action are pure technologies, they are dispensable if replacements can better ensure the vindication of private plaintiffs' primary (substantive) and secondary (remedial) rights.

3. *Private Law vs. Criminal Law.* Does deviating from the one-to-one adjudicatory model collapse the distinction between private law and criminal law? For those who conceive crimes as wrongs against the public as a whole, this concern is irrelevant.[16] But it must be addressed by defenders of the opposite view, who see criminal law as deployed primarily for the vindication of interpersonal rights. This view, however, limits criminal law's vertical dimension to its enforcement function and perceives the rights at hand as largely horizontal. Thereby, it indeed implies that criminal law should be understood as meant to extend, and even bolster, the force of private law.[17] In this conception, criminal law justifiably bears some resemblance to other regulatory schemes (such as those we discuss in Chapter 12), which have partially replaced traditional private law institutions of adjudication and enforcement.[18]

* * *

We thus return to the idea at the opening of this chapter: private law should be understood by reference to the capacities of law's subjects at the focus of the pertinent legal prescription. Identifying the conception of the person that underlies—or should underlie—its prescriptions can thus be consequential when evaluating the competing accounts. Earlier, we referred to the person of private law as a private individual rather than a citizen, but this distinction is too crude. We claim that private law, which governs our interpersonal relations in a variety of settings, is the law of the embedded person.

To clarify, as we noted above and elaborate below, the embeddedness of the person construed by private law entails implications that are by no means natural, inescapable, or deterministic.[19] Rather, the opposite: because people are embedded in society *as it is structured by private law*, law can—and indeed should—take their agency seriously. At its best, private law helps to *facilitate* people's autonomy and equal standing in relation to others.

To elucidate this image of the embedded person, we will sketch three competing—and more familiar—views that identify "private" with, respectively, the *dissociated person*, the *executive agent*, and the *civic person*. The first view probably reflects the traditional account of private law's subjects and is associated with a strict division of institutional and moral labor between private and public law. The second, antithetical view underlies the otherwise very different positions of the economic analysis of law and the left-leaning critics of liberalism and legalism. Finally, a third approach to private law smooths the rough edges of the first view by insisting that, in a democracy, citizens cannot relinquish their civic duties even when interacting in their private capacity and, therefore, they must respect the constitutional rights of others.

Private Law and the Dissociated Self

1. The Toronto School. Consider first the traditional account of private law, developed most compellingly in the Kantian (and corrective justice) theories of the Toronto school of private law. This school deserves great credit for resisting the tendency of previous theorists to perceive private law as the continuation of public law by other means. They attained this aim by highlighting the normative significance of private law's relational form. On this front, we join forces. What matters to us at this stage, however, is the substantive aspect of the Toronto school and its clear articulation of the dissociated person as private law's main character.[20] On that front, we part ways.

For these modern Kantians, the interpersonal respect we owe one another as free and equal persons means respecting each other's *abstract* personalities. The "particular features—desires, endowments, circumstances—that might distinguish one agent from another" are, as Ernest Weinrib claims, "irrelevan[t]" to private law.[21] Private individuals are free by virtue of their capacity to set and pursue ends by deploying their person and property without being subordinated to others' choices. Private individuals, moreover, are equal by virtue of having this capacity. They are thus "purposive beings who are not under duties to act for any purposes in particular, no matter how meritorious"; as such, they are subject to "a system of negative duties of non-interference with the rights of others"—namely, private law.[22]

The Toronto theory of private law, then, builds exclusively on one underlying ideal: freedom cast in terms of "independence from being constrained by another's choice."[23] As Arthur Ripstein clarifies, independence implies that "each person is entitled to be his or her own master . . . in the contrastive sense of not being subordinated to the choice of any other particular person." Accordingly, independence requires that no one gets to tell you what purposes to pursue and, therefore, is "not compromised if others decline to accommodate you."[24] Quite the contrary: "Because the fair terms of a bilateral interaction cannot be set on a unilateral basis, considerations whose justificatory force extends only to one party are inadmissible."[25]

The principle of independence and, accordingly, the requirement that the terms of people's interactions manifest the formal equal independence of each interacting party underlie the three building blocks of these modern Kantian accounts of private law: property, contracts, and torts.[26] They are not solely Kantian, however. Alan Brudner, a modern Hegelian, refers to private law as the "law for persons regarded as ends outside of human association—as morally self-sufficient atoms."[27]

Similarly, a recent major book on private law by a leading Toronto school scholar—Peter Benson's *Justice in Transactions*—defends a conception of "juridical autonomy" that "presupposes particular notions of freedom and equality specified in terms of the innate mutual independence of all persons in relation to others." This conception emphatically excludes any reference to the parties' self-determination, namely, their "forming and rationally pursuing a conception of their substantive good." It likewise rejects any consideration of substantive equality, subscribing instead to a formal equality wherein "the claims parties make in relation to each other must be absolutely the same." In this view, then, contractual fairness has no business protecting particular categories of individuals, be they "the economically or cognitively disadvantaged, the commercially inexperienced or the emotionally vulnerable," nor should it "aim to redress differences in bargaining power per se or unfair and unequal starting points" or "ensure the satisfaction of needs, however urgent."[28]

2. Three Pitfalls. This view of private law and its underlying conception of the person is to be rejected on three types of grounds: descriptive, jurisprudential, and normative. Descriptively, as we show in Part III, across a wide range of doctrines, private law is committed to enhancing a capacious vision of autonomy rather than merely safeguarding independence. It is not content with formal equality either but aims at positively establishing substantive equality. Numerous doctrines of private law are straightforward implications of the commitment to reciprocal respect for self-determination and substantive equality. Excluding these rules from private law and renaming them as public law or regulatory interventions entails a vast excision, leaving little of what usually passes for private law as deserving this title.

But the problems with the traditional view are even deeper. Not only does modern private law have little in common with its imaginary counterpart and with the dissociated self at its center. One profound difficulty relates to the role of law, which the Toronto school marginalizes and indeed obscures. This jurisprudential point is crucial for our account of the embedded person discussed at the end of this chapter. As for the normative pitfall of private law's traditional view, we deal with it here because of its embrace of the dissociated person.

A law of dissociated persons may be well-fitted to a world of morally self-sufficient atoms (to use Brudner's words), but this only means it is ill-fitted to the world as we know it. Two facts about our human condition—our interdependence and our differences—explain and indeed justify the expulsion of the dissociated person from modern private law. Both these facts indicate that the law governing our interpersonal relationships has profound implications for our ability to lead a successful life. They suggest that a law that authorizes people to ignore others' right to self-determination and substantive equality is dramatically—and indeed tragically—indifferent to the most basic features of the human experience and, therefore, ill-fitted to govern people's interpersonal relationships.

Our practical affairs are deeply interdependent. They are replete with interactions with others that range from fairly trivial transactions to the most crucial relationships in our lives related to family, friends, work, and positions we occupy in society. These interactions can be voluntary or involuntary. Thus, we invite others or are invited by others to join projects, be it because interpersonal interaction is critical to the project or because enlisting others is instrumentally helpful. Our projects could also affect the legitimate interests of others, including those beyond the privity of such joint endeavors. Indeed, the ability to lead one's life, and certainly to do so successfully, is influenced at almost every turn by both of these forms of interaction. A conception of private law befitting the human condition must not renounce responsibility for the construction of these interactions, given the significance of interpersonal relationships in people's lives.[29]

The significance of our standing vis-à-vis others also implies that the terms of interactions arising under conditions of interdependence should be assessed as just or unjust. Given that we all constitute our distinctive personhoods against the background of our peculiar circumstances, public law cannot be charged with sole responsibility for addressing our personal differences since private law cannot contend with the requirement that people respect each other as independent and formally equal individuals. Indeed, quite the contrary. Given personal differences and the significance of interdependence, private law must not specify the terms of interpersonal interactions in complete disregard of people's circumstances and their constitutive choices. As opposed to brute preferences, these choices pertain to features that make them who they are, including their ground projects, insofar as they are crucial for the interacting parties' ability to act as self-determining agents.

Any polity that takes people's rights to individual self-determination and substantive equality seriously, therefore, must not set them aside when structuring our interpersonal relationships. These rights, as we maintain in Chapter 3, are crucial to both our horizontal and vertical interactions, although they entail different implications for each of them. An appealing conception of interpersonal justice that guides a genuinely liberal private law must thus be founded on reciprocal respect for each party's claim to self-determination and, accordingly, cannot be exhausted by the duty of non-interference. At times, it may require private law to facilitate people's cooperative efforts proactively and, furthermore, impose on private parties certain affirmative duties of accommodation founded on such a robust notion of interpersonal respect. (We define duties of accommodation in terms of obligations that incorporate some measure of respect for people given the circumstances they face and the choices they make.[30])

Private Law and the State's Executive Agents

If the dissociated person is expected to see others merely as sources of normative constraints over her freedom to set and pursue her own ends, the executive agent is required to incorporate others' needs, preferences, and interests into her ends as if they were her own. The executive agent is the hero of those who see private law as simply one possible form of public allocation and regulation—"public law in disguise."[31] The person of private law, in this view, is thus no different from the duty-bearer in public law. Like the public official, the executive agent is expected to act to further the public interest writ large.

Typically, the executive agent is implicit in views that perceive the division of labor between private and public law as purely conventional. Many of these views are espoused by critics of the traditional conception of private law, who perceive it as a sheer delegation of public power, a legitimating device that only serves to obscure law's many injustices.[32] But a similar—and in a sense clearer—approach characterizes the economic analysis of law, which in many other contexts is viewed as the nemesis of critical legal studies. As Alon Harel notes, law and economics theorists tend to be indifferent toward—if not impatient with—any effort to differentiate between private and public law. Their basic approach is that "[t]here is work to be done and it ought to be done in the best possible way," with the choice between private or public agents a "pragmatic" one that "depends on a comparison between the expected efficacy" of these possible agents "in performing the job."[33]

On its face, presenting *homo economicus* as an executive agent seems confusing, if not ironic. Rather than pursuing everyone's interests, *homo economicus* is said to choose and behave *without* regard for anyone else's interests. But the *reason* offered for sanctioning (at times valorizing) this attitude is that people's rational pursuit of their subjective self-interest, narrowly defined, would yield the greatest good for the greatest number.

Private ordering, in this view, is a superior *social* mechanism of allocation given the expected failings of central planning, which faces unsurmountable difficulties in obtaining and processing pertinent information. The implication, however, is that all private law rights are necessarily contingent on a comparative institutional analysis. For lawyer economists, a market failure is often a valid reason for eliminating such rights. Similarly, new technologies that might eventually solve the epistemological and computational difficulties the market is supposed to overcome could justify obliterating both property rights and freedom of contract.[34]

The resulting despotic world is reminiscent of familiar liberal lessons. Lawyer economists are right when joining critical thinkers who repudiate the dissociated person of traditional private law theory. But the idea that society should "maximize the net balance of satisfaction taken over all of its members" conflates, as John Rawls famously argued, "all persons into one through the imaginative acts of the impartial sympathetic spectator." It thus fails to "take seriously the distinction between persons."[35]

People are not passive consumers or carriers of well-being. They are agents with projects who are entitled to govern their lives, and their choices and interactions matter because they are part of their life plans. Bundling people's property rights and their freedom of contract into one collective welfare package could lead to the nullification of their autonomy and dignity. The subjects of the canonical economic analysis of law are definitely executive agents, but not so definitely individual persons.[36]

This analysis may explain why some versions of the economic analyses of private law can be read as grounded in a commitment to people's self-determination (although, in most of them, this commitment is, at best, implicit[37]). A similar concern about effacing individuals while promoting the common good may likewise explain why some critics of the traditional conception of private law (at least those opposed to its sharp disjunction between the fundamental normative principles that apply to people and those that apply to institutions) do not dispute the distinction between our private and our collective responsibilities.[38]

Private Law and the Good Citizen

This last observation brings us to the good citizens of private law who take these collective responsibilities seriously, as indeed they should, according to Elizabeth Anderson, whose influential work on democratic equality is often referred to as relational egalitarianism.[39] Egalitarianism, argues Anderson, requires private individuals to bear direct responsibility for realizing the demands of justice given that they are citizens of a polity. The democratic ideal covers not only political engagement (such as voting and protesting against the government) but also requires social relations of equality in and around the institutions of civil society (such as public accommodations and the workplace).[40] Thus, in her thorough analysis of racial segregation, Anderson articulates a vision of social integration comprising the citizens of a democratic state, including its permanent residents.[41]

This shift, from the dissociated person of traditional private law to the civic person required to take responsibility for the justness of the polity she belongs to, closely aligns with the "materialization" path of European (especially German) private law, famously theorized by Jürgen Habermas.

While traditional private law sought to guarantee the negative freedom of legal subjects, its application, according to Habermas, requires a more fundamental right—"equal treatment according to norms that guarantee substantive legal equality." It thus introduces "a new category of basic rights grounding claims to a more just distribution of social wealth (and a more effective protection from socially produced dangers)." But these basic rights also have a "radiating effect" or "third-party effect": they prompt changes "in the classical areas of property law and contract law." Thus, materialization represents a "paradigm shift" from a facilitative "framework for private activity" that is "limited only by the contingencies of the quasi-natural social situation" to "the paternalistic provisions of a superior political will that, attempting to influence and shape these social contingencies, intervenes with the intention of enhancing the opportunities for an equal use of legal freedoms."[42] (Habermas is critical of materialization per se and suggests democracy as a redeeming approach.[43] But as we hint below, we do not think that democracy alone can be the solution.)

Like the two other approaches sketched above, this civic understanding of the person of private law offers a noteworthy insight. Because all citizens, as Rawls argued, are duty-bound to support just institutions,[44] they may not always be exempted from this obligation, even in their capacity as individuals.[45] This plausibly means that our vertical rights—the fundamental rights we hold vis-à-vis the state—may, legitimately, be somewhat extended to the private sphere and invoked against private actors as well. But the civic person, though certainly to be welcomed into the private law, cannot be its central figure.

One reason is that, although all citizens are subject to civic duties, introducing material justice into private law seems to impose the *disproportionate* burden of a *public* problem on a private actor whose negative (or republican) liberty is now constrained. The post-materialization of private law, therefore, even if democratically prescribed,[46] directly confronts a core justificatory query in the law of interpersonal relations: "Why me?" Why should *I* incur a significantly higher burden than all other members of this political community in the name of its overall justice?[47] The familiar answers are not always adequate since—barring a few exceptions—the duty-ower is not a public (or even a quasi-public) official and, in many cases, does not enjoy disproportionate market power or provide some essential good.[48]

Some duties may be owed to people by virtue of their membership in one's political community. Political communities may legitimately opt for a more stringent degree of interpersonal solidarity than the core minimal requirements of relational justice. A given domestic private law may thus express civic solidarity in excess of the core interpersonal injunction of reciprocal respect for self-determination and substantive equality.[49] But the thought that private law writ large is mediated by people's affiliation with a given polity is counterintuitive. It creates the false impression that the fundamental wrong inflicted by private discrimination is, for example, disrespecting another's privileged status of national citizenship (or, more broadly, membership in a political community).

The persons of private law do not interact as citizens in (or permanent residents of) the state but as private individuals *simpliciter*. A worker is not necessarily a member of the same polity as her employer, nor do consumer and producer/service-provider or, for that matter, pedestrian and driver, share membership in the same political community. These observations are not merely statistical or empirical but make a normative point: private law rights and duties are not grounded in citizenship or membership in a political community.

A weaker reading of the good citizen approach may counter this conclusion. In this view, while membership in a polity is the ground of private law responsibilities—and thus its proper boundary—these responsibilities can also emerge in contexts that have nothing to do with people's civic capacities.[50] But this restatement still leaves two objectionable implications, which we only identify here and discuss further in Chapters 3, 14, and 15. First, and most obviously, it artificially and unduly downgrades the responsibilities that private law (should) impose on members toward non-members of the community at issue. Second, it renders the responsibility of members of one's community unjustifiably conditional.[51]

The difference between the civic person and the executive agent implies that supporters of the former do acknowledge that the rights and obligations of private law are neither dependent nor founded on the common good of the pertinent collective as such. Rather than rethinking the persons of private law from the exogenous perspective of the constitutional order to which they belong, we need to reimagine them within the most charitable interpretation of private law as a domain of interpersonal justice. Finally, we arrive at the embedded person: the person that a liberal (properly understood) private law, grounded in the relational justice maxim of reciprocal respect for self-determination and substantive equality, should anticipate and serve.

Private Law and the Embedded Person

1. Lessons and Challenge. We hope we have established that the three conceptions of the person of private law considered so far—the dissociated person, the executive agent, and the civic person—are all unacceptable. Our critical analysis of these alternatives, however, yields important lessons. The major pitfall in viewing the person of private law as an executive agent or a member of a political community is that both these views discard a core insight of the traditional approach—private law deals with quotidian interpersonal interactions that neither need to implicate nor are tied to our capacities as members of a given political community or to the normative (or other) well-being of the polity as a whole.

The reverse side, of course, is that these approaches are correct in rejecting the indefensible account of private law's normative foundations endorsed by the traditional view. The moderate voices supporting the executive agent approach sensibly look for a middle ground between the unappealing ideal of formal freedom and equality and the troublesome vision of full collectivization. The civic person approach correctly insists that it is not enough for the state to respect its constituents as genuinely free and equal persons. A properly liberal polity must not abdicate its responsibility for ensuring people's substantive freedom and equality throughout the spheres of civil society.

Is there a way out from this tragic choice between the traditional Scylla of a normatively objectionable private law and the Charybdis of an unacceptable alternative fully subordinating the justice of private law to domestic constitutions or to a political community's public good? We think that the focus of private law on interpersonal (not civic) interactions can be preserved while discarding the disappointing normative commitments of the traditionalists' dissociated person. One way of elucidating this happy alternative is to refine the continuity between the jurisprudential underpinnings of private law before and after the development of work law and consumer law as robust legal fields.

2. Naturalized Traditionalism. This continuity is by no means conventional. Indeed, quite the contrary. Recall, for example, Habermas' discussion of the materialization process. Private law pre-materialization, in his narrative, was a "quasi-natural" bastion of negative liberty inhabited—exactly as imagined by traditionalists—by dissociated persons. Its normative rehabilitation, so the argument goes, was a "paradigm shift," effectuated only thanks to the intervention of the state superimposing its paternalistic provisions.[52]

Similar views on the workings of private law are widely shared among theorists. Thus, John Gardner claims that, like all law, private law's "main point" is to help "people to do what they ought to be doing anyway, quite apart from the law." Tort law, in this view, is about enforcing such *preexisting* norms of appropriate behavior, even though law can improve things "by rendering [them] more determinate." Gardner argues that the same applies to contracts, which "exist apart from the law and are merely recognised and upheld (under limited circumstances) by the law."[53]

But Habermas, Gardner, and like-minded theorists radically understate the role of private law in people's practical affairs. We recognize, of course, that some of our practices (the family, according to Hume, and some forms of transnational commerce) may have emerged independently of law, while others are unique creations of law. But regardless of how any specific practice has come into existence, many (albeit certainly not all) of our practices are legally governed.[54] Law—more precisely, private law—sets out the terms of interaction between the participants in these practices and, thus, a significant subset of the rules of the various games that structure and, at times, even constitute our everyday life.[55]

3. Power-Conferring Institutions. This role of private law is particularly conspicuous insofar as private law's power-conferring sections are concerned. A good starting point when considering this issue is H.L.A. Hart's famous definition of power-conferring rules and institutions. As Hart notes, besides laws that "impose duties or obligations" requiring "persons to act in certain ways whether they wish to or not," other laws—Hart discussed contracts, wills, and marriages—"provide individuals with *facilities* for realizing their wishes, by conferring legal powers upon them to create, by certain specified procedures and subject to certain conditions, structures of rights and duties within the coercive framework of the law."[56]

Thus, instantiating contract as a legal institution empowers people to solicit the commitments of other people, including total strangers, and insist on their performance even absent any detrimental reliance. Promisees enjoy this authority over promisors because once law renders certain types of promises enforceable, promisors are legally obligated to respect their contractual obligations and are subject to the coercive power of the law if they do not. As Hart implies, law's function here is both constructive and prospective. Contract law constructs promisees' authority: it prospectively sets up the rules of the contractual game wherein this authority is created and applied and prescribes its proper scope as well as the limits of its power. This authority is not—at least should not be—obvious (recall that it applies even absent detrimental reliance). Rather, as one of us argues elsewhere, it is premised upon, and thus circumscribed by, contract's service to people's self-determination and its commitment to securing their equal standing.[57] Property roughly shares, we think, the same conceptual structure.[58]

4. Terms of Interaction. The significance of these power-conferring institutions for people's right to self-determination implies that any humanist polity has a compelling reason for instantiating them.[59] Yet, both contract and property can take many forms, and an essential part of law's task in instantiating them is prescribing their constitutive terms of interaction.

These terms are neither limited to the ex-post response of private law to what parties in a particular interaction have done independently of it, nor do they replicate some "quasi-natural" analog. While contract law and property law vest people with private normative powers, law not only prescribes what types of promises and what categories of resources are, respectively, proper objects of contracts and property. It also—and necessarily—sets up the rules that circumscribe the scope of promisees' and owners' authority and thus its limitations and qualifications.

The ambition of private law's terms of interaction, then, is both *constructive* and *prospective*. Terms of interaction construct edifices of human relationships and are not merely ad hoc encounters between, for example, this or that employer and employee, seller and buyer, or driver and pedestrian. A constructive ambition of this sort entails a prospective one as well: private law's terms of interaction establish preconditions for interpersonal transactions by dismantling certain entry and exit barriers, outlawing some forms of impermissible behavior, and empowering parties to design their social and economic arrangements by forming rights and obligations.

In the vast areas of private law that, above all, are empowering, law *structures* our interpersonal interactions. Insisting that these structures should be just cannot plausibly be termed "intervention," as both traditionalists and many of their critics often call it. The language of intervention is appropriate for law's work in *re*distributing wealth, resources, or entitlements in order to correct deviations from distributive justice. By contrast, our private law rights precede any such intervention. If tax is law's primary *locus* of *redistribution*, private law is its main scene of *pre-distribution*.[60]

5. Duty-imposing Rules and Raw Morality. What about the duty-imposing sections of private law? Are not at least these sections shaped by "the contingencies of the quasi-natural social situation" as Habermas and Gardner suggest? Some sections of tort law—think about trespass as one example—obviously are not since the aim of their duty-imposing rules is to vindicate people's property and contract rights, which means that they either piggyback on or participate in the construction of the pertinent terms of interaction.[61] But even the other (core) sections of tort law, which vindicate people's most fundamental rights—say to their bodily integrity and good name—do not simply follow morality's preexisting norms of appropriate behavior.

One key role of any tort duty is to delineate an arena of permissibility so that even risk-creators, who owe a duty of care, are *entitled* to place others in harm's way insofar as they are discharging the duty. More importantly, tort duties are often used to facilitate valuable activities, including encouraging risky behavior (say, in the case of investigative journalism or the case of the business judgment rule).[62]

Many will certainly share Gardner's intuition that what he calls "raw morality" and "raw moral rights and duties" often provide us with a secure starting point. A critical contribution of law to morality, then, is to render an "already-constitutive (set of) norms" more determinate.[63] Given that all private persons have basic rights to a good name and bodily integrity, core aspects of the rights protected by such torts as battery, defamation, or negligence can be identified quite apart from the law, and yet they often require legal specification.

But even regarding these rules, Gardner understates law's significance by eliding a vital distinction concerning the epistemic role of law in giving effect to moral duties. To say that law's added value applies only at the margins implies that tort law merely reports what counts as wrongdoing, whereas, in fact, it turns raw morality into fully fleshed norms of respectful interactions.[64] The distance between the moral requirement to refrain from punching someone's nose and the mature tort of battery, with all its doctrinal complexities, comes closer to the latter pole. And so does much of tort law. Tort law is often needed to decide what behavior counts as appropriate interpersonal respect as well as whether victims have legal rights (and injurers correlated duties) to begin with.

6. Constructing Just Relationships. Notice where we end up: private law, even in its most conventional rendition, is in the business of structuring our interpersonal interactions in the various settings where we encounter one another as private individuals. It sets the rules of the various games of our social and economic lives. The market, the workplace, the neighborhood, the road—like many other interactional loci—are all partly constituted by the law governing our horizontal interactions, namely, private law. Because private law's function is both constructive and prospective, the persons of private law act in a legally structured universe, which in many ways transforms them into embedded persons.

People's embeddedness is related to a perception of them as substantively free and equal persons. People's constitutive choices and circumstances, as well as the variety of their mutual contacts in these daily contexts, make it normatively objectionable to think about their interpersonal interactions in abstract terms or as the seamless continuation of their political identities and affiliations.

Private law structures many of our daily interactions and thus tends to blend into our natural environment. Its existing instantiations, therefore, are too often perceived as necessary or at least neutral and acceptable. But their "thingification" (or reification) must be resisted since these contingent choices are by no means natural, inescapable, or incontrovertible.[65]

A legitimate private law—let alone an appealing one—must not abdicate its responsibility for shaping the terms of these interactions in compliance with the most fundamental humanist commitments. Private law should seek proactively to empower people's self-determination.[66] It should also construct these settings in compliance with the maxim that befits its embedded person, namely, reciprocal respect for self-determination and substantive equality, which we dub relational justice.

3

Relational Justice

Neither Corrective Nor Distributive

The purpose of this chapter is to flesh out our account of the underlying justice of private law. Our main focus is to expound our conception of relational justice and explain why this commitment to reciprocal respect for self-determination and substantive equality should guide the interpretation, development, and reform of private law. Before we embark on this task, however, we need to address an understandable concern: without conceptual space between corrective and distributive justice, relational justice would necessarily collapse into one of these two familiar forms of justice.[1]

1. Interpersonal, But Not Corrective. Some articulations of corrective justice perceive it as a purely remedial, backward-looking, and conservative concept calling for the annulment of both wrongful gains and losses.[2] These views do not even purport to offer a conception of justice that can guide private law in its core mission of setting up the rules of our interpersonal games. The dominant views in contemporary private law theory, however, are more informative. They construct an ideal of just terms of interaction around a formal conception of the free and equal person—the dissociated person of Chapter 2.

According to this ideal, people are equal in their interpersonal relationships if none is superior or subordinate to another, and every person is free as against all others—entitled to set and pursue their own conceptions of the good.[3] Die-hard libertarians subscribe to this position because, for them, independence and formal equality are the only legitimate commitments of law *tout court*.[4] Corrective justice does not need to subscribe to a libertarian theory of law, however. Indeed, some corrective justice views of private law—most notably that of the Toronto traditionalists—reject libertarianism as a political philosophy but insist that, so long as people respect one another's independence and formal equality, they bear no responsibility for one another's autonomy and need not be concerned with claims to substantive equality. It is the state, and not any particular individual, they insist, which must be responsible for providing "background conditions for a social world in which everyone is a full member."[5]

But private law traditionalism, which sanctions owners' sole and despotic dominion and strictly limits people's interpersonal obligations to duties of noninterference along these lines, authorizes—and thus perpetuates and at times even generates—severe vulnerabilities.[6] A radical division of labor between private and

Relational Justice. Hanoch Dagan and Avihay Dorfman, Oxford University Press. © Hanoch Dagan and Avihay Dorfman 2024.
DOI: 10.1093/9780191987762.003.0003

public law is therefore indefensible. Even assuming—a dubious assumption, to be sure[7]—that the state's tax and redistribution mechanisms flawlessly address these vulnerabilities, discarding the responsibility of private law for self-determination and substantive equality sheds the most fundamental liberal commitments from our interpersonal relationships.[8] The significant share of human interdependence in any life plan and conception of the good makes such a legal architecture unsustainable.[9] For instance, it amounts, as we argue in Chapters 13 and 14, to dismissing the central place of affirmative duties to accommodate disability or poverty as well as negative duties of non-discrimination in work, housing, and commercial settings.

Both the vulnerability and the valuable options to which our social condition gives rise imply that the liberal commitment to individual self-determination and substantive equality must not be excluded from private law. Only private law—the law of our interpersonal (horizontal) relationships—can form and sustain the variety of frameworks necessary for our ability to lead our chosen conception of life. And only private law can cast them as interactions between free and equal individuals who respect one another as the persons they actually are. Part of the burden of Parts III and IV is to demonstrate and render vivid these propositions and thus the stakes of the theoretical debates that occupy us in these early chapters.

2. Social and Economic, but Not Distributive. Some readers may worry that ours is yet another rendition of the familiar criticism of private law traditionalism that denounces its distributive injustices. Although that scholarship does inform some of our claims, both the grounds of our critique and the alternative ideal we offer do not rely on these distributive concerns. Our understanding of private law as the law of human relations does not imply that the justice of private law is distributive.

Distributive justice stands for an idea of equality in the overall distribution of resources and opportunities in society. It is a form of responsibility that—as John Rawls states—"society, the citizens as a collective body, accepts" for (under his scheme) "maintaining the equal basic liberties and fair equality of opportunity, and for providing a fair share of the other primary goods for everyone within this framework."[10] Rawls goes further, adding that with such a structure in place, "citizens (as individuals) and associations [can safely] accept the responsibility [only] for their ends and aspirations in view of the all-purpose means they can expect, given their present and foreseeable situation."[11]

Samuel Scheffler explains that this Rawlsian ideal of a moral division of labor builds on a commitment to value pluralism—appreciating that the values associated with justice form only one set of values among others—as well as on the concern that the demands of justice can become overly onerous.[12] He further notes that, while private law may well be part of society's basic structure, Rawlsian division of labor implies that "[i]ndividuals and associations must be free, within the basic structure, to be guided by the independent values and norms that apply to them."[13] Thus, at least on Scheffler's reading, Rawls ends up propounding the

Toronto School. Ronald Dworkin, another liberal champion of distributive justice, arrives at a similar outcome—some form of libertarianism, he argues, is the most adequate principle for the law governing the terms of interactions between private persons.[14]

There are other views regarding the effects of the (Rawlsian or other) demands of distributive justice on private individuals. Two prominent views insist on the responsibility of non-state agents. But even they—unsurprisingly—offer accounts very different from ours.[15]

One line of work comes from those who claim, with G.A. Cohen, that private individuals should not be exempt from realizing all or some of the demands of distributive justice. These critics of the Rawlsian division of labor extend the application of the full-blown demands of distributive justice to the choices of private individuals.[16] As we noted in Chapter 2, this view, in which (to use Cohen's words) "the personal is political,"[17] embraces a vision of the person of private law as if they were an executive agent. Thus, it erases the freestanding sphere of human and social interactions, thereby effacing—rather than extending—the obligations grounded in our interpersonal interactions as such.[18]

3. *Distinct from Relational Egalitarianism.* Relational egalitarianism is closer to our account but, again, significantly distinct. The term describes a bourgeoning body of philosophical scholarship elaborating on the familiar ideal that our relationships with others should be relationships between equals.[19] Thus, at a very abstract level, relational justice's substantive equality, which deals with a similar ideal—relating as equals—may seem a straightforward application of relational egalitarianism. Yet, the two theories diverge in their moral and structural characteristics. The differences between them pertain both to the parties' identity and to the standard of equality per se.

We address the latter point below when refining relational justice's conception of substantive equality. For now, it will suffice to recall that, contrary to leading accounts of relational egalitarianism, relational justice is *not* predicated on the democratic ideal of equality between members of a political community. Relational justice is not, in the terms of Chapter 2, the justice of good citizens. Instead, it simply concerns the interactions between persons in their private rather than civic capacity.[20] Hence, whereas certain leading relational egalitarians identify relational equality with *democracy*,[21] relational justice finds its grounds in *liberalism*.

A democracy-based account of just relationships prescribes relational duties that, ultimately, rely on the Rawlsian civic obligation to support just institutions, which makes these duties fundamentally accessory and conditional. They are accessory in the sense that social and political institutions (rather than private persons) are in charge of realizing the demands of justice so that these demands are fully specified *apart* from the role of private individuals. And they are conditional in the sense that individual (accessory) responsibility arises only because, *and only insofar as* private choices happen to contribute to the perpetuation of ongoing social injustices in the polity as a whole.

By contrast, relational justice-based duties are neither accessory nor conditional. For relational justice, the grounds of duties make essential reference to how the interacting parties relate to one another rather than to how, from a collectivist point of view, each party stands separately vis-à-vis all other members of the society. On these grounds, as discussed in Chapter 2, duties and burdens founded on relational justice are not even *a priori* vulnerable to the "why me" charge that properly limits civic obligations in a liberal polity.[22]

Thus, the distinction between relational justice as opposed to distributive justice and relational egalitarianism is not about the character of the duties they generate: both can give rise to relational duties. Nor is it necessarily the identity of the duty-ower that distinguishes between them since duties of distributive justice can attach to private persons, too. Instead, the basic distinction comes down to the *grounds* of their respective duties. Relational justice grounds relational duties in the importance of relating to others as substantively free and equal persons. By contrast, distributive justice and relational egalitarianism ground both relational and non-relational duties in their contribution to something broader. In distributive justice, the duties are grounded in their contribution to the achievement of fair equality in something (e.g., opportunity, resources, and others). In contrast, in relational egalitarianism, the grounds are one or another democratic ideal of equal membership in a political community.[23]

Indeed, it matters—and it may matter quite significantly—whether we focus on the most justifiable scheme of entitlements of a given polity or on other units of interactions (say, the workplace).[24] Focusing on the entitlements scheme may entail some reference to the workplace (if systemic injustices in the workplace undermine justice for members of a political community), and the latter may well contribute to the former (relational justice tends to promote both distributive justice and democratic egalitarianism). Yet, their differing perspectives necessarily imply some divergence.

A Relational Starting Point

1. Just Interpersonal Interactions. Private law is premised on people's engagement with one another to achieve the ends they each pursue and plays a key role in constituting, facilitating, and authorizing such interdependent interactions. Accordingly, relational justice approaches the question of whether private persons participating in an interaction relate to one another as free and equal as, in and of itself, a source of value and concern. Relational justice is not merely a fallback plan or a lesser option than distributive justice. Rather than addressing the concern for equality in the *overall scheme* of any given polity, relational justice takes up the question of whether the interacting parties (e.g., in a contract) relate to one another as free and equal. As we have reiterated, its concern is the *terms of the interactions* between individuals.

Both private law traditionalism and its distributive justice-based or democracy-based critiques undervalue the significance of private law arrangements for our ability to lead a successful life. Even in societies where all citizens have adequate opportunities to realize their full freedom in their private lives, this is a troublesome mistake. Our interdependence implies that our horizontal interactions are too significant to our autonomy and equal standing to be so easily supplanted by vertical arrangements, however just they may be.

The significance of interpersonal and interdependent engagements also highlights the separate significance of these interactions' specific terms. For persons to treat each other as equals, the terms of their interaction must not reflect prominent imbalances of power or advantage between the parties. To meet this demand, the terms of private law interactions must reference the participants' relevant personal qualities, including their distinctive characteristics and circumstances. Only if the private law's terms of interaction are predicated on the commitment to *take difference seriously*, contrary to what formal equality requires, can they guarantee the ability of the parties to relate as equals.

To count as just relationships, therefore, the terms of the interaction must take into account the parties' constitutive features, choices, and circumstances insofar as these are vital to their ability to interact as substantively free and equal persons. This prescription is critical of a legal order allowing legally governed practices that defy their participants' equal standing and autonomy and supports precisely the kind of accommodative structure precluded by the traditionalists' commitment to formal freedom and equality.

2. The Freestanding Significance of the Horizontal Interactions. Relational justice provides normative guidelines for private law's endeavor to structure the terms of our horizontal interactions. Both in close interpersonal contexts and in more impersonal ones, it participates in constructing the frameworks of these human and social interactions.[25] These frameworks may also be of interest for distributive justice. Rawls, for example, claims distributive justice is concerned with the basic structure, which includes state institutions but also other social institutions like the family.[26] But even when these two dimensions of justice address the same context of interpersonal interaction seeking to identify normatively required relational duties, their different orientations—more precisely, the different *grounds* of the duties they identify—imply that their overlap is likely to be only partial.

Relational justice focuses on the compliance of the pertinent legal framework with reciprocal respect for self-determination and substantive equality. Relational justice's scrutiny of both trans-statist and sub-statist frameworks, then, is not subservient to an overall goal of justice in any given political community. Our discussion of interpersonal human rights in Chapter 15 builds on the first (trans-statist) prong of this proposition. But the second (sub-statist) prong, which is pertinent here, is no less significant.

Take sub-state institutions or, more generally, social and economic institutions that are not organized as political communities (the family, the workplace, or the market). They are potential candidates for distributive justice demands as part of the basic structure if and insofar as they affect the normative well-being of the polity as a whole. These effects may be material or expressive, but their significance is always derivative because it is, as noted, accessory and conditional.[27] By contrast, for relational justice, these frameworks of interaction are primary. Its question is whether the basic rules of the game in this particular framework are justified as such rather than how local injustices might undermine the justifiability of a polity's institutions in general.

In this light, it is clear why, in some cases, the just terms of interactions between private persons may fall short of, or even violate, the demands of distributive justice. (The most conspicuous examples come up in our discussion of poverty in Chapter 14.)

3. *Relational Justice and Society's Structural Injustices*. Relational justice's orientation also highlights its sensitivity to systematic patterns of disadvantage, including those that are products of past injustices.[28] These micro-patterns of disadvantage usually escape scrutiny because their entrenchment in the structure of our everyday lives often renders them invisible.[29]

Relational justice forces us to see them for what they are—contingent practices that "*organize us* in ways that are unjust/harmful/wrong."[30] A commitment to relational justice requires us to examine the most fundamental building blocks of society—the scope of owners' authority, the preconditions of promises' enforceability, and what makes acts and omissions legal wrongs. Do the terms of interactions instantiated by these building blocks—those blocks that constitute the structures of our everyday life—comply with the injunction of reciprocal respect for substantive, rather than formal, equality? Do they truly take people as they are rather than as abstract bearers of generic personality?[31]

It is no wonder that the rights of disadvantaged groups recurrently surface in this book. We address them not only in Chapters 13 and 14, which are dedicated to discrimination and poverty, but also in Chapters 5, 7, and 9, which deal with mainstream doctrines of torts and contract such as the duty of care, compensation for loss of earning capacity, disclosure duties in contract, and unconscionability.

Relational justice theory helps to expose the *pre*-distributed burdens hindering members of these groups in the pursuit of their life plans and in relating to others as equals.[32] Once exposed, a genuinely liberal private law cannot remain agnostic. Its commitment to prescribing terms of interaction that comply with the injunction of reciprocal respect for substantive equality is discussed below. This commitment means that fixing the currently tilted terms of interactions becomes a requirement of relational justice and, therefore, cannot be satisfied solely by public law (and other institutions of distributive justice).

Reciprocal Respect for Self-determination

1. Reciprocal Respect. Relational justice stands for reciprocal respect for self-determination and substantive equality. Reciprocity in this context does not imply measuring how much each party respects the other. It is not about respect in the ethical sense of caring for one another or some other attitude of solidarity among intimates or friends. Nor does it imply that one party's obligation depends on the other's compliance with its own.

The requirement of reciprocity applies to the terms of interactions prescribed by private law. These terms must, we argue, take into consideration the impact of each party on the other in terms of self-determination and substantive equality. For instance, in the easy rescue case discussed in Chapter 6, we claim that private law must go beyond the independence of the would-be rescuer and consider the impact of protecting their independence on a person facing a life-and-death emergency. Here, reciprocity demands the juxtaposition of independence to the interest of the person whose life is at stake.

With this clarification in mind, we are ready to unpack the two core notions of relational justice as we employ them in this book, starting with self-determination.[33]

2. Self-determination and Private Law. We begin with the (uncontroversial, we hope) premise that people are entitled to act on their capacity "to have, to revise, and rationally to pursue a conception of the good."[34] They deserve to exercise some control over their destiny, "fashioning it through successive decisions through their lives."[35] Free individuals should be able to plot their own course through life—to have some measure of self-determination (or self-authorship—we use these terms interchangeably).[36]

A person, therefore—and here we clearly opt for liberal egalitarianism rather than republican freedom—is free not merely in the formal sense of non-subordination to the choices of another but also in the more robust sense of the ability to make meaningful choices about the direction of their life.[37] In the formal sense, a person can be "free" simply because no one else is in a position of dominance over them. But this conception neglects concern for the effective realization of that person's ability to form and pursue their own conception of the good. Self-determination is necessary for people to lead the fully human life they are entitled to. While this requires a measure of independence, self-determination "is not something automatically guaranteed by a structure of negative rights."[38]

Indeed, a meaningful right to self-determination is dependent on material conditions and also requires—as Joseph Raz famously argues—an adequate range of significantly different options for the choice to be genuine.[39] A body of law properly concerned with people's autonomy, then, must proactively support their ability to shape a life they can view as their own and cannot be contented with merely respecting their bare capacity for uncoerced choice.

This core responsibility of the state implies that public law must ensure the collective goods and the material, social, and intellectual conditions needed to enable people to become and remain self-determining individuals. These are necessary preconditions for autonomy, but they are not sufficient. Private law—most specifically, its power-conferring elements—also has an irreducible role in this fundamental state obligation. Because our practical affairs are deeply interdependent, our interpersonal interactions have freestanding significance. People's autonomy, in other words, is deeply relational.[40] Therefore, our self-determination cannot be fully secured by public law; private law must not abdicate its distinct responsibility to provide the variety of frameworks necessary for our ability to lead our chosen conception of life.

At their best, property and contract function as empowering devices for self-authorship. To see why, we need to briefly highlight private law's contribution to people's ability to plan and their ability to choose and thus act upon their own values and life plans.[41]

By allowing people to secure a temporally extended control of things, property facilitates people's ability to carry out meaningful projects—on their own or with the cooperation of others—and to pursue goals and objectives that typically require a temporal horizon of action. Similarly, by ensuring the reliability of contractual promises for future performance rather than merely protecting against promisees' detrimental reliance, contract enables people to extend their reach by legitimately enlisting others in their purposes and projects—both material and social.

Furthermore, contract expands our range of meaningful choices by expanding our repertoire of secure interpersonal engagements beyond the limited realm of gift-based and similarly close-knit interactions. Property and contract law further multiply the alternatives from which people can choose by constituting a variety of stable frameworks of interpersonal cooperation when different property and contract types support divergent forms of interpersonal relationships.

In all these ways, private law opens up possibilities for choice that allow people to make their own judgments about what they value and how they value it, what to own and how and with whom to own it, what to buy or sell, how hard to work, how much to save, and what to consume. It would be wrong to conclude that property or contract is strictly necessary for self-determination. A person could, for example, choose a radically ascetic lifestyle, opting to rely on the generosity of others. But it does not seem far-fetched to conclude that, by granting individuals the power to invoke a variety of property and contract types and employ them in the service of their life plans, private law makes a vital and distinctive contribution to people's ability to realize the right to self-authorship.

Indeed, the special standing conferred by the institution of property and the reliability of others' promises ensured by contract are best justified by reference to their service to people's self-determination. In other words, the justified claims of both owners and promisees are premised on their right to others' respect for their self-determination. Reciprocal respect for self-determination, and not for independence, is private law's most normatively defensible foundation.

3. Accommodation without Paternalism. The role of reciprocal respect for self-determination as the foundation of the power-conferring aspects of private law suggests that reciprocal respect for self-determination is a core commitment of property and contract rather than an external imposition.

Moreover, as we argue in the next section, without *some* attention to the distinctive features and predicament of the other, respect for self-determination is hollow. Substantive equality is thus also part of this justification of both property and contract. Attempts to enlist property or contract in the service of arrangements that undermine relational justice must be treated (at least prima facie) as *ultra vires*. They abuse the idea of property/contract by invoking it in defiance of its own legitimacy.[42]

In this light, relational justice-based rules of contract law successfully rebut their worrisome image as conveying unwarranted paternalism.[43] The concern is that these rules unfairly stigmatize the weaker parties as unable to protect themselves and prevent them from using contract in potentially empowering ways.[44] Paternalistic doctrines and policies should be resisted because, as Seana Shiffrin explains, they replace people's judgment and circumvent their will in an effort "to supplant or maneuver around an agent's agency . . . motivated by distrust of that person's agency." They thus "convey a special, generally impermissible, insult to autonomous agents."[45]

Prescribing a relationally just floor for the enforcement of voluntary undertakings, however, is not paternalistic. If enlisting law in the cause of contract enforcement must rely on an interpersonal obligation of respect for self-determination and substantive equality for its justification, then contract—or at least liberal contract—cannot legitimately contravene relational justice. The adherence of liberal contract to relational justice abides by the normative foundation of contract's legitimacy and is entirely unrelated to paternalism.[46]

4. The Place of Independence. Reciprocal respect for self-determination suggests, as noted, that our interpersonal relationships must not be solely governed by the negative duties of noninterference. At times, relational justice requires some affirmative interpersonal accommodation that takes account of choices or personal circumstances. However, replacing independence with self-determination at the normative foundation of private law does not imply that independence is purely instrumental.[47]

The contribution of independence to autonomy renders it non-contingently valuable and deserving of genuine consideration in every decent liberal polity.[48] Contrary to the Toronto school's embrace of an absolutist conception of independence, we hold, with Raz, that independence "admit[s] of degree."[49] Of course, properly safeguarding people's independence, while keeping in mind that what ultimately justifies (and requires) it is self-determination, is challenging. In shaping our private law (and especially in constructing our affirmative duties), we must undertake what H.L.A. Hart described as the "unexciting but indispensable chore" of distinguishing "between the gravity of the different restrictions on different specific liberties and their importance for the conduct of a meaningful life."[50]

Thus, an autonomy-based private law system may be willing to restrain the independence of some people when its significance to their self-determination is minimal and when upholding that independence could jeopardize their or others' self-determination or undermine substantive equality among persons. At the same time, a liberal private law would treat people's independence with greater caution in the absence of strong opposing normative pressure, namely, when there is no threat to others' self-determination and when formal equality roughly approximates substantive equality. It would certainly uphold independence when it is crucial for ensuring self-determination.

5. The Core Qualitative Distinction. This book does not offer a full-blown theory of autonomy accounting. For our purposes, it is enough to highlight the qualitative distinction between the features that make us who we are and our sheer preferences.[51] This core distinction guides our theory of relational justice in setting up the accommodative structure prescribed by Hart's analysis.[52]

Consider first sheer preferences. Choices driven by such preferences address the realization of people's superficial ends, whose frustration has hardly any bearing, if at all, on their broader plans, goals, and conception of self. Sheer preferences do not have a strong claim on accommodation, and people should fully internalize the monetary and non-monetary burdens they entail. One familiar example is that of a plaintiff whose choice of activity reveals risk-preferring attitudes. The tort doctrine of assumption of risk properly absolves defendants of the duty to accommodate choices made for the sake of experiencing risk, that is, choices that only risk-preferring plaintiffs would have made.[53]

Against sheer preferences, we posit a more diverse category of features that make us who we are. It includes what we referred to above as objects of people's most fundamental rights, namely, their bodily integrity and good name, as well as other immutable features, socially constructed conditions, and personal traits such as race, gender, and disability. Yet, some of the features most significant to people's identity reflect their own choices. After all, the idea of self-determination—the essence of leading an autonomous life—implies that decisions on what ground project to pursue should always be up to the individual.[54]

Not all choices belong in this category, but some clearly do. These are choices that pertain to people's most fundamental decisions. They reflect, to use Bernard Williams's conception of ground projects, "projects which are closely related to [an individual's] existence and which to a significant degree give a meaning to his life."[55] Unlike Williams' development of this conception, a ground project is not necessarily a life-and-death kind of choice for us. Indeed, in most cases, people have more than one ground project.[56] Still, ground projects are important in one's life story—religious, ethical, professional, and familial choices can plausibly be described in these terms. People's relationships with their loved ones or other constitutive features and choices, such as their vocation, are not on par with their preferences on mundane goods or daily services. If self-determination is a cardinal feature of private law, its doctrinal makeup must reflect the qualitative distinction between ground projects and sheer preferences.

This distinction implies that not all preferences are "sheer." Sheer preferences, such as the canonic choice of ice cream flavor, are relatively freestanding, but other preferences are not. Even seemingly small preferences may be intimately related to people's ground projects, and insofar as they are, they may deserve heightened respect.[57]

One may object to our favoring of vocation over, say, growing flowers, being a fan of a sports team, or improving one's ability to play the piano, especially given our disavowal of paternalism. Insofar as this critique suggests that "intensive hobbies" may also be distinguished from sheer intense preferences, we tend to agree. But this does not—and should not—imply that legal analysis will turn into free-floating, category-less reasoning.

Neither the Toronto view of respect for others' abstract personalities nor its economic counterpart, which views ground projects as merely preferences that happen to be highly intense, requires such categorization. But neither approach, as noted, offers an acceptable normative foundation for private law. Moreover, the need for such categorization flows from the distinctive task of private law discussed in Chapter 2: to structure interpersonal frameworks prospectively rather than improvise ex post interventions into people's affairs. If these frameworks, as we claim in this chapter, are to construct respectful interactions, private law needs to make some general assumptions about the types or categories of projects that are significant to people's identity.[58]

As long as interacting people cannot seamlessly observe one another's inner self and figure out what, in each person they encounter, is germane to their life plan—a rather despotic scenario—relational justice must rely on such assumptions. These assumptions are sufficiently thin—we reject smuggling in judgments as to the worthiness of human projects[59]—and should thus be no more objectionable than Rawls' assumptions regarding human nature and the goods that individuals prefer to have more of rather than less ("primary goods").[60]

Reciprocal Respect for Substantive Equality

1. Relating as Equals. Private law's proper conception of equality, we argue, is both relational and substantive.[61] It is relational, as opposed to distributive, in the sense that it concerns the parties' terms of interaction as opposed to equality in the overall allocation of resources in society. Equality in this context is not about what the parties, taken severally, have or should have but about how they stand vis-à-vis one another.

This conception of equality is substantive in the sense of taking the parties' interests and conditions into account. Given the differences between people, reciprocal respect implies that law must frame our interpersonal interactions as relationships between self-determining and substantively (rather than merely formally) equal individuals who respect one another for the persons they actually are. Our focus in this section is on this ideal of relating as equals.

At times, relating to other people as equals requires nothing more than formal equality. In contractual settings, for example, where commercial parties are more or less equally situated, formal equality is, all things considered, the best proxy for substantive equality, justifying the *local* application of formal equality when setting up their terms of interaction.[62] In most other cases, however, formal equality falls short of vindicating the parties' substantive equality.

To claim that substantive equality finds all deviations from a standard of strict equality objectionable, however, would be the antithesis of formal equality. By contrast, in private law settings, substantive equality is an ideal concerning just terms of interactions. The ideal of relating to others as substantively equal means, most abstractly, that terms of interactions must reflect some differences between the parties, particularly in two types—their respective interests and their respective conditions.[63] Both are closely related to self-determination.

2. Respecting Others' Constitutive Features and Choices. The first type concerns the qualitative distinction between sheer preferences and the features that make us who we are. Sheer preferences, as noted, do not justify claims of accommodation since differences on that front do not impinge on people's ability to relate as equals. By contrast, to facilitate respect for a person as substantively equal, just terms of interaction cannot allow the (monetary and non-monetary) costs of possessing constitutive features and choices to be borne solely by their possessor.

The implications of this injunction of accommodation depend on the context at hand. Often, reciprocal respect may require an interpersonal accommodation that takes account of certain personal circumstances or choices. At other times—notably in the context of discriminatory practices discussed in Chapter 13—it makes it illegitimate for private individuals to take account of certain traits, many of them publicly branded as inferior. In principle, however, the demands of relational justice depend neither on an existing public perception of inferiority nor on historical injustices that call for public remediation. A private law consciously guided by relational justice would thus be especially receptive to claims for accommodation raised by members of groups viewed as liminal.[64]

Translating relational justice's abstract injunction of accommodation into concrete terms depends on the substantive good (or goods) that the specific practice involved in the pertinent interaction is understood to embody. Given that practices are supposed to be rationally conducive to the pursuit of their underlying good(s), each practice will have its own internal logic as to how the specific terms of interaction in the pertinent practice are relationally just. In some cases, this logic could point to personal qualities that should determine the terms of the interaction to ensure relationships of substantive freedom and equality. Qualities relevant to cases of negligent infliction of physical harm in the context of transportation, for example, are the victim's physical, mental, and cognitive disabilities. Other personal qualities, even when they are rightly considered constitutive choices (say, religious affiliation), do not warrant accommodation simply because they are typically irrelevant.

Finally, complex cases may arise in contexts that fall between sheer preferences and ground projects. This intermediate category involves commitments that, although valuable, do not shape the overarching meaning of a person's life and, therefore, may be less significant to the definition of identity. The requirement to respect others on their own terms suggests that some accommodation duties may be in place. Nonetheless, given that the impact of these commitments on the person's self-determination is less profound than that of their ground projects, relational justice can (and probably should) insist on moderation in the demands for accommodation.

To illustrate, just terms of interaction between an employer and an employee could entail that, to relate to one another as substantively equal, the employer should reasonably accommodate the employee's absence from work due to essential family or religious commitments. Yet, this rationale does not apply to an employee who, for example, is unavailable for work on certain days because of her *casual* interest in watching migratory birds passing through. These kinds of leisure activities are not ground-project choices, and, as such, the employer bears no responsibility for accommodating them.

3. *Compensating for Imbalances of Power.* The second type of difference bearing on relational justice's ideal of relating as substantive equals has to do with imbalances of power. Power imbalance refers to the ability of one party to exercise controlling influence over the terms of the interaction. This form of relational superiority, which a genuine liberal law must address, can have many manifestations—for instance, a party may be better informed, more experienced, physically or emotionally stronger, or occupy a position of repeat player.[65] Relational justice's core prescriptions regarding contractual relationships, discussed in Chapters 9 and 10 below, exemplify this injunction.

For contractual parties to relate as equals, the terms of their interaction must reflect their relatively equal power to set such terms or (in many cases) to have reasonable expectations of safety, privacy, and relevant information to influence their setting. Identifying substantive equality with just terms in either of these ways is closely tied to self-determination, which again defines what it means to treat contractual parties as equals.

Thus, having the power to make or contribute to the making of contract terms offers a clear illustration. Substantive equality would then mean that the self-determining agency of *both* parties should be, more or less, equally evident in the authoring of these terms. We deliberately say *more or less* so as to emphasize that parties need not be situated strictly equally in terms of their powers (broadly conceived to include information, skill, and more). Instead, they must be situated *equally enough* for the terms of their interactions to reflect that both are in an authorship position.

Self-determination also features when assessing substantive equality in the absence of a party's contractual voice. In some categories of contracts—notably, those dealing with people's work or intimacy—the absence of voice can hardly be legitimate.[66] But in others—as those where consumers are term-takers facing adhesive contracts—it could be, as it is in tort law contexts featuring involuntary interactions.[67] Terms that respect the voiceless party's interest in safety, privacy, and relevant information aim to reduce the vulnerability imbalance between the interacting parties, focusing on these interests because of their key contribution to self-determination.

This relational justice conception of substantively equal terms of interaction departs from two leading accounts of what is wrong with relations of inequality centering on hierarchy and exploitation. According to Elizabeth Anderson, hierarchies of power, esteem, and standing are paradigmatic instances of relational inequality because they subject one party in the relation to an "inferior position."[68] For Seana Shiffrin, relations of exploitation denote a basic failure to relate to others as free and equal agents. Shiffrin emphasizes exploitation's relational grounds. In her account, contract law is morally required to refrain from facilitating one party's exploitation by the other.[69]

In our account of substantive equality, unjust terms in contractual relations rest neither on hierarchy nor on exploitation. Relations of hierarchy, as noted, are not necessarily impermissible. In many contract types, they may be legitimate if contractual terms show due regard for the security, privacy, and informational interests of the term-taker party in, say, an adhesive contract. The flip side is that contractual transactions could count as relationally unjust even when the parties are not in a hierarchical relationship.[70]

Finally, consider substantive equality vis-à-vis exploitation. We argue that exploitation is a specific case of the more general category of substantive inequality. The terms of a contract may thus be deemed unjust even when they do not include one party's exploitation by the other. Terms that fail (even inadvertently) to pay sufficient attention to a party's safety or privacy do not necessarily reflect exploitation. They should still be criticized, however, due to the failure to treat both parties as equals, given the moral import of safety or privacy to the parties' ability to interact as free and equal agents.

Inherent Limits

Relational justice is more demanding than the traditionalist prescription of no-boundary-crossing. In other words, it resists the view that interpersonal affirmative duties are always and necessarily duties of virtue.[71] The accommodation duties it prescribes, however, are not limitless. Some of their limitations derive from relational justice's embeddedness in law and its broader normative landscape and will thus be investigated in Chapter 4. Our focus here is on three limitations on the duty to respect other people's self-determination and substantive equality, which spring from this ideal itself.

1. No Respect for Disrespect. The first limitation emerges directly from the relational instantiation of equality that relational justice encapsulates. Relational justice focuses on the parties' equal standing in determining the terms of their interaction. Equality, here, is relational, not merely in its form, concerned solely with duties that persons formally owe to certain others. The relational ideal at the core of private law stands instead for the normative commitment underlying these duties. In particular, it picks out a commitment to the value of sustaining relations of respectful recognition with others.

This commitment constrains the class of conceptions of the good and other personal choices that may require interpersonal accommodation. Not all choices can be the object of interpersonal respect among free and equal persons: Some personal choices, policies, and conceptions of the good deny certain others the very standing to treat the deniers as equals—the animating ambition of both the murderer and the racist, for example, is the repudiation of their victims' equal standing. In short, choices that are inimical to the ideal of relational equality cannot lay a compelling claim as plausible candidates for interpersonal accommodation.

2. Actions, Not Motivation. Duties of accommodation are part of the terms of interactions of our horizontal interpersonal relationships. They thus purport to provide duty-holders with mandatory reasons for action, a justification for why it is necessary to act in a certain way.

A critical distance exists, then, between the normative grounds of a given reason and the motivation for conforming to its demands when the reason cannot actually lead to the motivation and, at most, can only influence people to acquire it. This gap between reason and motivation is particularly important for private law (as opposed to personal morality).[72] The enforcement of motives goes well beyond private law's proper mandate, at least in liberal societies.[73] However, relational justice does not threaten this boundary. It prescribes the parties' terms of interaction and thus requires conformity with its demand. Without dealing with the actual motivations of duty-holders, it argues that they have a reason to act in a way that is respectful of others.

3. *Not Overly Demanding*. The third limitation is particularly significant given the typical liberal concern noted above that placing demands of justice on individuals can become overly onerous.[74] But our discussion thus far—and the detailed applications provided in Parts III and IV of the book—show that this concern, while understandable, is unwarranted, at least regarding relational justice, both in its scope and its extent.

As for *scope*, recall that accommodation is not an all-encompassing requirement to accommodate every single person in every area of their practical affairs. The duty prospectively establishes fair terms of interaction in and around *one* sphere of action and applies to a particular context or event and with respect to *one* person (or class of persons) at a time.[75]

Moreover, while we insist on relational justice's role in guiding our legally structured practices, we readily acknowledge that it need not function as a categorical constraint. In Chapter 4 and throughout Part IV, we discuss cases where distributive justice concerns should limit the reach of relational justice. Yet, these competing justice concerns do not exhaust the reasons that may limit the reach of relational justice. There can be—indeed, there are—practices inconsistent with the ideal of relational justice that are nonetheless grounded on perfectly valid liberal foundations. In Chapter 13, we discuss the typical example: practices that strive for excellence and may—in proper, delimited circumstances—be properly insulated from the requirements of relational justice.[76]

Relational justice also sets inherent limits on the *extent* of the required accommodation. People, as noted, cannot be legitimately required to accommodate choices that repudiate the status of others as free and equal persons. This constraint also implies that the burden to perform an interpersonal duty cannot be excessive because it must neither undermine the autonomy of either of the parties involved nor create interpersonal subordination between them. Although relational justice's accommodating duties are costly, they must not be prohibitive.[77] Relational justice is a two-way street, implying that the obligations it imposes must be consistent with the self-determination and equal standing of those who owe them.

True, this limitation does not guarantee the degree of independence that a traditionalist private law regime would secure. The constraint is justified, however, because, in these cases, ensuring one party's independence would deny the other party equal power to determine the terms of the interaction and the substantive freedom to act as a self-determining agent.

Once we recognize that private law structures the relational frameworks that, to a significant extent, are the fabric of our daily lives, we must demand that relational justice serve as its basic guideline. Despite some noted justified exceptions, the freestanding significance of our horizontal interactions implies that, as the contract-independent duty of care established by the tort of negligence is an indispensable feature of private law in a liberal legal order, so is the more general obligation of reciprocal respect for self-determination and substantive equality.

This theme will be particularly pertinent in Chapter 13, where we argue for a new tort: private discrimination.

* * *

A liberal system of private law—the law of our interpersonal interactions—invites a conception of interpersonal justice that requires people to treat one another as self-determining and substantively equal. But translating this maxim of relational justice into the currency of law is not a straightforward undertaking. Before we turn to evaluate relational justice's manifestations in contemporary (mostly American) private law and its reform proposals, we need to study the challenges confronting it.[78] This is the task of Chapter 4.

4
Justice in Private Law

Law's Indispensable Role

Relational justice as a normative ideal seems independent of law and, in some sense, it is, which is why we were able to discuss its contours without referring to the institutions responsible for its instantiation and application. And yet, in a deep sense, it is not since it is law—specifically private law—that sets up many of the frameworks that structure our everyday life. In so doing, private law prescribes these frameworks' terms of interaction. Relational justice theory insists that *obligatory* reasons to accommodate others must be part and parcel of these terms of our interpersonal interactions.[1]

Social norms may suffice insofar as they comply with the dictates of relational justice and are taken to be obligatory. They would then govern people's interpersonal relationships but only because they would be properly regarded as law-like. If, however, that is not the case, as is likely given contemporary circumstances, relying on social norms amounts, at best, to an indirect and opaque endorsement of private law traditionalism. Fully delegating responsibility to social norms would thus threaten liberal law's commitment to individual self-determination and substantive equality.[2]

More precisely, the absence of legal duties of accommodation in an interaction framework that is, even if partially, legally constituted or regulated, *means* that legally, one person would determine whether to treat another as genuinely free and equal. The law would thereby *institutionalize* the potential subordination of the vulnerable (recall the facts of interdependence and personal difference) to the legal power or advantage of another private individual. This situation amounts to *structural* unfreedom and inequality.

Law, therefore, plays a critical role in instantiating and upholding relational justice. Thus, we often refer to law (or private law) as if it did something, even though we recognize that it has no independent agency. Law is formed, changed, and enforced by human agents, and at least some of those who participate in its making are strategic actors seeking to shape it in their favor.[3] Our task in this book is to offer the language and conceptual apparatus that can, at least to some extent, guide conscientious actors—be they the actual architects of private law or its critics and potential reformers—to do the right thing.[4]

Doing the right thing, however, is more complex than drawing a simple inference from the abstract maxim of reciprocal respect for self-determination and

Relational Justice. Hanoch Dagan and Avihay Dorfman, Oxford University Press. © Hanoch Dagan and Avihay Dorfman 2024.
DOI: 10.1093/9780191987762.003.0004

substantive equality. These complexities add limitations beyond the substantive ones discussed in the last section of Chapter 3. They also modify relational justice's accommodation requirements given their more specific contexts and other demands of the legal system at hand, and, finally, they require close attention to the legal institutions capable of implementing them.

Legality's Constraints

1. The Limited Reach of Law. Law's prescriptive effects are not limitless, and we begin with constraints that derive from the very nature of legal prescriptions. Crucially, activities that turn on authenticity and sincerity, such as romantic love or friendship, should lie beyond the reach of the law,[5] and treating them as mandatory reasons for action necessarily destroys their inherent value.[6] Other cases are more complicated. Legal prescription may crowd out internal motivations.[7] Displacing such motivations does not always justify law's abstention (relational justice, as noted, is about reasons for action, not motivations). But when it threatens to undermine the activity's intrinsic value or backfire by alienating law's addressees from the reasons for action it prescribes, abstention may indeed be called for.[8]

2. The Rule of Law. Translating relational justice into the language of law requires compliance with the two key elements of the rule of law, guidance and constraint, which feature in John Locke's argument: "Both the People may know their Duty, and be safe and secure within the limits of the Law, and the Rulers too kept within their due bounds."[9] The requirement that law be capable of guiding its addressees' behavior focuses on the subjects of law, while the injunction that law should not confer unconstrained power focuses on officials. But they both require that legal prescriptions be relatively clear, minimizing recourse to individualized knowledge and radically ad hoc judgments.[10]

While seemingly technical, this requirement is intimately connected with people's self-determination. As Joseph Raz argues, only a relatively stable and predictable law can serve as a "safe basis for individual planning," which is a prerequisite of people's ability to form definite expectations and future goals. Law's participation in securing stable "frameworks for one's life and action" increases predictability in one's environment and thus facilitates people's "ability to choose styles and forms of life, to fix long-term goals and effectively direct one's life towards them."[11]

Indeed, both the guidance of law's addressees and the constraint of officials' power are core expectations of the person of a liberal private law, which is committed to its constituents' self-determination. By requiring "people in positions of authority [to] exercise their power within a constraining framework of public norms," the rule of law "takes the edge off human political power, making it less objectionable, less dangerous, more benign and more respectful."[12] When legal decisions are "anchored in stable general legal doctrines, made for publicly available reasons, [and] applied faithfully," people may be able to "feel at home within the framework of the law, and . . . have the confidence and self-reliance to plan their life."[13]

The rule of law is often associated with the idea of the law of rules,[14] namely, that law's prescriptions must be concrete and sufficiently clear and determinate to be followed "without first resolving the very normative questions [they] are designed to settle" or "considering whether the local outcome of the rule conforms to the values [they are] supposed to advance."[15] Friends of bright-line rules are correct to criticize open-ended standards that invite judges to apply ad hoc discretion, which affronts the rule of law. In many contexts, bright-line rules do serve rule of law values best, yet in others, they do not. A better approach begins with the observation that there is ample conceptual space between ad hockery and bright-line rules and, within it, legal doctrines provide sufficiently clear guidance as to what the law requires.

Regulating a wide range of conduct is complicated and at times, an attempt to do so with bright-line rules generates technical, non-intuitive complexity, which could undermine law's guidance.[16] In such circumstances, commitment to the rule of law implies allowing or even favoring the use of what we call "informative standards." These standards enable their addressees (or their lawyers) to figure out their intended content, predict their possible applications, and modify their behavior accordingly.[17]

3. *External* and *Internal.* Both of legality's constraints—law's limited reach and the rule of law—also flow from our account of relational justice in Chapter 3. Law's limited reach replicates the focus of relational justice on actions rather than motivations. The rule of law is entailed by the last and most significant inherent limit mentioned above—relational justice duties must neither undermine the duty-owers' autonomy nor subordinate them to others.

Compliance with the rule of law, then, is not an external imposition on a private law regime guided by relational justice theory. The values of stability and predictability in the rule of law are entailed, as already noted, by the same commitment to people's autonomy and substantive equality. Moreover, the respect for other people's self-determination and equal standing demanded by relational justice *requires* respect for their ability to form expectations based on stable frames of reference. On its own terms, relational justice cannot be oblivious to the rule of law and, therefore, must not imply particularistic (thus necessarily post hoc) judgments.[18]

Final Incidents

1. *Justice and Incentives.* Relational justice focuses on the terms of our interpersonal interactions, and its legal instantiation is aimed at ensuring that our

horizontal relationships comply with reciprocal respect for self-determination and substantive equality. However, legal norms do not transparently translate into their intended actions because their potential addressees may have vested interests in circumventing these norms' intended effects. Well-informed and sophisticated parties are especially likely to take law's prescriptions, even if presented as reasons for action, as incentives rather than norms. They may behave like Holmes' image of the bad man, looking at norms as a list of prices for particular behaviors.[19]

Private law must not ignore these potential responses. Since the concern of relational justice is to set up just terms for people's interactions prospectively and constructively, any doctrine guided by relational justice must consider the contingency of such responses, with particular attention to the possibility that they could end up undermining the doctrine's goals. In order to prescribe rules (meaning reasons for action) able to secure just results, law's architects should shape private law with an ex ante perspective. They should carefully attend to the likely implications of its potentially contending configurations and thus take seriously their incentive effects.

But the possibility that private law's traditional processes and remedies are unlikely to secure relational justice does not imply that relational justice is necessarily beyond the power of private law. At times, it may point to nontraditional mechanisms that can serve as countermeasures that change the incentives of parties whose response threatens to frustrate relational justice.

2. Incentives Beyond Welfarism. This account of the way relational justice resorts to an ex ante perspective explains why some of the following discussions of specific private law doctrines resort to economic insights. But it also implies—and this should be explicitly stated—that relational justice theory is not welfarism in disguise.

The task of designing a private law that complies with relational justice differs dramatically from that of shaping a regime that maximizes social welfare. A welfare-foundationalist account of private law treats law as a technology for allocating resources and entitlements so as to maximize overall welfare. It thus enlists—as discussed in Chapter 2—the person of private law to act as the state's executive agent. When new technologies that could replace private law's economic functions emerge, both private property and freedom of contract can, and arguably should, be substituted by AI and big data.[20] Tort law could be subject to a similar fate.[21]

Relational justice, by contrast, focuses on the parties and the freestanding value of their interpersonal interactions, irrespective of private law's putative instrumental contribution to social welfare. Therefore, it offers lawmakers an alternative litmus test for success. While a genuine concern for social welfare would ultimately subordinate the parties' interaction to the dictates of the general interest, relational justice focuses on the parties' substantive freedom and equality.

3. Justice Beyond Equity. Like the canonic economic analysis of law, however, relational justice does not respond to ad hoc encounters between parties and adopts a clear ex ante perspective instead. Relational justice, as we have recurrently emphasized, seeks to guide private law on how to set up the terms of interaction that structure our interpersonal relationships constructively and prospectively. Ensuring the justice of private law must not be an afterthought of judges embarrassed by its inequitable results.

This proposition implies that relational justice theory is not a theory of equity. We do not ignore the fact that some of the doctrines covered in Part III originated in equity. Nor do we deny that some of them function as anti-opportunistic devices, which may remind the astute reader of Henry Smith's influential account of equity as meta-law.[22] But relational justice applies, as we will also see in Part III, throughout private law and not only in those of its domains historically governed by equity. Its workings are also wholly distinct from Smith's description of equity as meta-law.

For Smith, "equity addresses a special class of problems—those of high complexity and uncertainty, which lack foreseeability." Because "regular" law "seeks generality and ex ante certainty, it cannot handle such situations." In those cases, Smith claims, "equity will intervene" in "a particularized fashion," invoking a "second-order" system of "basic structures of domain, triggers, and ex post principles."[23]

By contrast, the doctrines we discuss in Part III (and IV) do not intervene in the second order because there are no prior, first-order rules they are supposed to operate on. The first time (or first few times) a court of appeals confronts a situation invoking relational justice concerns allows it to view this innovation as supplementing the first-order layer of rules with a second-order layer. But this added layer will, at some point, be assimilated into the former layer (and it does not matter, for our purposes, whether the first-order layer is formally called law or equity).[24]

4. *Trade-offs?* In some contexts, the relational injustice of a given rule may be legitimately compensated through another rule or set of rules affecting roughly the same parties. For example, a lower level of consumer protection in mundane, errand-like transactions may be justified if they come in a package that includes particularly demanding rules that vindicate workers' relational justice rights. Yet, the qualitative distinction between vocation and finance implies that the inverse proposition does not hold: our theory rejects relationally unjust work rules, even if they can be financially compensated by monetary benefits workers would gain in their capacity as consumers.

Background Regime

So far, we have addressed general features of law that refine the translation of relational justice into private law. Both legality's constraints and the possible gaps between law's prescriptions and its final incidents apply whenever we attempt to instantiate our normative commitments in law. We now turn to two sets of more specific challenges and refinements, starting with those that emerge from the background legal regime in which private law is embedded.

Though private law has a distinctive task, it is neither insulated from public law nor should it be. Two aspects stand out in their interdependence. One is that public concerns, such as distributive justice, may suitably override private law. The other is that the performance of the state's public law institutions when securing people's self-determination and substantive equality may affect the surrounding circumstances and impact the content of others' responsibility.

1. Overriding Public Values. At times, private law's commitment to relational justice will be inconsistent with external commitments of the liberal state, and, in some cases, the latter may well prevail. As we noted above, relational justice is private law's distinctive responsibility and thus justifiably privileged in its domain, but public purposes like distributive justice, democratic citizenship, and social welfare are also *potentially* relevant. Nothing in our insistence on relational justice's distinctive role in private law should be read to suggest otherwise.

To begin with, we do not deny that the jurisdiction of private law, and thus of relational justice, can be, and often is, circumscribed by public concerns. Constraints can work in both directions. Thus, in some contexts, a private law framework can be legitimately enlisted to serve irreducibly public values, whereby the state commandeers the support of private individuals to enhance collective goals. The incentives set by copyright law and patent law, for example, can (arguably) be understood in terms of delegating society's collective interest in fostering culture, research, and development to private individuals and firms.[25] But when private bodies are thus publicly enlisted to serve a public role, it is still meaningful, indeed important, to evaluate not merely their (external) regulatory performance but also their (intrinsic) performance—whether they establish, facilitate, and sustain the ideal of relational justice.

In turn, public concerns can justify restricting the practical domain of relational justice, although such overrides are not always legitimate. It is hard to imagine an acceptable legal regime that would eliminate the relational dimension of the simple tort duty against committing assault and battery, or all the normative powers allowing persons to create contractual obligations and control external objects as owners, to advance some collectivist end, however desirable. Yet, some types of cases, currently governed by private law, are different. For example, assuming that transitional concerns are properly addressed,[26] for a liberal law to limit the scope of potentially propertied resources in response to, for example, climate change, does not seem to evoke concern.[27]

Between these two types of categories, there are admittedly hard cases where relational justice and the most fundamental public commitments of liberal polities are in sharp conflict, and tragic choices seem unavoidable. A particularly difficult setting we address (without attempting to resolve it) in Chapter 15 arises in the context of societies afflicted by grave poverty, where the urgency of ensuring food and shelter to everyone may justifiably relax even Rawls' lexical priority of liberty.[28]

2. The Interplay with Public Responsibilities. The discrete status of relational justice, we argue, derives from the freestanding significance of people's horizontal interactions: private responsibility is necessary for the terms of the relevant interaction to reflect reciprocal respect for self-determination and substantive equality. Often, however, the public responsibilities to ensure self-determination and substantive equality will overlap the private obligations entailed by our conception of relational justice.

Thus, private law's commitment to relational justice should neither supplant nor dilute the implied public responsibilities and state obligations. The resulting interaction between private and public can assume various forms and raise various complications, but for our current purposes, addressing two typical ones should suffice.

One interplay between private and public responsibilities emerges in contexts where the primary responsibility should be private and relational, such as child support. Here, fulfilling the parallel public responsibility requires the state to assist in the enforcement of the relational responsibilities or even to provide some insurance against non-compliance with them.[29]

Another more general and more complicated private/public interplay applies across several private law contexts, clarifying why the scope of people's interpersonal duties at times depends on the state complying with its distributive justice duties. It also points out the limits of such dependence.

We assume that distributive justice theory allows for more than one option in matters such as the public provision of health, transportation, and other background conditions. This indeterminacy will, most likely, significantly affect the scope of private responsibility for accommodating people's predicaments that, in turn, is affected by the quality and level of public services.[30] (The dependency of relational justice's prescription on the public scheme of distributive justice is most clearly evident in the context of accommodating the poor, which we explore in Chapter 14.)

Two fixed prescriptions nonetheless remain. On the one hand, even if the state fully complies with its distributive justice obligations, the prescriptions of relational justice on the horizontal interactions constructed by private law remain. To appreciate this, we first need to introduce a distinction between the question and the circumstances of justice.[31] The question of justice is what relational justice or distributive justice requires. This question is posed against the backdrop of the circumstances of justice, namely, certain facts about the human condition, such as moderate scarcity and interdependence.[32] The question of justice—asking who is responsible for making the necessary accommodations—presupposes a number of such circumstances.

We recognize, as noted, that changed circumstances of justice may modify the question of justice and, therefore, that some such changes may even render it moot. For example, the question of justice concerning accessibility would vanish with a technology—such as teleportation ("transporter" in Star Trek or "apparition" in Harry Potter)—that eliminates the need to make places accessible. By contrast, as long as resources in a state are moderately scarce and their allocation for securing everyone's self-determination and substantive equality is not, at least to an extent, constitutionally guaranteed, the case of full state compliance is different. In other words, as long as interpersonal vulnerability remains a potential reality, the question of justice persists, and private responsibility remains indispensable.

It is now fitting to consider what relational justice requires when the state is only partially committed to compliance with the demands of distributive justice, an apt description of the world we live in. Is it permissible to impose private responsibility in *excess* of what the demands of relational justice already allow? From a relational justice perspective, the answer is no. In tort law parlance, we argue against invoking a regime of joint and several liability to tackle cases where distributive justice is judgment-proof.

The reason takes us back to our rejection (in Chapter 2) of the private law model as the law of state executive agents. In a tort law context featuring two defendants independently responsible for causing the plaintiff an indivisible injury, to regard both defendants as each other's surety may be justified by the fact that both are wrongdoers. However, the failure of private persons to make up for the state's retreat from its obligations to sustain distributive justice does not constitute wrongdoing, assuming, as we do, that these persons have fully discharged their relational justice duty.

Accommodation duties reflecting recognition of another person's self-determination and equal standing should not exceed the bounds set by reciprocal respect for each party's self-determination and substantive equality. Relational justice, however, does not necessarily cap people's responsibility in such cases. Private law need not—indeed, should not—be indifferent to demands of distributive justice that, in certain circumstances, may justify more responsibility, though not less. Relational justice does not eradicate people's civic duty to support just institutions.

More generally, the freestanding value of the justness of legally structured relational frameworks implies that a threshold for overriding relational justice's guidance is imperative but without implying, as noted, that relational justice should serve as a side constraint. Relational justice serves instead as the starting point, on par with the idea of threshold deontology. It is a deontological prescription regarding private law's unit of analysis: the pertinent human and social interactions.

Variability and Indeterminacy

1. Thin, Thick, and Contractual Engagements. So far, we have addressed how external legal doctrines, such as the state's tax and redistribution scheme, affect relational justice's injunctions in shaping (and often constructing) people's mutual relations. It is time to look inward. Private law covers a diverse range of contexts, and some of the differences between them are normatively significant.[33]

Our discussion in Chapter 3 implicitly addressed an involuntary interaction between strangers, which is indeed the setting of many private law doctrines, notably within tort law. Even in this setting of thin encounters, we insisted, private law must prescribe terms of interactions reflective of reciprocal respect for self-determination and substantive equality. This abstract injunction remains valid throughout private law. But in other, thicker interactions, the implications of relational justice—the accommodative burdens it entails—are particularly demanding.

A heightened requirement of relational justice thus clearly applies where the parties' capacity for autonomous choice is asymmetrical. In these cases—consider the canonic example of parental obligations—law legitimately prescribes heightened and immutable interpersonal duties to grapple with the parties' asymmetrical vulnerability.[34] Elevated interpersonal responsibility is also called for in thick types of private law engagements involving intimates and fiduciaries, which are also beyond the scope of our current discussion.[35]

Between these thin and thick engagements is the garden-variety contractual context. Two features distinguishing contractual from involuntary engagements are noteworthy for our purposes. On the one hand, the sequence of contract implies a close ongoing interdependence that, in turn, generates heightened interpersonal vulnerability. There are, as we will see in Chapter 10, different causes for this vulnerability, which also takes different forms, but their common denominator is that they invite one party to take advantage of the other. This potential for opportunistic behavior, which is ingrained in the sequential arrangement typical of contractual performance, is the contract-specific type of relational injustice.

Targeting these injustices requires law to prescribe contractual obligations beyond those that apply to people at large, meaning—and this is the second distinctive feature of the contractual context—that these rules must not be mandatory. All else being equal, then, contractual parties in a liberal legal system should not be forced to attend to one another's vulnerability more than other people should. When capable of fine-tuning the means for securing their future compliance with relational justice, they should be (and generally are) free to do so.

2. The Significance of Intentionality. Relational justice understands private law's basic role as prospective and constructive—it sets out to determine the rights and duties that constitute just terms of interactions rather than respond, after the fact, to wrongs and violations of previously fixed rights. Motives do not play a role in deciding what private law duties we owe to each other.[36] As such, assessing terms of interaction as just or unjust makes no reference to whether the behavior of duty-owers is motivated. One key virtue of this liberal commitment (to set motives aside) is that relational justice is acutely aware of injustices that arise independently of the deliberately bad behavior of this or that villain and is thus well-positioned to tackle structural injustices.[37]

The implication, however, is not that deliberate wrongdoing and malicious intentions should play no role in the legal analysis. Although their existence is not necessary for assessing terms of interactions as unjust, acting on such intentions can certainly warrant additional legal consequences, three of which stand out. As we argue in Chapter 7, deliberate wrongdoing can, and often should, ground supra-compensatory damages.[38] As for discrimination, the topic of Chapter 13, we argue that motives or intentions should not be necessary for determining what counts as wrongful discrimination, but they do affect the remedy and the allocation of the burden of proof in a prima facie case of discrimination.[39] Finally, deliberate wrongdoing also carries weight when assessing the value of the victim's right of action. As we noted in Chapter 2 and argue more fully elsewhere, entitlement to pursue the wrongdoer is often a means to the end of obtaining material redress. Yet, the value of this entitlement can become non-instrumental when what is at stake for the victim is not merely material redress but also the reassertion of agency vis-à-vis the wrongdoer. Deliberate wrongdoing, because it involves the rejection of the victim's very status as a free and equal being, invites response and thus elevates the moral significance of personal rights of action beyond their instrumental role.[40]

3. *Natural vs. Artificial Persons.* Does relational justice theory, which focuses on persons as human beings, apply to *artificial* legal persons (corporate bodies)? Since the individual human is relational justice's unit of analysis, we can confidently assume that our account of interpersonal duties applies to the horizontal dealings of these artificial persons with natural persons (e.g., as sellers or employers). Indeed, at least in some of these contexts, artificial legal persons may face more demanding obligations than their natural counterparts.

Admittedly, this proposition leaves vital questions unaddressed. Thus, it provides no guidance regarding further obligations toward individuals possibly imposed on incorporated bodies. (We deal with this issue in Chapter 11, where we defend the emerging case law placing a heavy responsibility on financial institutions for mistaken payments they made to individuals). In this book, we do not address cases involving corporations on both sides of the interaction nor cases involving natural persons' duties toward corporations.

Proper consideration of these questions requires a principled treatment of artificial persons. A theory of incorporated persons that transcends their economic function is urgently needed in private law theory, but this is a formidable task that must now wait. At this stage, we can settle for a rough distinction between, on the one hand, incorporations that serve as a ground project of a natural person or group of persons and, on the other, those that do not.[41]

4. Built-In Indeterminacy. Yet another source of gaps is that between the normative dictates of relational justice—even if properly calibrated along the lines articulated in this chapter—and full-blown specification of its legal implications. Relational justice theory does not—cannot, and indeed should not—prescribe detailed blueprints. Theories like relational justice, which aspire to apply across time and place, necessarily leave room for local adjustments based on the pertinent doctrinal landscape and the broader social, cultural, and economic circumstances as well as—and no less significant—democratic prescriptions[42] (and some measure of experimentation). This means that, while a genuinely liberal private law must take relational justice seriously, it can still accommodate other values. It also means that the remaining indeterminacy between the theory's guidelines for a justifiable system of private law and the concrete answers for as-applied, real-world questions is a feature rather than a bug.

In most of the doctrinal survey that follows, we analyze American private law. Using relational justice as our lodestar, we defend some rules, offer interpretations of others, and call for the reform of those contravening its prescriptions. We thereby hope to show that our theory can make a practical difference and, once operationalized in a given legal system, it can guide the architects of private law in their core mission of securing just horizontal relationships. But the built-in indeterminacy just mentioned requires adding a caveat: the prescriptions we sanction are not—at least not necessarily—the only ones that comply with relational justice. Different rules of other legal systems, with different choices and traditions, may also fit the bill.

This cautionary note will be particularly pertinent in Chapter 15, which examines the role of relational justice theory in setting a floor of acceptable terms of interaction in transnational settings. In that context, relational justice helps to develop a notion of interpersonal human rights, that is, a floor of the direct obligations incumbent on transnationally interacting parties that must be attuned to legitimate concerns of parochialism.

The Value of Private Law Institutions

The final aspect we will address regarding the translation of relational justice into concrete legal doctrines is institutional. Relational justice theory defends the non-instrumental value of the institution of private law. We argue that even the most generous scheme of (public law) rights against the state cannot supplant the rights, duties, and responsibilities underlying the horizontal dimension governed by the demands of relational justice. That said, not all the institutional components of the private law institution are equally valuable, and some of its core traditional components are valuable only instrumentally.

Some versions of private law theory claim that judge-made law should be the primary backdrop for interactions among individuals. In these views, judges bear the central responsibility for interpersonal justice, while legislation and regulation feature in the distant periphery as alien add-ons or late-coming policy interventions. As mentioned in Chapter 2, there are weighty reasons for this association of private law with adjudication, but they do not imply that private law only appears, thrives, or survives when run by judges. More specifically, they do not imply that adjudication is necessarily non-instrumentally valuable, let alone the *sine qua non* of private law.

Although adjudication is often a perfectly sensible mechanism for private law to employ, private law can be, is, and sometimes should also be made, applied, interpreted, and developed in other institutional arenas. In increasingly prevalent contexts in contemporary society, legislatures and administrative agencies rather than (or in addition to) courts are appropriate institutional settings for the articulation, development, and vindication of our interpersonal rights. Administrative regulation is useful and sometimes indispensable for establishing and maintaining the infrastructure of interpersonal interaction in complex societies.[43] The reasons for adopting an instrumental stance (subject to the exceptions we mention below) toward the distinction between legislatures, agencies, and courts indeed follow our theory of relational justice.

Enlisting agencies may be required for obvious but critical practical reasons: the existing private law institutions of adjudication (alternative dispute resolutions included) may fail to respond effectively enough to the demand for dispute resolution,[44] and their response may be disturbed by the parties' inability to pay or other asymmetrical limitations of the access to justice.[45]

Other reasons for taking an instrumental stance are more principled. In an increasingly interconnected social environment, it is increasingly hard for courts, whose *modus operandi* is *re*active and whose perspective and information on key categories of relationships—with employers, landlords, banks, and the like—is framed by the specific disputes they encounter, to face these challenges on their own. Private law's mission of developing and enforcing juridical infrastructures for people's interpersonal interactions compliant with relational justice frequently requires recruiting an administrative apparatus to complement or even supplant the courts.[46]

Regulatory underpinning may be necessary for ensuring the generality of legal prescription, maintaining the required technological expertise for legal decision-making, and targeting systemic market failures. It may also be necessary in order to establish effective tools for proactive (as opposed to reactive) ex ante guarantees of just interpersonal relationships in various settings and to ensure that they are sufficiently predictable so as to effectively guide people's behavior as required by the rule of law. Finally, in certain contexts, these reasons for handing over part of private law's mission to regulators expand when we recall that the challenge that confronts private law, rather than resist the influence of our public commitments, is to respond to the injunctions of relational justice while remaining sensitive to other vital public concerns.

Part of our task in this book, then, is to release private law theory from its conventional (in common law jurisdictions) judge-made law stricture. At the very least, a singular focus on the courts limits the institutional and procedural imagination as to how private law contributes to our interpersonal, horizontal relationships. The legal infrastructure of our human and social interactions—our private law—is and should be a product of a joint venture involving courts, legislatures, and administrative agencies.

Behind the choice between lawmaking institutions, as one of us argues elsewhere, is a non-instrumental value.[47] But we claim here that, from the standpoint of relational justice, the difference between various state institutions may often subject to instrumental considerations. We say "often" in recognition of categories of cases, noted above, where relational justice theory implies that a personal right of action—and thus the institutional choice—is non-instrumentally valuable.[48] Beyond such cases, however, the substance of private law comes first in the order of justification. Thus, private law should be designed keeping in mind the various institutional and procedural means that the pertinent legal system supplies (or can supply) for the optimal performance of its core task: relational justice.

Part III

The Familiar Terrain

5
Negligence and the Reasonable Person

The Road Ahead

We are now ready to move from legal theory to legal doctrine. Our mission, as discussed in Chapter 1, is to examine both the normative and the interpretive credentials of relational justice theory in a variety of actual cases. Although our coverage of (American) private law is necessarily partial, it seems broad enough to include major doctrinal areas where considered judgments can help to vindicate relational justice as the normative core of private law. While some of these areas call for legal reform, a sufficient number of others justifies treating relational justice theory as an interpretative theory of private law.

These diverse doctrines cast interpersonal interactions as frameworks for relationships between self-determining individuals who respect one another as substantively equal. The demands they place on people's conduct frequently go beyond respect for the independence of others, but they are not overwhelming. Often, these doctrines cannot be justified by reference to people's civic duties or by attributing to them the status of executive agents. They can be fully explained, however, once the freestanding requirements of relational justice are acknowledged.

We begin this doctrinal journey with tort law, a major focus of private law theorists in recent decades. Like private law more generally, tort law serves a constructive and prospective role. Its core mission is not that of responding to people's failures to comply with their duties, as civil recourse theory prescribes.[1] Rather, tort law is important even in a perfectly just society where people recognize the tension between their respective ends. Tort law purports to perfect this recognition and even to make it possible by determining the basic terms of interactions, including between complete strangers (e.g., between a driver and a pedestrian or between an accountant and non-clients who may come to rely on her audits).[2]

Tort law's primary duties, which are the subject of this chapter as well as of Chapters 6 and 8, are the main building blocks that law uses to construct terms of involuntary interactions. The existence of these duties, their content, and their scope of application determine what is the right way for people to engage in these types of encounters and, as elaborated in Chapter 7, partly determine the proper remedies and causes of action for their violation. Chapters 6 and 8 address tort law's intricate treatment of, respectively, nonfeasance liability and public nuisance. This chapter focuses on negligence and, in particular, on a key doctrine often called the reasonable person. The reasonable person is one of the two standards

Relational Justice. Hanoch Dagan and Avihay Dorfman, Oxford University Press. © Hanoch Dagan and Avihay Dorfman 2024.
DOI: 10.1093/9780191987762.003.0005

that, together, determine what constitutes a breach of the duty of care. The second standard decides what reasonable care requires, quite apart from the question of whether the actual skills of defendants and plaintiffs should have a bearing on the breach question.[3]

The negligent infliction of loss to life and limb is a—or the—paradigmatic tort in many developed countries since the days of the industrial and automobile revolutions.[4] The reason for that is not surprising. The tort of negligence addresses the problem of accidental harm. It is at the forefront of society's effort to mitigate the negative side-effects of people's otherwise legitimate pursuit of ends that, in turn, reflects the fact of interdependence that industrialization has intensified.[5]

For instance, going to visit a friend may involve acts, such as driving or crossing the road, which exposes us and others to accidental but substantial risk of harm—the most prominent type being bodily harm (including death). Negligence law establishes fair terms of interaction—standards of care—between individuals that respond to several demands, including preserving equal freedom for all those involved and generating incentives to take cost-justified precautions. Personal differences make this peculiar response particularly challenging, given that actual competence to constrain risky conduct may vary radically across individuals and throughout one individual's life.[6]

The Test Case

1. Proving Grounds. To fix ideas, consider *Fletcher v. City of Aberdeen*. An infrastructure construction worker who was about to leave the working area negligently forgot to mark the ditch he was digging on the sidewalk's edge with barricades. A pedestrian with a complete loss of sight walking with a cane failed to notice the ditch, fell into it, and, as a result, suffered serious personal injury.[7] The court ruled that the construction worker is answerable for failing to take the extra care involved in protecting the victim and that this victim is not expected to discharge the amount of self-care generally required from others under the circumstances.

In what follows, we focus on the category of cases where the capacities of one party to the interaction, such as the plaintiff in *Fletcher*, clearly and substantially fall below those represented by the objectively fixed standard of care. This category is the best proving ground for considering the way courts assess the conduct of defendants and plaintiffs in negligence law. It forces courts to take a clear position on what parties to a tort interaction owe each other.

Regarding the question of whether to accommodate the defendants' disability, this is clearly the case. But it is also and no less significantly so when a victim is a person with disability since the victim's disability can affect the terms of the interaction (and ultimately the resolution of this case) in two important ways.

First, the victim's disability can partially determine whether the injurer's conduct is at all negligent. Any non-arbitrary attempt, for example, at identifying the "reasonable" speed limit presupposes a prior judgment of what counts as reasonable conduct on the part of a potential victim reacting to an approaching car. In other words, the method of assessing the responding victim's conduct partially constitutes the contents of the duty of care owed by the potential injurer.

Second, the victim's disability may, under the doctrine of comparative negligence, determine the scope of the liability that can be imposed on a negligent injurer. Excluding the disability as a relevant consideration reduces the injurer's scope of liability and vice versa.

Our reason for stressing these two approaches to the assessment of the victim's conduct as partially constitutive of this victim's terms of interaction with the defendant is to preempt the familiar, though mistaken, view claiming that the victim's care is a matter of prudence rather than justice.[8] In this view, the potential victim has a duty of *self*-care. Therefore, the amount of care expected from her carries no moral implications for assessing both the level of care and the scope of liability owed to her by the defendant. However, as just mentioned, we lack a non-arbitrary way of determining the victim's care without thereby determining the terms of the tort interaction between this victim and the risk-creator. Self-care cannot be insulated from its other-regard dimension, which is why the question at issue is one of relational justice rather than personal prudence. This point is a concrete instantiation of the general point we made early on, namely, that one of the key animating concerns of relational justice is the fact of interdependence.

2. The Doctrine. The actual law of torts—contrary to what leading treatises and present and past Restatements of Tort Law claim—distinguishes the way it assesses the conduct of defendants from the way it assesses the conduct of plaintiffs, as one of us demonstrates in some detail elsewhere.[9] Tort law does not accommodate disability, physical or otherwise, regarding the vigilance expected from defendants (with two exceptions: sudden incapacitation and children engaging in non-adult activities[10]). The standard of care these defendants face is objective in the negative sense—it does not take into account the disabilities of the particular person whose conduct is being assessed.[11]

By contrast, a longstanding trend in tort law (shared by many common law jurisdictions, U.S. and non-U.S. ones) holds that the standard of care turns accommodative re assessing fault on the part of physically disadvantaged plaintiffs. For this class of plaintiffs, courts largely follow a subjective standard that makes some allowance for their disability. The plaintiff's physical disadvantage warrants a watered-down standard of self-care that, by implication, requires a heightened standard of defendant care. Thus, in *Fletcher*, the court rejected an objective measurement of the victim's negligence, saying that the defendant "is obliged to afford that degree of protection which would bring to the notice of the person so afflicted the danger to be encountered."[12]

The case of mentally disadvantaged plaintiffs is different. The conventional view is that mental illness and developmental disability are both irrelevant for setting a plaintiff's required standard of care.[13] On closer examination, however, the law reveals a growing trend toward subjective assessment of the conduct of mentally disadvantaged plaintiffs, in line with that of physically disadvantaged plaintiffs.[14]

Asymmetry as Relational Justice

1. The Bottom Line. Relational justice theory strongly vindicates the asymmetrical measurement of reasonableness in negligence law in the context of bodily security. Indeed, it treats it as a fixed point that helps to direct the architects of private law to steer the law's future path, as discussed in Chapter 1. The emerging trend regarding mentally disadvantaged victims is thus moving in the right direction, one that should be further amplified and stabilized.

Potential injurers and victims cannot be in a just relationship without allowing the diminished capacity of the victims to have some effect on the injurers' duty to moderate their risky activity when approaching a potential victim. Relational justice demands that risk-creators be held responsible for taking additional care—that is, incurring additional costs—to protect physically and mentally disadvantaged persons (not only non-disadvantaged ones) from their dangerous activities.[15] It also implies that no such accommodation is justified regarding physically or mentally disadvantaged potential injurers.

Our analysis does not seek to determine precisely, say, what notification method is most fitting in *Fletcher*'s factual circumstances. It is doubtful, as discussed in Chapter 4, whether a theory of private law can (and should) yield such a determination. Instead, relational justice sets the normative framework that should govern the legal practice of assessing due care—why and when is an objective (or subjective) assessment of due care required.

2. Qualitative Difference and Asymmetrical Requirements. As for why, we need to return to our core claims in Chapter 3. In setting up the terms of interaction, we argued, relational justice demands that we take one another as the persons we are rather than as abstract bearers of a generic personality and, more specifically, that the features that make us who we are should enjoy privileged status vis-à-vis all others. Unsurprisingly, bodily security is at the top of our list.

Bodily security takes pride of place because it is the prerequisite for the pursuit of most human goals and plans and thus to people's self-determination. Leading an autonomous life presupposes life itself, and the ability to pursue ends autonomously is significantly contingent on the security of the pursuer's physical and mental constitution.[16]

This priority of bodily security must inform negligence law in performing its core mission of establishing the terms of interaction between potential injurers and victims that, as noted, requires determining what qualities and circumstances of each party the other should accommodate. Negligence law, then, must treat the prospect of loss of life and limb to the risk-taker in terms qualitatively different from those it treats the risk-creators' marginal loss of freedom to pursue goals and plans that the duties it prescribes necessarily entail. The asymmetrical assessment of the standard of reasonable care is thus the proper response to the question of what it means for persons whose actions lead them to conflict to treat one another as *substantively* free and equal.[17]

Consider again *Fletcher* and imagine that the court had embraced an objective approach when assessing the victim's conduct. The construction worker would then not have been answerable for failing to take the additional care required to protect the physically disadvantaged from his dangerous omission, implying that contrary to our moral intuitions, negligence law views the freedom of the construction worker and the bodily security of the victim as equally valuable. Then, the symmetrical assessment of objective care across the defendant/plaintiff divide would not only have overlooked a normatively significant difference between the parties. It would also have *authorized* risk-creators to ignore it by relieving them of the requirement to accommodate their potential victims' disability by treating them as generic rather than full-blown persons whose constitutive features they are obligated to acknowledge and respect.[18]

As in *Fletcher*, courts justifiably find this result unacceptable. More than a century ago, the Iowa Supreme Court stated, "Whosoever did that which might injure [the blind person] should use more precautions than would be necessary where the one to be affected was not blind."[19] Only by determining the parties' terms of interaction partly by reference to the victim's physical disadvantage can the standard of care reflect the qualitatively privileged status of the features that make us who we are. The asymmetry the doctrine entrenches follows relational justice's prescription to accommodate other people's constitutive features and, thus, the normative priority of the right to bodily security over the right to pursue ends while exposing potential victims to risk to their life and limb.[20]

3. *Refining the Prescriptions.* This test case clarifies how relational justice theory can inform private law by reaffirming some of its existing rules (re the physically disadvantaged victim) and directing the doctrine's future development (re the mentally disadvantaged one). At the same time, it demonstrates some of the general claims of the theory, which were discussed abstractly in prior chapters.[21]

Thus, implicit in the previous paragraphs are some important limitations of the accommodation duties. The injunction to attentively consider the self-determination of the people with whom we interact and to respect them as they are rather than as abstract bearers of generic personality arises in myriad contexts. The relevant practices help to refine the appropriate scope and extent of required accommodation.

Crucially, the personal qualities that a duty of reasonable care requires us to accommodate must be connected to the kind of interdependence that brings the risk-creator and risk-taker together. In the context of the mundane conflict between driving and crossing the road, for example, the relevant qualities are those associated with the ability to decide where and when to cross and the competence to respond to the surrounding environment (notably, approaching cars). Physical, mental, and cognitive disabilities are the first that come to mind, along with other forms of insufficient ability to adapt to potential risks on the road.[22] Other personal qualities may not warrant accommodation because they do not rationally connect to the sort of interdependence relevant to the practice at hand. For instance, it makes no sense to take into account the victim's political sensibilities in setting the contents of the injurer's duty of care.

Inherent in the idea of just relationships, as we said, is a stopping point to the duty to accommodate the potential victim's circumstances. Converting the risk-creator into a mere instrument for respecting the risk-taker as a free and equal person is self-defeating. The notion of accidental harm implies that the risks at hand are incidental to the injurer's pursuit of an otherwise legitimate end.[23] Accordingly, a requirement to be extraordinarily careful about potential injuries to the physically or mentally disadvantaged might adversely affect a person's autonomy to pursue worthwhile ends. Therefore, although an accommodative duty of care should be costly for an injurer to discharge in light of—and in recognition of—the victim's peculiar condition, it must not be prohibitively so.

One limitation to this last requirement follows from the conventional threshold of reasonable foreseeability. Relationally just terms of interaction require that the duty of care an injurer owes to a victim be partially set by the victim's physical or mental capacity insofar as it is reasonably foreseeable. At times, the presence of a person with a physical disability within a zone of danger makes the threat particularly foreseeable. For instance, the tortfeasor knows (or can be expected to know) that she is driving in a closed community of older people. At other times, however, the presence of persons with a disability becomes a matter of statistical foreseeability (reflecting the frequency and distribution of a given vulnerability across society).

Negligent actors are surely not expected to know the exact numbers. But they are expected to be aware of the very existence of vulnerable people in their society and of the possibility that one or more of them might be within the zone of foreseeable danger relevant to their risky conduct. As the House of Lords stated in one case, "[in] view of the large number of blind persons who . . . are users of the road it cannot be said that the risk of causing them injury is so small as to be minimal and therefore to be excluded from the realm of foreseeability."[24]

Finally, we obviously recognize that not all bodily harms warrant an asymmetric assessment of care. Our argument takes serious personal injury (including, most extremely, death) as the paradigmatic case. Although articulating a test for telling serious from "light" injuries is possible, negligence law—for second-order, notably rule of law reasons[25]—treats *all* physical harms (except for trivial injuries) as falling within one category of setbacks to the person. Accordingly, although the rule at hand most acutely addresses asymmetric care in the context of serious personal injury risk, it is extended to all nontrivial personal injuries.

4. An Extension: Over-Skilled Defendants. The relational justice argument for asymmetrical care can be extended to cover other instances insofar as the interacting parties claim significant differences between them. Alternatively, it can rule out recourse to asymmetric assessment of due care when no such differences are present.

Thus, relational justice supports tort law's sharp distinction between under-skilled and over-skilled defendants for purposes of assessing due care. As noted, under-skilled defendants (including persons with disability) face an objective, i.e., non-accommodative, standard of care. Over-skilled defendants, by contrast, are sometimes expected to make their precaution-taking commensurate with their own special skills and knowledge. Essentially, they are required to adjust their care level upward because of their unusual traits, their special knowledge, or their ability to reduce the risk to the plaintiff more effectively than most other defendants engaging in their professions or their activities. Thus, a top-notch physician or a specialist may be required—by tort law and irrespective of contract—to exercise care that a mere physician or a general practitioner may not.[26]

Some courts would say that the special skills and knowledge of the over-skilled defendant set the background circumstances against which to apply the general standard of the reasonable person, but the standard is *not* grounded in external circumstances (e.g., stormy weather).[27] Rather, due to their traits, skills, and knowledge, over-skilled defendants are required to take extra care when compared to all the other defendants similarly situated. Here again, in line with what our test case showed, tort law applies a qualitatively different standard of care, this time distinguishing between under- and over-skilled defendants. This distinction is, again, responsive to the important difference between death and severe bodily injury on the one hand, and constraints on setting ends and pursuing them on the other.

In both cases, one person—the defendant—pursues an end that places the bodily security of another—the plaintiff—in danger. In the test case—a defendant who is a person with a disability—relational justice theory requires us to overlook the defendant's insufficient caring skills. In our current case—an over-skilled defendant—it requires that all else being equal, we should take the defendant's high competence into account.[28]

5. A Distinction: Private Nuisance. By contrast, consider the tort of private nuisance and, specifically, the standard of unreasonable interference with the enjoyable use of land at its doctrinal center. As in our test case, courts need to establish whether the plaintiff's idiosyncratic condition is a relevant factor when determining whether the defendant caused unreasonable interference with the plaintiff's use and enjoyment of the land.[29] Here—unlike in our test case—they do not.[30]

Thus, a typical nuisance dispute features a property owner seeking to enjoin the disturbing consequence of a neighbor's otherwise legitimate activity, be it loud noise, offensive odor, or some such annoyance. The typical statement on the court's part would then be that "[t]he activity complained . . . must be offensive to the person of ordinary and normal sensibilities. The result is not to be measured by its effect upon those of extreme sensibilities."[31]

Again, based on relational justice theory's core prescriptions, it would be objectionable for courts to insist here on *a*symmetric treatment of the clashing neighbors. The category of nuisance cases under discussion involves similar rights, namely, to use and enjoy one's premises. Compelling the defendant to accommodate the unusual sensibilities of the plaintiff would have expressed a preference for one party's right to the enjoyable use of his land over the other's *qualitatively similar* right. Insisting on such preference cannot be justified by relational justice's commitment to taking difference seriously because, at least typically, there is no difference.[32]

Neither Executive Agents; Nor Dissociated Persons

1. Comparative Performance of Competing Theories. Tort law and, more specifically, cases of negligent infliction of physical harm stand, as noted, at the forefront of private law theory. To some extent, the debates over negligence law frame private law's main schism, which we addressed in Chapter 2. The two dominant schools of contemporary private law theory—economic analysis and corrective justice –represent the views that conceptualize the person of private law as, respectively, an executive agent and a dissociated person.[33] (The third view, which conceptualizes the person of private law as a good citizen, will take center stage in Part IV.)

Relational justice focuses on the embedded person and thus rejects both alternatives. Relational justice theory seeks to render tort law's aspiration to do justice between persons both intelligible and normatively attractive in a way that the economic analysis' collectivistic aspirations and corrective justice's commitment to formal freedom and equality cannot.

The relational justice argument for caring asymmetry we have just articulated is our Exhibit A for the comparative performance of relational justice theory vis-à-vis its main private law rivals (Exhibits B, C, D, & c. will be discussed in the following chapters). We now turn to show that neither efficiency nor corrective justice welcome the introduction of a principled defendant/plaintiff differentiation of negligence assessment and discuss the greater difficulties this attitude reflects.

2. Relational Justice vs. Efficiency. The economic approach perceives the law of negligence as a scheme for regulating persons' entitlements to pursue risky activities meant to ensure that they do not engage in acts whose costs surpass their benefits. At first glance, this task implies a subjective standard because these costs and benefits cannot be fully specified apart from the idiosyncratic caring skills of the person who is called to take cost-justified precautions. But because the information costs this standard requires are often significant, economic wisdom suggests the presumptive priority of objective assessments of reasonable care. This presumption applies unless the divergence between the persons possessing the caring skills is both significant and relatively cheap to assess.[34]

We do not need to take a position as to where this line should be drawn or how it is affected by new information technologies that may significantly lower the costs of devising a purely personalized standard of due care.[35] The only point that matters here is that the economic reasons for employing either a subjective or an objective measurement of fault cut across the defendant/plaintiff divide. Thus, in principle, there should be no difference in assessing reasonableness on the part of the risk-creator on the one hand and the risk-taker on the other. Similarly, there should be no asymmetry in assessing reasonable care across the distinction between under- and over-skilled defendants. The economic approach requires courts to employ the same method of measuring fault when assessing the conduct of the defendant and that of the plaintiff.[36]

This economic wisdom may, and probably should, be softened. Whereas potential victims often create a risk of serious harm to their near and dear, one may plausibly argue that imposing on them a legal burden to take precautions is not always necessary: when faced with a life-and-death situation, rational victims act cautiously irrespective of the pertinent legal incentives. Furthermore, a careful economic calculus would be quite vigilant in deterring risks to bodily integrity, even when doing so inhibits otherwise socially desirable activities since "[a]ctions that result in premature death reduce overall welfare."[37]

It is difficult to divine the bottom line of these rather complex calculations. But it is easy to see that consistent commitment to welfare maximization is unlikely to yield the interpersonal injunction of priority to life and limb that existing law embraces. There are at least two reasons for this disappointing conclusion, both emblematic of the divergence between the economic analysis and relational justice theories.

The first reason lies in their different perspectives. True, both look at tort law from an ex ante viewpoint, and both seek to identify rules that can apply to categories of cases rather than require ad hoc judgments in particular ones. Their focus, however, is dramatically different.

Relational justice zooms in on the appropriate terms of interaction between risk-creators and risk-takers. By contrast, economic analysis must ultimately target the overall effects of these rules on society, including any potential and significant effects on third parties, such as consumers and employees. For example, whereas relational justice theory seeks to identify the just terms of interaction between physicians and their patients, economic analysis looks at the physicians' duty of care as one component in the production of the public good of safety that, in turn, is one piece of society's overall welfare that law should maximize.[38]

The second reason economic analysis seems unlikely to settle on the principled priority of bodily security—and the corresponding feature of the gulf between this account and ours—lies in its theory of value. The normative criterion that guides standard works in normative law and economics is the maximization of aggregate preference satisfaction.[39] Thus, the economic analysis of negligence necessarily treats risk-takers' bodily integrity and the forgone social welfare sustained by risk-creators and third parties as fully commensurable.[40] Relational justice theory does not dismiss the significance of preferences, of course. But it rejects such radical commensurability because the autonomy calculus it applies assigns sheer preferences a *qualitatively* inferior role to that of features that make us who we are.[41]

3. Relational vs. Corrective Justice. The corrective justice school—the other major approach to the standard of the reasonable person in contemporary academic discourse—consists of various tort theories. But the dominant modern Kantian accounts of torts typically follow Ernest Weinrib's proposition that "the equality of the parties corresponds to the irrelevance for the normative dimension in agency of the particular features—desires, endowments, circumstances, and so on—that might distinguish one agent from another."[42] They are thus guided by the traditionalist view that private law is in the business of upholding the parties' independence and formal equality, which identifies its conception of the person with the formally free and equal agent we referred to as the dissociated person.

The formal equal importance of each party's independence requires the terms of interactions prescribed in private law to be set objectively to preclude taking into account the specific skills, judgments, or attitudes of only one of the parties to the interaction. Negligence must be measured objectively because allowing its determination to be affected by the skills of one party is tantamount to enabling that party to fix the terms of the interaction with the other.[43]

Barring consideration of the victim's condition and idiosyncratic features indeed ensures formal freedom and equality. But it also, and necessarily, exempts risk-creators from attending to the risk-takers' special circumstances. "The unusually sensitive plaintiff," states Arthur Ripstein, "gets no solace from the law."[44]

Traditionalists who acknowledge the difficulty of burdening victims with the entire cost of their own particular circumstances may argue that rectifying the excesses of their conception of private law—through a public law solution, such as a national insurance scheme—is entirely the state's responsibility.[45] But both Weinrib and Ripstein seem to acknowledge that renouncing all responsibility for the implications of risk creation on the bodily security of another person who, through no fault of her own, is under-skilled is not an acceptable answer, at least not in all cases. So, they offer two escape routes from this uncomfortable position: either curb it or bypass it. Unfortunately, both proved unsuccessful.

The first route is to highlight that even a thin conception of agency assumes that persons can be guided by particular norms of conduct. This assertion means, so the argument goes, that subjective factors can, justifiably, carve narrow exceptions for three categories of cases in which this assumption does not hold: physical disability, unforeseeable lack of volition (such as an insane delusion or a heart attack), and infants.[46]

This route, however, is both too narrow and too broad. It is too narrow because it leaves intact the general, and we think unacceptable, repudiation of risk-creators' responsibility for respecting risk-takers as they really are. But it is also too broad because, like the preferred economic prescription, it applies not only to risk-takers but also to risk-creators. It thereby neglects the qualitative priority of bodily security, which requires *asymmetric* assessment of care.

The second route can be read as an attempt to overcome this difficulty. Comparing a plaintiff with a physical disability to icy road conditions, Ripstein claims that allowing the sensibility of this plaintiff to adjust the amount of care required from the defendant is as justifiable, in terms of formal equality, as adjusting the level of care to accommodate the changing road conditions. In fact, he argues, both a plaintiff's physical disability and icy road conditions are compatible with an objectively fixed standard of due care.[47]

Ripstein's analogy, however, does not hold up. The concept of formal equality cannot be coherently applied to inanimate road conditions and only makes sense in the context of the conditions and sensitivities of a human agent. Inequality concerns can only arise when the law allows for the idiosyncratic features of one *person* to determine the extent of care owed by another. To be sure, we do not argue that a person with diminished mental or physical capacity sets the terms of the interaction by exercising some pseudo-authority to decide whether to act.[48] Rather, the point is that the law fixes terms of interaction that are inconsistent with the formal equality of the parties if these terms require one party to tolerate the other's idiosyncratic features. Ripstein's failed analogy takes the traditional approach back to its point of departure. It prevents the plaintiffs' idiosyncratic features from playing any role in fixing the terms of their interactions with defendants.

The same conclusion holds regarding the distinction between under- and over-skilled defendants. The corrective justice commitment to formal equality is inconsistent with allowing these defendants' qualities (and infirmities) to have a bearing on determining the standard of reasonable care. Thus, whereas the law—and relational justice's account of this law—treats under- and over-skilled defendants asymmetrically, corrective justice calls for symmetry, which entails overlooking the skills that make persons the agents they are.

Varieties of Tort Law

The relational justice argument, we showed in this chapter, distinctly supports a crucial fixed point in the existing American law of negligence and offers compelling reasons for extending the asymmetric care doctrine to cases of mentally disadvantaged risk-takers too. But recall that demonstrating how relational justice theory can help to assess and guide existing law does not imply that this is the only way to vindicate relational justice. As we emphasized in Chapter 4, more than one translation of the theory's normative prescriptions into the language of law is possible.

Thus, like the traditional approach, our analysis presents negligence law as an expression of the commitment to relationally just terms of interaction in the context of accidental harm to life and limb. Unlike traditionalists, however, we do not argue that all aspects of negligence law are essential for this task. Relational justice only requires that risk-creators be subject to a duty of reasonable care to potential victims, which includes a requirement to accommodate them (within the limits discussed in Chapters 3 and 4) as the persons they actually are.

It follows that compliance with such a duty can, if necessary, be secured without the support of the adjudicatory and remedial aspects of contemporary negligence law. This conclusion could be particularly significant if these aspects turn out to be flawed in terms of public values such as distributive justice or social welfare, or even private law values insofar as the existing private law institutions of adjudication fail to respond effectively to the increasing demand for dispute resolution. For instance, New Zealand famously repudiated most aspects of the traditional tort of negligent infliction of bodily harm. It created, instead, a public insurance scheme subsidized by the general tax coffers.[49] The insurance system presumably promotes distributive justice and, according to some studies, attains efficacy.[50]

Tort theorists often invoke the New Zealand case as exemplifying a radical transition from private to public law.[51] However, these scholars overstate the shift in question and fail to recognize that negligence law's traditional scheme of adjudication is not a necessary condition for securing just relationships in the context of purely accidental risks to life and limb.[52]

To be sure, a "no-tort law system" lacking *any* rights of redress running directly between victims and their tortfeasors is deficient, even if the latter are properly deterred and the former appropriately compensated.[53] The reason, however, as we argued in Chapter 2, is that, in *some* cases, personal rights of action are necessary if relational justice is to be properly respected.[54] Consequently, while an outright abolition of the traditional model of tort law adjudication is unacceptable, modifying it—even significantly—need not be similarly criticized.

New Zealand may be a case in point. New Zealand has not abolished the legal doctrines—specifically injunctive relief and punitive damages—that ensure compliance with the reason for discharging the accommodative duty of care. Thus, a victim can seek punitive damages against an injurer who actively disregards the reason he must have for accommodating the victim by exercising appropriate care. Until recently, this same doctrine had been applied even in cases of negligence such as medical malpractice, and not only in assault and battery circumstances.[55]

The New Zealand scheme is, in fact, closer to home than many tort theorists imagine. It corresponds to relational justice theory's critical stance on the difference between various lawmaking and law-enforcing institutions and is thus, unsurprisingly, also manifest in other contexts where adjudication is not (or is no longer) a satisfactory mechanism for ensuring compliance with reciprocal respect for self-determination and substantive equality. Chapter 12, which addresses the American law of workplace safety, discusses the varieties of relationally just tort law in greater detail.

6
Nonfeasance Liability

The Traditionalist Starting Point

1. The Conundrum and Our Thesis. We turn now to nonfeasance, a doctrine traditionalists often invoke as their Exhibit A in the interpretive contest of tort law. Traditionalists frequently cite "the rule against tort liability for failing to rescue"[1] and regard it as "an organizing normative idea in private law."[2] They claim that the distinction between misfeasance and nonfeasance is a conceptual feature of private law and a stable point for legal analysis,[3] normatively crucial for "determining the structure of the obligations between private persons."[4] These propositions, taken at face value, suggest that the doctrine of nonfeasance liability in tort law strongly supports traditionalism's interpretive ambitions.

We accept the misfeasance/nonfeasance distinction as a matter of positive law[5] and its significance in determining the contents of interpersonal duties. We reject, however, the attempt to locate a foundational commitment in this distinction. The most plausible justification for the misfeasance/nonfeasance distinction, we argue, is consistent with our account of private law as the legal ordering of relational justice among substantively free and equal persons.

Our thesis in this chapter is that the doctrine of nonfeasance liability sheds light on the interaction between the normative commitments and the institutional constraints of private law discussed in Chapter 4.[6] We claim that the rule of nonfeasance liability is best interpreted as reflecting institutional rather than normative considerations. At the foundational level, tort law is not hostile to imposing duties of easy rescue on private persons. The reason why this stance does not surface in many situations is explained by reference to certain institutional limitations. It does surface, however, in the form of exceptions to the rule of no liability for nonfeasance whenever these limitations are eliminated or satisfactorily contained.

The task of this chapter is to show that this account explains the existing doctrine and provides lawmakers normative resources enabling them to develop it by recognizing additional exceptions to the rule. Before embarking on it, however, we need to clarify the meaning of the misfeasance/nonfeasance distinction.

2. A Revisionist Definition? Some traditionalists seek to show that the rule against liability for nonfeasance extends beyond the context of easy rescue cases to capture areas of nuisance law, pure economic loss, and instances of *damnum absque injuria*, more generally.[7] The key to this extension is a revised definition of nonfeasance as describing all cases where the defendant would be called upon to

Relational Justice. Hanoch Dagan and Avihay Dorfman, Oxford University Press. © Hanoch Dagan and Avihay Dorfman 2024.
DOI: 10.1093/9780191987762.003.0006

confer a benefit on the plaintiff. Misfeasance, in turn, describes all cases where the defendant actually injures the person or property of the plaintiff through a breach of duty.

This approach, however, is wholly conclusory and merely restates the crucial questions: *What* rights do we have, and, ultimately, *why* do we have them? Put differently, the claim that the misfeasance/nonfeasance distinction merely reflects an antecedent system of rights implies that the distinction between the two depends entirely on the applicable system of rights. But then the concept of nonfeasance adds absolutely nothing to the analysis—it all comes down to the question of whether the plaintiff holds a right against the defendant. If so, then by definition, this is a case of misfeasance. If not, then by definition, the case becomes one of nonfeasance.

3. *Back to the Familiar Definition.* We are back, then, to the use of the misfeasance/nonfeasance distinction in tort law, which characterizes the nature of the connection between a defendant and the risk that materialized into the plaintiff's injury. Misfeasance covers all instances where the defendant created or contributed to the creation of this risk. By contrast, nonfeasance captures all instances where the risk at issue exists entirely apart from any action (or inaction) by the defendant.[8] As one court has recently observed, "[c]lassically, a case of nonfeasance involves a situation when a bystander comes across someone suffering harm from causes not of the bystander's making."[9] Nonfeasance liability is about affirmative duties that private law imposes on people in the service of the self-determination and equal standing of others.

Normative Foundations

1. *Hard Cases.* According to this formulation, the rule against liability for nonfeasance stands for the absence of a duty to come to the plaintiff's rescue. This rule reaches its darkest normative moment when the rescue in question counts as easy. Thus, "the expert swimmer, with a boat and rope at his disposal, who sees another drowning before his eyes, is under no obligation to help him. Instead, he may sit on the dock and watch the man drown." And "an ordinary bystander is under no duty to rescue a child drowning in what he knows to be shallow water, or to prevent a neighbor's child from hammering on a dangerous explosive."[10]

These are not exaggerations,[11] and they are rightly decided by traditionalist standards.[12] But how can interpersonal justice require that no affirmative duty be imposed on private persons, not even the simplest duty of easy rescue (say, if you could save the life of someone about to fall off a hidden cliff simply by uttering "beware of the cliff")? Can this interpretation of the law—assuming *arguendo* it perfectly represents the prevailing doctrine—possibly strike a reflective equilibrium with our moral intuitions?

2. Ripstein on Easy Rescue. Arthur Ripstein maintains that it can and indeed does. Our claim-rights and powers with respect to our body and property "come as a package," he insists, because they are all "coordinate components of a system in which no person is in charge of another." Thus, "each of us is . . . entitled to decide whether to stand on our [negative] rights."[13]

But this assertion begs the normative question. Ripstein also suggests that abandoning the formal equality of the independence thesis and revisiting the notorious easy rescue doctrine implies the "remaking" of tort law. Maybe because he is (at least implicitly) aware of this proposition's potential problems, to which we turn shortly, he quickly adds that "[his] own view is that the idea that no person is in charge of another is normatively attractive."[14] Unfortunately, nowhere does he explain what makes this ideal attractive as the *sole*, fundamental normative premise of a just tort law (as opposed to an important component of a system that seeks to establish interpersonal relationships of reciprocal respect for self-determination and substantive equality).

It seems striking to see how Ripstein approaches the specific case of easy rescue—again, in a manner that cannot withstand the test of reflective equilibrium—by saying that "At the appropriate level of generality, [a duty of easy rescue] is no different from [all other cases of nonfeasance]: Absent a special relationship, you do not need to use your means in a way that best suits my preferred use of means."[15] Note that this statement fails to capture the easy rescue case because what renders this case so urgent and normatively important is that it is not about "my [i.e., the drowning person's] preferred use of means." In fact, *preferences* on "my" part have no bearing on the justice of the duty of easy rescue—rather, it is the very existence of the "mine" that calls for effortless help.

Indeed, to suppose that the moral idea of formal equal independence can bear the burden of justifying a strict requirement of no affirmative duties, categorically ruling out such private law duties even in cases of easy rescue, seems counterintuitive.[16] Of course, moving from such a simple case to the complexities of everyday life poses any number of difficult challenges to a legal system, raising compelling reasons for suspecting whether the misfeasance/nonfeasance distinction is indeed as fundamental as traditionalist theory suggests.

3. Relational Justice and Affirmative Interpersonal Duties. Pace Ripstein, there is no reason to suppose that the basic reason behind the distinction is necessarily that of sustaining formal equal independence. Quite the contrary: as we noted above and explain below, a legal system whose tort law is committed to self-determination and substantive equality may also be rightly cautious about imposing affirmative interpersonal duties to aid others, given certain systematic limitations on the enforceability of affirmative legal duties.

The availability of these alternative explanations implies that there is no straightforward way to take the doctrine of nonfeasance liability at face value. Worse still, casting these explanations in fundamentalist terms may essentialize what may properly be treated as contingent. This move also poses a significant risk because essential features are typically viewed as the theory's fixed starting points. A mistake in identifying the essential features might thus end up as a quietist exercise, unjustifiably shielding specific doctrinal details from critical scrutiny.

The easy rescue rule opens itself to alternative explanations partly because it does not stand on its own but is rather embedded in an elaborate legal doctrine. It gives way to several exceptions, none of which, as shown below, can be treated as trivial. Because the *doctrine* of nonfeasance liability combines a rule and exceptions, a successful interpretive account must explain what holds both the rule and the exceptions together.

Relational justice theory offers such an explanation. It begins with a simple moral intuition—an ordinary bystander seeing a child drowning in shallow water ought to do something to save the child. Relational justice finds this to be an easy normative case because its underlying commitment to substantive freedom and equality counsels against granting absolute protection to the bystander's independence necessarily at the expense of the drowning child.

But relational justice theory also explains why tort law's affirmative duties should be carefully circumscribed. Placing limits through a negative duty on a person's courses of action is typically less intrusive on that person's autonomy than dictating—through an affirmative duty—what this course of action should be. Put differently, it is one thing to require people to moderate their pursuit of ends when their ends put others at risk and quite another to compel them to make the protection of others their mandatory end.[17] This concern of excessive interference with duty-owers' autonomy is one of the major inherent limits on relational justice accommodation duties.[18] In our context, it implies that imposing a duty (say, of care) has different normative implications for the duty-holder's autonomy, depending on the category (mis- or nonfeasance) that a given case belongs to.[19]

The concern of non-excessive interference with autonomy tracks the distinction between creating, having a contributory role in creating, and having no role in creating the risk of harm to the life and limb of another. Its focus is on the relationship between a person's agency and another person's risk of being exposed to, most paradigmatically, risk to her person. The category of misfeasance picks out core instantiations of this relationship, whereas the category of nonfeasance features its absence.[20]

This understanding of the misfeasance/nonfeasance distinction does not imply that people should not bear private law duties to aid others. It does imply, however, that all else being equal, considerations of autonomy can be weightier when determining what people's moral and legal responsibility should be to aid others. This constraint clarifies that affirmative interpersonal duties must take into account the self-determination of both parties to the interaction. It singles out cases of easy rescue in which the responsibility placed on the duty-bearer certainly infringes on her formal freedom but does not seriously jeopardize her security or other autonomy-supporting interests.

Institutional Challenges

In principle, therefore, a private law committed to relational justice and attuned to the fact of interdependence must make the requisite normative room for affirmative interpersonal duties.[21] But the law, as we acknowledged early on, is far more restrictive. Although we hold it can and should be somewhat relaxed, we recognize that valid institutional reasons justify confining private law's affirmative duties much further than the purely normative analysis suggests.

In what follows, we claim that the doctrine of nonfeasance liability—the rule and its various exceptions—follows suit. The rule is grounded in institutional limitations rather than foundational commitments. The limitations come down to two basic challenges to the legality of imposing legal duties of nonfeasance: arbitrary enforcement and line-drawing. Either one is sufficient to trigger the rule of no liability for nonfeasance. Overcoming *both* is necessary for the exceptions to override the rule.

1. Arbitrary Enforcement. First, the challenge is identifying who owes duties, a task that, in turn, bears on the possibility of nonarbitrary legal enforcement. Since situations calling for rescue may involve any number of potential rescuers (consider a crowded beach on a hot summer day), singling out the defendant as the bystander whose failure to rescue should be deemed wrongful can become difficult.

This worry is not merely epistemic—how can we be sure that the defendant was at the forefront in the shoreline? Rather, it is also substantive—why pick the defendant when many others could have competently met the task of saving the drowning plaintiff's life? The "why only me?" question is directed at the law as a legitimate institution rather than specifically at the plaintiff. That is, the defendant did wrong the plaintiff by failing to assist her and thus cannot complain about being sued. His moral complaint charges the legal system for letting all other wrongdoers off the hook.

Typically, though not necessarily, the arbitrariness at issue is far less acute in connection with misfeasance: The fault line separating the wrongdoer from all other bystanders precludes the arbitrariness charge.[22] Accordingly, the compelling institutional consideration is to treat nonfeasance cases differently because (and insofar as) they face the problem of duty-ower identification. Simply put, the rule of no liability for nonfeasance answers an institutional, rule of law prescription against arbitrary legal enforcement. Indeed, *all* the exceptions to this rule pick out factual settings that face no such concern (on which more below).

2. Line-Drawing. Second, the liberal case for a legal duty to rescue must, as noted, be limited to easy rescues (contrastively defined as non-challenging rescues).

It cannot coherently require duty-owers to respect right-holders as substantively free and equal persons at the expense of their own freedom and equal status.

However, distinguishing easy rescues from overly demanding ones poses a serious challenge of line-drawing. It is serious because a tort duty, like most legal duties, must transcend ad hockery. If it is to guide other people's behavior, as respect for their self-determination requires, a tort duty should give would-be rescuers relatively clear reasons for action. [23] Is this a case calling for rescue, and if so, is there a duty to rescue, and what kind of action might it require? Typical cases of misfeasance, by contrast, do not introduce these difficulties since they feature tortfeasors creating the very risk for which they owe others a duty of care—for them, it should be reasonably clear (given that the duty element requires reasonable foreseeability) that their activities may put certain others in imminent danger.

What makes the line-drawing exercise especially challenging for both potential rescuers and courts? Expertise, broadly defined as including a person's abilities and knowledge, is crucial in determining whether rescue is needed in the first place and, if so, what rescue efforts count as sufficiently easy. Indeed, both determinations depend on the ability of the would-be rescuer to identify the situation as calling for rescue and assist the person caught in an imminently dangerous situation. To avoid case-by-case appeal to individualized knowledge about a particular person's expertise, courts need a category-based analysis concerning the kind of persons whose special training, knowledge, and position render them appropriate duty-owers.

Reconstruction

1. Tarasoff *Vindicated.* The celebrated *Tarasoff* case illustrates our claim regarding the doctrine's normative commitments and institutional limitations. A psychologist failed to warn or otherwise protect the intended victim even though his patient had told him that he planned to kill her. This example is a straightforward instance of nonfeasance since the psychologist had neither created nor contributed to the risk to the victim's life, and there was no special preexisting relationship between them. Indeed, unlike the traditional exception of "special relationship," say, between teachers and their pupils, the psychologist relates to the victim as no more than a bystander. The *Tarasoff* court, echoing relational justice's insistence on the fact of "interdependence," acknowledges the "general rule" of no liability for nonfeasance but carves out an "exception": a patient posing a "serious danger of violence" to another person.[24]

What explains the court's decision to carve out a nonfeasance duty to warn is that the two noted institutional limitations are muted. Concerning arbitrary enforcement, this worry can be set aside because only the psychologist, his supervisor, and two of his colleagues were privy to the patient's murderous plan. Concerning line-drawing, the psychologist here is not a mere stranger who happens to be aware of the killer's plan but a professional therapist treating a patient. Most importantly, the patient informed him of the plan during treatment. The psychologist thus occupies a unique position vis-à-vis the victim—he can assess reasonably accurately the gravity of the threat that his patient poses to her life and can act on his assessment—in what would count as an easy-rescue effort—simply by warning the victim.

In relational justice theory, therefore, the real difference between the *Tarasoff* exception and the general rule of no liability for nonfeasance comes down to institutional considerations rather than foundational moral commitments. As further support for our argument, it merits note that while "[t]he core holding of *Tarasoff* has been widely embraced,"[25] the very few jurisdictions that refused to follow *Tarasoff* grounded their reluctance in institutional rather than substantive (let alone corrective justice) terms.[26]

Tarasoff is not the only exception that fits this explanation, and all the traditional, common law exceptions are best seen in this light. These exceptions conventionally fall into three categories: undertaking, special relationship, and imperilment.[27] We set aside the first two since, to some extent, they can be explained by an appeal to the traditionalist commitment to formal freedom and equality.[28] Instead, we focus on the third category, imperilment, which completely rejects traditionalist teachings and illustrates the relational justice account of the nonfeasance liability doctrine: like *Tarasoff*, cases governed by the imperilment exception are not marred by the two institutional limitations mentioned above.

2. The Imperilment Rule. This rule deals with situations where a person innocently caused physical harm or innocently created a continuing risk of physical harm to another person. In such circumstances, that person may owe a duty of due care "to prevent or minimize the harm" to the other person, which is basically a form of a duty to rescue.[29] Consider someone who innocently struck a person hiding behind the bushes with a baseball. The injurer had carefully looked around before striking the ball. His conduct is absolutely faultless. Moreover, the injurer could not have owed the victim a duty of care because (recall *Palsgraf*[30]) there is no duty absent reasonable foreseeability with respect to the victim (or victim class).

According to the imperilment rule, the incident can nonetheless trigger a duty to mitigate the extent of the harm incurred by the victim. Note that this duty does not depend on the victim's fault or innocence and exists even when the victim has failed to act responsibly or even assumed the risk (say, hiding in the bushes hoping to be hit by the ball). Moreover, the duty does not turn on the victim being rendered helpless by the injury. In short, the harm is not tortious.[31] It is what the traditionalist approach would have to describe as *damnum absque injuria*. Imposing on the injurer a duty to rescue is, from that perspective, coercing one private person—the innocent injurer—to confer a benefit on another. Relational justice theory denies that the victim's normative situation should be cast in terms of benefit-holding.

The imperilment rule, and in particular the post-injury duty owed to the victim, affirms precisely this point.

The imperilment rule also demonstrates what the terms of the tort duty of rescue should be when the two pertinent institutional limitations—arbitrary enforcement and line-drawing—are muted. Imposing a duty to assist does not implicate the law in arbitrariness precisely because the imperilment rule works out a principled delineation of the category of duty-owers, viz., rather than recruiting all passersby, the rule singles out the (innocent) injurer only. In terms of the second institutional limitation, the imperilment rule assumes that all else being equal, the injurer is properly positioned, epistemically speaking, to appreciate the emergency. Since all else is not always equal, the imperilment rule only gives rise to a duty to rescue if the harm innocently caused to the victim is reasonably foreseeable.[32] Moreover, the content of the duty can ameliorate the second worry associated with line-drawing: A duty of rescue under the imperilment rule is one of reasonable mitigation, rather than elimination, of the innocently caused harm.

The imperilment rule, as one court has observed, "reflects the type of basic decency and human thoughtfulness which is generally characteristic of our people."[33] In relational justice theory, this statement is surely correct, and it is so for all instances within the universe of easy-rescue cases. Relationally just terms of interaction between a person imminently threatened and a passerby cannot ensure absolute protection to the independence of the latter at the total expense of the former's life and limb. Relational justice's commitment to reciprocal respect for substantive freedom and equality provides a relational interpretation of the notion of "basic decency and human thoughtfulness."

The imperilment rule removes one item from the universe of easy-rescue cases and makes it a tort duty to attend to the vulnerability of a person imperiled by the innocent conduct of the duty-ower. This removal concerns institutional limitations on the tortification of easy rescue's "basic decency and human thoughtfulness."

3. *Private Necessity*. A similar analysis applies to another common law doctrine rarely mentioned as an exception to the no easy-rescue rule, although it clearly is: the rule of private necessity, and in particular the entitlement of an individual in severe distress, to use another's property to save her person or property.[34]

In normal circumstances, private law plausibly assumes, and has no reason to doubt, that treating the interacting parties as formally free and equal justifies a requirement to secure the ex ante consent of the owner, and traditionalists may see no reason to change this assumption. Circumstances, after all, change only in the context in which formally free and equal persons set and pursue ends and, therefore, are irrelevant to law's terms of interaction.[35] Upholding formal equality between the parties in an emergency, however, amounts to empty formalism since disregarding the disadvantaged position of the distressed individual relative to the owner in question is implausible. Relational justice understands the role of formal equality as an imperfect proxy for its substantive counterpart.[36] When it clearly is not, there is no longer any reason for adhering to it.

The doctrine of private necessity contends with the parties' substantive inequality in a way that goes beyond the contract law doctrines of duress and unconscionability (that we address in Chapter 9). It sets aside the basic requirement of obtaining the owner's consent to the use of her property and permits a person in distress to make unilateral but reasonable use of that property to save their own person or property.[37] The law even holds a nonconsenting owner liable for interfering with such use of her property.[38] In these emergency cases, there is no doubt as to who is best positioned to incur the burden at hand and, consequently, no reason for concern about arbitrary enforcement. Furthermore, again in line with the imperilment rule, the law has a principled way of ensuring against excessive liability: the person in distress bears the property owner a duty to compensate for any damage caused during property use.[39] This rule corrects for the imbalance in autonomy that would arise were the nonconsenting owner left completely uncompensated for the unilateral use of her property.

4. Ownership and Responsibility. Relational justice theory can also illuminate another dimension of private law responsibilities: the burdens, rather than duties, borne by virtue of occupying the position of property right-holder (including, in particular, owner). The conventional wisdom, well-captured by the maxim "a person acts at her own peril," suggests that non-owners bear the entire risk of making mistakes with respect to property use.[40] By implication, owners are said to assume no responsibility for guiding non-owners in fulfilling their tort duty (such as the duty to avoid trespassing on land or chattels).[41] A commitment to formal freedom and equality renders this wisdom perfectly coherent, but our account rejects it, thus vindicating these prevalent burdens.

An a priori objection to owner responsibility is inconsistent with the accommodative structure of relationally just terms of interaction among substantively free and equal persons. Property rights-holders should not be exempted from making a reasonable effort (such as giving reasonable, clear notice) to reduce some accidental mistakes made by non-owners with respect to the property in question.

Fortunately, there is ample doctrinal evidence to this effect—for example, doctrines of consent, mistake, and proprietary estoppel, as well as burdens arising from registration or recordation law.[42] These and other carefully limited burdens—consider, for example, adverse possession and innocent accession doctrines[43] as well as the rules dealing with good faith purchasers for value[44]—are justified. They all derive from the owners' obligation to accommodate non-owners' self-determination and do not unduly impinge on owners' independence.

Similar affirmative duties and burdens proliferate in many of the following chapters. All are carefully circumscribed, and all respond to the important institutional limitations that we have focused on in this chapter. Together with the exceptions discussed above, they powerfully point out how the doctrine that, at first sight, appeared as traditionalism's most persuasive doctrinal support for its interpretive credentials actually follows the prescriptions of relational justice theory.

Reform

1. Relational Justice's Normative Pressure. This positive conclusion, however, does not justify complacency. The doctrines we considered above and will consider below demonstrate private law's commitment to relational justice while manifesting a cautious approach to the legitimate imposition of affirmative interpersonal duties. However, they also suggest that the existing approach of tort law is probably too cautious. These pockets of liability for nonfeasance do not fully satisfy the demands of relational justice, nor do they exhaust our private law's manifestations of the duty to aid.

Relational justice theory's understanding of the interaction between foundational and institutional considerations serves as a source of internal critique of the current law. It suggests that the nonfeasance doctrine should seek to eradicate unjustified gaps between the foundational commitment to interpersonal duties of easy rescue and its instantiation in the law of torts. Tort law, then, must not sanction, and thus approve of, a person failing to make a reasonable effort to rescue a child drowning in a puddle.[45]

Indeed, to count as relationally just, the doctrine of nonfeasance must not exceed the appropriate understanding of how the foundational and the institutional should interact as a ground for, and a limit on, the duty. We will not speculate here about further categories that should be added to the list of exceptions. For our purposes, it is enough to remember that "almost every civil law jurisdiction in Europe, as well as in Latin America, recognizes various types of duties to rescue and related tort actions."[46] One example of a category of cases that seems ripe for reversal is considered below.

2. A Case for Social Hosts Liability. Currently, social hosts do not owe a duty of reasonable care to third parties who might be injured by the hosts' intoxicated guests, to whom they had provided alcohol.[47] The relational justice account of the doctrine of nonfeasance liability implies that this rule must be radically revised.

A paradigmatic case is a gathering of adult friends at which the host, a noncommercial agent, serves alcoholic beverages. The host maintains the supply of drinks even though some of the guests are clearly intoxicated. Soon after the gathering ends, one visibly intoxicated guest drives home and accidentally crashes into another car. We argue that, contrary to current law, the social host should owe the injured driver a duty of care. The content of the duty—say, refraining from serving alcohol to visibly intoxicated guests or calling a taxi to take them home—turns on a highly contextual inquiry. The more important question here pertains to the very (in)existence of such a duty: why have such a duty—an *easy* duty of rescue—in the first place?

Recall that the basic reasons for tort law's usual reluctance to impose affirmative duties of rescue are institutional rather than foundational. It will, therefore, be apt to show that the two pertinent institutional constraints—arbitrary enforcement and line-drawing—can be met in the social host context. Accordingly, there is no reason for categorically insulating social hosts from liability for damages to victims of their intoxicated guests.

Begin with arbitrary enforcement. Unlike the case of a crowded beach, a social gathering poses no such problem since singling out the host is predicated on their very role as host of the party. Concerning line-drawing, the institutional case for imposing a moderate duty of care on the social host turns on this person's ability to identify the situation as calling for "rescue" and respond accordingly. Distinguishing commercial sellers of alcoholic beverages (say, pubs and bars) from social hosts will help to clarify this issue.[48] Typically, because social hosts lack the expertise, experience, and resources of commercial alcohol sellers, their duty of easy rescue should be less exacting than that of commercial sellers.

Against this backdrop, the major institutional constraints on the imposition of affirmative duties of easy rescue do not prevent deeming social hosts responsible, in some non-demanding measure, for the safety of third-party drivers or pedestrians. Their responsibility may amount, to use the two formulations mentioned above, to a duty to refrain from knowingly dispensing alcoholic beverages to their visibly intoxicated guests insofar as they are motorists or calling a taxi to take them home.[49] Discharging the duty, in these or some other non-demanding ways, is part of what it takes for tort law to fix terms of interactions that treat both parties—hosts and vulnerable third parties—as substantively free and equal persons.

7

Substantive Remedies

Rediscovering *Boomer*

1. A Trigger. Boomer v. Atlantic Cement Co.[1] has earned its place in "the legal canon"[2] as the exemplar of a proper "liability rule," namely, a form of entitlement-protection arguably conducive to economic efficiency.[3] But the distinctive regime of remedies it maps onto—substantive remedies—has escaped commentators. In this chapter, we use *Boomer* as a trigger to turn the spotlight on this hitherto obscure dimension of tort remedies that relational justice theory elucidates.

Substantive remedies do not aim to enforce or vindicate primary rights, nor do they seek to change them. Instead, substantive remedies adjust the remedial response for a right violation so as to ensure *post*-wrong justice—relational justice—in a manner that pays heed not only to the plaintiff's setback but also to the predicament of the defendant going forward.

The *Boomer* court, announcing that its role is to "do justice between the contending parties," declined to enjoin a large cement plant despite the finding that its operation amounted to a nuisance to seven owners of nearby properties and notwithstanding the damage it inflicted on these properties in the form of dust and vibrations. Instead of invoking the "drastic remedy" of injunctive relief, the court awarded "permanent damages" aimed at reflecting the "total economic loss to [plaintiffs'] property present and future" caused by the nuisance.[4] *Boomer* thereby resisted the idea that remedies should always serve to enforce the primary rights of plaintiffs, which in this case would have meant sustaining their right to use and enjoy their properties.[5] Yet, it also declined to enlist remedies law in the service of advancing "the general public welfare" by striking the optimal balance between environmental concerns and economic prosperity at the state and national levels.[6]

2. Misguided Controversy. Boomer made a big splash in the theory and study of private law remedies, forcing legal theorists to take firm positions for or against it. The ensuing debate understood the *Boomer* court to have enlisted the law of remedies in the service of aggregate social welfare by granting the remedy that would generate the most efficient allocation of resources.

Mainstream economic analysis celebrates *Boomer*, arguing that the court was correct in awarding compensatory damages in lieu of an injunction because the costs of enjoining this plant exceed the benefits of allowing it to maintain its socially productive operation.[7] Private law traditionalists conceptualize *Boomer* as

Relational Justice. Hanoch Dagan and Avihay Dorfman, Oxford University Press. © Hanoch Dagan and Avihay Dorfman 2024.
DOI: 10.1093/9780191987762.003.0007

an important but deeply unfortunate wrong turn: a troublesome collectivization of private nuisance law.[8] Both, however, are wrong.

A closer reading suggests that *Boomer* embodies the notion of substantive remedies while denying the accounts of both the economic and the traditional theories of private law. *Boomer* rests on a concern with the parties' rights, not with aggregate welfare, as both its friends and foes assume. But *Boomer*'s conception of rights is very different from the traditionalist one and is best cast in terms of relational justice.

Thus, contrary to what both debating parties suppose, the *Boomer* court rejects both the welfarist approach and the application of cost–benefit analysis to the dispute at hand. It insists that its role is to settle a "private controvers[y]" and "decide the rights of the parties before it," whereas the general "public concern with air pollution" requires the "full public and financial powers of government." The court explains that the reason for its decision is not merely one of institutional competence but an outcome of "its essential function," which is to "do justice between the contending parties."[9]

Furthermore, and unlike its familiar welfarist reading, *Boomer* does not question the primacy of injunctive relief in nuisance cases. It does not replace injunctive relief with cost-benefit analysis as a nuisance's primary remedy but, rather, substitutes a preexisting exception in the form of permanent damages for an injunction.[10] Moreover, and more importantly, cost–benefit analysis does not inform the legal analysis even when the exceptional situation of *Boomer* obtains.

The court invokes a baseline of "large disparity" to determine the (exceptional) desirability of damages over an injunction. The numbers cited to establish such a disparity—forgoing a $45 million investment and 300 jobs versus a total property damage of $185,000—vividly render the qualitative difference between mere cost–benefit analysis and the *Boomer* decision. The court is not interested in securing some positive surplus, not even one with generous margins. Instead, it is the catastrophic consequences of closing the plant that lead it to favor the exceptional remedy of awarding damages.[11]

3. *Second Look and Relational Justice.* In so doing, *Boomer* also dramatically repudiates core traditionalist maxims. Thus, not only did the court not look forward to the general interest of society to determine what remedy to grant, but it did not look back at the plaintiffs' primary rights either. *Boomer* deviates from the make-whole principle, in which "the primary remedial goal" is to try to restore "however imperfectly" the plaintiff's "rightful position."[12] The *Boomer* court took a second look at the respective conditions of the plaintiffs and the defendant at the *post-wrong* stage. The *Boomer* remedy is, accordingly, neither about what the plaintiffs had all along nor about what society should have; instead, it concerns the ex post predicament of the injurer as well as the setback to its victims.

Two key properties of the court's analysis of this predicament stand out. Contrary to the teachings of the economic analysis of law, *Boomer* takes a single-mindedly relational approach, implying that the defendant–plaintiffs' *interdependence* is a source of legal concern in and of itself, quite apart from its overall consequences for society. Contrary to the impersonal commitment of private law traditionalists, *Boomer* decides the remedies question by adopting a non-abstract conception of the interacting parties—that is, the decision to award damages in lieu of an injunction is influenced at every turn by "the particularity of the interaction."[13] *Boomer*'s sensitivity to the harsh consequences of incurring a disproportionately small property damage relative to the closure of this plant and the wholesale firing of its employees seems a fairly direct application of relational justice. Or so we claim in what follows.

Between Rights and Remedies

1. *Bifurcated Architecture.* Tort remedies are not always substantive. Many (perhaps most) simply look back, as the traditional account implies, at the infringed underlying rights. But as *Boomer* exemplifies, remedies law can, and at times should, take a second look at the terms of the parties' post-wrong interaction, and when it does so, it cannot measure their post-wrong conditions solely in terms of the make-whole principle.

The architecture of remedies law is, accordingly, bifurcated, consisting of remedies that look back alongside remedies that take a second look, or what we call substantive remedies. Substantive remedies are important in and of themselves, that is, apart from remedies' traditional role of enforcing or vindicating primary rights. They go beyond reinstating the parties' terms of interaction prior to a right violation. Substantive remedies adjust the remedial response to address both the plaintiff's setback and the defendant's predicament.

2. *Avoiding Remedy Reductionism.* The notion of substantive remedies contrasts two accounts of the relationship between rights and remedies—the traditional "make-whole" view introduced above and its disjunctive counterpart.

The celebrated Calabresi–Melamed framework of property rules and liability rules is the clearest articulation of the disjunctive approach since the recommended approach for setting remedies that protect entitlements is said to be fully independent of the initial choice of entitlements.[14] In this framework, which informs some economic analyses of remedies law, remedies are legal incentives designed to maximize overall social welfare.[15]

Variations on the disjunctive view have also developed outside the economic analysis, suggesting that some remedies are better understood as empowering private persons to enlist the court in the publicly administered vindication of their infringed rights.[16] These accounts begin with the truism that some remedies, such as compensatory damages for bodily injury, may not make the victim whole.[17] One account even compares remedies that award wrong-based damages to criminal law fines that supposedly communicate public acknowledgment of rights violations rather than making the right-holder whole.[18]

Remedies, however, respond to violations of just terms of interactions and, thus, contrary to the disjunctive view, cannot plausibly be understood independently of the rights they are grounded on.[19] While traveling back in time to eliminate past wrongdoing is indeed impossible, offering a second-best response that vindicates the legal rights the victim has had all along is part of what the concept of remedy means. The aim of the law of remedies is to address departures from private law's primary duties—it is the law's backup plan when these duties are ignored. The radically disjunctive view must, therefore, be rejected.[20]

Nevertheless, the traditional make-whole picture of courts focusing solely on the plaintiff's primary right when deciding what remedy to award does not necessarily follow.[21] To begin with, the provision of remedies may often be complicated due to institutional considerations bearing on how courts resolve disputes. Thus, while remedies law may attempt to enforce primary rights, it necessarily leaves some room for institutional considerations.[22] More importantly, our reading of *Boomer* suggests that disregarding the parties' post-wrong relational predicament is, at times, troublesome.

3. The Missing Category and Blind Spot. We argue that there is a fundamental non-institutional reason that justifies discontinuities between remedies and rights. Private law's conception of just terms of interpersonal interactions should entail immediate implications not only for the doctrines that establish primary rights and duties, such as the duty of due care, but also for those that address their violations.

That is, private law's remedial apparatus should give effect to the same normative commitments that determine the pre-wrong terms of interaction among private persons. The normative impact of reciprocal respect for self-determination and substantive equality on private law cannot stop at the stage of determining our primary rights. It must also inform the remedies for rights violations cases given the impact of these remedies on the respective conditions of the parties going forward.

Analyzing remedies from this perspective should seemingly be trivial since, as we argued in Chapters 5 and 6, these rights are already grounded in the tort law's commitment of relational justice. So why should the law not confine itself to looking at the parties' primary rights and resorting to the measure that reestablishes the plaintiff's pre-wrong condition?

This make-whole principle, typical of traditionalist accounts of private law remedies, is inadequate because it makes private law remedies strictly one-sided. The remedy, in this view, focuses solely on the victim's pre-wrong right vis-à-vis the defendant and thus only on the victim's post-wrong entitlement to be made whole again as if no wrongful damage had ever occurred. Thus, although traditionalism emphasizes the relational structure of remedies in private law, after the wrong, the wrongdoer is conceived as the agent of the victim's restoration, and the remedy is exclusively victim-oriented.[23]

Put differently, the make-whole principle is relational only in a purely nominal sense because, at the remedy stage, *nothing* in the defendant's condition makes any difference to the legal analysis. Its undivided focus on the victim's pre-wrong entitlement overlooks both the wrongdoer's self-determination and the consequent inequality should the remedial response place the latter in a relation of subordination to the former.[24]

Relational justice theory rejects such a result and responds by requiring courts to take a second look at the parties' interaction and examine its justness at the post-violation stage. A second-look principle expresses the substantive gaps between primary rights and the remedies provided in response to their violations, giving rise to what we have called substantive remedies.

Second-Look Remedies

1. Post-Wrong Relational Justice. Many remedies help to enforce and specify primary rights and duties further, thereby implementing the pre-wrong terms of private law interactions. Substantive remedies are different. They operate at the post-wrong stage to ensure that parties to an interaction that literally went wrong relate, at the remedial stage, as substantively free and equal private persons. Because private law's fundamental commitment to relational justice must not fade away at the remedial stage, it should adjust its remedial apparatus accordingly. A genuinely liberal remedies law thus endorses a second-look principle tasked with providing substantive remedies.[25]

The case for substantive remedies becomes especially powerful in the face of two facts mentioned in our account of *Boomer*: interdependence and personal difference. These facts, which undergird relational justice theory, are crucial beyond the level of primary rights and duties. Interdependence peaks when a defective interaction between a duty-ower and a right-holder places them in a wrongdoer–victim relation. At this point, the interests of the parties are firmly interlocked since, all else being equal, the injury of the victim and its rectification are deemed the wrongdoer's (rather than the state's) responsibility.

The relevant difference in the parties' factual and normative situations may loom large in the determination and size of the remedy, as the *Boomer* decision exemplifies. A theory of private law remedies should address the parties' post-wrong interdependence and personal differences and systematically articulate the implications of ensuring just terms in their post-wrong interaction. It is for this reason that this chapter emphasizes second-looking as an additional principle that, along with looking back, captures how remedies law should work.

The most fundamental proposition of this principle is that private law remedies should aspire to place the wrongdoer and the victim in a relationship of substantive freedom and equality. This account—in sharp contrast with the theories we have criticized—endorses a distinctively relational approach toward remedies law. Given that remedies determine the terms of post-wrong interactions between wrongdoers and their victims, a question arises as to the compliance of these terms with the demands of relational justice. The organizing idea for remedies' law, therefore, is to place the parties in a relationship of substantive equality between self-determining persons instead of restoration to the pre-wrong situation.

2. *Just Single-minded Looking Back.* Adding the defendant's post-wrong condition to the equation sometimes makes no practical difference. Making the plaintiff whole may not generate a post-wrong interpersonal injustice, and applying the second-look principle would, therefore, be redundant. In two categories of cases, more specifically, the law of remedies may justifiably pursue its looking-back function single-mindedly, disregarding the defendant's post-wrong condition.

One category pertains to ex ante voluntary allocations of risks, especially contractual ones. Many contractual remedies are off-the-shelf defaults for allocating the risks and costs of the parties' post-breach predicament.[26] Insofar as this category applies, then, remedies' law should respect this and refrain from second-looking.[27] (The mitigation principle, which we discuss in Chapter 10, is an exception, an instance of a second-look remedial response.)

The other category where remedies law should look back exclusively at the primary rights of the parties refers to egregious misconduct on the wrongdoer's part. Cases of malicious wrongdoings—where a wrongdoer exhibits (at minimum) reckless indifference to the plaintiff's right[28]—justify ignoring the defendant's post-wrong predicament when deciding on the remedy.

A clear case in point is the doctrine of punitive damages. One significant example is that of a calculated wrongdoer who knowingly employs an unsafe procedure based on a cost–benefit analysis.[29] The punitive damages granted in such cases are the functional equivalent of injunctive relief in the relational justice approach. In a sense, they are injunctive relief granted ex post.[30] Injunctive relief ensures against (gross) violations of the freedom- and equality-respecting terms of the interaction between the defendant, a risk-creator, and the plaintiff, the risk-taker whose bodily integrity is jeopardized. This idea cannot simply vanish after the risk materializes into injury.

As it commands ex ante intervention in the form of injunctive relief, so does relational justice require ex post intervention to reinstate just terms of interaction. A stand-alone remedy of compensatory damages would merely reinforce tortfeasors' strategy of reducing—and, indeed, commodifying—the life and limb of their victims to "a mere cost of doing business."[31] Super-compensatory damages provide the anti-commodification measure against the conversion of people's right to bodily security (correctly privileged, as emphasized in Chapter 5) into a standard of pay-as-you-go liability. A remedy of punitive damages appropriately adopts a looking-back approach to the determination of just terms of interaction at the expense of implementing a second look.[32]

Substantive Remedies in Action

1. The Remedial Toolkit. The argument has so far established the significance of a freestanding inquiry into the post-wrong interaction between parties in a private law dispute. We now look at how relational justice can be translated, at the remedial stage, into remedies law. In particular, post-wrong considerations of relational justice pick out a remedial ceiling as well as a floor.

a. Ceiling. Outside cases of contract and egregious misconduct, giving effect to a victim's infringed right cannot come at the expense of denying the wrongdoer their self-determination and equal standing when going forward. Defining a ceiling is important because the victim and the wrongdoer cannot relate to one another as substantively free and equal persons if redressing the setback to the victim requires the wrongdoer to sacrifice their basic ability to function as a self-determining and equal person.

More precisely, relational justice implies that remedies law should not (and, as we will see, by and large does not) confine its concern for the defendant's predicament to subsistence. A commitment to respect the defendant at the remedy stage as substantively free and equal calls for extending this concern to their self-determination as well (but obviously not to their convenience). This ceiling, therefore, differs from bankruptcy protections in both character and scope: it focuses on the wrongdoer's predicament vis-à-vis their victim rather than on the competing claims of many creditors. It does not apply only to insolvent debtors.

b. Floor. Remedying the wrong must be consistent with recognizing the victim as an equal, self-determining person. This prescription sets a floor that private law remedies cannot go below. It means that the compensatory damages awarded should not discount the victim's loss of future earnings, say, merely on account of her gender or ethnicity (given that the average wage of women or minorities is below average). It also means that a wrongdoer should be obligated to cover their victim's physical or emotional harm even when its extent was not reasonably foreseeable (given the latter's thin skull, for example).

2. Three Factors. Following our critique of ad hockery in private law more generally,[33] we reject the idea of open-ended "remedial discretion," let alone its celebration.[34] Remedial ad hockery not only offends the rule of law but also breeds indeterminacy in primary rights, undermining relational justice.

Recall, however, that objecting to ad hockery need not require remedies law to apply a strict regime of bright-line rules. In appropriate cases, it points out instead what we have referred to as informative standards.[35]

Bright-line rules may fit the gatekeeping function of voluntariness and egregious misconduct that, as noted, justify rigid adherence to the make-whole principle. In other cases, however, remedies law should set a stable framework directing judges to focus on the pertinent core factors and resort to the recursive structures that enable courts and their users to identify more or less definitive answers to particular questions. Three such factors stand out:

a. Defendant's predicament. Relational justice requires, as mentioned, to address the impact of liability on the wrongdoer's ability to function as a substantively free and equal person. (If the defendant is a corporation, it can sometimes stand in for its employees and other persons whose ground projects are substantially implicated in the defendant's condition).

One important consideration bearing on this factor is liability insurance. Can insurance against liability for non-willful wrongdoing dismiss this predicament, especially where compensatory damages involve a highly burdensome payment? Defendants should be estopped from seeking accommodation for their post-wrong predicament if, but only if, purchasing liability insurance is feasible. Feasibility in this context is a function of the availability of information concerning insurance options and, most significantly, the costs of purchasing insurance when many potential wrongdoers may lack the wealth to do so.[36] The extent of the insurance coverage can hinder even those who can afford some insurance but lack the means to insure themselves against substantial damages.

b. Plaintiff's setback. Remedies law's second look does not imply dismissal of the plaintiff's setback. As we claimed in Chapter 5, not all rights are substantively equal in the eyes of the law. Accordingly, tort law distinguishes pure economic loss from injuries to life and limb and, recently, from emotional well-being as well.[37] The core distinction that guides the relational justice account of our tort duties—injury to a person's all-purposes means versus injuries to features that make them who they are—is also present at the post-wrong stage of the parties' relations.

Courts are thus justifiably reluctant to take into account burdensome liability as a legitimate consideration when it comes to life and limb, a reluctance that (properly) vanishes when purely economic loss is involved.[38] Hard cases are easily imaginable, such as one where the injury to the victim is economic but severe and entails substantial compensation (or, in a nuisance scenario, injunctive relief) at the expense of respecting the wrongdoer as a substantively free and equal person.

c. Third-party effects. The preceding analysis insulates the parties' interaction at the remedial level from its effects on the rest of society. But remedies can carry important positive and negative implications for the *pre*-wrong stage, too, by changing the prices of the activities or goods that are the objects of the interaction for everyone. A familiar example is the imposition of strict tort liability for certain product defects.[39]

We make these third-party effects, not by chance, the last factor to be considered. An interaction governed by private law is, in and of itself, a source of concern.

However, nothing in relational justice theory, as noted, entails the total exclusion of countervailing considerations.[40] Hence, a private law's remedial framework is not oblivious to third-party effects if pursuing relational justice leads to violations of other dimensions of justice (say, when doing relational justice creates distributive injustice).

Just Remedies

1. Clarifying a Confusing Terrain. The actual practice of remedies law is ambivalent toward the defendant's post-wrong condition. A major area of remedies—compensatory damages—remains explicitly hostile to the admission of evidence on the defendant's situation when making remedial decisions.[41] This position is often used to support the interpretive credentials of the make-whole principle.[42]

Yet, the full picture is far more complicated. Consider the following: the legal construction of an expansive category of judgment-proof defendants,[43] a trend among personal injury lawyers to limit collectible compensatory damages to the sums available in the defendant's liability insurance,[44] the rise and spread of liability insurance,[45] the growing trend toward abolition of the collateral source rule,[46] and the juries' tendency to be more forgiving of individuals than of business corporations.[47]

As is often true, this list is a hodgepodge of doctrines and conventions. Not all of them can, or should, be part of a principled account of substantive remedies. Doctrines that limit recovery—notably medical malpractice caps that categorically limit the maximum amount of damages with no account of the plaintiff's post-injury condition or the defendant's ability to secure the funds necessary to make the plaintiff whole[48]—are not normatively justifiable. However, the diversified remedial scene does imply that the common view of the defendant's post-wrong condition as clearly and invariably irrelevant does not fit existing law.

The remainder of this chapter brings together a set of seemingly disparate rules and doctrines and shows that they are not embarrassing deviations from the make-whole principle. Rather, they all manifest—or, more precisely, can properly manifest once read and refined (or reformed) in light of this chapter's theory—the commitment of remedies law to relational justice. Relational justice serves as the regulative principle for the legal construction of respectful interactions between victims and wrongdoers at the remedy stage.

2. Crushing Liability. We begin with three sets of ceiling-setting doctrines, all following *Boomer*'s legacy of accommodating the defendant's post-wrong condition. These doctrines are, roughly speaking, akin to an excuse rather than a justification. Without presupposing the absence of a complete tort, they accommodate the defendant's predicament by reducing (in terms of liability) the consequences of the wrongdoing.[49]

If imposing liability on a defendant is likely to bring down her livelihood (or calling, or ground project), if liability is sought for an act of inadvertent neglect on her part, and if the damage inflicted by this neglect to the plaintiff—a business organization—is purely economic, a compelling reason exists for making some allowance for the defendant's predicament. Relational justice theory makes sense of the doctrine of crushing liability in terms of this line of reasoning.

Although this doctrine rests on liability rather than remedies, it should stand functionally, if not formally, for a remedial response to the negligent infliction of economic loss. Making allowance for the defendant's predicament cannot be satisfactorily explained as a no-duty decision, nor can it turn solely on the type of injury (economic loss) caused by the breach of duty. The doctrine does instead excuse, in part or in whole, the otherwise tortious act of the defendant when relational justice so demands.[50]

Indeed, Judge Cardozo's worry in the famous *Ultramares v. Touche* case was that of exposing the defendant "to a liability in an indeterminate amount for an indeterminate time to an indeterminate class."[51] But when this worry of crushing liability is not obtained, the court readily acknowledges the existence of a duty and does impose liability for the exact same misconduct and injury.[52] The special *Ultramares* allowance operates only to relieve defendants of *crushing* liability for negligent misrepresentation.

This allowance operates ex post in a manner reminiscent of the second-looking notion. It is indeed designed to have virtually no practical effects on the exercise of care by risk-creators. To begin with, the *Ultramares* court would have allowed full recovery for fraud, as opposed to negligence, insofar as it implicated the defendant in "willfully deceitful" conduct.[53] In line with relational justice theory, risk-creators cannot self-consciously convert a duty of reasonable care into a license to conduct themselves unprofessionally because doing so changes their wrongdoing from accidental into willful misconduct.[54]

Furthermore, Cardozo emphasizes that the case for relieving the defendant from crushing liability for purely economic losses would dissipate completely if the primary concern were "unreasonable risk of serious bodily harm."[55] Relational justice theory embraces this caveat and prescribes that the doctrine should be similarly muted were the plaintiff's economic grievance so severe as to place her ground project, not to mention subsistence, on the line. Arguably, a threat of this sort explains why, crushing liability to the contrary notwithstanding, some courts tend to award damages for the pure economic loss suffered by commercial fishermen as a result of the devastating and long-lasting consequences of oil spills.[56]

3. Collateral Sources. The collateral source rule proscribes the introduction of evidence from collateral sources (such as the plaintiff's first-party insurance) to reduce the defendant's damage payments by the benefits collateral to the tort action.[57] The more recent trend has departed from this rule and permitted defendants to submit evidence from collateral sources at trial.[58] Many forms of this trend are, as noted, unjustified. Other things being equal, the Vermont Supreme Court was right to observe that "[a]s between the insurer and the wrong-doer, in reason and justice the burden of making compensation to the injured party ought to be ultimately borne by the party thus in fault."[59] But things are not always equal.

Relational justice theory offers a principled way to single out cases where abrogation of the collateral source rule *is* justified: the collateral source rule should be set aside if, and only if, doing so is necessary and justified to accommodate defendants facing a genuine predicament, not to shield big corporations from liability.

For this to be the case, four conditions must apply. Two are straightforward. First, the deduction of collateral benefits is in place only if the plaintiff is about to receive sufficient compensation from the collateral source. Second, as usual, accommodation of the defendant's predicament is acceptable only with respect to negligence as opposed to deliberate wrongdoing.[60]

The third condition echoes the core distinction of relational justice theory recurrently surfacing in our survey of the law—between sheer preferences and features that make us who we are. In the context of this chapter, the relevant "we" are the defendants and, regarding the rule at hand, the specific distinction is between cases where awarding the plaintiff full compensation will force the defendant to forgo the pursuit of a ground project (say, their career or some other calling) and those that merely involve inconvenience, such as giving up on an equally expensive leisurely activity (say, a skiing vacation).

Relational justice theory implies that where the defendant's ground projects are at risk, accommodation may be justified.[61] By contrast, if fully compensating a risk-taker results in inconvenience—including a substantial one—remedies law is not required, and indeed not justified, in making any allowances.

The fourth and final condition is no less important. The collateral source rule must not be abrogated opportunistically by sophisticated and legally informed risk-creators to undermine their responsibility for exercising due care or purchasing liability insurance if feasible. Permitting such a defendant to submit evidence from collateral sources based on a post-wrong predicament must not lead to systematic underperformance of tort duties of care or to under-insurance.[62]

Remedies law must view a strategy of taking fewer precautions or reducing insurance coverage expecting partial exemption from liability as a form of non-accidental wrongdoing, allowing no second look. This policy is meant to prevent the erosion of private law's primary duties, thus undermining people's just terms of interactions.

4. Structured Payments. A similar analysis applies to the practice of installment payments in lieu of a lump sum, in use in most states.[63] Whatever this practice's institutional virtues,[64] relational justice theory is opposed to installment payments unless the following two conditions obtain.

First, paying a lump sum would severely undermine the pursuit of a negligent defendant's ground projects. Again, inconvenience alone cannot justify the deferral inherent in installment payments.

Second, installment payments must not leave the plaintiff worse off relative to receiving a lump sum. Specifically, periodic installments are an inadequate form of rectifying the wrong done with respect to some heads of damages, such as medical expenses accruing immediately after the injury or post-traumatic emotional harm. Usually, periodic installments should be limited to future medical expenses (including medical monitoring) and loss of earning capacity.

5. Loss of Earning Capacity. We now turn from ceilings to floors: categories where full compensation may be insufficient to re-establish relationally just interactions. Relational justice theory prescribes that, in these categories, the remedy must be set *beyond* the traditional view of what is required to make the plaintiff whole. Loss of earning capacity casts this issue into sharp relief.[65]

Making whole the injured earning capacity of the victim invites a court to predict "what career path the plaintiff would have taken and what he or she would likely have earned over a lifetime."[66] At times, prediction is relatively straightforward, as when the victim is already on a sustained career path. But at other times, as in a tort case featuring an infant suffering personal injuries, prediction rests on statistical evidence.

Traditionally, courts engaged in this pursuit adopted a troubling practice of reliance on traits such as race and gender as a statistical proxy for the victim's future earning capacity.[67] Empirically, race and gender are strongly correlated with substantial differences in earnings (as well as in other measures, such as life expectancy). In this approach, infant victims suffering from a similar personal injury may be awarded significantly different compensation simply due to their respective race and/or gender.[68]

Fortunately, a recently emerging trend argues that race- and gender-based predictions of future loss of earning capacity should be abandoned. One reason for this shift is the concerns about statistical inaccuracies triggered by overemphasis on current patterns of discrimination without factoring in the possibility of a far less prejudiced society in the future.[69] But courts and commentators also cite a non-contingent reason for opposing reliance on race and gender. Public law's demand of non-discrimination, so the leading argument goes, prescribes an external constraint on the tort law practice of determining damage awards.[70]

We do not dispute the power of this demand or the justification for imposing it on private law persons in their capacity as good citizens. But relational justice theory implies that private law need not—indeed, should not—be cast in the unacceptable terms that this recent trend rightly repudiates. Loyal to its indigenous normative underpinnings, a properly constituted tort law must never authorize, let alone enforce, baseless inequalities.

Relational justice theory rejects the assumption that both the traditional and the emerging trends share in common, namely, that tort law is the source of the difficulty. Its basic commitment to substantive freedom and equality rules out the problematic recourse to gender and race, irrespective of these traits' correlation with the victim's future earnings. Given relational justice's inherent sensitivity to society's structural injustices highlighted above, this approach is unsurprising.[71] Treating the victim as a genuinely self-determining, equal person is incompatible with tying future earning capacity to their gender or race.

Determining future loss of earning capacity, then, must begin with the normative assumption that for all self-determining and equal persons, a career path should not be dictated by such traits or by the (unwarranted) negative value assigned to them by some members of society. Engaging in race- and gender-based damages computation at the post-wrong stage runs counter to the demands of relational justice. This traditional practice violates these horizontal, interpersonal demands and not only the vertical ones prescribed by public law.

For relational justice theory, precluding defendants from relying on such obnoxious calculations is premised on private law's commitment to ensure the parties' post-wrong just relationship, which requires every defendant to respect the plaintiff as a self-determining, equal human being at the remedial stage. Our account thus preempts the concerns that haunt private law rules, which rely on people's civic duties—the "why me?" question[72]—and makes the emerging trend independent of the ebb and flow of constitutional jurisprudence.

6. *Thin-skull Rule.* The foreseeability of an act's adverse consequences partially affects the extent to which it might count as wrongful. According to the thin-skull rule, the scope of tort liability incurred by tortfeasors extends broadly to cover harm, even when its magnitude is not reasonably foreseeable since it reflects an idiosyncratic condition—the victim's thin skull.[73]

This unforeseeability introduces *normative* discontinuity between the wrongdoing and the exceptional magnitude of the victim's harm, which cannot be ascribed to the wrongful risk-taken by the risk-creator.[74] The thin-skull rule, then, deems the risk-creator liable even for adverse consequences that could *not* have figured ex ante in her (or in any other reasonable risk-creator's) decision about the kind and scope of precautions that should have been taken. It is, in other words, a rule of damages rather than of proximate causation.

If tort courts are only looking back at the victim's primary right to bodily integrity, they cannot justify recognizing the predicament of thin-skulled victims as rooted in the defendant's duty of due care and the liability for its breach. By contrast, relational justice theory explains, first, what in the post-wrong interaction invites a second look, and second, what the proper scope of the thin-skull rule is.

Concerning the first, pitting the defendant's predicament against the plaintiff's setback reveals an imbalance in their post-wrong conditions: compensating the thin-skulled victim is both a means of reclaiming (the economic equivalence of) her bodily integrity and an economic shortfall on the tortfeasor's part. Thus, the monetary value of a damage award implicates the freedom interests of the parties in vitally different ways. Accordingly, if, at the remedial stage, the parties are to relate to one another as substantively free and equal, the law must respond to this difference by holding the tortfeasor liable for the injury to the victim's thin skull.[75] The thin-skull rule, in other words, builds a second-look mechanism into the remedies law.

This explanation entails immediate consequences for the rule's proper scope. It supports extending the rule to include "emotional thin skull," given the normative significance of emotional well-being for living as a genuinely free and equal agent that, like bodily integrity, has priority over the defendant's economic costs. Extrapolating from the normative significance of bodily to emotional integrity is amply supported in the case law.[76]

Relational justice, however, rejects extending the rule to "proprietary thin skull." The (scarce[77]) case law and the limited comments on the thin proprietary rule tend to downplay the difference between the plaintiff's person and property.[78] This shift, however, disregards that moving from bodily (or emotional) integrity to property integrity affects how the law should assess the balance of freedom and equality between the interacting parties. This move transforms an asymmetric interaction, where accommodating the plaintiff's bodily predicament normatively precedes the resulting economic setback to the defendant, into a more symmetric one, where the proprietary predicament of one party may be normatively indistinguishable from the setback to the other.[79]

Hence, owners should not be entitled to full recovery of the losses to their property if, due to its unexpected fragility, the unusual magnitude of the damages could not have been reasonably foreseen.

8
Public Nuisance

A Timely Challenge

In this last chapter on tort law, we rely on relational justice in an attempt to make sense of the tort of public nuisance, which seems to have gone astray in recent years. Emerging from the early modern common law crime of public nuisance,[1] this tort imposed liability primarily for obstructing public highways and navigable waters.[2] Moving beyond this narrow case, however, has proven challenging. Although it is widely acknowledged that all cases of public nuisance turn on the infringement of public rights[3]—rights "common to the general public"[4]—what these rights include was and still is far from clear. In particular, how do they differ from the rights that feature prominently in all of tort law, such as the right to bodily integrity, reputation, property, and privacy? The latter are clearly private rights in the sense that they protect individuals, taken severally. Do public rights form a genuinely different category of rights, and if so, why should tort law give effect to it?

This ambiguity of public nuisance's core concept, which neither the Restatement of Torts nor torts' leading treatise resolves,[5] has been a major factor in its transformation into a "super tort"[6] tasked with addressing a "laundry list of social ills,"[7] including "the most vexing legal controversies of our time."[8] Indeed, resorting to public nuisance is "all over the place," and courts confront complaints of interference with public rights in connection with seemingly unrelated matters, including corrupting public morals,[9] undermining law and order,[10] threatening peaceful coexistence,[11] risking health and safety,[12] burdening government resources,[13] and destroying the natural environment.[14]

Public nuisance's expansion without foundations raises important doctrinal challenges, but here, we focus only on the existential threat it poses to its own legitimacy.[15] According to this critique, public nuisance should either return to its traditional, narrow focus on highway obstruction[16] or tear down tort law's mask to show what it really is—"public action . . . subject to the control and direction of the legislature," uniquely positioned to "spell out what is prohibited, the sanctions for violation, and which entities have authority to enforce the law."[17]

Relational Justice. Hanoch Dagan and Avihay Dorfman, Oxford University Press. © Hanoch Dagan and Avihay Dorfman 2024.
DOI: 10.1093/9780191987762.003.0008

Public Rights for Private Persons

1. The Relational Justice of Public Nuisance. Fortunately, neither alternative is called for since the (widely shared) view on which they are premised, contrasting the public rights at hand with private rights, is misguided. We argue that the adjective "public" in public right, rather than revealing the supposedly "essentially public nature"[18] of public nuisance, concerns the context or the domain that right-holders are entitled to use and enjoy, namely, the public space.

More specifically, we claim that relational justice theory is the normative source of these public rights and that it conceptualizes them as private rights like any other right in the law of torts since they protect private persons, *taken severally*. This entitlement, as both Arthur Ripstein and Jason Neyers have observed, is wholly individualistic since it attaches to discrete individuals and not to the public as a whole. Moreover, and in sharp contrast with the respective accounts developed separately by Ripstein and Neyers, we argue that it is wholly private in another crucial sense. Specifically, its grounds make no essential reference to membership in a political community and, accordingly, its holders hold and exercise it as private persons rather than as members of a single political community (or as would-be sovereigns or public authorities).[19]

These private rights, however, are also distinctively public in the sense that they protect the interests of private persons to use and enjoy the *public space*. All human beings, regardless of nationality, identity, and so forth, have a right to make the public space integral to leading their lives as substantively free and equal persons. This right is grounded in the moral significance of being a person rather than a member of this or that political community.[20] Hence, relational justice theory conceptualizes the tort of public nuisance as a crucial component in the construction of an inclusive and facilitative domain—the public space—where people interact in terms that respect them as free and equal persons.

2. The "Public" of Public Right: Public Space. Indeed, the public space is a source of value not merely because of its centrality in political and democratic lives but simply because it is crucial to our ability to act and interact as substantively free and equal private persons. Main street and the green are important venues of political action, but they also support our social and economic lives.

In the public space, we engage—as private persons, not necessarily as members of a political community—in valuable activities. Some are instrumentally valuable, as when we use a public road to get to work, whereas others are non-instrumentally valuable, as when we explore the great outdoors. The significance of public space in the pursuit of private affairs is even greater for low-income urban residents, whose private spaces may not afford them opportunities to manifest their agency in the world. Not everyone has a backyard with a playground or a private beach from which to watch sunsets.

But the public space is also, and simultaneously, a cause for concern. Using it may sometimes be too dangerous or too difficult due to the conduct of, or the conditions created by, other people, including private persons. Accordingly, we argue that the public nuisance tort plays an important role in establishing and protecting fundamentally private rights to fundamentally public spaces. In determining ex ante terms of respectful interactions between free and equal private persons, the tort not only imposes ex post liability for violating these rights but, first and foremost, constructs a *liberal public space.*

Conceptualizing the object of the tort along these lines suggests that the emphasis of historical cases on public highways and bodies of water should be taken to represent only one set of paradigmatic instances of the public space.[21] They do not exhaust the public space given that, in principle, any physical or virtual space[22] that is not privately owned could count as a public space. Hence, both publicly owned spaces and open commons (including *un*owned spaces) within a territorial jurisdiction could count as public space.

Furthermore, our broad definition of the public space reflects the basic commitment to substantive freedom and equality. Those who defend public rights on grounds of independence and formal equality might argue that only rights to pass and repass on public highways and certain other essential public goods are required to protect people's independence when they seek to move from one private place to another using a highway.[23] By contrast, relational justice concerns itself with protecting substantive freedom and equality, which means that public nuisance should protect the right to use the public space *even when* using it does not implicate people's independence.

Currently, people must use public highways to get to work, and therefore, their independence is necessarily at risk if they lack public rights to use them. However, this necessity may lose momentum given that technological progress may allow us to dispense with current habits and practices (consider the recent trend of working or studying remotely). More generally, people do not, as a matter of necessity, have to visit natural parks, walk in the wild, or enjoy the beach (be they publicly owned or *terra nullius*). If their public rights are grounded in independence, they may not have a compelling case for having public rights to such spaces in the first place. Accordingly, this view of the tort of public nuisance may not afford them protection.

By contrast, relational justice's commitment to substantive freedom and equality suggests that the tort of public nuisance can and should protect people's interest in using and enjoying these spaces—being able to relate to others as free and equal is not reducible to being free from relations of dependence (or domination).

The public space (properly conceived as extending beyond publicly owned spaces) may be subject to varying degrees of regulation and law-like rules. Some public spaces, such as modern highways, are heavily regulated through rules that specify, often in detail, permissible and impermissible ways of using and enjoying them. In these cases, the public space is not merely a physical (or virtual) platform wherein private persons pursue their natural or pre-political rights to use and enjoy the space. Instead, the rules of the sphere at issue partially determine our rights of use and enjoyment. For instance, we do not have a right to picnic on a highway, and drivers could certainly complain that our doing so interferes with their right to use and enjoy that public space. The public space thus provides a normative rather than merely a physical context for giving effect to private persons' use-rights.[24]

Other public spaces may require less specific determination of our public rights. The coordination rules they provide leave a greater role for pre-political rights (such as freedom of movement and freedom of occupation) to define our rights to use and enjoy the public space. For instance, an oil company negligently releasing vast quantities of oil into the ocean interferes with commercial fishermen's basic freedoms of movement and occupation. Neither the content of the fishermen's public right nor that of the duty breached by the oil company derives from the state's effort to fix the "rules of the road" for open waters. Rather, these state rules can be said to incorporate the already recognizable wrong of public nuisance committed by the oil company against the fishermen.[25]

Finally, note that our right to use and enjoy the public space need not apply to all its constituting parts with equal force. Law courts are public spaces, but unlike streets and public squares, we generally do not possess rights to use and enjoy them. Even quintessential spaces for usage and enjoyment by the public—parks, beaches, national parks, libraries, and so forth—may have limited availability. For instance, a park may be open from dawn to dusk, the number of visitors may be limited for various reasons, and it can even be indefinitely closed for maintenance or for animal nesting or denning activity. As rights in general, rights to the public space are not absolute. Countervailing considerations—in the form of competing rights and interests—may limit the scope of the right at issue or weaken its force.

3. The "Private" of Public Right: Private Rights of Private Persons. Moving beyond the spatial dimension of public rights, the next question concerns the nature of this right. Contrary to the approach adopted by some courts and commentators,[26] relational justice theory relies on the simple understanding of rights in private law: public rights are claim-rights (to use and enjoy the public space) that individuals hold *severally* in their basic capacity as *private* persons. To appreciate the sense in which public rights are both severally and privately held, we turn to *Tate & Lyle*, a leading English authority on public nuisance.

An authorized user of jetties in the bed of the river Thames engaged in a costly operation of dredging a shipping channel that had silted up due to the defendant's lawful construction of two ferry terminals elsewhere in the river. To undo the reduced depth of water and make the jetties operational again, the plaintiff incurred substantial dredging costs and sued the defendant for this loss. Since the plaintiff did not own the river bed,[27] it relied on a public nuisance theory. Notice that doing so implies that this plaintiff did not suffer purely economy loss since public nuisance presupposes interference with a right to use a public space, meaning that the plaintiff's economic loss was consequential rather than "pure." It further implies that the plaintiff cannot maintain a claim of *private* nuisance because the object of its use and enjoyment rights—the river Thames—is not the plaintiff's private property. To maintain a cause of action in public nuisance the plaintiff had to show that the silting amounted to interference with a public right.

The court noted that the public holds "a right to pass and repass over the whole width and depth of water in the river."[28] Such a "public right"[29] is not held in common. Instead, it is held by every single individual making up "the public." It entitles the plaintiff to use and enjoy the navigable water of the river, be compensated for infringement of this right, and sue the wrongdoer to obtain such compensation. Moreover, and more importantly, this set of rights is individualistic in another sense—it has a robust *personal* dimension. Both its existence and practical bite do not depend on whether persons other than the plaintiff could be affected by the defendant's conduct. Although to suppose that the silting adjacent to the plaintiff's jetties interfered with the public rights of others to pass and repass over the water of the river seems unrealistic, there is no reason to deny the plaintiff's cause of action for public nuisance. A materially similar factual setting would be to (inadvertently) drop liquid asphalt on a public road that, when dry, was to block access to and from a dwelling's private driveway.

What the preceding discussion helps to clarify is that the "public" in public right speaks for the domain—public space—to which individuals hold usage rights. Other than that, a public right operates on the same model of rights that figures prominently in the law of torts and in all of private law.[30]

Holders of public rights, besides holding them discretely, are also private persons. Historically, public nuisance was characterized—and by some, still is—as conduct that "obstructs or causes inconvenience or damage to the public in the exercise of rights common to all His Majesty's Subjects."[31] This characterization may support the impression that, unlike most other torts, public nuisance is tort law for members of a political community: their right to use and enjoy the public space is theirs to keep, as it were, *because* they are members of the political community.[32] But *Tate & Lyle* implies that this is no longer the case: the claimants' status as right-holders and the grounds for having such a status makes no essential reference to membership in a political community or, indeed, any other community, thick or thin.[33]

Relational justice theory, as we argued above, insists that in a liberal legal order, this is the only acceptable reading of this, or any other, tort.[34] Passing and repassing on a highway, and indeed being with others in the public space, does not single out people with a certain membership in a political community. Interfering with the rights of visitors to tour a national park by, say, putting a pole across the entrance road does not count for less (let alone for nothing) if some (or even all) the visitors happen to be foreigners.

Discriminating between visitors based on their membership in a political community is impermissible, not due to epistemic difficulties in verifying who is who but based on the substantive rejection of any distinctions between the rights of members and foreigners to use and enjoy public spaces. Private law adheres to this commitment by consistently refraining from insisting on membership in a political community as a prerequisite to owning and exercising private law rights.

4. The Value of Public Rights: The Construction of a Liberal Public Space. Why should private persons, taken severally, hold rights to use and enjoy public spaces? More precisely, why are the rights to use and enjoy our private spaces never enough? We reject the answer of corrective justice to the second question and defend the relational justice ideal of the public space. The corrective justice approach views the relations between public and private spaces in terms of a sharp divide, whereas that of relational justice views them in terms of supplementation and enhancement. We take each in turn.

The corrective justice answer presumes a qualitative difference between the public and private spheres. Whereas the public space is structurally egalitarian in the sense that its terms of interaction must be all-inclusive, the terms of interaction in the private sphere entitle right-holders to decide unilaterally whether others can make use of it.[35] At first glance, the distinction seems to match our intuitions concerning the difference between the town square and a dwelling—the square is fundamentally inclusive, whereas the dwelling is (and is perhaps even designed to be) exclusionary.

This perception of the relationship between public and private spaces, however, fails *on two counts.* It fails because private spaces neither are nor should be identified with exclusionary terms of interaction. We explain the relational justice account of this characteristic of property in liberal legal order in Chapter 13,[36] but for our purposes, two familiar examples will do. Places of public accommodation—big and small—are formally and substantively private entities. However, their owners' freedom to run their businesses as they see fit does not include an absolute right to exclude, discriminate, or fail to accommodate the needs of specific others. Another case in point is the prohibition of private discrimination in the housing market, stating that the selling and leasing decisions of private right-holders must be consistent with the duties of anti-discrimination.

The corrective justice approach fails regarding the other side of the distinction as well. The public space is often a context for radically egalitarian interactions. However, it can also serve as a platform for facilitating highly exclusionary social interactions. A family gathering for a picnic in a public park, friends going for a hike in a national park, or a dating couple strolling on the lakeshore typify valuable human activities hinging on their exclusivity, including a right to discriminate against those who are not welcome into such circles of intimacy or friendship.[37]

The (dual) failure that results from perceiving the distinction between public and private spaces in contrastive terms suggests that these spaces are better understood as mutually complementary.

Relational justice theory offers such a view. At the most abstract level, rights to use and enjoy spaces, private *and* public ones, give effect to people's rights to substantive freedom and equality. They entitle private persons, users of physical and virtual spaces, to write and rewrite their life stories; moreover, they ensure that autonomous persons use and enjoy such spaces as substantively equal persons. This fundamental liberal commitment carries—as is often the case—both vertical (public law) and horizontal (private law) implications.

Vertically, they imply that the state must construct and maintain public spaces, and not only private ones.[38] The public space is a resource or a good that provides private persons a facility for extending their agency in space. Using and enjoying public spaces is necessary for people to lead their lives as substantively free and equal persons. From a freedom perspective, they affect their ability to act as self-determining agents. At times, we need to use the public space to reach various private spaces, be it our place of employment, a friend's house, or the grocery shop. For most people (i.e., non-hermits), doing so depends on being entitled to pass and repass on the public space. At other times, using and enjoying public spaces is intrinsically valuable, not only for those who engage in political activism but also for private individuals, for whom a specific public space is not merely a platform or a stop on the way but the thing itself. Cruising the ocean or a great river, walking the continental divide, or participating in other less extravagant activities may be valuable precisely because they take place in the public space and, often, with other persons (ranging from intimates to complete strangers).

From an equality perspective, the instrumental and non-instrumental value of using and enjoying public spaces is not measured in absolute terms, and the same activity—say, jogging on the shoreline—may feature more or less prominently in a person's autonomous life. At times, this variance does not raise concerns integral to the person's ground projects, choices, or preferences. It may, however, be an upshot of the person's social condition, and the relative value of using and enjoying the public space may then pose a normative difficulty. For instance, the less affluent may be starved for spaces allowing them to exercise autonomous choice since they may be unable to obtain private substitutes for the facilities and opportunities that public spaces commonly offer. The public space's significance for the pursuit of valuable activities is then relatively greater.

However, the vertical dimension of the legal construction of a liberal public space is still insufficient. A horizontal dimension—which is, of course, the one that is crucial for our purposes—is indispensable. To begin with, using and enjoying the public space is hardly possible in insulation from other users. At times, users voluntarily engage with one another by entering commercial transactions or social interactions in and around public spaces. At other times, the users' interdependence comes forth in involuntary encounters when one user's activity undermines another, as in double parking.[39]

Public spaces, then, are not only sources of value for their users but can also be a potential cause of concern. The right to use and enjoy the public space, together with the correlative duty of other private persons to respect it, are therefore part of what is incumbent on a liberal legal order to ensure that all users are free to pursue their affairs as well as treated as equals by their peers. By dictating terms of voluntary and involuntary interaction between free and equal persons, the public nuisance tort builds a horizontal dimension in the public space. In this dimension, private persons must conform with a basic commitment to reciprocal respect for one another's self-determination and substantive equality, thereby completing the legal construction of a liberal public space.

As noted above, the significance of this account of public nuisance could be examined in many socially important contexts. But none of them is more urgent than climate change.

Public Nuisance and Climate Change

1. An Existential Challenge and Two Unacceptable Approaches. Since the beginning of the industrial age, environment-related harm has been at the center of the law of public nuisance. Air and water pollution issues are major causes of interference with people's right to use public spaces, and lawsuits to prevent or abate smoke pollution, for example, were successfully litigated as early as the late nineteenth century.[40]

The harms associated with global warming and the resulting climate change, however, are quantitatively and qualitatively different. Greenhouse gases (such as carbon dioxide) may not traditionally count as air pollutants, but they can certainly destroy our ability to use and enjoy the public space. Unlike typical incidents of air or water pollution pointing to localized departures from environmental equilibrium, global warming poses an existential threat. And yet, public nuisance may still be making a "big comeback" since both private individuals and public entities employ this cause of action to tackle global warming, among other "truly enormous social problems,"[41] mostly (as of now) to no avail.[42] Can, and should, public nuisance play a role in grappling with global warming? We will offer a critique of the two antithetical approaches currently available and suggest a middle ground.

In one extreme approach, public nuisance (and perhaps the common law of tort law more generally) either cannot or should not be employed to deal with global warming.[43] The basic argument is that public nuisance lacks the suitable normative resources to take up such a challenge effectively: its tort law doctrines, especially causation and injury, do not suffice to hold governments and polluting industries accountable. Furthermore, even to the extent that this tort can be revised, given that the common law response to global warming is judge-centered, it will likely be inferior to the potential regulatory and statutory responses to this challenge.

Although caution might be advisable, this defeatism is inappropriate not only due to the urgency of the challenge but also because—as our account of it thus far implies and as its application below further demonstrates—the tort of public nuisance is far from toothless in this regard. In fact, public nuisance law can play a role in addressing the existential challenge of climate change.

The other extreme approach turns the tort of public nuisance into a wide-ranging tool for handling global warming issues, arguing that it is certainly fit (or can be made fit) to face the looming threat of climate change.[44] In this view, given the current emergency, neither the question of institutional competency nor the bar of legitimacy should stand in the way of the public nuisance tort. To succeed, the underlying right of public nuisance must be substantively revised, replacing its aspiration to sustain relationally just terms of interactions between free and equal persons in and around public spaces with that of providing background justice on a universal scale.[45] Thus, rather than focusing on the right to use and enjoy public spaces, the revised tort protects no less than the right to "the use of the atmosphere and [to] a safe climate."[46]

This definition of the revised tort is so broad and abstract that it becomes almost useless. It is not only over-inclusive in that it cuts across the distinction between the protection of public and private spaces[47] but also in that it applies to vertical rather than merely horizontal interactions. States, be it jointly or separately, are among the first to owe us a duty to see to it that the atmosphere remains usable and safe.[48]

2. What Public Nuisance (Properly Reconstructed) Can Do. Contrary to these two approaches, our account of public nuisance has the normative resources to turn this tort into a meaningful legal framework for addressing aspects of global warming. We outline here (rather than fully pursue) this framework and its potential implications. Part of its appeal, we argue, is its ability to overcome two doctrinal hurdles commonly associated with climate change litigation, namely, proving causation and injury.

But before we address these challenges, we need to clarify that our analysis here focuses on the primary right of claimants—their right to use and enjoy the public space. Primary rights of private persons to, say, bodily and emotional integrity, privacy, and good name are, as we argue elsewhere, at the moral center of tort law.[49] It further extends, with limits, to the secondary right of repair. By contrast, as we claimed above,[50] the tertiary right of action does not always single out the victim as its exclusive bearer. In some instances, the real value of the right of action is that of securing adequate enforcement or vindication of the victim's primary right. It, therefore, does not require that the victim herself be in legal or actual control of the suit against the tortfeasor.

Indeed, for relational justice theory, the "primary" right is primary because it is normatively prior to the other rights. In particular, the primary right dictates what might count as a wrong in the first instance and what, all else being equal, should be the proper way of rectifying its violation.[51] The priority of the primary right warrants not only remedial measures when things go wrong and injuries result but also preventive measures (including injunctive relief and preemptive mitigation) when things *might*, with some degree of certainty, go wrong, even in years to come.

The public nuisance tort fits this understanding of the relationship between primary, secondary, and tertiary rights. It is also a paradigmatic case for extending (and at times for limiting) the standing to sue to non-victims and, in particular, to public entities holding official responsibility for constructing and maintaining the public space.[52] What matters is that private persons should be able (either directly or indirectly through a public authority acting on their behalf) to complain against an entity emitting carbon dioxide or some other greenhouse gas, thereby creating or participating in the creation of a substantial risk of destruction to public lands, infrastructure, and other public spaces they are entitled to use.[53]

The complaint is forward- rather than backward-looking in that it seeks to prevent or reduce potential interference with people's entitlement to use public spaces. The remedy sought, then, could be injunctive relief, enjoining the defendant from discharging unreasonable amounts of greenhouse gases,[54] or can somehow mitigate the effects of global warming on people's right to use public spaces. Building seawalls exemplifies the reliance on mitigating options as feasible measures for protecting the safe usage of the public space.[55]

Our reconstruction of public nuisance does not seek to change the primary rights underlying this tort and calls instead for extending its protection by affording rights of action to eliminate or reduce the future (though imminent) risk to these rights posed by global warming.

3. *Line-Drawing and Causation.* Two key challenges confront this approach to the role of public nuisance in tackling global warming. The first concerns the question of what constitutes a nuisance. It will require tort law to set a standard for greenhouse gas emissions (and also determine whether past statutory permission to pollute could count as a defense against liability). As in the standard of reasonable care in negligence or that of community rule in private nuisance, where tort law prevents some risky activities while enabling others, not all greenhouse-gas-emitting activities should be deemed wrongful. The difficulty of drawing the line is not unique to tort law and is certainly surmountable. One option may be to piggyback on binding and other authoritative standards, as courts already do in the context of negligence when they treat violations of statutory and regulatory safety provisions as negligence per se.[56]

The second challenge concerns causation. It involves both the legal standard of causation and the science—i.e., climate change attribution science—that enables it. As a cause of action in public nuisance employed above all to prevent or mitigate the adverse effects of climate change, causal inquiry does not focus on the connection between conduct and injury. Instead, it addresses the three-place relationship between the defendant's conduct, climate change, and the conditions this change imposes on the plaintiff's right to use and enjoy the public space. Moreover, as we argue presently, rather than identifying but-for causes, it invokes nuisance law's traditional standard of "nuisance due to many."

We begin with the three-place relationship between conduct, climate change, and potential nuisance. Liability to public nuisance in connection with global warming depends on the nature of the change constituting the alleged nuisance. Whether it is raising sea levels, inundations, or some other extreme weather conditions, the case for causation must begin with the proposition that the change is anthropogenic.[57] Science firmly suggests that this is the case, both regarding long-term changes like raising sea levels[58] and regarding some discrete catastrophic events such as a storm or a heat wave.[59] To this extent, progress in the science of climate change attribution holds a promise of bringing more long-term impacts as well as one-off events under the umbrella of public nuisance causation inquiry.[60]

The next stage addresses the questions of whether the change at issue can undermine the plaintiff's right to use a certain public space (say, a public shoreline) and, more critically, whether the *defendant* contributes to this potential outcome. Identifying contribution depends on the fast-advancing science of climate change attribution, a sustained attempt to study the "relative increase in the probability of occurrence, or intensity, of a given outcome."[61] One way of assessing the contribution to climate change is to compare the outcome's "likelihood of occurrence in simulations of the present-day climate with some modeled estimate of a counterfactual climate where some or all anthropogenic influences have been removed."[62] Scientific progress on this front is further motivated by the fact that key greenhouse gas emitters, viz., some of the giant fossil fuel producers, understood the causal connection between *their* activities and global warming at least as early as 1980[63] and by studies that trace the substantial share of a relatively small number of energy companies in anthropocene climate change.[64] According to one study, two-thirds of the world's greenhouse gas emissions originated in only ninety companies, and roughly half of them were released after the 1980s when global warming was already a consensus view in the scientific community.[65]

Building on the success of attribution science in establishing a robust linkage between big emitters (such as "carbon majors"[66]) and the adverse consequences of climate change, the legal question is what counts as "contributing" to enjoin or mitigate the effects of a defendant's activity. Notice that, traditionally, the torts of (public and private) nuisance have not followed negligence's but-for test of causation.[67] As in other torts that subject the causal inquiry to a less demanding standard,[68] some courts have relaxed the standard at issue to what is known as nuisance due to many: "a number of persons contribute . . . in each case an infinitesimal share to that which becomes in the aggregate a grievous nuisance."[69]

Resort to "infinitesimal share" incorporates an implausible principle of individual responsibility into the law of torts. Accordingly, leaving out infinitesimal shares of the standard of "nuisance due to many" avoids this deficiency. In our revision, "a defendant will not be exempted from liability on the grounds that they were simply one of many causing a nuisance. This will be so even if the defendant's actions in isolation would not amount to a nuisance or of itself cause any harm."[70]

"Nuisance due to many" is not a prototype of familiar standards of causation developed in and around the tort of negligence (and product liability) in connection with uncertainty. The rationale behind this standard does not lie in uncertainty with respect to the identity of the tortfeasor (as in the doctrine of market share liability)[71] or with respect to the existence of a causal link between wrongful conduct and injury (as in doctrines such as loss of a chance). If anything, "nuisance due to many" is structurally similar to the case of multiple sufficient causal sets in negligence law, namely, a set of actors whose combined emissions suffice to undermine the right to use and enjoy particular public spaces.[72]

However, even structural similarity should not subject "nuisance due to many" to the causal logic underlying the tort of negligence. Unlike the tort of negligence, "nuisance due to many" aims to address instances where multiple emitters *presently create a future condition* that is deemed to be inimical to the use and enjoyment of public spaces. It concerns the creation of a harmful *condition* as opposed to a one-off harm or a "single-hit" event such as a car collision. In addition, the causal contribution under assessment concerns itself with a *future* (rather than past or present) harmful condition. Preventing or mitigating the adverse effects of greenhouse gas emissions, therefore, is a legal response to wrongdoing that takes place in the here and now but manifests itself only in the future.

Against this backdrop, the tort of public nuisance can adapt its workings to protect the rights of private persons to use and enjoy the public space from industries and other major greenhouse gas emitters. Incorporating climate change attribution science, implementing the traditional causation standard of nuisance due to many, and drawing more robustly on injunctive relief and other preventive measures[73] could turn public nuisance into a meaningful private law framework for addressing important aspects of the imminent threat of global warming.

We do not underestimate the significance of these doctrinal adjustments. Yet, addressing the reconstruction of the tort of public nuisance in relational justice theory as a major element in the construction of a liberal public space of respectful interactions between free and equal private persons implies that these adjustments are not only possible but also necessary.

9
Precontractual Justice

The Justice of Contract

In this chapter and the following one, we move from torts to contract, but our task remains the same: demonstrating the normative appeal and interpretive credentials of relational justice theory. A just contract law must set the floor for acceptable ways of people treating one another in and around contracts. In this chapter, we discuss relational justice's role of gatekeeping, focusing on the justice-oriented doctrines governing contract formation—the "grey zone" in which relationships between strangers start leaning toward contractual ones but are not yet there.

1. Vulnerability in Contract Formation. Relational justice's requirement of reciprocal respect for people's self-determination and substantive equality is particularly appropriate in setting people's terms of interaction in the process of contract formation. The responsibility of contractual parties goes beyond the tort duty of reasonable care that applies to strangers. Contractual liability is typically strict (with only limited reasons for excuse).[1] It extends to each other's expectation interest, that is, "having the benefit of his bargain by being put in as good a position as he would have been in had the contract been performed."[2]

This heightened responsibility brought about by contract formation empowers people: the enforcement of wholly executory contracts makes contract a major interpersonal planning device and, thus, a key tool in the realization of their higher-order projects.[3] At the same time, it makes people particularly susceptible to the risk of others taking advantage of their ignorance, exploiting the harsh circumstances they may be placed in, or their vulnerability in general.

2. Contract's Autonomy-Enhancing Function. The demand of relational justice that potential promisees refrain from such abuse is also particularly called for. A return to the first principles underlying the legitimacy challenge of contract will shed light on the reasons for this demand.

Enforcing contracts is an obvious feature of our legal environment but is far from trivial. Justifying the application of law's authority and power against promisors even before promisees have been harmed and even if the promisees' expectations have not been met for reasons beyond the promisors' power, would be difficult if interpersonal obligations were exhausted by the traditionalist maxim of reciprocal respect for independence. Reneging on a wholly executory contract that has not yet been relied upon frustrates the expectations of promisees, undermining their ability to use contract as a planning and, thus, autonomy-enhancing device.

Relational Justice. Hanoch Dagan and Avihay Dorfman, Oxford University Press.
DOI: 10.1093/9780191987762.003.0009

In a regime of interpersonal independence, however, people are entitled to ignore others' needs and advantages, and these setbacks cannot qualify as a legitimate reason for obligating the promisor.[4]

One way of explaining contract legitimacy, which we take as a given, is to discard the traditionalist view in favor of a less rigid principle of interpersonal relations. When going beyond the harm principle, contract law imposes a burden on prospective promisors that, though modest, is highly significant to their promisees' ability to use contract as a planning device. In a liberal polity, people can justifiably be expected to incur this reasonable burden to benefit others they interact with. Thus, the puzzle of contract legitimacy is solved when we recognize a duty of reciprocal respect for people's right to self-determination and substantive equality.

3. Contract's Legitimacy and Relational Justice. One of us has defended these propositions in greater detail elsewhere,[5] and we will only note here that their implications for the present account are dramatic. They suggest that reciprocal respect for self-determination is *not* related to contract only externally. Moreover, without *some* attention to the distinctive features and predicament of the other, respect for self-determination is hollow, and therefore, substantive equality is also part of this justification of contract. Reciprocal respect for self-determination and substantive equality is thus the premise of contract legitimacy.

Attempts to enlist contract in the service of arrangements that undermine relational justice must, therefore, be treated (at least prima facie) as *ultra vires.* They abuse the idea of contract by invoking it in defiance of its own legitimacy.[6]

4. The Floor of Contractual Justice. Relational justice is thus endogenous to (liberal) contract, part and parcel of its normative DNA. Hence, as usual in a genuinely liberal private law, the requirements of contract law must not be specified in complete disregard of the parties' circumstances and constitutive choices insofar as they are crucial for the interacting parties to relate as equals and to act as self-determining agents.[7] As usual, this reality may entail not only duties of abstinence but also (modest) affirmative obligations.

More specifically, as noted, relational justice theory requires that, when setting the floor for contractual justice, law should ensure that imbalances of power and vulnerability do not corrupt contract formation.[8] Consequently, if the terms of interaction governing contract formation are to comply with relational justice, they must reflect what would have been agreed if the parties had relatively equal power or if reasonable expectations of safety, privacy, and relevant information had influenced their making.[9]

Situating Relational Justice Theory

1. Traditionalism. Before we move on to examine in some detail the contemporary doctrines that regulate the parties' bargaining process, we will situate our account vis-à-vis four major competing views. We begin with the traditional one, where the contrast could not be clearer. For traditionalism, the exclusive requirement of the justice of contract is respect for interpersonal boundaries, and, accordingly, it is limited to the proscription of one party's active interference with the other's free will.[10]

We hope that our normative objections to this view are by now clear, but as a preview, we should add that modern contract law is dramatically divorced from this laissez-faire vision.[11] The question of whether the traditional common law of contracts ever followed this vision is highly controversial. Patrick Atiyah, for example, insists that contract law had "little more than a brief flirtation with" this position in the early nineteenth century and, from the start, had to contend with "serious opposition" from some judges, who ultimately won out.[12] But even if Atiyah is wrong, we must not discount the possibility that what *ancien régime* traditionalists celebrated was not based on principled grounds but triggered mostly by the institutional limitations of the judiciary, once the sole architect of contract law.[13]

Either way, contemporary contract law, as discussed in Chapters 2 and 4, is not reducible to common law,[14] which explains why some of the law that follows is not—or not solely—the product of the judiciary. Moreover, even insofar as judge-made law is concerned, contemporary precontractual doctrines often impose, as Melvin Eisenberg noted, "a duty to rescue," that is, "a duty that is imposed by law upon one actor, *A*, to bestir himself to take a low-cost, low-risk, and otherwise reasonable action that will forestall a major loss to another actor, *B*, although *B*'s peril of prospective loss is not created by *A*'s fault."[15]

Indeed, the prevalence of these rules and the significance of their split from traditionalism undercut the interpretive credentials of not only libertarians but also those of traditionalists. The latter seek to reclassify these rules as part of public law and thus external to contract law.[16] As we will see, however, these attempts would imply an extensive deletion and renaming exercise that artificially limits the domain of contract law and dilutes its normative appeal.

2. Equality in Exchange. The relation between our theory and traditionalism is one of sharp antagonism, and its connection to James Gordley's account of equality of exchange is a possible, but probably unwelcome, elaboration.

Gordley offers a modern articulation of just price theory, which focuses on the uniqueness of the parties' decisions regarding price. Unlike the parties' subjective preferences, which determine all other aspects of their transaction, he argues, the decision as to the proper price is one that "all potential buyers and sellers face whatever their aspirations and circumstances." A party who does not "use the market price" is thus assumed to be "either unaware of [it] or unable to use the market," which means that a contract price that deviates from the market price can only be explained by reference to "ignorance or necessity." Because neither party has a "moral or equitable claim to the benefits that exchange confers" on the other, this conclusion implies that parties should not be free to decide the price in a contract.[17]

One way to read this argument—the reading that seems more loyal to Gordley's—is as an entailment of the principle against unjust enrichment, in which neither party should be "enriched at the other's expense."[18] But this makes the claim either wholly circular or normatively indefensible. To decide whether an enrichment is unjust necessarily relies on a prior decision as to what renders changes in distribution just.[19] And if the answer to this query relies, in turn, on prevalent market prices, it ends up begging—or worse, obscuring—our normative inquiry since market prices are the product of the legal infrastructure we are trying to establish.[20] Obscuring private law's pre-distribution by reference to market prices is particularly worrisome given the scale dynamics of contemporary markets, which tend to make the market a site of power and domination.[21]

A more charitable reading of the argument emphasizes the normative pitfall of benefitting from another's ignorance or necessity. This reading invites the (unwelcome) elaboration by relational justice theory that, as we saw, clarifies the justification for holding the benefitting party responsible for taking measures to protect the disadvantaged party and—as we show below—refines the circumstances (that do not only refer to ignorance and necessity) as well as the scope of this responsibility.

3. *Distributive Justice.* Consider next Aditi Bagchi's claim that distributive justice should be central to contract.[22] Bagchi calls for "a duty not to take advantage of distributive injustice and make it worse." Her argument does not deny that exploiting an injustice is not equivalent to creating one. Nonetheless, she insists that "bad conduct does not become benign just because it was preceded by still worse behavior."[23]

Bagchi accepts that duties that infuse contract are "ultimately interpersonal moral duties." But she also argues that the content of the duties encumbered upon those who seek to interact with the poor and the disadvantaged through a direct, profitable exchange—the prohibition against exacerbating or exploiting distributive injustice—"turns on the normative state of the world (i.e., distributive justice or injustice) and related facts about distribution."[24]

This does not mean that contract law rules should be set "instrumentally with an eye to distribution," but it does mean that they should turn on "background distribution, as well as prospective effects on distribution."[25] Existing law, she claims, follows suit and is appropriately "less sympathetic to those whose weak bargaining power reflects bad luck rather than distributive injustice."[26]

We agree that a theory of contractual fairness can hardly be oblivious to the exploitation of a party's poverty or disadvantageous predicament. Hence, we also share Bagchi's claim that distributive injustices should inform the justice of private law in general and contract law more particularly. Relational justice theory is an obvious home for the prohibition of exploiting the poor and the disadvantaged, given its inherent sensitivity to society's structural injustices discussed in Chapter 3.[27]

Relational justice theory sustains this prohibition without endorsing two potentially difficult assertions in Bagchi's framework. First, it does not imply that poverty and disadvantage exhaust the list of predicaments whose exploitation is unacceptable. Structural injustices should be high on our list, which is why we dedicate two chapters (13 and 14) to discuss their amelioration in private law, but there is no justification for summarily dismissing all others.

The second difficulty that relational justice theory avoids comes from the familiar futility challenge that haunts contract, given its notorious susceptibility to frustrate distributive justice-oriented rules. Rules of contract law are particularly vulnerable to this concern with final incidents[28] since repeat players tend to price their obligations so that seemingly progressive rules might generate a regressive cross-subsidization.[29]

For various reasons, this difficulty may be less common than this economic wisdom suggests.[30] However, a commitment to distributive justice would require the architects of contract rules to address this systemic effect, follow the final incidents of each potential measure, and define illegitimate exploitation accordingly. Our theory, by contrast, insists on the freestanding status of relational justice.

The warranted inference is not that relational justice should never give way to considerations of distributive justice. Sufficiently pressing distributive concerns may, as discussed above, legitimately override the demands of private law's relational commitments.[31] But grounding these commitments in distributive justice precludes such (certainly complex) judgments altogether because it implies a lexical priority of distributive justice over relational justice that we find unacceptable.

4. Efficiency. In analyzing contract law, relational justice theory resorts to insights from extensive economic analyses of the potential effects of alternative contract rules on the contracting parties. Attending to these effects may be surprising to readers who expect a theory of justice to take the ex post position. But the focus of relational justice theory on the ex ante construction of just contractual relationships makes the expected consequences of legal doctrine a foremost concern.[32]

That said, the consequences we are interested in are, as noted, very different from the welfarist consequences associated with the economic analysis of law.[33] First, a genuine concern for social welfare would go beyond the interests of the parties and, indeed, ultimately subordinate the contractual interaction to the dictates of the general interest. As Liam Murphy notes, because "[t]here is no guarantee that what is best for each contracting pair is best for all of us," a genuinely welfarist account must not take for granted that an appropriate contract rule would be the one that is best for each contracting pair.[34]

Murphy's claim implies that a welfare fundamentalist account should attend not only to clear cases of externalities but also focus on contracts' effects at the macro-level.[35] Thus, for example, it should assess the effects of consumer law on workers and of employment law on consumers, given the pertinent numbers of both workers and consumers. As with other public concerns, these possible effects may be relevant to contract law, but they are not part of a theory of contractual justice.

The second, even more, fundamental distinction between economic analysis and relational justice theory derives from the qualitative difference between focusing on the welfare of the parties and addressing their substantive freedom and equality. A liberal contract law should not content itself with attention to the welfarist implications of the parties' interaction. It must also ensure that the terms of these interactions comply with the maxim of reciprocal respect for self-determination and substantive equality. Contract law, then, must carefully distinguish the features that make us who we are—our immutable and socially constructed characteristics and our constitutive choices (the choices that define our ground projects)—from our brute preferences.[36]

Preferences are "active attitudes which people hold for reasons,"[37] and these reasons refer back to their plans, projects, and goals or their normative convictions. Situating the satisfaction of people's preferences in their life stories explains both the normative significance of this satisfaction and why it cannot be foundational or even freestanding. People's preferences are meaningful *because* of their role as features of personal self-determination. The maxim of equality explains why preferences of equal intensity should be counted equally, regardless of their holder's identity. Appreciating how some of our preferences are grounded in our normative convictions further refutes the plausibility of treating all preferences as "opaque natural events."[38] Both directions thus suggest that, at times, it is *in*appropriate to be guided—or solely guided—by the criterion of maximizing preference satisfaction.

Hence, notwithstanding the overlapping (ex ante) perspective and the convergence of some of the prescriptions that follow with those of the economic analysis of contract law, other (significant) prescriptions of our account differ from those favored by lawyer economists. Thus, as we show below, relational justice (unlike economic analysis) accounts for the immutability of safety warranties, the emphasis of unconscionability on the weaker party's vulnerability, and the focus of disclosure doctrine on cases of clear asymmetry between the parties' capabilities.

***

We now move on from legal theory to legal doctrine, focusing on the most basic legal rules of precontractual justice. Our tasks are clear-cut. The first is to show that the liberal commitment to relational justice can justify a broad swath of core contract doctrine and account for its shape and direction. Though the theory-to-doctrine fit is not perfect, it is closer than that between economic analysis and these doctrines and superior to all competing accounts of the justice of contract. Our second task is to demonstrate that although translating the abstract maxim of relational justice into specific legal prescriptions is a complex and subtle assignment, it does not pose an insurmountable challenge, at least when judges, legislators, and regulators cooperate in the attempt to meet it.

Ignorance and Non-disclosure

1. From Traditionalism to Relational Justice. Some parts of the law of fraud need not rely on an understanding of interpersonal relationships in relational justice terms. Like active misrepresentation, both manipulative half-truths and concealment of undisclosed information are offensive even in a laissez-faire vision of interpersonal independence—all involve someone wrongfully attempting to influence another's behavior.[39] They can thus easily be viewed as a misrepresentation because neither one imposes an affirmative duty to attend to another person's predicament, nor both are consistent with *caveat emptor*.[40]

A different justification is needed for the rule currently enshrined in the Restatement, which imposes a duty to disclose if a party "knows that disclosure of the fact would correct a mistake of the other party as to a basic assumption on which that party is making the contract and if non-disclosure of the fact amounts to a failure to act in good faith and in accordance with reasonable standards of fair dealing."[41]

This rule, which typifies contemporary law even though it is not universally followed,[42] reflects an attempt to repudiate *caveat emptor*.[43] It defies the Supreme Court's proud declaration of 1871, stating that "No principle of the common law has been better established, or more often affirmed" than "the maxim of *caveat emptor*."[44] (This normative shift also underlies the doctrine of unilateral mistake).[45]

Delineating the scope and contours of this vague and open-ended duty of disclosure is not always simple. Thus, determining what facts must be disclosed to the buyer in the classic casebook example of selling a private home may not be trivial given that most homeowners have vast and unique knowledge of their property and of myriad factors that can affect its value. Some of these question marks can and have been alleviated through the accumulation of case law.[46] Common law, however, given its casuistic method and incrementalist progress, may not always be the appropriate tool for this task.

2. From Adjudication to Regulation. Adjudication, then, may no longer be the sole or even the main source of disclosure law. After the judicial establishment of a precontractual disclosure requirement for private homes, most states—following California's lead—have set up statutory schemes detailing the mandatory disclosures in a Real Estate Transfer Disclosure Statement.[47] While these statutes "do not purport to pre-empt the evolving common law,"[48] they provide a complying seller some reasonable assurance.[49]

In other contexts, notably regarding securities, action has dramatically shifted to a specialized regulatory apparatus. Thus, the Securities and Exchange Commission (SEC) requires "public companies to disclose meaningful financial and other information to the public" so that investors can "have access to certain basic facts about an investment prior to buying it, and so long as they hold it."[50] Resort to institutional expertise is likely to gain even more traction given the current knowledge about the systemic difficulties confronting mandated disclosures.[51]

These operational challenges are crucial for creating and sustaining a legal regime supportive of just precontractual relationships.[52] But our focus here is more foundational: to fine-tune the normative commitment underlying precontractual disclosure duties as a principled basis for these architectural refinements to flourish.

3. Relational Justice in Action. The literature offers two prominent attempts to account for the emerging (residual) case law of precontractual disclosure: one is based on social welfare, and the other on distributive justice.

The premise of Anthony Kronman's analysis is that social welfare is served when the most accurate information on the relative value of commodities and other entitlements reaches the market as soon as possible. A precontractual duty to disclose casually discovered information is thus justified because this obligation creates an incentive conducive to allocative efficiency. By contrast, no such duty should be imposed when the information involved was deliberately acquired so as not to discourage the costly production of this type of data.[53]

Kim Scheppele focuses on allocative fairness rather than efficiency. She argues that the precontractual disclosure duty is aimed at a distributive ideal of equal access, which ensures that the parties "(1) have equal probabilities of finding the information if they put in the same level of effort and (2) are capable of making this equivalent level of effort." To ensure equal access, Scheppele argues, law must impose a duty to disclose "deep secrets," meaning relevant information that the other side neither knows nor even suspects exists. Other types of information—"shallow secrets"—do not threaten equal access and, therefore, are not subject to a similar duty.[54]

Both accounts face a descriptive difficulty. Kimberly Krawiec and Kathryn Zeiler's thorough empirical analysis of disclosure cases demonstrates "that courts are no more likely to impose disclosure duties when the information is casually acquired as opposed to deliberately acquired, and that unequal access to information by the contracting parties is not a significant factor that drives courts to find a duty to disclose."[55]

The pattern of liability for non-disclosure developed in the courts, according to Krawiec and Zeiler's account, is best justified in relational justice terms. Refuting the descriptive power of both Scheppele's and Kronman's accounts, Krawiec and Zeiler conclude that what makes courts "significantly more likely to force disclosure" is the *combination* of clear asymmetry between the parties' capabilities—where one was "illiterate, elderly, severely ill, or extraordinarily mentally deficient in some way (although still competent to contract)"—and casually acquired information.[56] This pattern applies to all contract cases—and particularly to those that are not governed by domain-specific rules that would be reflected in market prices—and is thus especially helpful for exposing the normative intuitions underlying disclosure law.

Krawiec and Zeiler's account of the actual workings of the law echoes the prescriptions of relational justice. It reflects an understanding of the parties' interaction as an exercise in interpersonal cooperation, where each party enlists the other in pursuit of its goal while respecting the other's self-determination and substantive equality.

Where formal equality can serve as a proxy for substantive equality, each party can legitimately focus on its own interests. But where formal equality no longer ensures substantive equality, a duty of accommodation (here, of disclosure) may arise, as is clearly the case where one party's capability for finding relevant information is dramatically lower than the other's.

Finally, as is usually true of relational justice, the burden of its accommodation duties must not be excessive and, in particular, cannot undermine the other party's autonomy and equal standing. Therefore, not every case of asymmetry justifies the imposition of a disclosure duty, especially when such a duty would preclude the parties' use of valuable information they have legitimately acquired in pursuit of their own life plans.

Harsh Circumstances and Duress

1. The Common Law of Duress. The idea that duress overrides the promisor's free will may seem appealing.[57] Following Justice Holmes, however, courts and commentators largely acknowledge that duress must be defined by the fact that the promisor has "to choose the lesser of two evils."[58] Hence, the baseline for duress is necessarily normative.[59] A contract is voidable by a victim of duress if their "manifestation of assent is induced by an *improper* threat by the other party that leaves the victim no *reasonable* alternative."[60]

The common law of duress developed gradually, expanding along two dimensions, both of them relevant here.[61] First, while courts originally "restricted duress to threats involving loss of life, mayhem or imprisonment, . . . these restrictions have been greatly relaxed and, in order to constitute duress, the threat need only be improper."[62] Contemporary duress law goes far beyond threats to commit a crime or a tort to include cases that "amount to an abuse of [the bargaining] process."[63] Second, while the impact of the threat was for centuries judged against the standard of "ordinary firmness,"[64] contemporary law looks at "the person claiming to be the victim of duress" and considers all "attendant circumstances" and "infirmities," including such matters as the age, background, and relationship of the parties.[65]

These pronouncements of the Restatement (Second) of Contracts, which reflect much of the judicial discourse on duress, echo our conception of contractual justice, both in their broad understanding of improper threats and in their explicit reference to the parties' pertinent features. But a critical reading of the cases may lead to a more cautious conclusion: duress doctrine, as one commentator noted, "remains largely unused," and courts continuously "struggle with defining [its] parameters."[66]

In particular, most courts still require the promisee to assume some responsibility for the promisor's distress so that sheer exploitation of this distress is not deemed to be duress.[67] This limitation cannot be interpreted as a normative endorsement of traditionalism, which is incompatible with duress law's broad understanding of "wrongful" threats, including its famous inclusion of threats to do what one has a legal right to do.[68] This doctrinal under-inclusiveness, however, is still disappointing. To exploit another person's harsh circumstances may indeed be less wrong than to create them, but, in some cases, taking advantage of another is outrageous enough to run afoul of relational justice.[69]

2. The Challenges: Line-drawing and Final Incidents. And yet, except for extreme cases, this consistent *judicial* position[70] may be understandable. Although exploitation and duress often go hand in hand, providing a clear criterion independent of market considerations for what constitutes illegitimate exploitation that courts can invariably rely upon can be challenging.[71] Besides this line-drawing problem, duress is a paradigmatic instance of the risk of potentially counterproductive consequences discussed above.[72]

According to Oren Bar-Gill and Omri Ben-Shahar, who study this difficulty, when a promisor surrenders to a *credible* threat—that is, when the threatening party is likely to carry out his threat if his demands are not met—"her wellbeing might be better served if the law were to deem her act voluntary and give it ordinary effect." The reason is that, if "antiduress rules would later invalidate the threatened party's surrender," the threatening party "would not bother to make the threat" but "simply do that which he would otherwise threaten to do." A rule with this effect, then, sets aside "a choice between two evils" only by leaving the threatened party with "the greater of the two evils." To evaluate cases that raise this dilemma, one needs to inquire whether contract law's refusal to enforce expensive, coercive transactions such as loans could lead putative lenders to make the loan for a lower rate of return or leave potential borrowers without any loans at all.[73]

This "feasibility constraint," as they call it, implies that the traditional judicial response to duress can effectively address relational injustice only insofar as it relates to threats that are not truly credible (namely, bluffs). For credible threats, a more robust remedy is needed to change "the incentives of the threatening party, by inducing him to refrain from either carrying out the threat or making it in the first place." Such credibility-reducing policies may resort to nonlegal sanctions or to legal ones (civil or criminal) that go beyond the threat of invalidation, and, at times, even this expanded repertoire may not suffice.[74]

The analysis of Bar-Gill and Ben-Shahar focuses solely on the threatened party's well-being. They imply that, for this category of cases, when law cannot affect the threatening party's incentives, enforcement is the sole normatively credible way, and allowing a duress claim is unambiguously counterproductive. For us, this category incorporates a set of (possibly divergent) hard cases that raise a difficult choice: either allowing the use of contract for interactions that undermine relational justice or limiting it in ways that could prove severely detrimental to the well-being of the weakest segments of society.

3. *Relational Justice After All.* Many (most?) other cases, however, are different. Sheer invalidation may be counterproductive, but contract law—properly understood as the law governing contractual relationships, whatever its institutional pedigree—can resort to other (or further) means. Neither the need for line-drawing nor the potentially complex credibility analysis dismisses law's *principled* judgment of contractual justice. Both, however, imply what lawyers already know: proper translation of the demands of justice into legal doctrine often involves complex questions of fact and legal architecture. As usual, these complications suggest that, at times, it is other legal actors rather than judges who enjoy a comparative advantage in the creation of contract law rules.[75]

Usury is a familiar case in point. As Alan Wertheimer notes, usury laws, which specify a ceiling on allowable interest rates,[76] "may be thought of as a second-best device for preventing certain forms of deception and duress that cannot be attacked more directly."[77] But legislation on this topic has gone further. Anti-price-gouging laws have been enacted to date by thirty-five states and the District of Columbia, using a variety of legal techniques that include restitution, civil penalties, and criminal sanctions. Like usury law, these laws play a role in prescribing the floor of contract law by precluding "merchants from selling certain necessities such as food, medicine, fuel, or other emergency supplies for . . . a price significantly higher than the average price on a day prior to the natural disaster or state of emergency."[78]

These legislative schemes should not imply that judges cannot or should not take part in this complex endeavor. Indeed, as early as 1857, the Supreme Court held in *Post v. Jones* that "Courts of admiralty will enforce contracts made for salvage service and salvage compensation [only] where the salvor has not taken advantage of his power to make an unreasonable bargain," but "will not tolerate" contracts in which a salvor "avail[s] himself of the calamities of others to drive a bargain."[79]

As Bar-Gill and Ben-Shahar explain, by nullifying the agreement and replacing the exorbitant contract price with a lower, court-determined fee, *Post v. Jones* was able to ensure the substantive fairness of the contract while avoiding discouraging salvage in similar situations. Furthermore, the ensuing "doctrinal guidelines determining the magnitude of this reasonable fee eliminate the potential credibility of the salvor's threat to sail away," thus ensuring that "performing the salvage operation is incentive compatible for the salvor."[80]

These three important categories of relatively tailored ways that contract law (properly understood) resorts to in cases of duress should not be viewed as aberrations or as merely "regulatory" exceptions. Instead, they exemplify a principled position for the law of contractual duress, stressing its broad understanding of improper threats and its attention to the contracting parties' pertinent characteristics. The task of this law is not to guard people's interpersonal independence but to preserve the integrity of the bargaining process or, more specifically, its compliance with relational justice.

4. Reform. Duress doctrine—by no means fully, let alone perfectly—faces the complex challenge of complying with relational justice while attending to its feasibility constraints and adhering to the rule of law. Appreciating the normative commitment that should guide the law of duress, its challenges, and these three stories of (relative) success implies that current law already possesses at least some of the resources needed for addressing and hopefully reforming its remaining shortfalls.

One context that reformist attention should be channeled to is spousal agreements, which—especially in an environment that is still typified by pervasive gender inequality—at times implicate significant bargaining-power disparities. Unfortunately, the (sometimes conflicting) existing doctrine is often inadequate.[81] By contrast, the American Law Institute's *Principles of the Law of Family Dissolution*[82] point in the right direction, as demonstrated by its rules for premarital agreements.[83]

Thus, rather than requiring the party challenging the agreement to prove a duress claim, the *ALI Principles* prescribe that "[a] party seeking to enforce an agreement must show that the other party's consent to it was informed and not obtained under duress."[84] The *Principles* also helpfully instruct courts to apply particular suspicion towards last-minute (namely, less than a month prior to the marriage) opt-outs of default rules governing marital property. A similar suspicious attitude justifiably applies, as per the *Principles*, where a party's consent to an agreement whose language is not "easily understandable" was granted without having a reasonable opportunity to obtain advice from independent legal counsel. The *Principles* correctly add that a spouse who lacks money "is without reasonable opportunity to obtain counsel."[85]

Vulnerability and Unconscionability

1. Relational Justice Par Excellence. We now turn to our third and last precontractual doctrine—unconscionability, which showcases both the normative and the interpretive prongs of this chapter.

Unconscionability doctrine represents a dramatic departure from the laissez-faire understanding of the parties' interpersonal responsibilities in terms of non-interference.[86] A contract "should not be enforced," as per the famous holding in *Williams v. Walker-Thomas Furniture*, "when a party of little bargaining power, and hence little real choice, signs a commercially unreasonable contract with little or no knowledge of its terms." In other words, a contract or a contract term will be invalidated, even without *active* interference with the weaker party's will, when two conditions apply to it: "an absence of meaningful choice" *and* "contract terms which are unreasonably favorable to the other party."[87] These two conditions are sometimes identified as procedural and substantive unconscionability, a distinction coined by Arthur Leff to refer, respectively, to "bargaining naughtiness" and to "evils in the resulting contract."[88]

This canonical formulation explains why relational justice—the requirement of reciprocal respect for self-determination and substantive equality—is unconscionability's obvious home. To begin with, it manifests contract law's attempt to draw a line between legitimate forms of taking advantage of one's superior bargaining power on the one hand and exploitation, which implies using the other party's vulnerability to secure a benefit, on the other. The exploitative interaction of another being exceeds legitimate advantage-taking because it degrades the other's value.[89] Since contract relies on a requirement of reciprocal respect for self-determination and substantive equality, contract law must ensure that contracts do not become a tool of exploitation.

Thus, as the Restatement notes, while a bargain "is not unconscionable merely because the parties to it are unequal in bargaining position," it may become so in cases of "gross inequality of bargaining power," as when the weaker party suffers from "physical or mental infirmities, ignorance, illiteracy or inability to understand the language of the agreement."[90] These features are largely irrelevant from a welfarist perspective that views a lack of meaningful choice as merely a potential source of misallocation.[91] But they are obviously significant to relational justice.

The replacement of "unequal" with "gross inequality" as a threshold for triggering unconscionability is also sound in terms of relational justice's underlying commitment to substantive equality. Recall that this commitment does not require tackling all deviations from a standard of strict equality. Rather, substantive equality requires contracting parties to relate as equals either by *co*-authoring/influencing the determination of the terms of the interaction or by satisfying the reasonable expectations of typical term-takers. Contracting parties must be situated *sufficiently* equally so as to enable the weaker party to understand the economic and legal risks implicit in these terms or assume responsibility for their possible materialization.[92] Judging what counts as sufficiently equal is fundamentally open-ended, which justifies setting the legal bar of unequal bargaining power no lower than "gross inequality."

2. *Supplementary Regulatory Schemata.* Implementing a legal doctrine of unconscionability, however, is far from simple. Consider Walker-Thomas' celebrated cross-collateralization clause. When a term is one-sided, abstaining from enforcing it could end up depriving weaker parties like Williams of the opportunity to transact (by making credit less available or prices higher) rather than cleansing such transactions from injustice.[93]

Insights from behavioral law and economics do demonstrate that such counterproductive consequences are less frequent than what a simple pricing analysis might suggest. Most buyers, not necessarily only vulnerable ones, tend to rely on heuristic techniques and make their choices based on just a few critical attributes. They may also underestimate, due to characteristic judgment biases, the risk-adjusted costs of potential defaults. In both cases, the implication is similar: buyers are likely to underprice the cost of inconspicuous offensive clauses, and market forces are expected to encourage sellers to include them in their contracts.[94] But even when these potential effects are considered, the concern remains: refusing to enforce these clauses could be most harmful precisely to the most disadvantaged.

This difficulty, along with the rule of law concerns that unconscionability is particularly vulnerable to, may account for the post-*Williams*' institutional shift of the doctrine's evolution. As Anne Fleming demonstrates, the *Williams* litigation "catalyzed a process of legislative change." Reformers, Fleming reports, "sought to preserve unconscionability as a defense for poor borrowers but also pushed for statutory protections that would create bright-line boundaries for installment sellers and buyers." Thus, "*Williams* played a role in creating a 'law of the poor' consumer in the District of Columbia" by triggering the "enactment of statutory reforms" aimed at injecting "some measure of equality and fairness" into "the low-income marketplace."[95]

Relational justice is indeed the scene for addressing regressive pre-distributions that translate into structural imbalances of bargaining power.[96] Addressing such structures to ensure interpersonal terms of interaction that comply with the maxim of reciprocal respect for self-determination and substantive equality does, at times, require the supplementation of common law with tailored statutory schemes and specialized regulatory apparatuses such as the ones currently governing consumer contracts.

Thus, the States' Unfair and Deceptive Practices Acts[97] establish a personal right of action and entrust government officials (usually the state attorney general and, in some cases, also municipal consumer protection officers at the city and county level) with the authority to administer and enforce these rules.[98] The Federal Trade Commission also actively regulates consumer transactions, taking action in areas like misleading advertising, coercive or deceptive sales techniques, and marketing campaigns preying on the young, the elderly, or the infirm.[99]

Finally, consider the Consumer Financial Protection Bureau (CFPB). Title X of the 2010 Dodd–Frank Wall Street Reform and Consumer Protection Act created the CFPB,[100] investing it with "rulemaking, enforcement, and supervisory powers over many consumer financial products and services, as well as the entities that sell them."[101] Part of its rulemaking activity relies on a set of (eighteen) preexisting federal statutes, such as the Truth in Lending Act, the Truth in Savings Act, the Fair Credit Billing Act, and the Fair Debt Collection Practices Act. In addition, the CFPB enjoys "organic authority" to define "certain acts and practices as unfair, deceptive, or abusive."[102]

The Act explicitly includes under the rubric of abusive acts or practices not only one that "[m]aterially interferes with the ability of a consumer to understand a term or condition of a consumer financial product or service," but also one that "[t]akes unreasonable advantage" of the consumer's "lack of understanding" of "the material risks, costs, or conditions of the product or service," their inability to protect their "interests in selecting or using a consumer financial product or service," or their "reasonable reliance" on an intermediary "to act in the interests of the consumer."[103]

3. The Emerging Common Law Doctrine. All these regulatory schemes, as noted, supplement rather than replace the common law doctrine of unconscionability. This doctrine is far from clearly settled, but two emerging patterns in it match the interpretation of it we have suggested here.

First, the judicial test for substantive unconscionability asks whether a contract term, analyzed independently from the rest of the contract, is "overly harsh," "unduly one-sided," or "shocks the conscience." As Russell Korobkin observes, this question may help to identify offensive terms that, due to features of consumers' behavior noted above, cannot be disciplined by market forces.[104] Refusal to enforce such terms would thus not confront the feasibility constraint highlighted by Bar-Gill and Ben-Shahar.

The second pattern goes beyond the point of convergence between accounts—like Korobkin' s—solely focused on the parties' wellbeing, and others—like ours—committed to constructing people's contractual relationships as interactions between self-determining and substantively equal agents. Relational justice, as stated above, provides a normative bulwark against the self's welfarist subordination by drawing a qualitative distinction between the features that make us who we are and our sheer preferences. It calls for particularly exacting scrutiny of terms that might undermine the weaker party's ability to pursue a meaningful life.[105]

Thus, this qualitative distinction between people's constitutive and welfarist interests can justify the courts' willingness to strike out facially offensive terms in lease contracts and employment contracts.[106] It also vindicates the rule whereby "[l]imitation of consequential damages for injury to the person in the case of consumer goods is prima facie unconscionable but limitation of damages where the loss is commercial is not."[107] This trend has been developed still further in the modern products liability law, which has transformed warranties of safety into *immutable* duties owed to consumers.[108]

The same core distinction between people's constitutive and welfarist interests that guides relational justice theory makes its interpretation of unconscionability doctrine particularly receptive to Sabine Tsuruda's plea to read this doctrine as a platform for recognizing and resisting structural injustices, namely, addressing cases in which transactional exploitation leverages on social subordination.[109]

10
Good Faith and Related Doctrines

Rediscovering *Jacob & Youngs*

1. Justice in *Contracts?* The mission of justice for contracts may seem to be solely gatekeeping and thus fully exhausted in Chapter 9. As long as the justice of the bargaining stage is secured, contract law, in this (conventional?) approach, must simply follow the parties' preferences. Doctrines that govern contractual performance and breach by appealing to justice considerations are thus either confused or misguided. The justice rhetoric is either a cover for other, notably economic, considerations or undermines contract law's liberal underpinnings.

Though perhaps the accepted platitude, this perception is wrong. Contractual justice, which, as just described, is a species of relational justice, does not step down once the contract is formed—quite the contrary. Responding to the contract-specific form of relational injustice associated with the heightened interpersonal vulnerability that sequential contractual performance gives rise to, modern contract law properly solidifies a cooperative conception of contract performance, which guards against relational injustices. This conception is implicit in a significant body of doctrines that set up contract law's rules of the game, epitomized by the duty of good faith and fair dealing.

We begin this chapter, which delves into this body of law, with Judge Cardozo's celebrated *Jacob & Youngs v. Kent* decision.[1] Although *Jacob & Youngs* is a veteran member of the contracts canon, one of its vital contributions that also inspired the elaborate discussion that follows, has hitherto gone unnoticed.

2. Enter Cardozo. Jacob & Youngs stands for the substantial, as opposed to absolute, performance doctrine for service contracts.[2] Where the promisor's "innocent" performance defects are "of trivial or inappreciable importance," making them "insignificant in . . . relation to the project," Cardozo ruled, that omission "will sometimes be atoned by allowance of the resulting damage, and will not always be the breach of a condition to be followed by a forfeiture."[3]

This rule is prompted by "[c]onsiderations partly of justice and partly of presumable intention" but for Cardozo, the former—preventing "harshness" and "oppression"—dominate the latter: "The transgressor whose default is unintentional and trivial may hope for mercy if he will offer atonement for his wrong"; and from the proposition "that promises may not be treated as dependent to the extent of their uttermost minutiae without a sacrifice of justice, the progress is a short one to the conclusion that they may not be so treated without a perversion of intention."[4]

Relational Justice. Hanoch Dagan and Avihay Dorfman, Oxford University Press. © Hanoch Dagan and Avihay Dorfman 2024.
DOI: 10.1093/9780191987762.003.0010

Cardozo does not prescribe this norm of accommodation as an immutable, mandatory rule. Sensibly, he acknowledges the ability of the parties "to effectuate a purpose that performance of every term shall be a condition of recovery." But he also insists that "[t]here will be no assumption of a purpose to visit venial faults with oppressive retribution." Accordingly, Cardozo holds that "the law will be slow to impute the purpose, in the silence of the parties, where the significance of the default is grievously out of proportion to the oppression of the forfeiture."[5]

Thus, even though it is a default rule, the substantial performance doctrine is particularly sticky and difficult to change through bargaining.[6] "Intention not otherwise revealed may be presumed to hold in contemplation the reasonable and probable. If something else is in view, it must not be left to implication." Contracting parties can overrule a normative default only if they use "apt and certain words."[7]

Cardozo has been criticized for not observing the parties' attempt to do just that[8] and—more broadly—for failing to provide proper guidance as to how future parties might effectuate such a purpose.[9] We take no issue with the former critique and agree that specifying the altering rule[10] for a sticky default—or, for that matter, any other default—is indeed generally desirable. Nevertheless, we think that *Jacob & Youngs*, if charitably interpreted,[11] fully deserves its status as a landmark case.

3. Jacob & Youngs' Unnoticed Legacy. Specifically, *Jacob & Youngs* and the substantial-performance rule it stands for epitomize contract law's inventory of rules that serve as anti-opportunistic devices. Cardozo's more general lesson relates to this inventory as a whole.

For Cardozo, justice and preferences serve wholly different purposes: the former provides the *justification* of the rule, whereas the latter sets out a possible *constraint* on its scope of application. Cardozo, as noted, prescribes the substantial performance default *because* it is a rule of justice among contractual parties and, therefore, likely to accord with the parties' intentions. He then concludes that if this rule does not work well for any specific contracting parties, they can signal their dissent, and once their signal is clear enough, courts will honor their individualized arrangement. This outline distills a notion of normative defaults, which is key to this chapter, and explains their characteristic stickiness.

As noted in Chapter 4,[12] the rules of the contractual game that instantiate relational justice go beyond private law's floor of acceptable interpersonal relationships. Therefore, parties may generally opt out from many of these rules and from the specific obligations, which are understood to derive from the general duty of good faith and are not immutable either. Yet, liberal law is nonetheless justifiably bothered by the systemic impediments through which contract-specific relational injustices hinder contract's ability to perform its autonomy-enhancing function. It is thus no wonder that these rules tend to be resilient even where they do not follow the actual or presumed preferences of the contracting parties or of most parties. Liberal contract law embraces these rules as normative defaults: rules whose status need not depend on their responsiveness to majoritarian preferences, even though they are offered to the parties as defaults that they are free to reject.

Contractual Injustices and Normative Defaults

1. Heightened Vulnerability and Contracts. In order to defend Cardozo's insights, it is apt to begin with some economic wisdom that refines the heightened interpersonal vulnerability contract typically entails.

Consider first contracts involving relation-specific investments where "at least one of the parties is required under the contract to make an investment that is more profitable in the relationship than elsewhere," such as "the production of specialized goods, the development of human capital specific to a particular deal, or research to acquire information about future costs or prices." Legal enforcement is particularly acute for these contracts because after one party makes its relation-specific investment, the other's "incentive to cooperate vanishes." Rather than perform under the original contract, the non-investing party will have "an incentive to renegotiate the contract price downward."[13]

The lesson of cases with relation-specific investment applies more broadly. The vulnerability to opportunism that contracts generate is endemic to any case of sequential performance because opportunism "becomes more likely when one side has taken affirmative, costly steps or has foregone unique alternatives which expose that side to exploitation by the other side."[14] Sequential performance (as opposed to simultaneous performance) is obviously a defining feature of relational contracts.[15] Sequential performance, however, typifies many other contracts as well and also entails many moments of asymmetrical contract-specific investments. The implication is that the less-investing party faces post-contractual opportunistic incentives to renegotiate the original terms to capture more of the bargaining surplus.[16]

Whenever performance is sequential, and whenever reputational, ethical, or ethos-like commitments create insufficient incentives to perform, the party performing first is vulnerable to "the problem of contract opportunism."[17] Finding a solution to this problem is complicated, and, in some contexts, social norms and communal legal systems, rather than state law, take center stage.[18] At this point, however, the main issue is only that the intertemporal dimension of contract tends, systemically, to turn increased vulnerability into opportunism.[19]

This phenomenon, though typical of contract, is not a necessary feature of all contracts. First, in some contracts, performance is simultaneous rather than sequential, and they involve no such intertemporal-based vulnerability. Second, for the (large) subset of cases where performance is sequential, the parties may still deploy means that extinguish, or at least dramatically diminish, the risk of opportunism. This is at least the promise of smart contracts.[20]

Nonetheless, intertemporal-based-vulnerability-turned-opportunism *is* an especially important instance of relational injustice in contractual relationships and properly encapsulates the notion of contract-specific relational injustice. The reason is not merely that this phenomenon is prevalent, although its prevalence is surely important, but its intrinsic connection to the autonomy-enhancing and equality-sustaining underpinnings of contract. To see why, we need to return to first principles, namely, contract's core mission and the premise of its legitimacy.

2. Contract's Intertemporal Core and the Threat of Relational Injustices. Contract's intertemporality is key to its empowerment function.[21] What renders contract a major interpersonal planning device and, thus, a key means for people's ability to carry out their higher-order projects—to self-determine—is the *reliability* of contractual promises. Contract allows people to legitimately enlist one another in pursuit of their goals by exchanging promises for *future* performance.

The irreducible intertemporality of contract explains why the enforcement of wholly executory contracts is the signature feature of modern contract law. In turn, the implication—as noted[22]—is that the legitimacy of contract itself is grounded in the commitment of liberal law to reciprocal respect for self-determination. Put differently, rather than externally related to contract, relational justice is an intrinsic contract value entailed by contract's own foundation of legitimacy. Liberal contract law, then, must not limit relational justice's jurisdiction to matters of gatekeeping. Committed, as it must be, to proactively facilitating people's ability to take part in cooperative endeavors that might engender heightened interpersonal vulnerability, liberal contract law must also undertake the mission of ameliorating risks of relational injustice even if they do not reach the level of outright abuse.[23]

The typical intertemporal unfolding of contract, which is the immediate outgrowth of its empowering mission, is also the source of its specific forms of vulnerability to opportunism. Where a wholly executory contract takes the form of a spot exchange projected to the future, as in the case of a seller's future delivery of a widget for an agreed-upon price, this vulnerability is avoided since no sequential performance is involved. But because sequential performance typifies other forms of sales contracts as well as even the most banal forms of service contracts, where the object of the parties' agreement is the pursuit of a project (say, the promisor will build the promisee's home), limiting contract's empowering potential to the widget-like cases would dramatically curtail contract's current autonomy-enhancing work.[24]

The contract-specific relational injustice that opportunism generates does not threaten the legitimacy of contract. Therefore, it neither does nor needs to trigger mandatory relational justice-based rules. But opportunistic abuses of intertemporal-based vulnerability threaten to impinge on contract's ability to perform as one of society's major autonomy-enhancing and equality-sustaining institutions. Therefore, liberal contract's intrinsic commitment to relational justice implies that law must not remain agnostic.

3. *From Relational Justice to Normative Defaults.* This is exactly the befitting context for the application of normative defaults along the lines of *Jacob & Youngs*' legacy. Normative defaults do not depend on their responsiveness to majoritarian preferences but derive directly from the normative commitments indigenous to liberal contract.[25] The normative defaults we explore in this chapter rely on considerations of relational justice.[26] However, given that the implications of these considerations for the life of ongoing contracts go *beyond* the floor of relational justice,[27] and given that law's impetus to address them springs from its facilitative mission, these rules are offered to the parties as defaults.

Thus, unlike doctrines that manifest the floor of relational justice, allowing opt-outs from *these* rules—think, for example, about the substantial performance rule of *Jacob & Youngs*—is not tantamount to an authorization to disregard self-determination. Parties may, for example, legitimately prefer to devise other, possibly contextually better, means to protect themselves from each other's opportunism. Because opportunism is an elusive concept, and since opportunistic behavior, even if clearly defined, is not easily verifiable, they may prefer to rely on extra-legal means such as reputation, social norms, or technology or even decide that it would be best for them to price this risk into their contract.[28] As long as these decisions themselves are not blemished by relational injustice, liberal contract law need not, indeed should not, insist on requiring the parties to resort to its own anti-opportunistic default devices.[29]

That said, the normative pedigree of this category of defaults—more specifically, their unmediated reliance on contract's own normative DNA—implies that when parties enter the contractual domain, they are presumed to accept their jurisdiction. Although the parties are free to reject these rules, such repudiation would not—given this normative presumption, which Cardozo properly highlights—be concluded lightly. Unlike majoritarian defaults, therefore, normative defaults are sticky so that the option of opting out requires, in Cardozo's famous phrase, "apt and certain words."[30]

Facing Up to Economists' Challenges

Is there any room for relational justice to affect the doctrines governing the life of ongoing contracts, as we claim it should, and is this claim correct? Before we turn to our doctrinal survey, we will address these challenges, starting with the economists' suspicion that our account is, at best, marginal to contract law. This position does not need to rely on the welfare-foundationalist position, which we criticized above.[31] Instead, it is premised on a mainstream contemporary economic analysis of contract law, which emphasizes the incompleteness of contracts and thus bases the choice of defaults on an assessment of what the parties would likely have wanted.

The relevant question to this approach is whether the rule at hand would be one that most contracting parties prefer or—more precisely—one that maximizes the joint surplus (in terms of preference satisfaction) of most parties.[32] This view avoids the pitfalls of welfare-foundationalism while hardly leaving room for normative defaults or their underlying concern for relational justice. It may thus explain why the idea of justice-based normative defaults is rarely used in current contract scholarship. Alan Schwartz seems to represent this approach when arguing that normative defaults should be applied only where typical party preferences are unknown. Otherwise, he claims, their enactment would unfairly impose (opting out) costs on the majority.[33]

The commitment of these economic analyses of contract to the parties' joint maximization rather than to the economic canon of aggregate welfare makes them indeed much closer to our theory. But even if we set aside the necessary reliance of this approach on the normative underpinnings of self-determination along the lines of our account,[34] the added value of our theory is not, as Schwartz suggests, marginal.

First, it is unclear why Schwartz's distributive concern should *necessarily* outweigh concerns of relational justice. Furthermore, Schwartz's own work vividly shows that it is often difficult to observe and verify typical party preferences,[35] implying that prescribing defaults that are truly majoritarian is much more complex than is usually assumed. Many economic accounts bypass this problem by *ascribing rational* preferences to the parties and thus *assuming* they have no other tastes (say, for wagering or altruism).[36] Although this exercise is often valuable, it can hardly justify the pursuit of joint maximization when it could depart from relational justice.

The gap between our account and the economists' is less significant than its friction with traditionalist prescriptions, to which we turn next. There are differences, however, at times even significant ones. Some differences result from the economic analysis' marginalization of the notion of normative default, which explains why, for example, its practitioners tend to (unjustifiably) condemn the principle against forfeiture. Other differences—regarding the different burdens of mitigation these two approaches prescribe—are due to the gap between the modest other-regarding obligations implied in relational justice and the more demanding ones prescribed by joint maximization, as well as from our insistence on the qualitative difference between ground projects and sheer preferences, which has no room in the economic calculus.

Finally, and just as notably, our account seems to fare better than its economic counterpart, given the institutional concerns that economic analysts such as Schwartz properly highlight. The reason is that the same concern that explains why generalist courts are not well-equipped to identify typical party preferences also suggests they may not be well suited to engage in the economic analysis of transactions required by the mainstream majoritarian defaults paradigm.

In fact, concerns of institutional comparative advantage suggest an *inverted* hierarchy to the one Schwartz prescribes. Judges are well-positioned to set rules for the performance of contracts and the consequences of their breach based on what seems normatively justified for interpersonal interactions vulnerable to the endemic risk of opportunism. At the same time, because parties' preferences do matter in these contexts, and since judges are often ill-equipped to track (empirically or theoretically) the preferences of *most* contracting parties, judges should focus on the *particular* parties' indications of their preferences. When these parties do prefer alternative arrangements, judges should allow them to opt out of (most of) these rules.

Resisting Traditionalists' Objections

1. Markovits' Pushback. If the economists' pushback against our thesis is one of marginalization, traditionalist contract theorists who insist that contract law, as part of private law, must adhere to the vision of reciprocal respect for independence and formal equality push back even deeper. For them, reliance on relational justice is thoroughly objectionable.

Even Daniel Markovits, who thinks of contracts as collaborations,[37] harshly criticizes any attempt to rely on substantive fairness (or, for that matter, efficiency) to conceptualize good faith—the flagship of the body of doctrine we analyze in this chapter and, in his view, of contract as a whole. Rendering good faith "the doctrinal pathway for making the ideal actual," he claims, "undermine[s] rather than promote[s] contractual values" because it paternalistically substitutes "the actual contract that the parties' intentions established" with "the *utopian* contract that it would have been optimal for them to establish." Markovits offers a very different understanding of this core doctrine of contract performance. His is "a pedestrian ideal," whose content is determined "according to the actual intentions of the imperfect parties."[38]

Pedestrian good faith, Markovits writes, is "of a piece with contract law's negative libertarian elements" and thus properly "corresponds to the formal equality that contract law embeds elsewhere in doctrine." Therefore, it does not require contracting parties to display "even modest affirmative other-regard": good faith does *not* imply that they should assist each other in the face of new contingencies. Rather, "good faith allows contracting parties to remain as self-interested . . . within the contract as they were without it, *except* that they must accept, as a side-constraint, that the best interpretation of what they agreed to in contracting binds them to limit their self-interest." Good faith requires the parties "to respect each other's contractual intentions even where they, preferring manipulation, are disinclined to do so."[39]

Markovits celebrates this minimalism. Pedestrian good faith resists the utopian temptation by qualitatively distancing itself from the altruistic obligations of fiduciaries, which may paternalistically override beneficiaries' choices. Instead of "impos[ing] on the parties a bargain that they did not make," good faith "*promotes* freedom of contract [by protecting] the parties' actual contractual intentions against *ex post* exploitation, thereby allowing the parties to project their intentions into the future."[40]

Pedestrian good faith, then, neither determines "the *content* of contract obligation" nor does it "help in drawing a line between permissible and impermissible conduct." Therefore, good faith in this view is *not* a rule of decision: it "cannot be called on to identify the reasonable expectations in terms of which it is defined." Rather, because pedestrian good faith stands for "an attitude of respect for the contract relation"—the attitude of intent to obligate, which implies "taking [the] contractual obligation appropriately seriously"—the boundaries of good faith in particular cases must be fixed by "the actual intentions and expectations of the [particular] parties." Thus, "pedestrian good faith simply directs a court to contractual intentions whose content must be gleaned from elsewhere, using other means."[41]

This account of good faith—this understanding of the justice in contracts—is misguided because it relies on two indefensible binarisms and paradoxically yields a conception of good faith that betrays contract's most fundamental commitments.

2. Relational Justice, Not Virtue. Pedestrian good faith assumes—and this is Markovits' first binarism—that in order to distinguish its good faith duty from the altruistic obligations of fiduciary law, contract law must adhere to the ideal of interpersonal independence (rendering offensive even a requirement of "modest affirmative other-regard"). In that, Markovits implicitly subscribes to a specific delineation of the distinction between our legally enforceable duties and our strictly moral duties of virtue.

We agree that contract law should not enact duties of virtue but deny what Markovits assumes, namely, that legally enforceable duties are *only* duties of abstention, whose delineation requires strict adherence to the parties' explicit allocation of rights. Relational justice rejects the negative conception of rights whereby concerns for independence and formal equality exhaust the considerations that ought to determine our legal rights and duties. In its stead, relational justice establishes our private laws' terms of interactions on the liberal commitment to individual self-determination and substantive equality.

Because this commitment, as noted, also strengthens the normative DNA of contract, following its prescriptions has (as usual) nothing to do with paternalism.[42] And since relational justice is inherently limited only to modest affirmative obligations and properly avoids excessive impingements on independence,[43] it does not threaten—as might other theories of substantive fairness—the liberal commitment to freedom of contract.[44]

Accordingly, relational justice's prescriptions for justice in contract go beyond duties of abstention and—in sharp contrast to Markovits' notion of pedestrian good faith—do set up informative guides for conduct that can (and do) decide cases. The rules we discuss below, including those that derive from the good faith duty that Markovits focuses on, are not rooted in the parties' intentions, but this does not denigrate their agreement. Rather, these rules of the contractual game are all normative defaults, and, as such, they function in ways obscured by Markovits' second binarism—between a utopian contract and freedom of contract.

3. *What (Liberal) Contract Is Not.* Recall that Markovits treats the application of such rules as an imposition on the idea of contract. To see why they are not, consider his preferred instruction to courts: to divine ex post the *real intentions* of the particular parties at the moment of contracting. This instruction is an exacting, fact-intensive inquiry involving verifiability (at times even observability) difficulties and is thus particularly costly and susceptible to error. Such inquiries risk diminished predictability in contract law and expand the discretion of judges. Consequently, they tend to destabilize contracts and thus frustrate the expectations of many contractual parties.[45]

By contrast, setting up normative defaults that target systemic vulnerabilities in opportunism is much less intrusive on the parties' contractual freedom as long as these rules are not too open-ended. Even if these rules of the game do not correspond to the majoritarian preferences (as is often the case), they only add up the costs of opting out without significantly affecting the parties' agreement.

This difference highlights how Markovit's pedestrian ideal and relational justice diverge in their expressions of loyalty to the idea of contract or, more precisely, do not share a common view of that idea. In refining his critique of utopian conceptions of good faith, Markovits notes that "contracting parties might, *in some instances*, form the actual intention that gaps in their contractual understandings shall be filled in using ideal terms."[46] But as one of us shows elsewhere, this approach, which indeed follows from Markovits' adherence to ideals of interpersonal independence and formal equality, renders suspect some of the more conspicuous features of existing contract law—notably its objective approach and its extensive gap-filling apparatus that law's commitment to reciprocal respect for self-determination does explain well.[47]

Modern contract law proactively empowers people, and its default rules are thus designed along the lines of its liberal DNA of reciprocal respect for self-determination and substantive equality. The prescriptions of contract law's normative defaults are founded on this very same commitment that, as noted, is also the basis for the legitimacy of contract itself. Normative defaults respect freedom of contract when properly conceived.

* * *

As with the law of precontractual justice and other sections of private law, much of the contemporary doctrine governing both the performance of contracts and their breakup can be charitably understood and should thus be further developed in line with relational justice theory.[48] All the rules we discuss in this chapter are part of the robust gap-filling apparatus that typifies modern contract law, but they are not, at least not necessarily, informed by the parties' preferences. In other words, these rules prescribe obligations implied-in-law rather than implied-in-fact, which apply regardless of the parties' intentions.[49] Moreover, these defaults are not (at least not necessarily) based on their correspondence to the preferences of most parties. Rather, these are all normative default rules chosen on account of their compliance with relational justice.

Conditions

1. The Doctrine. The good faith doctrine is obviously the main scene for the appearance of these contract-specific relational justice rules, but the fit beginning is the law of conditions that *Jacob & Youngs* belongs to.

We start with a relatively specific rule. "Where a duty of one party is subject to the occurrence of a condition," prescribes the Restatement, that party may *also* be obligated to refrain from "conduct that will prevent or hinder the occurrence of that condition" and at times take active "affirmative steps to cause its occurrence."[50] Thus, as Allan Farnsworth writes, "if a party has conditioned a duty to pay on honest satisfaction with the other party's performance," and "the party to be satisfied refuses to look at the performance," its refusal "would amount to a breach that would excuse the condition and make the duty of pay unconditional."[51] The required cooperation is not limited to duties of abstention, as the traditionalist vision would imagine. As noted, parties are "often expected to take affirmative steps to see that the condition occurs"; for example, a "purchaser who conditions the duty to close on obtaining a mortgage is expected to take suitable steps to obtain one."[52]

Indeed, the obligation to cooperate suits our account well since it preempts the contingency of an opportunistic abuse of power.[53] Similarly, it follows relational justice's norm of *modest* accommodation: the purchaser in our example only needs to take "suitable steps"—its duty to see that the condition occurs is only one of "best efforts."[54] Finally, the obligation fits our theory not only in substance but also in form—it is a normative *default*, which does not apply "if the risk of such a lack of cooperation was assumed by the other party."[55]

While this obligation to cooperate is relatively limited in scope, the principle against forfeiture, which *Jacob & Youngs* invokes, is not. This principle has two prongs. The first sets up a presumption stating that "doubts as to whether an event is made a condition of an obligor's duty, and as to the nature of such an event" are to be resolved by favoring the interpretation "that will reduce the obligee's risk of forfeiture, unless the event is within the obligee's control or the circumstances indicate that he has assumed the risk."[56] The second prong of the anti-forfeiture principle is one of "excuse [of] the non-occurrence of a condition" if (but only if) the occurrence of such condition "was not a material part of the agreed exchange" solely "on the basis of the forfeiture that would otherwise result."[57]

2. Anti-forfeiture Beyond Equity. Robert Scott and Jody Kraus harshly criticize both of these prongs, as well as *Jacob & Youngs*, which they perceive as invitations to engage in "individual justice," guided by "the moral logic of the ex post perspective."[58] This critique is justified insofar as it refers to cases where courts invoke an equitable discretion in order to excuse—or, at times, divine an implicit ex post waiver of—"an express term that unequivocally creates a condition."[59] There are indeed such cases, mostly within the second prong of the anti-forfeiture principle,[60] and they do deviate from private law's mission of setting up the *terms* of our interpersonal interactions. Furthermore, they threaten to undermine planning, the autonomy-enhancing core function of contract.

But anti-forfeiture doctrine need not take this form and, in many cases, does avoid this trap.[61] Indeed, even the second prong of the anti-forfeiture principle need not go that far. Applying this prong can, and we think should, take seriously the blackletter law requirement just noted, allowing no excuse where the clear condition *is* "a material part of the agreed exchange." Thus applied, the two prongs should be reconstructed as a means for addressing the concern of intertemporal-based vulnerability to opportunism. Combined, they create a strong presumption that the parties' agreement follows the requirements of relational justice. The presumption is strong, but it neither is nor should be irreversible: it neither applies where the clear language of the agreement indicates otherwise nor to conditions whose materiality the parties have clarified.

Scott and Kraus may still resist our position. They think that the anti-forfeiture norm is irredeemable because it is premised on two troublesome assumptions: that "parties are unlikely to select terms that create the risk of forfeiture" and that "express conditions sometimes are not material at the time of formation." Both assumptions, they insist, are wrong since parties often favor such precise terms, which "create rule-like obligations that are easy for the parties to verify and enforce in court."[62]

This response works against the anti-forfeiture principle, however, only if it is examined within an analytical framework that classifies contract rules as either mandatory or majoritarian defaults. But neither the claim (that we agree to) whereby the anti-forfeiture rule should not be mandatory nor the fact that this rule does not reflect majoritarian preferences (Scott and Kraus focus on sophisticated commercial parties) justifies obscuring the role of the anti-forfeiture principle as a normative default. Furthermore, the gradual crystallization of *categories* of "suspicious" clauses—three notable examples from the existing case law include acceleration clauses, time clauses, and the requirement of a written notice in lading contracts[63]—implies that the doctrine can be further distanced from the ex post individual justice posture, which Scott and Kraus rightly criticize.

Legally informed, sophisticated firms that set up commercial contracts may, as Scott and Kraus explain, prefer otherwise. These contractors should thus be able—as they indeed can where normative defaults are at hand—to opt out by using "apt and certain words."[64] But contract law applies to idiosyncratic and legally uninformed parties as well. Therefore, *general* contract law—as opposed to statutes or doctrines meant strictly for commercial contracts—must respond first and foremost to the real people it serves and who are subject to its authority and coercive power. Contract law, then, should set up its normative defaults with individuals in mind and allow sophisticated commercial firms to adjust in the ordinary course of legally informed contract drafting.

One conspicuous example of the successful application of the anti-forfeiture principle comes from the law of insurance. In order "to avoid what would amount to a forfeiture of otherwise-provided coverage," courts have declined to read literally the liability insurance policy provision stating that "notice of a claim or suit against the policyholder must be given to the insurer 'as soon as is practicable.'" Even in cases of significant delays, "the majority of courts hold that coverage is not forfeited unless the liability insurer has been prejudiced by the delayed notice."[65]

Good Faith

1. Two Strands. We turn now to the primary home of justice in modern contract law: the good faith doctrine. "Every contract," declares the Restatement (echoing the U.C.C.[66]), "imposes upon each party a duty of good faith and fair dealing in its performance and its enforcement."[67] The "office" of this doctrine, explained Judge Richard Posner, is "to forbid the kinds of opportunistic behavior that a mutually dependent, cooperative relationship might enable in the absence of rule." In other words, good faith responds to the fact that "contracts do not just allocate risk" but also "set in motion a cooperative enterprise, which may to some extent place one party at the other's mercy."[68] Contractual parties, writes Posner in another opinion, "are embarked on a cooperative venture, and a minimum of cooperativeness in the event unforeseen problems arise at the performance stage is required even if not an explicit duty of the contract."[69] This "minimum of cooperativeness," we claim, nicely reflects our notion of contractual relational justice.

Good faith is, of course, a vague standard that can be—and has been—variously applied. Thus, "while some States are said to use the doctrine 'to effectuate the intentions of parties or to protect their reasonable expectations,' . . . other States clearly employ the doctrine to ensure that a party does not 'violate community standards of decency, fairness, or reasonableness.'"[70] Whereas the former strand seems to fit Markovits' account of pedestrian good faith we discussed and criticized above, the latter is reminiscent of our own competing account. Although it is not fully articulated, many of its characteristics aptly fit the prescriptions of relational justice theory. This strand vindicates the robust doctrinal presence of the relational justice account of good faith, making it a viable alternative to Markovits' theory not only normatively but also descriptively.

Good faith, in this view, is an umbrella and a potentially doctrinal hook for a set of contractual conduct rules.[71] Markovits himself cites many of the pertinent rules of both the U.C.C. and the Restatement. We cannot offer a full catalog here, but relying mostly on a subset of Markovits' examples reorganized into three categories, we show that, despite his claim to the contrary, good faith does prescribe an informative guide of conduct.

2. Three Categories. The first category of good-faith-rules-of-the-game applies in contract types that characteristically "invite" opportunistic behavior. One set of examples comes from insurance contracts, as in the case of an insurer who rejects "reasonable settlement offers near the policy limit, on the ground that it bears none of the litigation risks associated with rejecting the offers."[72] Two other classics involve requirements and output contracts. In these two contract types, one party is systemically subject to the other's discretion in cases of significant changes in the market price.[73] This feature explains why the U.C.C. specifically mentions in the context of these contracts the duty of good faith and helpfully clarifies its content by adding that "no quantity unreasonably disproportionate to any stated estimate or in the absence of a stated estimate to any normal or otherwise comparable prior output or requirements may be tendered or demanded."[74]

The second category of good-faith rules involves specific moments in the life of contracts where one party is typically vulnerable, namely, moments that are particularly susceptible to the other party's opportunism. Three such particularly sensitive moments involve specification, termination, and renegotiation.[75] Thus, "where a contract leaves the particulars of performance to be specified by one of the parties, that party is constrained to make the specification in good faith, which . . . entails that 'the range of permissible variation is limited by what is commercially reasonable.'"[76] Likewise, at least where the contract does not establish any specific regime, "termination is governed by good faith," which means that "[a] party seeking to terminate may not do so before the nonterminating party has had 'reasonable notification,' which is to say a 'reasonable time to seek a substitute arrangement.'"[77] Finally, repudiating the traditional pre-existing duty rule, the U.C.C. prescribes that a modifying contract "needs no consideration to be binding," but rather "must meet the test of good faith."[78] As it helpfully explains, this rule is aimed at facilitating renegotiations that are triggered by "unforeseen difficulty as would make out a legal excuse from performance," while making "ineffective" any attempt "to escape performance on the original contract terms [through] the extortion of a 'modification' without [such a] legitimate commercial reason."[79]

Topping all these more specific rules and informative standards is a residual category of "freestanding" bad-faith contractual behavior. Because conduct here is neither related to a particular contract type nor to a specific moment on the contractual horizon, the lists of examples mentioned by the Restatement are quite vague but still not uninformative. Good faith is violated, we learn, in cases of "evasion of the spirit of the bargain, lack of diligence and slacking off, willful rendering of imperfect performance, . . . and interference with or failure to cooperate in the other party's performance."[80] Good faith is also violated by such behavior as "conjuring up a pretended dispute, . . . harassing demands for assurances of performance, [or] rejection of performance for unstated reasons."[81] Admittedly, these lists do not exhaust the cases where a justice-based good faith requirement may invite intervention, and commentators also advance a duty to warn of a potential loss as well as an even broader duty to cooperate.[82] The relative open-endedness of these duties, which potentially destabilizes the parties' expectations, may explain why courts are less willing to adopt these additional obligations.[83]

3. *Good Faith as Relational Justice.* Both the substance and the form of this robust body of good faith doctrine fit relational justice theory. On the substantive side, it is worthwhile to highlight aspects related to the doctrine's content as well as its scope and source. These anti-opportunistic and cooperative prescriptions, whose bite seems to grow as performance unfolds and circumstances change,[84] embrace what Markovits explicitly repudiates,[85] namely, a "requirement of certain, usually minimal, restraints upon self-interest in deference to a much heavier interest of another party."[86]

In turning from content to scope, good faith goes beyond abstention duties. Good faith, as Farnsworth explains, "may not only proscribe undesirable conduct, but may require affirmative action as well," so that a party may be under a duty to take some affirmative steps to cooperate with the other party's performance.[87]

Finally, these good-faith-based prescriptions do not necessarily follow only the parties' intentions. As some courts openly acknowledge, the doctrine's underpinnings are normative, which explains their references to "ethical norms" or to "standards of decency, fairness, and reasonableness."[88] Again, contrary to the pedestrian view of good faith, all these prescriptions live comfortably with the conventional position where the covenant of good faith and fair dealing, as it is often called, is imposed *by law* rather than implied in fact.[89]

The doctrine also reflects the form side of our account, which centers on the notion of normative defaults. Thus, whereas the good faith umbrella "may not be disclaimed by agreement," the parties can contractually "determine the standards by which the performance of those obligations is to be measured if those standards are not manifestly unreasonable."[90] The parties can, more specifically, "grant the right to engage in the very acts and conduct which would otherwise have been forbidden by an implied covenant of good faith and fair dealing."[91] Moreover, some courts appropriately insist that such an opt-out requires explicit language and that the rigidity of this requirement depends on the nature of the contractual power at issue.[92]

Mitigation

1. An Obvious Implication of Relational Justice. Relational justice not only refines the contracting parties' rights and duties of performance. It also helps to delineate the scope, and often the type, of relief for breach of contract. The continuity between performance rules and remedial rules should not be surprising.[93] Like contract law's rules on performance, its remedial rules allocate risks and responsibilities to the parties and, in a sense, are thus part of their joint plan. They should, therefore, be—and indeed are—by and large defaults,[94] either majoritarian or normative.

The mitigation principle, which bars the injured party "from recovery for loss that he could have avoided" by "reasonable efforts" (unless he has made such efforts unsuccessfully), is relational justice's main representative at this stage of the contractual drama. As the Restatement clarifies, this rule does not impose a duty to mitigate—there is no liability for failure to do so—but rather only a burden, so that "[t]he amount of loss that [the aggrieved party] could reasonably have avoided by stopping performance, making substitute arrangements or otherwise is simply subtracted from the amount that would otherwise have been recoverable as damages." In that, the mitigation doctrine—like the doctrine of good faith—participates in shaping the parties' expectations from one another. It implies, more specifically, that the non-breaching party "is expected to take such *affirmative* steps as are appropriate in the circumstances to avoid loss."[95]

This expectation may seem out of place for relationships of reciprocal respect for independence—it may, on this view, even be "morally distasteful."[96] But it follows quite naturally if the parties' relationships are to be governed by relational justice.

2. The Efficiency of Mitigation. While mitigation is anathema to traditionalism, economic analysis finds it far more appealing, as Charles Goetz and Robert Scott's majoritarian default rule account suggests. In their view, mitigation mimics "widely suitable risk allocations" because most contracting parties "would agree in advance to minimize the joint costs of adjusting to prospective contingencies, assigning the responsibility of mitigating to whoever is better able to adjust to the changed conditions." The mitigation rule follows this "joint-cost minimization" principle by "den[ying] a mitigator recovery for losses he unreasonably failed to avoid," while "allow[ing] him full recovery for costs incurred through any reasonable affirmative efforts to minimize losses."[97]

Goetz and Scott seem to celebrate the mitigation doctrine but are fully aware of the limits of their account. One difficulty is that, if most parties indeed aim at joint maximization, as the majoritarian default paradigm assumes, mitigation is over-inclusive. As Goetz and Scott explain, the challenge of adjustment to prospective contingencies requires balancing the costs of evading contractual obligations with the costs of opportunistic bargaining whenever unanticipated cooperation is needed. In situations "lacking a good substitute market," this tension is acute, and mitigation is indeed called for. But in other settings, "where a developed market for substitute performances exists," much of the problem can be resolved without the mitigation doctrine.[98] Moreover, the difficulty of ascertaining mitigation's fit to the majoritarian preferences is further exacerbated if we seriously address the parties' *actual* preferences. They might include tastes for wagering or for altruism, which Goetz and Scott's discussion—as most economic analyses of contract—*assumes* that they do not.

Furthermore, some of the doctrine's rules "diverge from the joint-cost minimization principle." As Goetz and Scott acknowledge, "[m]ost courts have declined to impose any duty on a mitigator to deal with the breacher, even where the breacher offers the best readjustment option."[99] Moreover, and even more fundamentally, the standard of mitigation is not as demanding as the joint-cost-minimization principle would have prescribed. Mitigation is only expected if the loss can be avoided "without undue risk, burden or humiliation."[100] The non-breaching party is not expected to "sacrifice any substantial right of its own in order to minimize the loss of the defendants" or to "disregard its own interests or exalt above them those of the defaulting defendants."[101] For the mitigation duty to apply, it is not enough that a cost-effective alternative or substitute is available; it must also be *easily* available.[102]

3. Back to Relational Justice. Both these core features of the doctrine and its broad scope of applicability can be accounted for if mitigation, rather than as a majoritarian default rule, is understood as a normative default guided by relational justice. This alternative understanding is also echoed in the language of some courts, which justify the doctrine by reference to notions of "basic fairness"[103] and explain its role in terms of doing "justice between the parties."[104] As noted, and similarly to the other relational-justice-based doctrines discussed above, the mitigation doctrine does not shy away from expecting one contracting party to "take reasonable affirmative steps"[105] that would benefit the other.[106] But—again like these other doctrines—it limits this expectation to *modest* affirmative other-regard, which explains why mitigation arises only "when the effort is not great."[107]

As a normative prescription of relational justice, this maxim need not depend on the preferences of most contracting parties and is not contingent on the structure of the market. Furthermore, its modesty vis-à-vis the more demanding principle of joint maximization need not, indeed should not, be conceptualized as a blemish, especially given that the mitigation doctrine sets up a default,[108] which the parties can refine at will. Likewise, the fact that courts "have tolerated cost-increasing refusals to deal with the contract breacher"[109] is also understandable since relational justice surely does not require the aggrieved party to put himself vis-à-vis the breaching party "in a position that will involve humiliation, including embarrassment or loss of honor and respect."[110]

Finally, conceptualizing mitigation in terms of relational justice implies that the strict limitation of its applicability to the post-breach stage is probably unjustified.

Given that there are parallel pre-breach opportunities to avoid loss, relational justice implies that contract law should recognize, as Ariel Porat suggested, a defense of comparative fault.[111] Implementing such a defense without detrimentally injecting broad judicial discretion and possibly destabilizing contractual expectations may not be easy.[112] But we see no a priori reason to assume it would be impossible, especially given that many courts have managed to operationalize the duty of good faith by translating it into more precise contractual duties.

Expectation Damages

Relational justice affects not only the *scope* of remedial relief but, where a market is available for the contract goods, it also informs the *type* of remedy appropriate for breach of contract.[113] Specifically, we claim that relational justice provides an important justification for the position of common law, claiming, in sharp contrast with its civil law counterpart,[114] that expectation damages rather than specific performance is the aggrieved party's proper remedy.[115]

Like many other commentators, in most of these cases, we see no justification for preventing the contracting parties from proactively choosing specific performance as their remedy of choice. Unlike some of these critics, however, who find common law's preference for monetary recovery morally embarrassing,[116] we hold that contract's underlying liberal commitments require law to adopt a normative default that indeed privileges monetary recovery over specific performance.

Scott and Kraus carefully explicate the reason for this stance, though they seem to suggest it as grounds for choosing expectancy as a majoritarian default. "Once a regret contingency has occurred," Scott and Kraus explain, the promisor faces a choice mainly between two options—"perform and lose" and "breach and pay"—and is thus "motivated to choose the least costly option." Other things being equal, namely, where both parties are equally situated to acquire substitute goods, promisors are likely to perform because breach would entail not only liability for the promisee's expectation but also "bad feelings, loss of business reputation, good will, etc." Other things, however, are not always equal. Thus, when the promisor has a reason to believe that the promisee "is better able to cover in the market and thus reduce [her] anticipated losses on the contract," she is likely to choose the breach option. This "'benign' vision of breaching behavior," Scott and Kraus conclude, conceptualizes breach as a "cry for help" by the promisor, a request for the promisee "to salvage the broken contract at least cost and to send [her] the damage bill."[117]

A regime that makes specific performance widely available "invites" an opportunistic response by the promisee. The default preference of common law for expectation remedy preempts such a response, in compliance with relational justice.

11
Restitution

What Renders Enrichments (Un)just

The principle of preventing unjust enrichment is conventionally presented as the grounds of liability in restitution.[1] But despite its very long legacy in the history of private law, separating just from unjust enrichment remains challenging, as noted in Chapter 9. As one of us shows elsewhere, prominent attempts to do so without relying on an open-ended intuitionist sense of right and wrong fall apart upon scrutiny. Some are normatively suspicious; others are, at best, meaningless or, at worst, a disguise for unaccounted-for doctrinal choices.[2]

In this short chapter, we seek to rehabilitate the notion of *unjust* enrichment with respect to at least two of the most paradigmatic categories of the law of restitution by setting it within the theoretical framework of relational justice.[3] This should not be surprising. One could expect that private law's judgments regarding the justice of enrichments or lack thereof would hinge on the same underlying principle that prescribes the just terms of interpersonal interactions. The conceptual fit of relational justice theory to the key question of the law of restitution may thus account for the theory's interpretive credentials established below.

Mistaken Payments

1. Challenging Traditionalism at the Core. We begin with the category of mistaken payments, which is often described as the law of restitution's "core case."[4] The basic rule governing mistaken payments prescribes that, in principle, a recipient of such a payment "is liable in restitution."[5] Absent negating considerations, notably the recipient's reliance, restitution is generally deemed appropriate, and this form of restitutionary liability is broadly accepted.

Traditionalists are hard-pressed to account for the paradigmatic case of this doctrine, one where the transfer is unmarred by the mistake so that it gives the recipient good title to the money, and the recipient "did not participate in the claimant's cognitive preliminaries to the act."[6] Indeed, efforts to accommodate this canonical rule of the law of restitution to the traditionalist account of private law necessarily fall short. If private law is to address only our independence and formal equality, it must, by definition, be indifferent to whether the transferor's mistake

Relational Justice. Hanoch Dagan and Avihay Dorfman, Oxford University Press. © Hanoch Dagan and Avihay Dorfman 2024.
DOI: 10.1093/9780191987762.003.0011

thwarts the attainment of her own intended goal as long as the mistake was not forced or manipulated by fraud and the like.[7] Moreover, imposing liability in such cases offends the parties' formal equality because it requires the recipient to use her means for the benefit of the transferor.[8] This difficulty is not ameliorated (without begging the question) by adding the recipient's knowledge of the transferor's mistake, her free acceptance of the payment, or her retention thereof.[9]

Either way, the recipient, who is purely a passive beneficiary, is enlisted in the remedying of the transferor's unfortunate mistake—the consequences of her own freely willed activity—for which the recipient bears no responsibility. If private law is to be strictly guided by reciprocal respect for independence and formal equality, restitutionary liability for mistaken payments becomes indefensible since the transferor's demand of restitution is tantamount to unilaterally subordinating the recipient to the transferor's ends.[10]

This conclusion deals a strong blow to the traditional conception of private law. James Penner subscribes to this conception and suggests that, because liability to return mistaken payments is a duty of virtue that singles out the defendant to contribute to the collectivity's concern for everyone's welfare, it is the outlier of restitution. Unlike restitution's paradigmatic case, mistaken payments law ends up, in this view, as a doctrine that might be good to have but is not part of our core (let alone necessary) expectations from a just system of private law.[11]

We argue, by contrast, that mistaken payment law deserves its status as restitution's core case even though it cannot be defended on the grounds of independence and formal equality. Instead, it is entailed by the adherence of private law to relational justice that, as previous chapters demonstrate, guides the private law of a liberal legal order.

2. *Modest Affirmative Interpersonal Obligations.* As reiterated above, a private law guided by the demands of relational justice supports affirmative interpersonal obligations without necessarily ignoring people's independence. Traditionalists, because they affirm an absolutist conception of independence, view this as a contradiction in terms. Relational justice theory's qualitative distinctions between people's differing interests and its prescriptions on inherent limits to interpersonal accommodation demonstrate that it is not.

Thus, rather than presenting itself as a duty of virtue in private law, the law of mistaken payments imposes a duty of right: an affirmative legal duty of rescue, requiring the payee to return the payment to the payor. Relational justice theory clarifies why this particular duty is unobjectionable. For a private law concerned with self-determination, "to be free is to act from purposes that are self-authored and to be able to view one's life as broadly expressive of one's projects and goals"; therefore, such a private law—the currently prevailing private law—pays heed to "the misalignment between the [payor's] reason for acting and the outcome she produced."[12] Furthermore, restitutionary liability is also conducive to self-determination because it expands people's freedom of action by reducing the overly chilling effects of making mistakes in a no-liability regime.[13]

Finally, while imposing on any other person an affirmative obligation of responsiveness to the payor's predicament would have been harsh and intrusive, the restitutionary burden that the mistaken-payment law imposes on recipients is quite modest. Recipients' frustrated expectations should not be dismissed outright (see below), which means that implementing restitutionary liability for mistaken payments might pose some challenges. But in the paradigmatic case, the doctrine anticipates that when the time that elapses between the mistaken conferral and the transferor's claim is not too considerable, restitution neither jeopardizes the recipient's self-determination nor seriously undermines her independence.[14] Moreover, it raises neither the concern of arbitrary enforcement nor the challenge of line-drawing that limit the scope of nonfeasance liability, as discussed in Chapter 6. Therefore, reciprocal respect for self-determination and substantive equality justifies such a duty, which basically compels one party not to be oblivious to the predicament of the mistaken other.

Justifying the law of mistaken payments on relational justice grounds not only accounts for the presumptive rule of restitution but also clarifies other aspects of this doctrine. We focus on two of them. One is the familiar restitutionary defense of change-of-position, which is almost exclusively confined to cases of mistaken payments.[15] The other and much less familiar is the emerging doctrine applicable to the (increasingly important) categories of mistaken payments to individuals by financial institutions such as banks, brokers, or insurance companies. While the former rule illustrates the ex post significance of relational justice, the latter demonstrates relational justice's amenability to qualitative distinctions between parties' interests.

3. Change-of-Position as a Substantive Remedy. As a defense, the change-of-position rule is part of the remedial apparatus of restitution law. It does not belong, however, to the part of remedies law directly premised on the parties' primary rights. Instead, the change-of-position rule belongs to the family of remedial doctrines that, as discussed in Chapter 7, are normatively important in and of themselves. Substantive remedies, as we dubbed them, incorporate mechanisms of "second-looking" at the post-payment condition of both parties to adjust law's response to their defective interaction, seeking to address both the plaintiff's setback and the defendant's predicament.

What triggers the change-of-position defense is the mundane fact that, typically, mistaken payments are neither immediately nor costlessly discovered. Recipients sometimes fail to notice the mistake and dispose of their income in the belief that the conferred payment is rightfully theirs. Requiring recipients always to be prepared to return any benefits they receive would hamper the security and stability of their affairs. Such a regime severely deviates from the modest, and thus acceptable, burden of the recipient's prima facie restitutionary liability because it might disrupt recipients' plans and goals.[16] The law precludes such an unacceptable result by prescribing a second look at the recipient's predicament, thus reducing their liability if the pertinent receipt has led them "without notice to change position in such manner that an obligation to make restitution of the original benefit would be inequitable to [them]."[17]

4. Carving Out Financial Institutions. Consider finally a seemingly deviant line of cases where professional financial institutions—banks, brokers, or insurance companies—are the transferors, and individuals are the recipients of their mistaken payments. As shown elsewhere, in many such cases, courts make extensive efforts in order to preclude restitutionary recovery: they overlook the change-of-position requirement of causation, skirt the irrevocability of the mistaken payment, or "creatively" find compromises.[18] While these cases may be dismissed as doctrinally erroneous, we think that they should be read more charitably.

This emerging body of case law expresses an unarticulated judicial intuition, stating that mistaken payments by sophisticated financial institutions invite different normative accounting than those made by ordinary, private persons. This new accounting justifiably precludes recipients' liability and thus obviates the need for a second look at their post-receipt predicament.

A restitutionary doctrine that is premised on reciprocal respect for self-determination and substantive equality should respond to the shift from individuals to financial institutions. When transferors are professional profit-maximizing institutions, they cannot validly invoke a relational justice-based requirement of accommodation by the recipients of their mistaken payments (especially when recipients are ordinary, private persons). Requiring *this type* of transferor to take *full* responsibility for their payment would not impede their self-determination and equal standing (even if we set aside the difficult question as to the status of autonomy and equality claims of incorporated persons[19]). Not only are banks, brokers, and insurance companies the cheapest cost-avoiders and superior risk bearers of these mistakes but they are also structured to function as such. The transferors' avoidance capacities and their abilities to spread the costs of mistakes among the beneficiaries of the activity that generated those mistakes (e.g., the banking system) are intrinsic to their raison d'être.[20]

Insofar as *these* transferors are concerned, therefore, taking full responsibility for any such mistakes is fundamental to the story of their (institutional) life. Financial institutions, then, even before we examine the power imbalance that typifies these cases, have no standing to expect recipients to incur any burden on their behalf. Where unsuspecting individuals receive payments that were transferred by financial institutions, frustrating their expectations is unjustified. They should be able to feel free to adjust their modes of living—their decisions about consumption, as well as their responses to income-earning opportunities—to what they believe are their resources.[21]

Self-Interested Conferrals of Benefits

1. Interdependence and Collective Action. Rules in the category of self-interested conferrals of benefits involve cases where the interests of a group of people are interlocked, such as all sharing an interest in the same piece of property or all being subject to a common liability.

Suppose one group member incurs some expense in this joint project—she pays for repairs to the damaged roof of a shared house—and thereby benefits the other members since it is impossible or infeasible to exclude them from this collective good. In some instances, the beneficiaries might actively indicate their unwillingness to pay for the benefit. In others, the expense-incurring member and the beneficiaries might never have communicated about the expense. If the law of restitution were to discount people's self-determination and focus solely on upholding their independence, it would be difficult to justify a requirement for beneficiaries to make restitution. In the typical case, the claimant can show neither harm inflicted by the defendant nor the defendant's consent to the exchange.[22]

Fortunately, the law does not take this approach. When the parties' interests are sufficiently interlocked to prevent the claimant from reasonably pursuing their self-interest without benefiting others, the law typically requires (under certain conditions that we will shortly address) restitutionary payment to one who confers an economic benefit on another in performing a joint obligation or in holding jointly held property.[23] By forcing the beneficiaries to pay their proportionate share of the collective good, the law of restitution neutralizes the potential free-riding that could undermine the jointly beneficial collective action and, thus, the parties' self-determination. This role of the law of restitution is justified in terms of its underlying liberal maxim of reciprocal respect for self-determination.[24]

The typical features of collective action problems,[25] which exemplify the significant impact of human interdependence on self-determination, illuminate the gap between the commitments to independence and self-determination. Although promoting the parties' self-interests when these problems arise requires cooperation, the absence of legal intervention might hinder jointly beneficial action because the individual interest of each party usually overrides their interest in the collective good. (This will be, more precisely, the expected outcome if no single member of the group is likely to derive sufficient personal benefit from the collective good to justify paying the entire cost of supplying it alone, and no coalition of members can feasibly divide the costs among those members.[26]) If properly fine-tuned, a restitutionary recovery is the proper remedy since it requires people's independence to recede in order to ensure their self-determination.

2. Private Law's Autonomy-enhancing Mission. But why should a liberal polity allow the use of law's coercive power for this purpose? Should not the parties resort to the normative powers instantiated by contract law to secure such cooperation, to the exclusion of restitution law? To answer these questions, we need to appreciate the insights of both lawyer economists and critical scholars.[27]

The economic analysis of private law forcefully demonstrates how many of our existing practices rely on legal devices for overcoming various types of transaction costs (information costs, bilateral monopolies, cognitive biases, and heightened risks of opportunistic behavior) that generate the participants' vulnerabilities in most collaborative interpersonal interactions. Merely enforcing the parties' expressed intentions would not be sufficient to neutralize the inherent risks of such endeavors. If many of these endeavors are to become or remain viable options, the law must provide assurances to establish the trust so crucial for success. Even where parties follow their own social norms in their interaction, these background legal guarantees serve as a sort of safety net in the event of future conflict and thereby foster trust in routine interactions.

The law's effects are not only material but also, as Chapter 2 implies, structural and, at times, even constitutive. Because private law often blends naturally into social reality, the categories it creates construct our daily interactions. Thus, many of our conventions—including social practices we take for granted (think bailment, suretyship, and fiduciary)—are, especially in modern times, legally constructed. Even putting aside the transaction costs entailed in constructing these arrangements from scratch, were these conventions not to be legally coined, people would face "obstacles of the imagination" that could preclude these practices. Indeed, private law plays an important cultural role. Like other social conventions, it both consolidates people's expectations and participates in constructing core categories of interpersonal relationships around their underlying normative ideals.

The material and structural functions of private law imply that contractual freedom, albeit significant, cannot do all the work that is to be done. Hence, for many cooperative types of interpersonal relationships, some measure of further and more active legal facilitation is both desirable and necessary. Lack of such legal support may sometimes undermine—perhaps even eliminate—these types of interactions and, in turn, people's substantively equal ability to pursue their conception of the good.

The unbridgeable gap between strict adherence to independence and private law's twin commitment to autonomy and substantive equality is rooted in people's fallibility, most notably their bounded rationality, cognitive failures, and the fact that they tend to prefer their self-interest over the interests of others. These human imperfections are not merely of peripheral concern. At least in the doctrinal areas under consideration, they pose a systematic difficulty. Ignoring this difficulty would thus be self-defeating for any theory that aims to guide or justify these doctrines.

Traditionalists who adhere to their commitments to understand private law in terms of relational independence need not be alarmed by these propositions. As we have seen, they can—and, to be normatively consistent, should—insist that defendants' liability be limited only to what can be reliably founded on their actual (explicit or implicit) consent.[28] But taking this (radically reformist) path would be normatively unfortunate given the significant impact of private law on people's ability to pursue their plans, goals, and conceptions of the good as free and equal persons. Thus, taking a hands-off attitude is tantamount to undermining the liberal commitment to self-determination and substantive equality.

3. *Cases of Justified Override of Independence.* When law's inaction is likely to frustrate goals that require collective action, a liberal law should consider overriding defendants' explicit reluctance to participate in collective action and pay their share. For the law to justifiably impose such a restitutionary obligation, however, two conditions must be met.[29] *First,* it must be objectively evident that the defendant's proportionate benefit exceeds their proportionate share of the cost of providing the benefit and that the law's intervention is necessary to facilitate the jointly beneficial collective action. *Second,* a defendant must be unable to point to any (credible) nonstrategic motive for not contributing to the collective good.

Together, these conditions ensure that restitution defendants are better off receiving and paying for the collective benefits than doing without them and have no legitimate objection to the restitutionary obligation. The first condition refines the circumstances in which law's inaction is likely to hinder goals requiring collective action—that is, cases in which individuals may refuse to pay their fair share based solely on the expectation that the efforts of others will yield them the same good free of charge (or more cheaply). The second condition ensures that the divergence between the defendant's explicit preference (not to participate in the collective action) and their presumable self-interest (to participate) is due to the payoff structure to which they and the other potential participants are subject and does not reflect their genuine subjective preferences.

The second condition, which echoes the doctrine of subjective devaluation, clarifies (again) law's departure from the traditionalist embrace of uncompromising independence. The reason for this is that—as Alan Brudner and Jennifer Nadler argue—traditionalists "cannot fill the gap [of the defendant's consent or wrongdoing] by deeming a benefit incontrovertible, because this simply bypasses what needs to be established: the defendant's active involvement in the transaction" that, for an independence-driven private law regime, is a strict prerequisite for liability.[30]

4. *Self-determination, not Welfare.* The rules of subjective devaluation also help to refine the departure of the law of restitution from another contending account. In this approach, solving people's collective action problems is justified, but not as a legitimate way of respecting their freedom and equality (a way that follows the dictates of relational justice). What drives the work of the law of restitution in this alternative view is society's aggregate welfare, the concern that free-riding would bring about the underproduction of collective goods.[31]

This welfarist perspective is very responsive to restitution claimants, indeed far more responsive than its relational justice counterpart. In this view, restitution should only be denied if the utility loss to the defendant, if forced to pay, exceeds the gain to the plaintiff from the collective action that restitution could facilitate. Doctrinally, this approach implies a restrictive interpretation of the subjective devaluation defense that potential realizability in money can overcome because, even if the beneficiary does not appreciate the conferred benefit, the market's appreciation will ensure that restitution does not generate a utility loss.

By contrast, relational justice's commitment to self-determination precludes restitution in cases of potential subjective devaluation, even when there is relative certainty that the action is jointly beneficial overall. Insisting on people's right to order their own priorities means that a benefit's value is deemed incontrovertible only if it has been converted into money or "it is inevitable that the defendant will [in fact] realize the benefit."[32]

These two alternatives were offered, respectively, by the two great authorities on the English law of restitution: Goff & Jones and Peter Birks.[33] In line with the analysis of the preceding pages—and with relational justice's insistence on conceptualizing welfare as a means (to self-determination) rather than an end[34]—contemporary law largely endorses the latter approach. This view is reflected in the orthodox position that denies restitutionary liability for the improvement of a defendant's existing interest, as opposed to its preservation, which does yield (at least in some cases) liability.[35]

5. Collective Action and Workers' Organization. Appreciating the prevalence and significance of these collective action mechanisms for a genuinely liberal private law offers important critical insights. It shows, for example, why, for labor unions to thrive, they should be able to negotiate so-called "agency shop" contracts, requiring employees to pay union dues as a condition of employment. A genuinely liberal conception of private law must consequently repudiate the Supreme Court *Janus* ruling, which prohibits agency shop (at this stage in cases of public employers).[36]

Forcing unions to allow nonmembers to free-ride—to be able to pay no fees for the services the unions must provide them—proactively frustrates their collective action. Accordingly, *Janus* is not only deeply problematic from the viewpoint of a just political economy[37] but also runs against one of the most fundamental commitments of liberal private law, and it is an aberration within the existing domain of private law doctrines dealing with collective action problems.

An agency shop arrangement should be authorized, as are the other existing legal mechanisms for addressing these problems, because it does not meaningfully reduce individual autonomy. It results in an ex ante reduction in the amount of money belonging to an employee who has to pay dues in return for higher wages, increased benefits, and better working conditions. Even assuming that some employees are unwilling third-party beneficiaries of agency shop provisions, a sufficiently competitive labor market ought to empower employees to seek out employers with desirable union agreements.

Part IV

Beyond The Familiar

12
Regulating Workplace Safety

Private Law's Proper Domain

In Part III we demonstrated that relational justice is the appropriate normative lodestar of private law across significant subsets of its familiar terrain. The purpose of Part IV is to challenge the limited scope of private law in the conventional legal taxonomy. Private law's proper domain, we argue, encompasses *all* the—existing and potential—legal doctrines governing people's interpersonal relationships in their capacity as individuals. Put differently, as we argued above, private law is the law of human relations.[1]

This claim should not be surprising at this stage. The pointers to private law's unchartered territories were noted in previous chapters in the recurrent argument that private law is not reducible to common law. As we hope to demonstrate in this chapter, which studies workers' compensation schemes and regulatory safety agencies, relational justice is often manifest beyond judges' chambers.

Chapters 13 and 14 shift to two social ills—discrimination and poverty—that are conventionally presented as inviting a quintessentially public law remedy grounded in distributive justice or other collectivist commitments. We disagree. Given that some of their instantiations dramatically affect interactions between individuals apart from their overall consequences, continuity is also evident between the proper legal treatment of poverty and discrimination and the way private law addresses other interpersonal differences such as ignorance or necessity. Therefore, discrimination and poverty should be, and to some extent already are, important concerns of private—and not only public—law.

Finally, the domain of private law is typically tied to the law governing interactions among members of the same political community. But this limitation again fails to fully realize that private law is in charge of constructing just terms of interactions between and among private persons as such. This failure is particularly consequential when addressing grievances of victims of grave transnational wrongs, as we argue in Chapter 15.

The proper delineation of private law's domain to include these areas matters because, as we noted at the opening of the book, each mapping of private law's domain impacts the application scope of the reasoning deemed typical of private law. The unjustified capitulation of private law's domain, therefore, hinders the critical reach of relational justice reasoning. By resisting these unjustified limitations and reforming our mapping of private law's domain, we hope to expose blind spots

Relational Justice. Hanoch Dagan and Avihay Dorfman, Oxford University Press. © Hanoch Dagan and Avihay Dorfman 2024.
DOI: 10.1093/9780191987762.003.0012

and dogmatic assumptions that obscure the freestanding significance of people's interpersonal interactions. As usual, the payoff is explanatory or transformative. In some cases, our reconstructive argument helps to make sense of existing doctrine, while in others, it places private law's resources at the service of the doctrine's desired reform.

Regulating Relational Justice

Establishing and maintaining a just scheme of interpersonal relationships has never been simple. Modern societies are complex, and setting up an effective legal infrastructure that vindicates relational justice in key social and economic contexts—dealing with people's relationships with their employers, landlords, banks, and the like—poses a daunting challenge to courts given their comparative institutional disadvantages, discussed in Chapter 4. The heavy involvement of legislatures and administrative agencies in this core task of private law in addition to or instead of courts is thus neither surprising nor objectionable.[2]

The responsibility for securing just relationships differs from the other—and more obvious—responsibility of these legal actors for serving the public interest. This concern requires legislators and regulators to ensure not only that the state respects its constituents as free and equal persons but also that the interaction frameworks constructed (or regulated) by law abide by the maxim of reciprocal respect for self-determination and substantive equality.

Indeed, one takeaway from this chapter is to discard the scholarly schism over the primary regulatory schemes dealing with interpersonal relationships, such as workers' compensation programs or the Occupational Safety and Health Administration (OSHA) that defines the duties of employers to provide safe workplaces. Traditionalists oust them from their purview altogether (or cast them as public law limitations on private law), while critics are not careful to ensure that these schemes are *relationally* just. But both these regulatory projects play a key—probably *the* key—role in implementing the employers' tort duty of care to ensure workplace safety for their employees.

Proper appreciation of this role implies resisting the "public law reductionism" typical of their analysis. We do not claim that publicly regarded concerns should be irrelevant in these contexts but insist that they must not overshadow the private law duties these schemes are tasked to fulfill. The legal actors in agencies whose responsibility focuses on such tasks should "think horizontally" and adjust the substantive and procedural features of their *modus operandi* accordingly.

Fortunately, the two bodies of law we discuss in this chapter do so by and large. Some of their rules may seem confusing if understood as devices attending solely to the public good (however defined) and only become apparent when viewed from a relational justice perspective. Refining the relational justice underpinnings of these legal schemes thus helps to make sense of existing practice and, indeed, vindicates features of it currently under attack, mainly on collectivist (notably economic) grounds.

Workers' Compensation

In abstract terms, the duty of employers to ensure the safety of the workplace for their employees is in no way unique, meaning that the common law of negligence is a simple way of implementing it. Traditional one-to-one litigation, however, is not essential for this task, and using other means to secure compliance with this duty does not imply repudiation of this relational justice prescription. What relational justice does require, as we argued above,[3] is that a potential injurer be subject to a mandatory reason to accommodate, within limits, the person the potential victim actually is. If necessary, compliance with a reason to accommodate can be secured without making exclusive reference to the adjudicatory and remedial aspects typical of negligence law.

We thus have reason to doubt the historical narrative portraying the rise of workers' compensation acts as a legislative doing-away-with-torts in a traditional core area of application.[4] Typical workers' compensation schemes indeed prescribe that injured workers are not entitled to sue their employers or coworkers for work-related injuries.[5] They have *not*, however, eliminated the interpersonal tort duty of care that employers owe to employees.

Workers' compensation schemes do not release employers from their traditional tort liability for injuries caused by their *non*-accidental (i.e., intentional or even merely reckless) misconduct.[6] In sharp contrast to their economic readings, these schemes do not leave to the employer the decision of whether to invest the cost of exercising the requisite care. How do we know this? Because they do not strip employees of their tort law right to bodily safety, which allows them to compel their employers to ensure a reasonably safe work environment, that is, they have not abolished injunctive relief[7] and punitive damages[8] (which, as noted, is a form of injunctive relief granted ex post[9]). Barring these doctrines, the reason that the duty gives to the employer would prove spineless, lacking the mechanisms that render it de facto mandatory rather than merely de jure. As with the case of tort liability for non-accidental injuries, ex ante and ex post injunctive relief are doctrinal manifestations of the duty's mandatory character.

The view that workers' compensation schemes repudiated tort law is especially puzzling given that this rendered the tort duty of employers to secure a reasonably safe working place for their employees far *more*, rather than less, demanding.[10]

A major reason for repudiating the traditional common law order in matters of workplace safety has been the notorious feebleness of the employer's duty of care. Prior to the rise of workers' compensation schemes (and even before them, in the famous English case of *Winterbottom v. Wright*[11]), the dominant judicial approach was to subordinate this duty to some (certainly problematic) idea of freedom of contract. According to this paradigm, a person's conscious choice to enter an employment contract in the first place or to go on working in the face of a known risk is reason enough to bar the employee from suing the employer for negligence. The doctrinal hook of employers' immunity from violations of their duty of care was often assumption of risk.

The reformist agenda behind the rise of workers' compensation schemes has gradually and steadily made the duty of care far more adequate, and the doctrine of assumption of risk has been substantially modified. Persuading courts dealing with workplace safety (and other non-recreational contexts) that the mere conscious choice to expose oneself to an unreasonably dangerous environment is sufficient to absolve the injurer of liability for negligent infliction of bodily harm is now almost impossible.

OSHA

1. The Significance of Ex Ante Risk Regulation. A similar analysis applies to the main tool contemporary law uses to vindicate workers' relational right to their employers to secure a safe and healthy working environment, namely, the regulatory scheme prescribed by the *Occupational Safety and Health Act* of 1970 (OSHA).[12] Like workers' compensation law, the point of OSHA is to *strengthen* employers' ex ante compliance with this interpersonal duty rather than to mimic the results of traditional negligence law.[13]

Indeed, the common law of torts, with its traditional requirement of a completed wrong, is particularly inapt for this task because it cannot properly respond to the irreparable harms at hand, and workers' compensation schemes do not obviate this difficulty. No award of monetary damages can restore to victims of wrongful death their lost life, and this is also true of injuries such as mangled limbs or blindness. Ex ante regulation of risk is, at least in principle, the proper response to this predicament.[14]

Accordingly, the OSHA regime structures the relationships between employers and employees by ensuring the foundational status of employees' right to safety and health.[15] These expansions beyond the traditional apparatus of the common law of torts do not imply that the OSHA regime is divorced from private law's relational focus.[16] Rather, they mean that, despite its regulatory *form*, this regime is in tune—in fact, more in tune than its adjudicatory counterpart—with the interpersonal focus of private law and, indeed, with what the maxim of relational justice requires.[17]

2. OSHA's Substantive Requirements. The interpersonal perspective is key to both the substance and the form of the OSHA regime. Its clearest substantive manifestation is OSHA's prescription of feasible risk reduction.[18] OSHA "requires the elimination of 'significant' risks, when they can be eliminated without threatening the long-run health of the activity to which the risks belong."[19] As Gregory Keating explains, this feasibility analysis "looks to achieve the lowest level of risk practically"—that is, technologically and economically—"attainable, not the level of risk that minimizes the combined costs of injuries and their prevention."[20]

This requirement is understandably puzzling, if not irrational, for theorists who tie adjudication to private law and regulation to public law.[21] As a public law measure, this requirement seems dubious from an aggregative perspective since, as Cass Sunstein argues, "one OSHA regulation protects a large number of lives at relatively low cost, while another regulation protects a small number of lives at a relatively high cost."[22] But OSHA's feasibility test makes perfect interpersonal sense, in line with the underpinnings of private law's relational justice. Private law's focus on the terms of human and social interactions, rather than on the aggregate public pie, entails, as we saw in Chapter 5, an *asymmetrical* treatment of physical harm and financial costs, which is what the standard of due care in the common law of negligence requires.[23]

The implication is not that costs are always irrelevant. As usual, relational justice does not categorically exclude general welfare concerns, which explains why its feasibility requirement does not apply to insignificant risk. A "background level of risk" is "worth bearing," as Keating notes, because eliminating all discernible risk "requires the elimination of all discernible activity"—"a cure worse than the disease it treats."[24] But relational justice does not subscribe to the economists' cost–benefit analysis, and OSHA rejects it too. Where "the essential conditions of effective agency" of the employees are at stake, risk-creators *are* required to "press precaution beyond the point of marginal cost-justifiability."[25]

The same interpersonal logic and commitment to relational justice explain and justify the regulation providing workers a right to refuse hazardous work if "the condition clearly presents a risk of death or serious physical harm, there is not sufficient time for OSHA to inspect, and, where possible, a worker has brought the condition to the attention of the employer."[26] A similar analysis supports OSHA's attempt to force accommodation of workplace conditions to workers' known susceptibilities.[27]

3. *OSHA's Relational Form.* Furthermore, although OSHA does not establish a one-to-one litigation regime, the relational foundation of the OSHA regime can also be traced in many features of its form. OSHA defines its "general" mission as the assurance of "safe and healthful conditions for working men and women" and its role as one of "setting and enforcing standards and providing training, outreach, education and compliance assistance." At the same time "*employers* are responsible for providing a safe and healthful workplace for their workers."[28]

This division of labor is not one whereby the state commandeers the support of employers to enhance its public goals; rather, it rests on the relational logic typical of private law:[29] "Because employers control the conditions of employment, the onus of protecting workers from occupational disease and injury was to rest with them as well."[30] Indeed, as the "general duty" clause of the OSH Act prescribes, each employer is obligated "to furnish to each of his employees employment and a place of employment which are free from recognized hazards that are causing or are likely to cause death or serious physical harm to his employees."[31] This relational emphasis accounts for the rough correspondence between the list of employers' responsibilities and that of employees' rights, as well as for the fact that the OSHA regime does not cover self-employed workers.[32]

4. OSHA's Modus Operandi. OSHA's focus on constructing just workplace relationships involves its compliance with the requirement of the Administrative Procedure Act on stakeholders' participation in its rulemaking procedure.[33] Both employers and labor representatives can recommend that OSHA initiate standards.[34] OSHA also conducts public hearings or round tables, where both sides can provide their input.[35] Two representatives of each side also sit on the National Advisory Committee on Occupational Safety and Health (NACOSH), which advises the Secretary of Labor and the Secretary of Health and Human Services on occupational safety and on health programs and policies.[36]

The connection between process considerations and relational justice is complex. One conceptualization of the democratizing element of OSHA's advisory committee is as a mediating feature, which recognizes the multiple potential forms of compliance with relational justice. Indeed, under modern industrial conditions, safety policy is a hybrid category offering a range of arrangements that accord with relational justice, all meriting consideration. Reasoning about those arrangements is not a mere exercise in expressing preference or exerting interest group power, and situated perspectives affect our choices. Allowing significant representation, then, is a step toward allowing participants to understand the system as one of their own authorship, an integral part of the infrastructure of just relations.

The same relational justice rationale also explains "OSHA's priority system for conducting inspections," which "is designed to allocate available OSHA resources as effectively as possible to ensure that maximum feasible protection is provided to working men and women."[37] It also explains, indeed justifies, OSHA's authority to seek a restraining order if it finds "conditions or practices" that "could reasonably be expected to cause death or serious physical harm before normal enforcement procedures could eliminate the hazard."[38]

Finally, the noted sensitivity of relational justice to society's structural social injustices[39] underpins OSHA's outreach priorities. It explains its focus on "vulnerable, hard-to-reach workers in dangerous jobs to enhance their knowledge about their rights and the hazards they face" as well as on "temporary workers" and "limited English proficiency workers—a population that typically experiences a higher rate of injuries, illnesses, and fatalities in the workplace."[40] OSHA's mission of constructing just workplace relationships is also clear from the extension of its reach to foreign workers, who are thereby also encouraged "to exercise their rights under occupational safety and health laws."[41]

Outreach has rarely been the focus of scholars dealing with OSHA. It is, however, a telling example supporting our claim. When people affected by the ground rules of interaction are unaware of their rights, the very basis of just relationships is threatened. Outreach is crucial for establishing the basic conditions for just work relationships. Furthermore, it is particularly inaccessible to courts; it may occasionally be a byproduct of sensational litigation but can only be pursued systematically by an administrative agency. OSHA's outreach regime recognizes the importance of creating the conditions for just relationships by assuming responsibility for generating an informed workforce.

Relational Regulators

As one of us demonstrated in a co-authored work with Roy Kreitner (that the previous section also draws on), workers' safety is but one example of a much larger inventory of interpersonal relationship categories subject to regulatory schemes, which vindicate private law's normative DNA of relational justice.[42]

Relational regulators abound, and often, like OSHA, they respond to their private law duties. Although most of these regulators have proactive enforcement powers, they generally aspire to provide satisfactory responses to relational wrongs. Thus, they take individual complaints seriously, either as (partial) substitutes for private lawsuits or in parallel to potential lawsuits. The continuity between common law and these horizontal agencies goes beyond that, as our case study of OSHA illustrates. The substantive norms they apply and their technique toolkit are guided by relational considerations, as is to be expected given their vital role in shaping important categories of interpersonal relationships.

The common law conception of private law, which we rejected in Chapter 2, makes judges primarily responsible for the justice of people's interpersonal affairs and treats legislation and regulation as alien add-ons or late-coming policy interventions. Thereby, it obscures this increasingly important area of private law and unduly limits the borders of institutional and procedural imagination concerning law's potential contribution to our interpersonal, horizontal relationships.

Moreover, by implicitly presuming that the regulatory apparatus should focus solely on aggregative goals, this view indirectly reifies the prevailing regulatory theory, which is blind to the contribution of (a subset of) the modern regulatory apparatus to relational justice.[43] Due to this blindness, this theory tends to perceive any interpersonal attention as a distraction from its public role. This misguided (but unfortunately prevalent) reductionist account of regulation in public law is behind the increasingly strict and insufficiently discriminating cost–benefit analysis of administrative agencies' requirements.[44]

Even for agencies like OSHA, whose task is mostly interpersonal, the relevance of such analysis is undeniable. The closer we come to that pole of the regulatory universe, however, the more troubling an outcome where the cost-benefit analysis overshadows interpersonal considerations—or, more specifically, the demands of relational justice—that should guide private law, whatever its institutional pedigree.

The role of relational justice is most prominent in regard to two major agencies that deal with discrimination: the Equal Employment Opportunity Commission (EEOC) and the Office of Fair Housing and Equal Opportunity in the Department of Housing and Urban Development (FHEO). The EEOC, whose vision is to secure "Justice and Equality in the Workplace," enforces "federal laws that make it illegal to discriminate against a job applicant or an employee"[45] and works "to prevent discrimination before it occurs through outreach, education and technical assistance programs."[46] The FHEO "administers federal laws and establishes national policies that make sure all Americans have equal access to the housing of their choice."[47]

The prominence of relational justice in this context is hardly surprising since discrimination is a relational wrong. Appreciation of this proposition is both theoretically important and practically significant, as we argue in Chapter 13.

13
The Tort of Discrimination

From Denial to Partial Acceptance

1. A Missing Tort. The law of interpersonal responsibility for workplace safety outlined in Chapter 12, like much of the law on precontractual justice discussed in Chapter 9, is the result of a cooperative effort involving judges, legislators, and regulators. In these (and other) legal areas, the first move came from the bench. But often—as in the familiar tort of negligence per se[1]—the path of private law goes in the reverse direction, with judges building on previous statutory and regulatory measures. In this chapter, we argue that the statutory and regulatory apparatus dealing with private discrimination should inspire judges to fill a major gap—indeed, to change the normative starting point on the legality of private discrimination—in contemporary tort law.

Tort law protects some of the most fundamental rights we hold against others, but the list of these rights is not static. Straightforward illustrations are the twentieth-century additions to the law of torts of rights to privacy, product safety, and emotional well-being. One right, though, has been missing:[2] *the right to be treated as equal* to the other party to an interaction as well as to all others interacting with this party.[3] This right entitles one to interact with another private individual in terms that respect both of them as substantively free and equal persons.

A claim-right held against other private persons, this right implies that all else being equal, our traits and choices must not be held against us in a wide range of voluntary interactions, especially (though not exclusively) market ones. It aims to dismantle transactional barriers set up by others when applying their normative powers, thus implying that these voluntary interactions must conform with the maxim of reciprocal respect for self-determination and equality. This approach entails a corresponding duty against wrongful discrimination and warrants *a tort of discrimination* that further entrenches this duty and addresses its breach. Note that we use "discrimination" not only in the narrow sense of reluctance to employ, sell, lease, or include but also in the broader sense of failure to accommodate the constitutive choices and traits of another.

The reference to voluntary interactions could be misleading, creating a perception uncritically accepted by almost all moral accounts of discrimination, namely, that wrongful discrimination in contexts such as employment, consumption, housing, and educational institutions can be specified independently of the property and contract laws governing these interactions. In this perception,

Relational Justice. Hanoch Dagan and Avihay Dorfman, Oxford University Press. © Hanoch Dagan and Avihay Dorfman 2024.
DOI: 10.1093/9780191987762.003.0013

the difference between discrimination in the choice of a friend and an employee pertains to the context where the choice is made. It suggests that the right to make discriminatory choices is already implicit in the freedom to choose one's friend, employee, and others. Hence, the only live question seems to be one of legal intervention: should the law impose limits on the freedom to choose friends, employees, and others? The answer may vary depending on the context, but the structure of the problem remains the same: discrimination is an integral aspect of our freedom to engage in voluntary interactions.

We reject this view because it rests on an indefensibly reductive understanding of private law. Rather than merely tracking or even facilitating our extra-legal voluntary interactions, private law—as we argued in Chapter 2—sometimes plays a constitutive role in making these interactions possible in the first place. It does so by introducing legal powers and correlative vulnerabilities that do not merely preserve our rights and duties but empower us to change them and create new ones. The institutions of property and contract, as we claimed in Chapter 3, do precisely that—they vest right-holders with the power to make choices that change the normative situation of others. Voluntary interactions that are partially constituted by law, therefore, cannot be analyzed relying on a model of such interactions existing apart from this legal fiat.

Consequently, the view of discriminatory choices as inherent in freedom of choice is untenable when this freedom is not a natural right but a normative power artificially manufactured through the operation of the law.[4] Empowering some people—private proprietors, employers, and lessors—over others suggests that normative powers must not undermine the status of parties to voluntary interactions as free and equal agents. Unlike the case of choosing a friend, property and contract laws cannot legitimately grant employers, for example, normative power to subject employees (or potential employees) to impermissible behavior on their part, including wrongful discrimination.

Accordingly, the tort of discrimination we propose in this chapter establishes and protects the right to be treated as an equal by preventing holders of legal powers from incorporating the freedom to discriminate against others into their legally constructed voluntary interactions. This tort does not interfere with people exercising legitimate normative powers; instead, it denies the very existence of *any* power to make discriminatory decisions to begin with. Wrongful discrimination, then, rather than merely one more example of substandard behavior, should be treated as an instance of *ultra vires*, namely, acting beyond one's legal power.

Not only is our argument for a tort of discrimination not limited to the defense of new philosophical grounds for wrongful discrimination in private voluntary interactions, but it also makes a significant practical contribution to the design of contemporary anti-discrimination law. Currently, the right to be treated as an equal receives some protection from various isolated statutes that tackle discrimination on a *retail* basis—one set of statutory provisions focuses on employment, another on housing, a third one picks out places of public accommodation, education provides yet another, and so forth.[5] In addition, wrongful discrimination in law is specified on a narrow basis, detailed in a closed and exhaustive list of grounds, be they race, gender, and so forth.[6]

This cluster of retail duties suffers from a range of substantial shortcomings. To mention but a few: liability for wrongful discrimination is typically predicated on deliberate behavior, to the exclusion of negligence;[7] private contractors and gig-economy workers are not entitled to anti-discrimination protections afforded to all other workers;[8] unjustified gaps in pay between occupations of comparable worth are currently not illegal even when the disparities reflect racial, gender, or other biases;[9] and, according to some courts, virtual places of public accommodation (like online stores) are not duty-bound to make their websites accessible to people with disabilities (such as deaf and hard of hearing individuals).[10] A tort of discrimination helps address these and other pitfalls—bluntly put, it changes the normative starting point, thus bridging all the gaps left open by the existing retail duties. In that, this tort gives judges, juries, and regulators more control and agency over the construction, application, and enforcement of duties of non-discrimination.[11]

2. The Traditionalist Permissibility of Private Discrimination. The right to be treated as an equal is not a story of neglect or of an otherwise respectable right, having to, perhaps tragically, give way to other, more important rights. Instead, denying this right is a feature, rather than a bug, of private law traditionalism, which denies this right's very existence. For traditionalism, a right to be treated as an equal undermines private law's normative order.[12]

Consider a restaurant that refuses to serve green-eyed customers. Should this practice be legally permissible? Traditional private law answers this question in the affirmative. Normatively, this answer rests on a sharp distinction, already noted,[13] between public and private in terms of a distinction between inclusion and exclusion. In this account, the public space that includes institutions, entities, and goods governed by public law norms is structurally egalitarian. Discrimination against green-eyed persons, say, when recruiting new government employees or when entering a public park, for example, is not merely unethical but also illegal. The all-inclusive character of the public space contrasts with the private one: voluntary transactions between private persons should not be governed by public law norms and, consequently, should not be subject to prohibitions on discrimination.

The key to this picture is the idea that the justness of an interaction between private persons should be assessed by reference to independence and formal equality. Private persons are thus absolutely free to choose partners for voluntary transactions as they see fit, and it is up to restaurant owners to decide who to serve. Precluding this prerogative undermines the independence of the owners, who are now subject to other persons' choices regardless of whether green-eyed customers have visited the restaurant. It is the very existence of a right not to be discriminated against due to one's eye color that makes the owner subject to others. At the same time, the absence of a duty of non-discrimination does not impinge on the independence of green-eyed diners because it only affects the *context* wherein they could still set and pursue ends. For instance, they can eat elsewhere or cook for themselves. A duty of non-discrimination violates the maxim of reciprocal respect for independence and formal equality because it entitles customers to demand service from the owner.

This analysis can escape the discrimination-friendly prescriptions just noted in two ways. One is to preclude discrimination indirectly, attributing to the restaurant owner a different wrongdoing, such as misrepresentation or even deceit. The argument is that the restaurant, like many other "public accommodations," extends "a general invitation to the public to come in and do business" without being able to "choose which customers to serve."[14] It thereby implicitly undertakes to be open to the public and, therefore, presents itself as fully committed to serving people irrespective of eye color. Excluding green-eyed customers is certainly wrong, but not because it discriminates against green-eyed diners. Rather, the wrong lies in deceiving green-eyed customers who had relied on the owner's representation.

The second escape route takes the form of publicization.[15] Instead of analyzing this as a horizontal transaction between two private persons, it emphasizes its public aspects, highlighting the function on offer. In this argument, specific private entities cannot discriminate against green-eyed customers because they fulfill inherently public functions. Common carriers are a familiar case in point.[16] Shopping malls and, more recently, major social media platforms share, for free speech purposes, several public characteristics with the traditional town square.[17] Another public aspect concerns monopolistic market power in the provision of basic goods—for instance, being the sole grocery or pharmacy in a small, isolated town can elevate this business to a position of dominance.[18]

Neither of these escape routes, however, explains why our restaurant owner should not be legally entitled to deny service to green-eyed customers.[19] The owner can avoid liability for misrepresentation simply by explicitly announcing their discriminatory policy. In turn, redescribing the owner as a quasi-public official and the restaurant as fulfilling an inherently public or government function is highly artificial. In any event, resorting to a logic of misrepresentation or publicization merely explains away what is wrong about the discriminatory policy in question—to wit, that when applying their normative powers, restaurant owners must not treat would-be customers as unequal to them and other customers simply because of the color of their eyes. This failure is inherent in the uncompromising commitment to independence and formal equality.[20] We argue, by contrast, that green-eyed customers have a basic right to be treated as equals and that this right, like any other basic right in the law of torts, is necessary and sufficient to impose a prima facie duty of non-discrimination on their discriminator.

3. *The Civil Rights Acts: Revolution Incomplete.* The civil rights revolution of the 1960s—and especially the creation of statutory duties of nondiscrimination in

connection with public accommodations, employment, housing, and education—set out to change the traditional identification of voluntary interactions between private persons with independence and formal equality.[21] Thus, instead of the broad entitlement to choose their parties as they see fit, various Civil Rights Acts impose duties of nondiscrimination on providers of goods, services, and employment. Other liberal jurisdictions have followed suit.[22] And yet, what to make of this change and, specifically, what its nature and scope is less clear, at least in its conventional reading.

This accepted reading follows the model of the good citizen approach we discussed (and criticized) in Chapter 2.[23] It thus understands prohibitions on discrimination in public accommodations, housing, education, and employment markets as extending the reach of constitutionalism to some areas in the private sphere[24] by enlisting rights-holders in the service of meeting the demands of public justice.

Concretely, the state commandeers the support of certain private persons—commercial providers, landlords, and employers—to realize collective goals associated with democracy and distributive justice. The animating concern, therefore, is the justness of society as a whole rather than the justness of interactions between persons. The underlying rationale is that some private institutions, although perhaps less powerful and coercive than state institutions, profoundly influence society's democratic credentials. The citizens' ability to claim they have an equal say in politics and other dimensions of public life is largely contingent on the inclusiveness of markets for goods and services, employment, education, and housing.[25] In this approach, the Civil Rights Acts are primarily intended to remedy political inequality, thereby reinforcing the equal footing of citizens in a democracy.[26]

Advocates of this approach can discern some supporting evidence in the Acts. For instance, the Acts do not set a general duty against discrimination and, instead, identify a limited number of prohibited grounds while also placing limits on the identity of duty-owers. Unfortunately, however, this interpretation of statutory duties of non-discrimination falls short of fully addressing traditionalism's pitfalls. Moreover, this interpretation is troublesome for another and more fundamental reason, which reflects our critique (in Chapter 2) of the good citizen model. Its civic foundation renders its prescriptions contingent on the need to remedy political inequality in our society. The case for these Acts loses momentum when political inequality recedes or even sufficiently narrows. Barring people from a restaurant due to the color of their eyes would then be unethical but entirely legal as long as the number and gravity of such instances remain relatively low. What makes discrimination legally wrong is *only* the *cumulative* effect of discrete instances of discrimination rather than each one of them severally.

Furthermore, thus perceived, these Acts are mere means to the ends of political equality and a thriving democracy. They can, therefore, be replaced by other means—either legal or extra-legal—that may prove capable of attaining these ends in more effective and less costly ways.[27] Thus, generous programs of public housing and robust social practices of ethical consumerism could provide effective substitutes for existing statutory prohibitions of, respectively, private discrimination in housing, places of public accommodation, and employment. Indeed, under certain circumstances, these alternatives may emerge as plausible strategies for promoting political equality. Yet, though plausible from the perspective of the justice of the political community as a whole, they unacceptably relieve employers, lessors, sellers, and other holders of property or contractual power from the *duty* to refrain from discriminating against other private persons.[28]

A Tort of Discrimination

1. Reinterpreting the Civil Rights Acts. The tort of discrimination we advance in this chapter builds on a reinterpretation of the Civil Rights Acts and their corollaries in other jurisdictions.

By reinterpreting the Acts, we do *not* mean to imply that the public law of antidiscrimination sketched above should be set aside. Rather, we claim that, besides their important public role, the Acts can and should be viewed as also instantiating an internal reform of the traditional private law approach. The private duties of non-discrimination and the private rights of action against discriminators stand for a transformation of the balance of legal power enshrined in the traditional private law rules of trespass on land, ownership, and freedom of contract aimed at securing the status of the interacting parties as substantively free and equal persons.

The interacting parties, as is usually the case throughout this book, are viewed here as private persons who are not necessarily members of the same political community. The prescriptions at hand, therefore, focus on how things stand between them rather than only on the collective effects on the political community.[29] This reading of the Acts further implies that their closed list of prohibited grounds and relatively narrow scope need not mean that other types of discrimination are permissible.

Insisting that we must not take the Acts' statutory duties to be exhaustive is important because their retail-based strategy of tackling discrimination leaves, as may be expected, significant gaps.[30] For instance, gender and sexual orientation are not listed among the grounds prohibited in Title II (concerning discrimination in places of public accommodation), but that is no reason to render discrimination on these bases legally permissible. Moreover, many courts interpret Title II as mandating equal access to places of public accommodation but do not extend this norm to prohibiting inferior treatment or service.[31] Their exclusion from the purview of Title II, however, does not entail that they are legally permissible.[32] Finally, existing statutes (Title II and the Fair Housing Act, for instance) may not be suited to deal with a range of discriminatory practices, including discrimination in the enforcement of contracts of adhesion as well as in the platform and gig economies.[33] Allowing discrimination, for example, in ride-sharing and short-term rental platforms cannot be justified on the grounds that statutory duties of non-discrimination may fail to capture their business models.

2. The Pitfall of a Retail-based Strategy. A tort of discrimination could be claimed to go beyond what these instances of legislative omission require. We agree but insist on the significance of adding a wholesale duty of non-discrimination atop whatever list of retail duties exists at any given moment.

To start with, the failure to recognize the (wholesale) right to be treated as an equal is one of the reasons for the fact that, as noted, even particular rights, such as being treated as an equal in commercial settings, receive (at best) partial protection.[34] Moreover, a comprehensive scheme of retail duties that could address all conceivable forms of discrimination is hard to imagine since discrimination, like negligence, is an *evolving* phenomenon. Just like the failure to discharge a duty of care is bound to take new forms as society changes, attempts to use normative powers in defiance of others' right to be treated as equals can (and likely will) also be manifest in different, including unanticipated, ways. Technological progress only reinforces this difficulty by improving the ability to implement discriminatory practices far beyond the reach of current law.

The evolving nature of discrimination poses unique challenges in the realm of structural or systemic discrimination. This discrimination can persist because (retail) duties of non-discrimination outlaw *some* discriminatory practices while leaving all others in place and, thus, overlooking the intersectionality dimension of some discriminatory practices. Given that discrimination is sometimes structural or systemic, the absence of a wholesale duty amounts to passive authorization of discriminatory practices that fall beyond the reach of existing retail duties.

Recognizing a wholesale duty of non-discrimination addresses this significant lacuna. Since a wholesale duty is, by definition, inclusive of wrongful discrimination of any sort, it can breed dynamism into the law of discrimination and its specific retail duties. A wholesale duty can thus perfect the ability of discrimination law to tackle wrongful discrimination by propelling retail duties to make desirable changes. A stream of claims against the violation of the wholesale duty can, for example, expose a vulnerability in the existing law and direct the adaptation of retail duties. For instance, employment discrimination law should add political views and affiliations to the list of prohibited grounds.[35]

A wholesale duty can also help identify the need for and lead to the creation of *new* retail duties of non-discrimination. One case in point emerges when, out of a motley collection of discrimination claims, a substantial number of lawsuits happens to form a coherent category. A cluster of discrimination claims raised by gig economy workers (or contractors), for example, can move the legislature or courts to create a new duty of non-discrimination appropriately attuned to the realities of this economy.[36]

3. The Wholesale Duty of Non-discrimination. These methods of revising the law of discrimination suggest that a wholesale duty is not merely a rule of conduct but also a potentially powerful engine of legal change. They also imply that, as discussed below, a wholesale discrimination duty does not anticipate a legal path of ad hoc decision-making. Rather, as regarding the other standards at the heart of private law (negligence law's reasonableness or contract law's good faith, discussed in Chapters 5 and 10, respectively), we assume that the law's daily operations will mostly be governed by a list of established categories with relatively well-defined retail duties, to be adapted and refined incrementally.[37]

Indeed, we do not argue against distinguishing between instances of discrimination based on context (such as employment, commerce, housing, education, and so forth). Neither do we claim that legal standards for unlawful discrimination should ignore suspicious classifications and grounds for discrimination. Nor, finally, do we object to distinctions between types of discrimination, dividing instances of discrimination into disparate treatment, disparate impact, or failure of accommodation (as in instances of disability). Rather, we argue that the *success* of a retail strategy hinges on the prior recognition of a tort of discrimination that protects our basic right to be treated as an equal by other private persons whenever they hold (and therefore can exercise) normative powers like those associated with property and contract.

Moreover, a wholesale duty changes the nature of law's commitment to the elimination of wrongful discrimination. A multiplicity of retail duties of non-discrimination implies that private persons can be effectively protected against discrimination in specific spheres of action taken severally. Missing from this picture is a more holistic commitment against wrongful discrimination in the application of normative powers, irrespective of its context. To this end, freeing the right to be treated as an equal from its various contextual manifestations springs from its moral significance as a basic right, on par with the right to bodily integrity, privacy, good name, and so forth.

Indeed, wrongful discrimination should be a tort because, like a breach of the duty of due care at the core of the tort of negligence, it is an instance of grave relational injustice. The right to be treated as an equal is an entitlement that cannot be affected by a person's constitutive choices and traits when other private individuals this person engages or seeks to engage with apply their normative legal powers. The significance of this right derives from the freestanding role that our voluntary interpersonal interactions play in our ability to lead a life, let alone a successful one, as free and equal agents. Wrongful discrimination is a violation of this right. Discrimination is analogous to the erection of a transactional barrier and is thus wrongful if this barrier prevents the discriminatee from interacting with the discriminator in terms that reflect the status of both parties as substantively free and equal persons.

In the remainder of this chapter, we defend these propositions and explore their implications. We claim that because wrongful discrimination should include any overstepping in the discriminator's normative power beyond what relational justice allows, it goes further than what current law prescribes. It is neither contingent on the discriminator's deliberation or mental state nor on any specific harm inflicted on the discriminatee, on a particular social group, or on society as a whole. Yet, its scope is not overly broad given the right's intrinsic limitations (grounded in the foundational commitment to *reciprocal* respect for self-determination and substantive equality itself), as well as its extrinsic ones (grounded in other important values and ideals). Based on this theoretical foundation, we conclude this chapter by drawing on existing doctrines in and around tort law to identify the legal tools necessary for prescribing the proper elements—duty, breach, injury, causation, and remedy—of a tort of discrimination befitting a liberal legal order.

Wrongful Discrimination as Relational Injustice

1. An Irreducible Relational Dimension. Contrary to accounts of wrongful discrimination that view the discriminatee as a member of a certain social group,[38] relational justice theory makes no such essential reference—the discriminatee figures as a person *even when* not a member of one or another social group.[39] Moreover, unlike the perception of wrongful discrimination as a failure to treat the discriminatee as equal to others in society,[40] our account suggests, as we presently explain, that this failure is ultimately relational—the failure of the discriminator is not treating the discriminatee as equal to the discriminator.

This relational failure is measured, as usual, against the baseline that views persons as substantively, rather than formally, free and equal agents (thus rejecting the reductive view of persons as possessors of a capacity for choice or as preference maximizers). It thus relies, as can be expected, on the core distinction that guides us throughout this book between the features that make us who we are and our sheer preferences.[41]

Hence, while discrimination based on a person's sheer preferences may be frustrating, discrimination based on their ground projects is prima facie wrongful because it is an instance of failing to relate to people as who they really are.[42] Besides such constitutive choices, recall that unchosen conditions also partially define who we are in our own perception, which is partially shaped by how others see us. These conditions consist of personal and socially constructed traits and may include a person's height, race, disability, and socio-economic condition. Many of these traits are socially salient because they immediately link individuals to a social group, subjecting them to the expectations, assumptions, and biases held regarding that group. Other traits, however, lack social salience and may be purely personal—eye color, for instance, is a trait that may cut across social groups. But even these personal traits may become socially salient (including negative stereotypes) or serve as a proxy for other socially salient traits.

That said, a personal trait is literally part of who people are, and holding it against them is, therefore, prima facie wrongful.[43] For instance, barring a person from a restaurant or rejecting someone's job candidacy on this basis is inconsistent with treating them as who they really are, and the fact that this trait (currently or even potentially) carries no badge of social inferiority does not launder the wrong.

In relational justice theory, private discrimination is wrongful when it violates a person's right to be treated as an equal. This right, which places the constitutive choices and traits of the right-holder at its moral center, implies that people are prima facie entitled not to have their constitutive choices or traits held against them when others exercise their normative power. In other words, the terms of possible interactions enabled by these normative powers—for example, the interactions they facilitate with owners, employers, and market actors—must conform with the maxim of reciprocal respect for self-determination and substantive equality. Using these powers in defiance of this maxim is thus wrongful discrimination. We elaborate on this claim below by reference to three sets of distinctions: motive versus conduct, harm versus injustice, and process versus outcome.

2. Motive versus Conduct. The motives of wrongful discrimination vary. Discriminators are often moved by attitudes associated with bigotry or animus toward their discriminatees. At times, discriminators act out of rational concerns, such as the economic prospects of their business, as when a business owner realizes that she will lose many white customers if she does not discriminate against black ones. Another motive for discrimination is ethical or religious beliefs that oppose serving, hiring, or simply interacting with another person in a particular context or in general.

Should motives matter, then, for deeming a discriminatory act wrongful? We say no.[44] Discrimination can be wrongful even when it is *un*motivated. Discrimination should count as wrongful not because it is driven by a specific motive (or attitude) but because it is an act of a certain kind—it denies the discriminatees' ability to interact with the discriminator in terms that reflect their status as substantively free and equal persons. We certainly do not argue that motive never matters. It does matter, for instance, for the purpose of determining the fitting response—in terms of a proper remedy—to an instance of wrongful discrimination, as shown below. But ill motive should not be necessary for determining what counts as wrongful discrimination.

To see why discrimination can be unmotivated and, at the same time, wrongful, consider a straightforward instance of indirect discrimination (a.k.a. disparate impact). It features a rigorous audition process for a professional orchestra that, year after year, ends up admitting mostly (or even only) white male players.[45] The auditors could be motivated solely by a desire to recruit the best-qualified candidates and, therefore, the failure to select musicians who are neither white nor male is unrelated to any discriminatory motivations. In tort law parlance, this procedure reflects inadvertence on the part of unconsciously biased auditors.

Inadvertently failing to include non-trivial numbers of female and non-white musicians is, prima facie, an instance of wrongful discrimination. The wrongness lies in the holding of certain traits—race and sex—against musicians who, although as good as those selected, were not chosen. Rather than the motives, the "holding" represents the terms of the interaction that seem to govern the job selection process, implying that certain musicians are less likely to be considered solely on the basis of their professional qualifications because of who they are. Adopting these terms is akin to erecting a transaction barrier preventing candidates from interacting with their auditors (or would-be employers) as substantively free and equal persons.

We do not argue that this barrier reflects a conscious, let alone deliberate, decision to exclude female and non-white musicians. Instead, using their normative powers in a way that denies certain candidates their right to be treated as equals reflects inadvertence on the part of the auditors, who *could* have adopted a more impartial selection process. Neglecting the right of female and non-white musicians to be treated as equals—like similar neglects pertaining to other fundamental rights (say to our bodily integrity) that we hold against other private persons—is, in and of itself, what turns this process into wrongful discrimination.

3. *Harm versus Injustice.* Influential accounts of discrimination often identify its wrongfulness with one or another harmful consequence. One such approach states that discrimination is wrongful because it is demeaning or subordinating.[46] Other accounts locate discrimination's wrongfulness in the cost it imposes on certain freedom interests of the discriminatees. For instance, discrimination can undermine the discriminatees' ability to deliberate freely about where to work, live, or dine.[47] It can also undermine another aspect of freedom when it limits or reduces the range of available options to choose from.[48] Without denying that wrongful discrimination can often lead to these (or other) adverse consequences, discrimination can count as wrongful even when none of these consequences do or are likely to follow.[49]

Consider a "harmless" instance of discrimination featuring a baker who refuses to bake a wedding cake for a same-sex couple.[50] A discriminatory act of this sort could generate any number of harms to the couple, perpetuating (by themselves or by others) the social and political subordination of the social group they are associated with. Yet, if the market for wedding cakes faces robust competition *and* the society where the parties live is overwhelmingly liberal and inclusive, these effects could be avoided.[51] The refusal at issue, then, does not reflect the baker's "social power" to subordinate the couple.[52] He does not intend to relate to the couple as unworthy or in any way inferior, nor is his message interpreted by most members of the society as an attempt to do so.

The same holds when we switch from accounts that emphasize the demeaning impact of subordination to those which take discrimination to be wrongful because it might mark the social group the discriminatees belong to as inferior while perpetuating the superiority of the discriminator's social group.[53] The case under consideration does not generate any concern about group subordination since the social and political power imbalance works in precisely the opposite direction. Indeed, it is the baker who may be part of a small and vulnerable religious community. His refusal reflects—and is widely understood to reflect—his attempt to preserve a traditional way of life in the face of strong cosmopolitan pressures.[54] If wrongful discrimination is identified with its demeaning connotations or with its contribution to group subordination, the baker is not necessarily guilty as charged.

Moreover, making the demeaning aspects of this hypothetical case the root cause of what makes the discrimination wrongful is troublesome not only because it is unnecessary, as we just intimated. It is also problematic because appealing to indignities and emotional setbacks immediately opens the door to the discriminator's own complaint.[55] His complaint, recall, is grounded in a sincere religious or ethical commitment, and coercing him to serve the couple could be experienced by him and his fellow adherents as demeaning and even humiliating, especially given the existence of many other equally competent bakers out there.

Does this baker harm the freedom of the couple by inviting, or even forcing them, to "factor into their deliberations" their conception of marriage and family life "*as costs*"?[56] That is, is the couple indeed wronged by being forced to "always have before their eyes, as they deliberate" their traits or conceptions of the good?[57] Alternatively, does he harm their freedom by limiting the range of available options to advance their autonomous life or by undermining a public culture of autonomy?[58]

The answer to both these questions is no. Given that the alternatives available to the couple are nearly unlimited, discrimination at the hands of *only* one baker does not threaten their freedom to deliberate without having to internalize the cost of their conception of the good. A similar conclusion applies when the consequential harm is cast in terms of a diminished range of options and a weakened public culture of autonomy: one less option will not destabilize the range itself and the multitude of attractive possibilities. The baker's refusal will not derail the public culture of autonomy since the impact of his discriminatory practice is more than offset by the inclusive commitment of all other service providers in this and all other market contexts.

That said, this discrimination may be harmless and still wrongful due to the baker's use of his normative powers in a way that is disrespectful to the couple's right to be treated as equals. This instance is strikingly analogous to deeming a physician's interference with their patient's bodily integrity wrong without their consent (when it could have been secured), even if otherwise harmless.[59] Validating the use of normative powers in defiance of the couple's right to be treated as equals would imply *entitling* the baker to turn a constitutive choice of the couple (concerning marriage, family, and love) into a transactional barrier. An entitlement to erect such a barrier is incompatible with interacting with the persons making up this couple as the persons they are.

The baker's wrongful conduct (again, as that of the physician who failed to secure their patient's consent) reflects a normative shortfall in how things stand between the parties, irrespective of its harmful consequences. Therefore, private discrimination is wrongful regardless of whether it carries overtones of contempt or diminishes opportunities. The only way out of this relational injustice is to take back the entitlement in question and hold commercial bakers independently responsible for making their services sufficiently inclusive. The baker should owe the couple a duty to refrain from holding their constitutive choice against them. Their terms of voluntary interaction in applying their normative powers must meet the basic threshold of treating the couple as self-determining and substantively equal persons.

4. *Process versus Outcome*. The question of what renders discrimination in the exercise of legal powers wrongful typically focuses on outcomes rather than processes. It considers the permissibility of final decisions concerning exclusion and inclusion, or favorable and unfavorable treatment. Left outside is the *process* leading up to such decisions. Relational justice theory, by contrast, focuses on both outcome and process: because it places the exercise of legal powers at the center, it must also address the question of how these powers are exercised.

A key process-based concern arises in connection with discrimination based on statistical inferences. Power-holders often resort to statistical knowledge about persons when making hiring, renting, selling, and other similar decisions.[60] For instance, resorting to reliable data showing a high correlation, say, between eye color and work productivity, or between age and ability to complete difficult manual tasks, represents one way of making informed hiring decisions.

We argue that a power-holder should either set aside statistically reliable data or deploy it in ways that are consistent with the demands of relational justice. Opting for the latter, power-holders assume the burden of shifting from generalizations to a person's particular situation. For instance, when a moving company seeks to hire movers, it may be rational, economically speaking, to prefer younger to older candidates given the probability of a statistically significant correlation between old age and poor performance in the moving industry. But the pertinent hiring officer must also be open to consider senior candidates based on their actual physical condition. Thus, while statistical data can establish a default decision-making rule, a real option for rebutting it must be available so that the ultimate hiring decision is based on the candidate's specific data.[61]

As long as this process does not overreach—as long as it does not undermine duty-owers' pursuit of their own self-determination—it should apply to everyone and not only to members of a disenfranchised or otherwise socially marginalized group. Thus, our hiring officer cannot use reliable statistical data—say, that people with a graduate degree in the humanities are highly likely to be physically weak—to refrain from considering a candidate with a Ph.D. in history.

Yet, this all-encompassing accommodation burden may go beyond the requirements of relational justice or may be ruled out for other—substantive or institutional—reasons. Then, as in other contexts discussed in this book, both rule of law and relational justice concerns justify—indeed, require—placing burdens and accommodation duties in distinct categories that trace the pertinent vulnerabilities of the parties involved. (Recall, for example, our discussions of disability in the tort doctrine of the reasonable person, and of asymmetries in capabilities in the contract law doctrine of disclosure).

The relevant concern here—the most acute vulnerability in the context of reliance on statistical data—is the dignity of the candidates considered. The basic intuition suggests that resorting to statistical data with respect to humanities graduates is quite different from doing so with respect to a member of a disenfranchised social group.

Thinking about people in terms of damaging generalizations reflects a failure to deal with them as the persons they really are, disregarding relational justice's basic demand of reciprocal respect for self-determination and substantive equality. But failing to do so with respect to a member of a marginalized group aggravates the relational injustice by attaching to this person a label of social inferiority.

Thus, the substantive burden of shifting from generalizations to a person's particular situation is not unitary. It should reflect, in some measure, the expected vulnerability of individuals to inferences about who they really are drawn on the basis of their (actual or perceived) membership in disenfranchised groups. *Those* inferences are unacceptable even in contexts where reliance on statistical data is generally justified.[62]

Scope: Intrinsic and Extrinsic Limits

Thus far, we have focused on the prima facie case for identifying wrongful discrimination with relational injustice. What makes discrimination wrongful in this account is that it represents a failure to interact with discriminatees as the persons they are, including the constitutive choices and traits that shape them. It is for this reason, as noted, that discrimination's wrongfulness dispenses with the discussion of the discriminator's mental state and deliberative process, disentangling wrongful discrimination from the consequential harms it often inflicts on discriminatees, on certain social groups, or on society as a whole. Releasing the tort of discrimination from the shackles of intentionality and harmful consequences is necessary for it to contend with the basic wrong of discrimination: overreaching the power that property and contract can legitimately confer in a liberal society.

We now take up the scope of the discrimination tort, explaining why and when duties of nondiscrimination must give way to countervailing considerations. We argue that the combination of a wholesale duty of nondiscrimination and a set of (internal and external) limitations on its scope of application reflects a legal structure resembling that of negligence law. The tort of negligence features a general or wholesale duty of reasonable care, though its scope is not limitless. In fact, it deliberately leaves out domains of human behavior (such as contact sports) that ought not to be governed by a legal duty of due care.[63] The structure of the discrimination tort is similar—a wholesale duty that, nonetheless, carefully avoids encroaching on human relations that should not be governed by it.[64]

1. Intrinsic limits. Begin with considerations that are integral to relational justice. As we have reiterated, relational justice sets not only a floor but also a ceiling for people's interpersonal obligations. Ensuring that people's normative powers do not contravene the maxim of *reciprocal* respect for self-determination and substantive equality requires the interactions structured by these powers to respect both parties' rights to self-determination and substantive equality. Compelling owners, employers, and market actors to abide by a duty of utmost accommodation of their parties' constitutive choices and traits could ultimately destroy their substantive freedom and equality.

When the cost of refraining from wrongful discrimination is relatively small, the need for a ceiling remains latent. When duties of nondiscrimination become excessively costly, however, the necessity of a ceiling claims center stage. It will be impossible for a restaurant owner to tailor the height of the restaurant's tables to the precise height of every potential customer, to render the restaurant accessible to every possible condition of physical disability, or to create a menu that meets all existing dietary restrictions. Performing all these tasks is (arguably) technically feasible but still normatively undesirable. Imposing on restaurant owners' terms of interaction that incorporate a requirement of utmost accommodation is incompatible with treating them as substantively free and equal persons. Hence, a duty of nondiscrimination grounded in relational justice theory does not require more than a reasonable measure of accommodation.[65] Were the costs of accommodation to drop substantially (say, due to technology), duty-owers may have to extend reasonable accommodation of constitutive choices and traits *beyond* the current status *quo*.

Limiting the duty of non-discrimination to a requirement of reasonable rather than utmost accommodation, however, cannot vindicate acts of discrimination that reflect a *categorical* rejection of the discriminatee's standing to relate to the discriminator as substantively equal. The baker case discussed above fits this description: even though the baker may not refuse to sell the couple a generic cake, his refusal to bake them a wedding cake is, nonetheless, categorical in the sense that it involves rejecting the couple for who they really are. Another instance is that of a racist restaurant owner who singles out people of color for inferior treatment or simply exclusion.

Indeed, unlike discrimination against unusually tall restaurant patrons in the design of tables, chairs, and bathroom sinks, a categorical refusal to serve them because of their constitutive choices or traits should get no solace from the morality of relational justice. Whereas the former reflects the need to consider the freedom and equal standing of both parties, the latter repudiates the discriminatee's equal standing outright. Departing from a standard of utmost accommodation in the former case may thus be fully compatible with the demands of relational justice while doing so in the latter case is inimical to everything relational justice stands for. As discussed above, relational justice theory insists that choices and ground projects inimical to the ideal of relational equality cannot be plausible grounds for limiting the nondiscrimination duties of liberal private law. According to relational justice theory, we insisted, there is no respect for disrespect.[66]

Finally, another intrinsic limitation on the scope of the nondiscrimination duty was noted above when pointing out that the daily operations of a wholesale duty of non-discrimination should be governed by a list of established categories with relatively well-defined retail duties. This limitation reflects not only legality's constraint of the rule of law. As discussed in Chapter 4, the values of stability and predictability in the rule of law are also endorsed by relational justice, which requires respect for duty-owers' self-determination and, thus, for their ability to form expectations based on stable frames of reference. Relational justice, in its own terms, cannot be oblivious to the rule of law and, therefore, must not imply overly particularistic ad hoc judgments.[67]

2. Extrinsic limits. Two external limits stand out. Contrary to the previous ones, their grounds are values and ideals that do not derive from relational justice but are nonetheless compatible with the core liberal commitments to self-determination and substantive equality. Adjudicating the demands of relational justice and these competing values and ideals would require presenting a *complete* theory of justice in a liberal society, which is beyond the scope of this book.

The first category of external limitations is evident in social practices whose value turns on what would otherwise count as a core case of wrongful discrimination. An easy example in this category, anticipated briefly in Chapter 3, comes from friendship and romantic love. Choosing friends and loved ones is deeply influenced by people's choices and traits. We are often attracted to people possessing specific traits or adopting specific ways of life as opposed to those who do not. Friendship and romantic love might thus lose their intrinsic value when subjected to the demands of nondiscrimination.

Another practice whose value (in liberal societies) turns on authentic choice is art. Deciding what to paint, or what poems to write, and for whom, may require that painters, or poets, be free to define their creative work as they see fit. Regulating such authentic choices by imposing duties of nondiscrimination is inimical to the value of art. The category of art, however, has a firm center but also soft and constantly evolving edges. Hence, alongside the traditional center—the fine arts (such as painting and music)—art and artistic expression can take any number of forms. Defining the boundaries of artistic expression is beyond the scope of our argument. We do insist, however, that it cannot be wholly subjective. A snow plower cannot invoke artistic freedom to justify a refusal to remove snow from a person's adjacent sidewalk. The person doing the plowing may sincerely see their work as art but that cannot turn snow removal into a new art form. We set aside the question of whether cases that fall between the painter and the snow plower—consider the bakers, website designers, photographers, architecture firms, and other professional service providers—engage in artistic activity. We remain skeptical as to whether a typical goods or service provider can count as an artist or as engaging in artistic expression.[68]

Between practices that hinge on intimacy and/or authentic choice, and those that do not, are borderline cases.[69] They involve voluntary interactions that could not be formed independently of law's normative powers, which also create the conditions for the formation of relations that lie somewhere between the legal and the personal. Consider an instance of co-housing where a private owner rents out a room in her dwelling to a stranger.[70] A landlord/tenant interaction, wherein the right to property is constitutive, creates the conditions for another form of relationship to evolve. Note that the former interaction does not merely allow the latter to arise but also creates a social dynamic that typically leads the parties to experience one another as more than landlord and tenant. The leasing transaction leads the parties to forms of intimacy and rapport since they literally share a living space (not to mention a relationship as roommates).[71]

One option when addressing in-between cases of this type is to draw on their particular legal and extra-legal contexts, such as the physical structure of the building subject to the co-housing practice. Sharing a living space in a small apartment differs from co-housing in a large building with multiple dwelling units when the former might suggest that property is predominantly incidental to, and the latter predominantly constitutive of, the parties' interaction. We leave the operational difficulties of coping with these situations for another occasion.

Other practices may pose more challenging dilemmas. The value of these practices does not hinge on intimacy and authentic choice. Thus, they could incorporate duties of non-discrimination, although doing so will necessarily transform them in radical ways. Take practices striving for excellence, as in sports or ballet. It is possible to insist on all ballet companies respecting everyone's right to be treated as an equal. These companies would then comprise dancers of varying levels of performance, including dancers that, for objective reasons (say, not being flexible enough), cannot exhibit the aesthetic value that accompanies the skill, discipline, and self-expression of superb ballet dancers. The trade-off between egalitarian and excellence-striving ballet practices clarifies the dilemma at hand: whether the value inherent in professional ballet or professional soccer merits its inherently discriminatory character.[72] While relational justice theory cannot resolve this question, we hope that this example demonstrates what *might* count as an extrinsic consideration that potentially justifies judging these instances of discrimination as *not* wrongful.[73]

A second set of extrinsic limits on the right to be treated as an equal arises in connection with affirmative action. The justificatory foundation of contemporary programs may well be over-determined. In particular, many of these programs may be justified in relational justice terms given the systemic and structurally unjust tilting of many admission practices, as evident, for example, in the orchestra auditions discussed above.[74] This type of case poses no real dilemma for our account since affirmative action *removes* a structural barrier to relational justice. Its *absence* implies the unjustifiably favorable treatment of majority group members (white men) at the expense of other candidates.[75]

But there are, or might be, more difficult cases where relational justice does not entail affirmative action. Here, increasing the participation of systemically marginalized persons and communities in major private and public institutions requires employers, universities, and other entities to reject competent candidates simply because they happen to be members of non-marginalized social groups. Yet, the unjust distribution of opportunities that still prevails in many societies is so overwhelming that, although these programs flout the demands of relational justice, they still seem justified. Hard cases may (hopefully) emerge once this competing (distributive justice) consideration has significantly shrunk so that affirmative action can rely only on past injustices rather than on their current consequences.

Toward a Doctrinal Framework

1. Beyond the Familiar. Contemporary legal doctrine tends to classify retail duties of non-discrimination into two forms—direct and indirect discrimination, often referred to, respectively, as disparate treatment and disparate impact.[76] The distinction is considered qualitative since it reflects the difference between approaches to the responsibility for discrimination—motive-based and outcome-based responsibility—echoing the distinction between deliberate and strict liability torts.[77] Many philosophers and legal theorists view this distinction as fundamental to the normative analysis of discrimination.[78] Accordingly, large sections of the practical and theoretical debates about what renders discrimination wrongful are organized around it.

Relational justice theory challenges the terms of such debates. Discriminatory motivations should be neither necessary nor sufficient to characterize discrimination as wrongful. Rather than strict or absolute liability, the basis for rendering discriminatory outcomes prima facie wrongful is negligence. In our account, the generic tort duty of non-discrimination is akin to—though crucially, not coterminous with—negligence law's duty of care, or here, a duty of accommodation.[79]

The duty at hand requires holders of legal powers (e.g., in their capacity as providers of goods and services, employers, and educators) to take reasonable measures to make their voluntary interactions inclusive of the constitutive choices and traits of others. Failure to meet this requirement can be deliberate or inadvertent.[80] We do not argue that the difference between the two is negligible but rather that it should not matter at this stage of the legal analysis and will only become crucial at later stages, notably for the purpose of shifting the burden of proving causation and imposing punitive damages for incidents of flagrant discrimination. Moreover, our objection to limiting the tort of discrimination to instances of deliberate wrongfulness does not mean that liability can be assigned when discriminatory outcomes are not reasonably foreseeable.[81]

Driving a (partial) wedge between wrongful discrimination and motivation is reinforced by the psychology of discrimination. Empirical studies suggest that unconscious or implicit bias—viz., when "people act on the basis of internalised schemas of which they are unaware and thus can, and often do, engage in discriminatory behaviours without conscious intent"[82]—figures prominently in our lives.[83] Tackling such implicit discrimination challenges the approach that identifies wrongful discrimination with antisocial or immoral motivations but not the account of wrongful discrimination posited in relational justice. Structurally, implicit bias can prima facie be deemed as wrongful discrimination, just as a motorist may be deemed prima facie negligent (i.e., in breach of a duty of care) for inadvertently speeding in a pedestrian's vicinity. Although the tort of discrimination is not a debiasing mechanism, it does give potential discriminators a mandatory reason—a legal duty—to be vigilant about the impact of their decisions on the rights of others to be treated as equals.

To prepare the ground for this new tort of discrimination, we address the elements of duty, breach, injury, and causation. We take each in turn, raising key questions and identifying ways of addressing them.

2. Duty. This element determines the identity of duty-owers. Two important aspects guide this inquiry. The first is that discrimination presupposes some normative power held (or claimed to be held) by the discriminator vis-à-vis the discriminatee. This power manifests itself in the allocation of goods and services, broadly defined to include opportunities, and operates by fixing the normative situation of those with whom they engage. Property and contract are, as discussed in Chapter 2, straightforward examples of legal institutions whose animating rules are power-conferring in the sense that they empower right-holders to fix the entitlements of others concerning certain goods.[84]

As a first approximation, therefore, the duty of nondiscrimination is incumbent on holders of normative powers but not on all such holders; hence, the second aspect of the duty inquiry. The paradigmatic instance of duty-owers is the for-profit and non-profit provider of goods and services. By contrast, some normative powers may fall outside the purview of any liberal legal order insofar as they are personal choices in intimate relationships, such as those of friendship and romantic love, or in the pursuit of artistic creation. Other instances of exercising normative powers may be exempt from legal oversight due to substantive or institutional considerations.

Substantive considerations have to do with free agency.[85] A consumer deciding not to purchase certain goods because the seller is Jewish may reach the exact same decision for other and perfectly legitimate reasons, such as the price of the goods. Thus, there is a space between motives and actions, that is, between why they refuse to do X and doing X. It means that free agents *could*—rather than merely would—change their minds before consummating the act. To respect free agency, therefore, a liberal legal order must furnish consumers with an arena of revisability in the domain of motives or attitudes, allowing them an opportunity to act more appropriately after revising their current attitude. They can, then, decide to do X or to refrain from doing X for perfectly good reasons (such as to remain reluctant to purchase the thing at issue for the legitimate reason that it is too costly for them). A liberal legal order cannot hold them legally responsible on the *sole* basis of forming and acting on repugnant motives. Notice that the same free agency-based analysis does not apply to the buyer's seller: a seller who is not willing to interact with the buyer typically faces only two options, namely, refrain from doing so or close down the business.

However, the free agency case for relieving consumers from nondiscrimination duties is limited.[86] It focuses on the case of a consumer deciding whether to buy a particular product from a particular seller at a particular time. It does not extend to the very different case of a buyer who sets up a procedure (say, an auction) to be regularly used in its purchasing activity. Unlike the former case, there is no principled basis to relieve buyers engaging in the latter market activity from antidiscrimination duties.

Institutional considerations that might support exempting consumers from legal oversight derive largely from the epistemic difficulty of verifying discriminatory decisions on the part of consumers.[87] This class of considerations, by its very nature, is contingent.

These substantive or institutional considerations (arguably) explain why existing duties of nondiscrimination do not apply to how consumers, employees, lessees, and students exercise their normative, contractual powers vis-à-vis their respective providers. In *these* cases—but not, as noted, in more regularized purchasing activities—discriminating in the choice of provider can be ethically wrongful, though not necessarily legally impermissible.

Subject to these exceptions, relational justice theory implies that providers of goods and services are duty-bound, no matter how big the provider or how essential the provided goods are. It applies to common carriers as well as to small businesses held by sole proprietors, irrespective of the availability of equivalent options furnished by other market providers or by the state.

3. Breach. The breach element fills out the content of the duty. It tells us what duty-owers owe in terms of measures they have to implement and decisions they have to refrain from to lower and, at times, even eradicate transactional barriers. Doing so, as noted, requires a reasonable accommodation standard of conduct. This standard is made up of epistemic, substantive, and legality conditions.

a. The Epistemic Condition. The first, epistemic condition, is known in tort law as reasonable foreseeability.[88] To refrain from wrongful discrimination, duty-owers must be able to know what they are required to do or abstain from doing so that the terms of their interactions with others are not discriminatory, that is, that they do not hold the others' constitutive choices or traits against them.

At times, knowing is relatively simple—for instance, when an ice cream parlor refuses to serve foreigners, the owner is fully aware that such an interaction is discriminatory. At other times, foreseeability may be less straightforward—for instance, if auditions to professional orchestras are governed by terms of interaction that, though not by intentional design, turn out to be discriminatory. Reasonable foreseeability, then, becomes the only relevant question. If duty-owers cannot reasonably be cognizant of the pertinent fact, holding them strictly liable in discrimination necessarily undermines their status as free and equal agents since there is nothing they can do in terms of accommodation to avoid liability for the discriminatory outcome. If, by contrast, they might be aware of a non-trivial possibility that the audition process treats women and non-whites much less favorably than white men musicians, duty-owers can be required to take some measure to rule out that possibility.

Although possible in theory, voluntary interactions resulting in unforeseeable indirect discrimination will rarely exist in practice. We could imagine that, at some historical moment, no reasonable auditor had realized the discriminatory character of the audition process. When complaints and studies begin to pile up, however, appeals to ignorance will not do, and this statement applies not only to auditions for orchestras but almost everywhere. The reason is that today, people are (or can reasonably be assumed to be) acutely aware of the ever-present risk of potentially discriminatory implications, even in generally applicable terms of interactions. The threshold set by the epistemic condition of foreseeability is thus low, which happily implies that a tort of discrimination would be especially receptive to claims by members of liminal groups.[89]

b. The Substantive Condition. The second, substantive condition, is more demanding and is meant to insulate the standard of reasonable accommodation from the exacting demand of utmost accommodation. As discussed above, utmost accommodation is inconsistent with relational justice because it threatens to destroy the duty-ower's self-determination and equal standing. For this reason, the duty-owers' awareness of discriminatory overtones in their interactions with others will not suffice. Defusing these overtones, however, must be made commensurate with the resources available to duty-holders (including in the form of state subsidies).

Again, the burden of conforming with a duty of nondiscrimination is often negligible, such as simply refraining from excluding green-eyed people from one's restaurant, and thus can, and indeed should, be demanded from duty-owers. Yet, some cases are more challenging and may involve costly accommodations, such as structural changes to the built environment or substantial adjustments of production processes and modes of operation in the workplace. A key role of the standard of reasonable accommodation in these instances is to set a ceiling beyond which no additional accommodation is required. A ceiling can be set directly by the standard of accommodation or indirectly by introducing state subsidies that lower the (economic) burden that the duty of nondiscrimination imposes on duty-owers.[90]

c. The Legality Condition. The substantive condition immediately invites a third one—the legality condition, which concerns the rule of law implications of a reasonable accommodation standard. Attempts to meet the standard of reasonable accommodation might collapse into the ad hoc tailoring of dos and don'ts. But taking this path is, as noted, unacceptable for rule of law reasons as well as for relational justice ones, and to avert this, the presence of recursive structures should be built into the standard of reasonable accommodation, enabling courts and duty-owers to identify clear answers to particular questions.

This difficulty is not unique to our context; indeed, it typifies doctrines that impose not only prohibitions but also affirmative interpersonal obligations. Resort to regulation provides a straightforward solution, as in the analogous case of disclosure law, discussed in Chapter 9. Helpful examples *in pari materia* come from the work of two major agencies that deal with discrimination, whose regulations are aimed at shaping the pertinent parties' rights and obligations in compliance with the injunctions of relational justice: the Equal Employment Opportunity Commission (EEOC) and the Office of Fair Housing and Equal Opportunity in the Department of Housing and Urban Development (FHEO).[91] Courts can further reinforce the prescriptions made by these (and other) agencies by treating their violations as discrimination per se, in line with the familiar doctrine of negligence per se.

4. Injury. Infringing a person's right to be treated as an equal can give rise to any number of consequential harms. Some of them are pecuniary, such as lower earnings. Others are non-pecuniary and concern emotional distress as well as other forms of non-monetizable suffering, including stigmatization and feelings of inferiority. But the right in question is not reducible to any of these consequences, all of them being surface manifestations of a deeper setback to victims of wrongful discrimination: denying them the possibility of relating to others—employers, providers, educators, lessors, and so forth—as substantively free and equal persons.

This characterization of the injury element puts this aspect of the tort of discrimination closer to torts like assault and battery rather than negligence. Thus, breaching the duty of reasonable accommodation is per se a violation of the discriminatee's right to be treated as an equal, as when the victims are denied bakery services based on their sexual orientation.

Two clarifications are in order. The per se quality of the tort of discrimination does not deny the victim's entitlement to recover the legally cognizable consequential harms that may result from the discriminator's failure. Moreover, our account is consistent with a practice of awarding super-compensatory damages (often called punitive damages) under the right circumstances, as discussed in Chapter 7.[92]

5. *Causation*. Finally, failure to conform to the standard of reasonable accommodation and the injury the discriminatee complains of must be causally connected. Neither the act nor the injury can, alone, satisfy a prima facie case of wrongful discrimination, and the injury must result, in the right sense, from a (deliberate or careless) failure of reasonable accommodation on the discriminator's part. Failure to render the workplace reasonably accommodative of job candidates with physical disability does not mean that turning down one of them necessarily amounts to wrongful discrimination since the reasons behind the rejection may be irrelevant to this person's disability.

The causation doctrine, as practiced in the common law of torts and as further developed in the context of contemporary anti-discrimination law,[93] is up to this task.[94] The epistemic difficulties that may arise in proving causation here are not qualitatively different from those addressed in contemporary anti-discrimination law.

* * *

When a general, privity-independent duty of care was first pronounced in *MacPherson v. Buick* (or, for English tort law, in *Donoghue v. Stevenson*), it added a wholesale tort to the retail duties of care prescribed in preexisting law. This decision is now rightly viewed as both a paradigm shift in the history of tort law and as an indispensable feature of private law in a liberal legal order.[95] The private law of discrimination, we claim, is in its pre-*MacPherson* moment. The gaps between its existing retail duties are indefensible, and its retail structure fails to vindicate people's fundamental right to be treated as equals by those exercising their normative powers over them. As in the tort of negligence, a wholesale duty does not call for an all-encompassing scope, given the many spheres of action and human relations that should remain beyond the purview of legal oversight. Yet, again, as in the case of negligence, nothing short of a general tort of discrimination can suffice if the revolution instigated by the Civil Rights Acts is to be completed.

This chapter shows that existing doctrines in and around tort law offer important tools that can be utilized for prescribing the proper elements—duty, breach, injury, and causation—of this new tort. Relational justice theory offers the missing piece for this crucial endeavor: a clear articulation of the normative foundations of a discrimination tort as an integral, indeed indispensable, part of private law in a liberal society.

14
Poverty

Accommodating the Poor

1. Poverty as Social Exclusion. Like discrimination, poverty is one of the most important and urgent challenges of our time. As is the case with discrimination, its alleviation is widely conceived as a matter of public law or, more specifically, distributive justice, that is, as part of a broader effort to bring about fairness in the overall distribution of resources or opportunities in society (and even beyond). Some private law theories, identified mostly with a view of the person as an executive agent, insist that private law—and not only public law—should certainly address poverty's distributive injustice.[1] The canonical view, however, follows John Rawls' claim that "since the market is not suited to answer the claims of need, these should be met by a separate arrangement."[2]

In this chapter, we argue that relational justice requires private law to include rules that accommodate the poor. Our claim can be read either as a direct challenge to Rawls' proposition (if strictly interpreted) or as an exercise in giving it a charitable interpretation. Either way, we argue that poverty has an irreducible relational dimension.[3]

Poverty is not merely a matter of material destitution. Insufficient access to basic needs such as food, clothing, and shelter can certainly lead to physical and material deprivation (a matter of distributive justice). However, the concern with human subsistence underlying this definition, which is often associated with an absolutist measurement of poverty,[4] does not exhaust the evils of poverty because poverty can, and often does, lead to social exclusion, and that is also an evil.

Adam Smith, the champion of the social exclusion view, famously distinguishes what is "indispensably necessary for the support of life" from "whatever the custom of the country renders it indecent for creditable people, even of the lowest order, to be without." On this basis, he identifies social exclusion with the inability "to appear in public." Smith's concern is not with brute presence in a public space. His living example for identifying the proper baseline—the "creditable day-labourer"—refers to people on a lower subset of the middle-class whose poverty does not threaten their survival but rather their ability to engage in everyday interactions surrounding employment, housing, consumption, and credit markets.[5] Thus, poverty implicates a person's inability to participate with *dignity* in customary social and economic interactions and includes insufficient access to such interactions or unfair terms in them.

Relational Justice. Hanoch Dagan and Avihay Dorfman, Oxford University Press.
DOI: 10.1093/9780191987762.003.0014

Careful not to overstate the case for poverty as social exclusion, Smith locates the latter between subsistence and convenience, a distinction equivalent to that between survival goods and "luxuries." He illustrates this point through a person whose financial situation compels him to "abstain totally" from purchasing certain alcoholic beverages. Such drinks are not "necessary for the support of life," so that lack of access to them does not undermine that person's subsistence. These goods are, moreover, mere "luxuries" and, therefore, "custom nowhere renders it indecent to live without them."[6]

This last observation is most striking regarding a subset of luxurious goods, namely, Veblen goods (viz., goods for which the demand increases as the price increases). A ridiculously expensive watch is a Veblen good if its economic value does not reflect intrinsic quality but rather a desire to set its owner apart from most people. The inability to purchase it may result in inconvenience rather than indignity.[7]

One can read Smith's account from a political or civic perspective, which emphasizes the relational standing of the poor vis-à-vis other members of their political community.[8] Unsurprisingly, in this chapter, we opt for a more strictly relational reading,[9] focusing on the legally constructed relationships between employer and employee, landlord and tenant, and the like, which brings home the way poverty should impact the law of our interpersonal interactions, namely, our private law.

Indeed, poverty affects the poor's ability to interact with other people in terms of reciprocal respect for self-determination and substantive equality throughout the various (legally constructed[10]) markets they routinely participate in—employment, housing, consumption, credit, et alia, both inside and outside their political communities.

2. Beyond the Rawlsian Framework. This understanding of poverty as social exclusion implies that poverty is a genuine source of concern for relational justice and, thus, for private law in a liberal legal order. We do not argue that poverty does not lay claim to distributive justice. Instead, we claim it is a matter of relational justice *as well*, with an irreducibly relational rather than merely distributional dimension. Accordingly, the poverty-related demands of relational justice hold even in a society that, in distributive terms, is unreservedly just.

The prescription of a relational justice perspective on the problem of poverty is, as Chapter 3 explains, qualitatively different from one grounded in distributive justice. Whereas distributive justice is primarily concerned with the overall alleviation of poverty and inequality in society in general, relational justice focuses on whether the terms of interactions between people address poverty properly. Relational justice insists that employers, landlords, retailers, lenders, and others are duty-bound to address, in some measure, the poverty of their employees, tenants, buyers, and borrowers. This obligation is incumbent on them not only as part of their responsibility to society along the Rawlsian lines of a fair system of cooperation among free and equal people. Rather, they also have specific duties integral to what it means for parties in employment, housing, consumer, credit, and other relationships to relate to one another as free and equal persons.

These duties, we argue, are necessary features of a just private law for the same reason that justifies all other interpersonal obligations and burdens discussed in the previous nine chapters of this book. Private law, as recurrently emphasized, does not address ad hoc encounters between, for example, this or that employer and employee; instead, it sets up—constructively and prospectively—the terms of their interaction. It constructs the actual category of the employment relationship as well as many other frameworks of our social and economic life so that, conceptually, private law cannot take a neutral standpoint vis-à-vis socially constructed conditions such as poverty, disability, and so forth.

For private law, the crucial question is necessarily the normative question: what are the terms of the relationship that respect the interacting parties as free and equal persons? Our answer is that these terms must treat the parties as self-determining and substantively equal, and, therefore, a condition of poverty is integral to these terms as a matter of relational justice.

Relational justice provides a distinct normative framework for accommodating the poor when compared to its distributive counterpart. It insists that poverty is not just an allocative or distributional problem (although it is certainly that, too). It invites us to see that our responsibility to accommodate the poor cannot be exhausted by leaving it to the government, entire industries, or communities to tackle poverty. Further, relational justice theory shows that poverty can count as a defect not only in the overall distribution of resources in society but also in the way private persons relate to one another in their day-to-day social and economic affairs. Again, our theory tackles structural injustices at their roots.

In principle, poverty should not be treated differently from other socially constructed conditions and personal traits, which merit accommodation by virtue of their importance to the parties' ability to interact as self-determining and substantively equal persons. What makes poverty distinct is *not* a matter of principle, which is why Rawls' proposition need not be read as an endorsement of the (Toronto) thesis of strict division of responsibility. Instead, Rawls' proposition can, and we think should, be understood as a cautionary note that highlights the *operational* difficulties involved in implementing private responsibility for poverty.

In other words, morally absolving people from any responsibility for others' poverty is as unacceptable as authorizing private discrimination or, for that matter, nondisclosure or price-gouging. The operational difficulties of implementing such a responsibility in cases of poverty, however, are indeed particularly challenging. The institutional constraints of operationalizing poverty's claim to relational justice are admittedly more prominent than other types of social conditions calling for interpersonal accommodation. All these limitations, however, are not entailments of justice but unfortunate impediments to its legal implementation, which we should do our best to overcome.

From Disability to Poverty

1. Analogous Cases. The analogy of poverty to physical disability may shed light on our case for accommodating the poor and clarify the distinctive difficulties it faces. Indeed, poverty's effects on people's transactional freedom and equality are strikingly analogous to those of physical disability and other social conditions and personal traits that, as noted in Chapter 13, make private discrimination relationally unacceptable.

The poor person is bound to find certain establishments inaccessible and thus be effectively excluded from many contexts providing everyday, non-luxurious goods and services. Under certain circumstances, these may include trains, taxis, bookstores, restaurants, museums, sports arenas, and the like. At times, social exclusion is manifest in a radical separation between communities so that the poor are excluded from the social and economic hubs of the rest of society. At others, it is enforced at the point of entry, as when showing a ticket is a prerequisite or a certain dress code is de rigueur. And yet, at other times, poverty results in exclusion from some service or good but not necessarily from the venue where the service or the good is provided and not immediately, as when people are thrown out of a restaurant after their condition is discovered.

The reason for exclusion in all its manifestations is the socially constructed condition affecting this person—poverty. While the form of exclusion in the case of poverty differs from that experienced by the person with a physical disability—financial as opposed to physical inaccessibility—substantively, it is very much alike.[11] Poverty, like discrimination, is a social condition whose impact on self-determination and substantive equality is anything but negligible. Terms of interaction between private parties that make no demand to take poverty into account are, therefore, unacceptable. They undermine reciprocal respect for self-determination and equality by entitling one party (say, a service-provider) to turn the poverty of the other into a transactional barrier.

One possible counterargument is that a fully complying state could obviate the need for holding private people responsible for accommodating the poverty, unlike the physical disabilities, of their customers. Generous state support for the poor could diminish poverty and extend equal opportunities, rendering private accommodation superfluous. This bottom-line perspective, however, fails to capture the freestanding importance of relational justice and its special role in addressing poverty at the transactional level. As we concluded above,[12] as long as resources in a state are moderately scarce, poverty remains a real possibility, and consequently, the justice question persists. Concomitantly, insofar as poverty *could* become a reality, relational justice should remain an actual option as a source of interpersonal duties.

2. Why Me? The relational justice case for accommodating the poor addresses the "why me?" charge often raised in private law's traditionalist schools. The accommodation duties of employers, landlords, retailers, lenders, and the like are not grounded in their moral responsibility for the predicament of their employees, tenants, buyers, and borrowers or in their being enlisted as the state's executive agents or good citizens. Instead, they are (or should be) encoded in the terms of the interactions of a private law regime guided by relational justice. Such terms, as noted, are at odds with ignoring a person's poverty precisely because of poverty's profound impact on people's ability to manifest their self-determination in the world. They preclude a reading of private law as empowering individuals to apply their transactional powers in ways that undermine others' substantive equality.

Indeed, treating a poor person as *not* poor fails to respect this person as a self-determining agent. Accordingly, giving no weight to poverty in the determination of the terms of an interaction between an employer and employee (or a storeowner and a customer, and so forth) is inconsistent with substantive equality's basic commitment to take relevant differences seriously when fixing interpersonal duties, responsibilities, and burdens.[13] The specific method for discharging the private responsibility of employers (and others) can vary. The conventional one—remuneration as in minimum wage—is perhaps the most familiar, but (as Chapter 12 clarifies) indirect methods are also plausible. What must remain intact (in a genuinely liberal legal order) are the freestanding demands of relational justice, which imply that employers must not be entitled—read, legally authorized—to disregard the socio-economic condition of employees when setting up their employment terms.

3. *Responsibility for One's Condition*? Does this prescription ignore people's responsibility for their own condition? This concern, we argue, is misplaced not only because poverty-caused social exclusion is typically a matter of socio-economic structural circumstances or bad luck so there is not much the poor can do about this predicament. It is also inappropriate because reciprocal respect for self-determination and substantive equality does not depend on such considerations.

To see why, return to the analogy to disability and consider the impact of the past conduct of people with physical disability on their entitlement to accommodations. Although storeowners should not be held morally responsible for accommodating a chosen disability if the purpose of this choice was to become eligible for accommodation, the owners' responsibility is choice-insensitive in the face of less absurd instances. Thus, if a person has genuinely chosen to become physically disabled (say, because her conception of the good life requires her to forgo the ability to walk), owners should still be responsible for rendering their place accessible to this person as part of respecting her self-determination and equal standing. A person who recklessly harmed himself into a state of disability (say, to be exempted from mandatory army service) is also owed a duty of accommodation because treating him as a self-determining, equal agent includes a measure of respect for his ability not only to write but also to rewrite his conception of the good life.[14]

Hence, insulating the duty of accommodation from the individual responsibility of the person with a disability does not reflect epistemic difficulties (or the fact that an accessible entrance serves not only this person but also all the people facing a similar condition). Ascertaining the role of people with disabilities in developing or aggravating their condition may be very costly, but that is not the reason for deeming this inquiry irrelevant. Instead, the reason is that, for a discrete transaction to meet the bar of reciprocal respect for self-determination and substantive equality, the owner must treat the person with disability as the person they are.

Poverty is again analogous because, like being disabled, being poor is an important aspect of a person's condition, and—again, similarly to disability—its importance cuts across the distinction between choice and circumstances. Poverty may be a choice if, say, someone joins a Franciscan order or practices voluntary privation for environmental or other reasons. For such individuals, living in a state of poverty is part of their ground project. Being poor is a constitutive feature of their identity and, therefore, profoundly impacts their self-determination.

Obviously, poverty is rarely chosen in this fashion and, indeed, rarely chosen at all. Moreover, as in the case of a chosen disability, the fact that poverty has been chosen is not sufficient to relieve the store owner of responsibility. What is necessary is that the choice to be poor was made opportunistically, that is, for the purpose of being eligible for accommodation. By contrast, other cases of chosen poverty—such as when it is constitutive of the person's conception of the good or when it reflects a mistake made in the past—are consistent with holding the store owner duty-bound to respect the self-determination of the poor. This means that, as in the case of disability, any reasonable rule of law-based system would ignore the marginal cases in which accommodation could have been denied due to a person's opportunistic choice to become poor.

Finally, poverty (chosen or unchosen) has a profound effect on the poor person's self-determination and substantive equality, which grounds the owners' duty of accommodation. First, poverty severely limits the available options, hindering people's autonomous functioning and their ability to relate as substantively equal.[15] Second, poverty often invites adverse reactions from other members of society, thus limiting self-determination and equal standing even further since many of our plans are frequently heavily dependent on the voluntary cooperation of other people.

4. Why Poverty Is (to Some Extent) Different. Relational justice's case of a free-standing private responsibility for accommodating the poor does not settle the practical implications of this responsibility, even before the more contextual stages of a blueprint that, as usual, exceed our scope here.

First, the accommodating duty is circumscribed by relational justice's inherent limits. These limits, as discussed in Chapter 3,[16] ensure that accommodation efforts reflecting recognition of another person's self-determination and equal standing should not exceed a reasonable investment. In this regard, nothing distinguishes poverty from, say, physical disability, nor are the (real) practical challenges of turning this prescription into a legal doctrine complying with the rule of law unique to this context.

By contrast, the institutional considerations discussed in Chapter 4 are significantly more challenging in this case, given the epistemic and substantive difficulties of implementing private responsibility for accommodating another person's poverty. Unlike physical disability, for example, a condition of poverty may not be easily verifiable, and this epistemic burden makes implementation especially challenging.

Ascertaining a person's economic situation and then acting on it may be epistemically demanding, possibly overly intrusive, and at times even demeaning[17] when impersonalized government entities oversee collecting and processing the information (as, for example, when establishing food-stamps eligibility). It can become far more intrusive and potentially demeaning, however, when private people share the government's information or process it by themselves (which is also epistemically complicated and demanding).

These difficulties—to be contrasted with the conventional view that poverty cannot be mixed with private law because it is purely a matter of distributive justice—may help to explain why implementing the demands of relational justice in private law is anything but straightforward. This means that the most challenging part of the relational-justice case for accommodating the poor concerns the legality, rather than the justice, of private responsibility for poverty.

The argument is not that being epistemically demanding, intrusive, and demeaning are necessary features of any private law scheme for accommodating the poor. Rather, we claim that these aspects can constrain the course of private law's attempts to accommodate the poor, challenging it to consider ways of reducing, bypassing, or even eliminating their potentially unwarranted effects.

Indeed, there are both direct and indirect strategies designed to address (some of) the operational difficulties of accommodating the poor. Besides them, several preventive measures are also required, given that both strategies may be vulnerable to attempts to sidestep or shirk the implementation of this responsibility. We now turn to these strategies and measures.

Strategies

1. Direct Accommodation and its Operational Constraints. The most straightforward way to fulfill the relational justice promise is to accommodate the poor directly, that is, by tailoring the duty to the social condition of its beneficiary. Although direct accommodation does pose operational challenges, these can be met under certain circumstances.

Accommodating the poor by imposing direct affirmative private duties to support them in the context of *involuntary* interactions poses coordination difficulties. Consider, for example, the implications of a passerby owing a legal duty of financial support to homeless people occupying sidewalks. The combination of substantial numbers of destitute people and the multitude of duty-owers requires an organizing scheme to meet two fairness demands, which do not apply in the context of the one-off easy rescue duties discussed in Chapter 6. The first demand is that all beneficiaries should receive a more or less fair share (as determined by each one's needs). The second is that all duty-owers contribute a more or less fair share (as determined by each one's condition). This demand is integral to relational justice, whose basic task is to determine just terms not merely for a discrete case but for any similar pairwise interaction. Coordination thus emerges as a real operational obstacle.

Other operational constraints can still loom large even when we scale down complexity by reducing the number and the heterogeneity of the participants involved, as the shifting from an involuntary to a voluntary modality of private law interaction will prove. A direct (or tailored) strategy for accommodating the poor within a voluntary interaction, such as contractual dealings between retailers and consumers, means that the duty to make reasonable accommodations is bound to exhibit high variance. In other words, the object of the duty—whom it is owed—and its subject matter—what is owed—would need to reflect the circumstances of the person for whom accommodation is considered, a practice that, as noted, raises concerns about demandingness and intrusiveness.[18]

Focusing on three barriers to the direct implementation of private responsibility for accommodating the poor will help to clarify these concerns as well as the contexts in which they could render direct accommodation unwarranted. Three properties of goods and services make accommodation a challenging endeavor: publicity, hybridity, and fungibility. Consider, for example, these three properties in the context of a distinction between buying groceries and entering a tuition agreement between an applicant and the admitting (private) university.

- *Publicity*. The store/university distinction stresses different institutional ways of addressing the mentioned epistemic and moral difficulties: the impersonal and discreet financial-aid procedures of a typical university starkly contrast with what (we suspect) grocery stores would do to fulfill their private responsibility for accommodating the poor.
- *Hybridity*. This distinction also highlights the varying complexity of telling basic from luxurious goods. Whereas many grocery stores exhibit a large degree of hybridity and sell both types of goods, a college education can typically, or more easily, be defined as providing one basic good. Imposing a duty to accommodate the poverty of grocery buyers may hinge, therefore, on

solving the preliminary question of enforcing accommodation with respect to what products.

- *Fungibility.* The distinction at issue emphasizes a difficulty that could be specific to fungible goods: the possibility of re-selling the goods in the market (including black markets) opens an option for price reduction beneficiaries to become arbitrageurs with respect to the goods they purchase in the grocery store.

The grocery/university example helps to uncover the multidimensional complexity confronting the implementation of a direct strategy. It suggests that retailers and other providers of commercial goods and services may justifiably be exempt from implementing a direct strategy of accommodating the poor. Yet, it also points out that providers of other goods and services—notably education, housing, and legal services, which we discuss below—are less susceptible to the obstacles set by publicity, hybridity, and fungibility and thus are, or at least should be, legally responsible for accommodating the poor.

2. *Indirect Accommodation: Proxies, Floors, and Ceilings.* An indirect (untailored) strategy utilizes a proxy instead of an individualized assessment of need. An intriguing example would be adjusting retail prices to local economic conditions. For instance, a supermarket chain can vary the prices of a basic product according to the location of its stores, thereby accommodating the poor without facing the operational obstacles mentioned above. The drawback of this and other indirect strategies is not necessarily related to economics. Indeed, from a purely cost-benefit analysis, departing from uniform pricing could benefit retail chains.[19] Indirect strategies could emerge as legally problematic, however, particularly if the proxies they invoke rest on highly contingent factors or prove impractical, as when the distance between poor and rich zip codes is relatively small. These proxies may consequently become too complicated for a legal system to enforce without violating rule of law commitments to provide duty-owers effective guidance and constrain the power of public officials to enforce them.

A promising way of avoiding these operational constraints is to endorse a *structural* strategy. A strategy is structural when accommodation is *built into* the terms of the interaction, becoming an indelible aspect of what it means for the parties to respect one another's self-determination and substantive equality. Private law's recourse to adequate floors and ceilings thus implements this indirect strategy of accommodating the poor.

Begin, once again, with the case of physical disability. The responsibility of business owners to make their facilities reasonably accessible to persons with disabilities takes the form of structural accommodation. It sets a floor to the terms of the interaction between the parties below which they cannot go, conducting their interpersonal dealings in terms that allow the person with a disability to enter, face the owner, move around, and so forth. This accommodation of physical disability protects one dimension of the parties' terms of interaction—the infrastructural dimension—against breaches of the reciprocal respect bar for self-determination and substantive equality set by relational justice. There are other floors—consider workplace safety—the law uses for this purpose, which cover additional dimensions of the interaction.

Setting an adequate floor to accommodate poverty is meant to sustain another dimension of compliance with relational justice, introducing a measure of consideration for the socio-economic condition of a party to the interaction. As usual, this measure goes beyond an ad hoc individualized judgment of one side's particular situation and becomes a structural feature, a mandatory floor of the parties' terms of interaction. It thereby extends individual responsibility beyond physical and other conditions to include the impact of poverty on the possibility of interacting in terms of reciprocal respect for self-determination and substantive equality. Doctrines like minimum wage and implied warranty of habitability, as we show below, can be reconstructed and defended in this way.

This argument also applies to the imposition of ceilings to accommodate poverty within the terms of interaction. As is true of floors, ceilings—such as price control and usury laws, which we also discuss in this chapter, and the tort doctrine of crushing liability discussed in Chapter 7—can tackle an existing economic predicament or prevent its evolvement. They do so by capping some of the costs incurred by one party's actions when interacting with the other if such actions can indeed address a concern with poverty.

3. *The Necessity of Maintenance.* Both direct and indirect strategies of accommodating the poor in horizontal, voluntary interactions require maintenance. Maintenance, in turn, demands much more than the micro-level judicial enforcement of victims' rights in discrete cases. Specifically, there are foreseeable regressive consequences at the *macro* level, including, most importantly, "redlining" practices involving providers of goods and services structuring their business operations to avoid transacting with the poor.[20] In the absence of preventive measures, therefore, the private responsibility for accommodating the poor can be systematically flouted with impunity.

To forestall redlining, reverse redlining,[21] and other avoidance practices, private law cannot rely solely on victims asserting their rights individually or in class actions. The shortcoming in this common law way of enforcing private rights is twofold. First, it takes an ex post orientation and thus depends on articulating and proving an actual injury. Second, private individuals often lack the institutional competence—resources, expertise, and power—to gather and assess the information necessary for pursuing redliners.

Thus, law's preventive function must expand its reach beyond the adjudicatory modality to deploy (at least) two further enforcement mechanisms. One is to authorize the relevant administrative agency or other public entities to pursue redlines on the victims' behalf.[22] The other, potentially more significant mechanism is to establish a rigorous ex ante enforcement regime parallel to the OSHA regime discussed in Chapter 12. Here, administrative agents assume responsibility for preventing redlining (et alia) by resorting to various means, including setting clear standards for what counts as redlining, conducting audits, requiring periodic disclosures of data, revoking licenses, and other administrative sanctions.[23]

Accommodating the Poor Directly

With these normative and institutional building blocks in place, we are ready to show how, and to what extent, what is morally required on relational justice grounds can also be made legally obligatory in several prominent spheres of social and economic life. We begin with the direct strategy of accommodation, which can be implemented regarding goods and services when their provision can overcome the operational challenges we noted—the publicity, hybridity, and fungibility of goods or services. The provision of some of these goods and services can accommodate the poverty of their consumers or users while preserving a satisfactory level of publicity, limiting transactions to one basic good or service, and preventing arbitrageurs from setting in.

1. *Inclusionary Education.* Private universities can, as noted, adjust their tuition fees for poor applicants.[24] Currently, a need-blind approach to admissions is the practice in most private and elite American institutions as a matter of policy rather than as a legal duty.[25] It should be mandatory, however, for the same relational justice reasons that require these institutions to be reasonably accessible to students with a physical disability.[26] Moreover, this argument should also be extended to the provision of educational goods by private schools more generally.

Consistent with the demands of relational justice, private educational institutions—nurseries, primary schools, middle schools, and high schools—are duty-bound to make their facilities reasonably accessible to persons with a physical disability, irrespective of whether they receive government funding.[27] Poverty calls for a similar approach, and the only question for a relationally just private law concerns operational difficulties. Assuming that, like universities, admission processes in these schools are sufficiently discreet, implementing their private responsibility through a direct strategy for accommodating the poor can, and therefore, should be legally required as well.[28] The relational justice case for identifying who is in charge of accommodation does not settle the question of who should bear all (or even some of) the costs of discharging this duty. What relational justice does settle is the duty's upper bound—to wit, it must not repeal or severely diminish the self-determination of the institutions' owners and their agents.

2. *Affordable Housing.* Residential developers offer another example of direct accommodation overcoming operational obstacles concerning publicity, hybridity,

and fungibility. Municipalities often issue inclusionary ordinances requiring or encouraging developers of new housing units to designate a number of units for sale or lease at reduced prices to low- or moderate-income families.[29] They thereby order or entice private developers to make good on their public responsibility for accommodating the poor.[30]

This way of deploying developers represents, in the words of the New Jersey legislature, one "technique" for advancing "the provision of the [municipality's] fair share"[31] that, from a distributive justice perspective, may even count as inferior given its regressive impact on housing prices overall.[32] Moreover, the resort to distributive justice lacks a principled basis for distinguishing between those who benefit from the developer's duty of accommodating the poor and the many other low-income families that will necessarily stand beyond the reach of the developer's duty.

Relational justice, by contrast, construes developers' responsibility as horizontal and *strictly transactional*, requiring them to make some of their units affordable to poor home-seekers. As with the responsibility to provide reasonably accessible dwelling units to people with a physical disability, providing affordable housing for low-income families is grounded in the *developer*'s duty to respect *buyers* rather than the entire class of low-income family members as self-determining and substantively equal persons. What matters is not whether the developer contributes to the alleviation of poverty but whether the terms of her interaction with buyers reflect reciprocal respect for self-determination and substantive equality.

Relying on a direct strategy of accommodating the poor can overcome the three obstacles of publicity, hybridity, and fungibility. Consider publicity: unlike the buying of goods at a grocery store, buying a house can be made discreet by insulating the buyer's economic condition from other buyers and by limiting access to information on the buyer to most of the seller's agents. The two other obstacles, hybridity and fungibility, pose no challenge in this context as the good at issue—an inexpensive housing unit—is a basic good purchased for its real market value.

3. *Affordable Legal Services.* The demand for low-cost legal services in the United States has long exceeded the supply of services available.[33] The response of the organized bar to the legal needs of the poor has shifted from acting "as a club against lawyers whose clients were urban poor, immigrants and working class"[34] through deciding that providing free legal services to the poor is no longer ethically objectionable,[35] up to ultimately urging "every lawyer" as a matter of "professional responsibility" to provide pro bono services to the poor.[36] Responsibility for providing free or reduced-fee legal services, however, remains voluntary, though, from a relational justice perspective, it should be made mandatory (subject to the qualifications below).

The operational challenges can also be met. Legal services are typically neither hybrid nor fungible, to begin with. If anything, the real challenge here might be publicity—can legal service providers identify, consult, and represent eligible clients without engaging in epistemically demanding, intrusive, and demeaning screening processes?[37]

One way to meet this challenge is to resort to referring organizations that (ideally) make detached and informed identification of cases meriting free or reduced-fee legal services. Law firms could then discharge their duty to accommodate poverty by choosing from this class of cases (say, according to their subject-matter expertise). Finally, a duty to provide free or reduced-fee legal service should come with an upper limit to render the terms of legal-service interaction compatible with the self-determination and equal standing of the attorney. For instance, pro bono legal services by medium to large private law firms, as opposed to a small-town solo practitioner, may likely uphold this relational justice limit.[38]

* * *

The provision of affordable education, housing, and legal services lends itself to direct accommodation in the private law terms of the relevant interactions. In principle, any category of horizontal interactions concerning the provision of important goods or services should follow suit insofar as the operational constraints just discussed can be overcome. Thus, parallel to the practice of inclusionary zoning, consider one of inclusionary employment requiring big employers to provide professional training to those who were not lucky enough to benefit from a proper education.[39] Similarly, there is no reason for limiting the coverage of the "patient anti-dumping" rule, which stopped hospitals from refusing emergency care to low-income individuals, solely to hospitals that receive federal funds.[40] Technological progress may bring further opportunities for direct accommodation of the poor.

The Workplace: Minimum Wage

1. *In Search for a Rationale.* We next turn to four legal doctrines that represent the other form of accommodating the poor: indirect or, more specifically, structural strategies that build a floor or a ceiling into certain contractual and property transactions.[41]

Minimum wage—our first case study—exemplifies the general point we are making about poverty's relational dimension. Its early years mark a clash between those who associate the contractual relationship of employment with independence and formal equality[42] on the one hand and, on the other, those who call for enlisting this nexus in the service of advancing overall justice in the distribution of resources.[43] Although the former has been overwhelmingly repudiated by legislatures and courts,[44] the latter has been found wanting.

In particular, minimum wage may violate rather than advance justice in holdings because of the possible regressive effect of increasing the costs of employment for employers, who would then be forced to cut jobs, including of the least well-off, namely, the low-skilled workers.[45] The regressive effects are harder to defend from a distributive justice point of view when the means—minimum wage—turns out to fare poorly in comparison with state-administered schemes of direct, need-based support, such as the earned income tax credit.[46]

Against this background, it is not surprising to find that even liberal egalitarians, who would normally be wary of formal equality, disapprove of minimum wage[47] or develop alternatives for reconciling minimum wage with the basic commitments underlying prevailing liberal theories of distributive justice.[48] In particular, some liberal egalitarians justify minimum wage as a civic instrument in the service of a collective goal, such as improving democracy or securing the equal standing of employees as members of the political community.[49] Minimum wage law thereby commands employers to achieve a public purpose—e.g., democratic equality—that really falls within the moral responsibility of the polity rather than the employers' class.

2. Relationally Just Workplace. Relational justice provides a different, non-statist justification for minimum wage. Indeed, an employment relationship is an interpersonal source of concern and value in and of itself rather than merely a means for achieving greater distributive justice, democratic equality, or some other state-based goal. A minimum wage requirement could make the terms of employment interactions between private persons—including those of different nationalities or political communities—relationally just.

Our focus on the interactions between private persons acting as employers and employees, as opposed to agents of the state or members of a particular political community, fits the Universal Declaration of Human Rights' prescription: "Everyone who works has the right to just and favourable remuneration ensuring for himself and his family an existence worthy of human dignity."[50] This foundational legal norm does away ("*Everyone* who works") with any essential reference to citizenship, democratic equality, and other renditions of the employment relationship that depend on membership in the employer's political community.

Minimum wage thus adds poverty as another source of concern (along with accessibility, workplace safety, anti-discrimination, and others), which ought to inform the terms of employment interactions. These concerns apply regardless of the parties' nationalities or democratic loyalties. From a relational justice perspective, the minimum wage should be mandatory even if the employee is a guest worker or some other non-resident alien, typically from a developing country.

Our claim, however, is not limited to the rights of migrant workers. To see that, consider whether the direct transfer of state funds to employees could render sweatshop-based employment just or even merely legitimate. We do not think so since sweatshops undermine relational justice in ways that cannot be laundered by state efforts to achieve (distributive) justice.[51] Poverty raises a justice concern with a relational twist—it is not only about the "total income of the least advantaged (wages plus transfers)."[52] Rather, poverty picks out the terms of the *employment* interaction because such terms ought to reflect reciprocal respect for the self-determination and substantive equality of the interacting parties.

Because the poverty to which relational justice responds is social exclusion rather than merely material destitution, the appropriate level of minimum wage must be sufficiently attentive to the socio-economic context in which the employment interaction takes place. On the employee's side, a unitary, nationwide minimum wage might fail to provide an adequate floor for employees facing unusually high costs of living due to their place of residence.[53] On the employer's side, a unitary minimum wage may inflict a substantially different economic burden depending, in part, on the employer's overall financial resources.

Relational justice provides the justification and the theoretical framework for assessing what should count as a minimum. The actual math depends on the circumstances of the particular society and, if necessary, locality. Adjusting minimum wage to reflect these two relational justice concerns, however, must be consistent with rule of law commitments to provide effective guidance to employers and constrain the discretionary powers of public officials in charge of the regulation, enforcement, and adjudication of minimum wage matters. Failing that, structural accommodation in the form of a floor would effectively collapse into employers tailoring their accommodation duties ad hoc.[54]

The Home: Warranty of Habitability

A warranty of habitability in residential leases obligates landlords to keep the tenancy premises safe and livable at all times.[55] In most states, this warranty is *non*-waivable, which means that the habitability requirement sets a floor to the terms of the landlord/tenant transaction.[56] Although this warranty and the minimum wage laws operate in different interpersonal contexts, the structural similarities between them are significant. Therefore, we will only focus on a few of the warranty's distinctive characteristics.

The warranty of habitability justifiably does not treat the parties as formally equal and free given the qualitative difference between the autonomy interest of landlords (in enhancing their wealth) vis-à-vis that of their tenants (in having a home), the substantive inequality between landlords and tenants resulting from information asymmetries, and the typical gap in resources, experience, and bargaining powers.[57] Yet, the remedy of imposing a non-waivable warranty of habitability has been widely criticized, both for failing (at least in theory) to promote distributive justice and for its inefficiency.[58] On both grounds, the criticism goes, it would be less regressive and more effective for the state to transfer subsidies directly to those in need.[59]

Relational justice provides a freestanding argument—independent of both efficiency and distributive justice concerns—justifying the need for the warranty, including as a duty of the landlord to the tenant. As Joseph Singer observes, this warranty enforces a measure of "fairness," not necessarily in the overall allocation of society's resources but in the "ongoing relationship" between landlords and tenants.[60] A requirement to provide "premises that are safe, clean and fit for human habitation"[61] incorporates a concern for the impact of the tenants' economic predicament on their self-determination because a basic level of healthy and safe living conditions is *crucial* for enjoying meaningful freedom. In that, the warranty also tackles inequality in the landlord/tenant relationship as it addresses a relevant difference in the parties' economic conditions and, to that extent, aspires to treat them as substantively equal.

Basic Products: Price Control

1. Relational Justice and Consumption Goods. After work and home, we turn to basic products. Price regulation of consumption goods has been criticized for generating gross inefficiencies.[62] Exceptionally, however, using a central planning mechanism has been justified as a means for fixing market failures or tackling unusual circumstances created by wars or natural disasters.[63] The introduction of price control at such times is meant to reinstate the competitive prices that would have obtained had the market been operating properly and is justified on welfarist grounds: the loss society incurs due to the inefficient allocation of goods.[64] Whether price regulation is, all things considered, cost-effective hinges on the administrative costs of implementing it compared to alternative mechanisms.

From a relational justice perspective, the case for price regulation is very different, given that it seeks to build accommodation into the terms of market transactions by setting prices' upper limits. This would be the case when the price at which a consumption good is sold might challenge the transaction's congruence with the demands of relational justice, namely when we are dealing with basic goods supplied mainly through markets. Basic goods are, in Adam Smith's terms, non-luxurious goods[65] whose lack leads to poverty—a condition of social exclusion no less than material destitution. Some goods are inevitably basic—staple food, medicine, or clothing. Some goods count as basic in some societies but not in others—consider bicycles in the Netherlands vis-à-vis San Francisco. We will not specify a comprehensive list of them. We will focus instead on the implications of viewing price regulation of basic goods as a structural strategy of accommodation grounded in relational justice.

Charging poor consumers excessively high prices for basic goods sets the terms of the interaction between consumers and providers at odds with the demands of relational justice because affordable vegetables or medicines are crucial for sustaining an active, healthy life conducive to individual autonomy. Affordable prices correct the predicament of poor consumers by allowing them to transact despite their economic vulnerability, thus treating them as substantively equal. Rather than ignoring the impact of this vulnerability imbalance on the interaction with them, this measure seeks to reduce it.

A price control system captures an important element (along with accessibility and other anti-discriminatory provisions) of justice in consumption transactions. By imposing a ceiling, price control provides an indirect means for dealing with the relational injustice resulting from charging excessive prices for basic goods. Substituting the market price with the ceiling makes basic goods more affordable to the poor without forcing providers to face the multidimensional complexity—publicity, hybridity, and fungibility—entailed by the direct strategy of individualized accommodation.

2. Implementation Challenges. Putting a price control scheme into effect poses challenges regarding the basic goods to be included as well as the administrative costs of determining and enforcing the ceiling. The regulator would need to extract credible information about the costs of producing particular goods, including research and development costs, to reach a sensible pricing decision.[66] Moreover, such a decision would need to be periodically reevaluated, as production costs typically vary with changing economic and technological conditions. Substandard exercise of these regulatory tasks is bound to generate inefficient (and possibly regressive) allocation of resources, resulting in supply shortages and black markets.

Faced with this regulatory challenge, should not price control be supplanted by cost-effective means of bringing about affordable prices? This question highlights the distinction between the institutional and moral considerations at play in a comparative assessment of price control versus other alternatives. The most familiar alternative means of ensuring affordable prices takes the form of state subsidies paid directly to consumers. A universal basic income is the most radical example,[67] while a less ambitious scheme is the Supplemental Nutrition and Assistance Program (or SNAP, formerly known as the Food Stamps Program).[68]

One criterion for assessing price control, then, is institutional competence. The administrative costs of running SNAP and other safety net schemes may be higher or lower than implementing a price control system. Systems can also differ in the cross-subsidies and incentives triggered by each of them. Any adequate comparison will turn on fact-dependent variables, which will likely diverge across contexts (as there are different markets for different basic goods in different societies and under different sets of legal and extra-legal governing rules). The most we can say on the institutional competence front is that price control schemes are up and running without necessarily causing recurring supply shortages or black markets.

The UK's schemes for state "control of maximum prices to be charged for any medical supplies" is a case in point.[69] Through these schemes, the state (by negotiating with the industry or by operation of the law) becomes the price setter for prescription branded medicines.[70] The recently enacted Inflation Reduction Act requires the Centers for Medicare and Medicaid Services to negotiate the prices of certain prescription drugs.[71] Another instance is the statutory price control for staple foods (such as eggs, milk, and bread) in force in Israel.[72]

These cases do not imply that price control is overall the most efficient and distributively just way of ensuring affordable prices for basic goods. Indeed, direct subsidies are held to be more efficient than price control,[73] whose role in the fair redistribution of resources among consumers remains unclear. On the one hand, both the poor and the rich enjoy the same affordable prices for basic goods, and on the other, the rich may be paying higher prices for luxurious goods to compensate for the revenue lost in the sale of basic goods. The institutional assessment of price control versus direct state subsidies to consumers, therefore, remains undecided.[74]

Beyond the institutional dimension, however, a non-contingent consideration is at the moral center of the relational justice case for price control of basic goods—who is responsible for accommodating the poor? Price control implements the relational justice idea of *private* responsibility for it. Identifying sellers and manufacturers as legally responsible for accommodating the consumers' poverty by selling their products at controlled prices does not address the question of cost allocation—who should pay the bill? (the providers' shareholders, their employees, the consumers of other products they sell who end up cross-subsidizing these, and so forth). Nor does it rule out direct subsidies, safety net programs, and other welfare state interventions (including anti-trust law). Instead, the argument is that it is (in part) the moral obligation of providers to accommodate poor consumers in connection with the sale of basic goods. Price control is the legal doctrine that enables—at least in some cases—the shift from the justice to the legality of accommodating the poor.

The Credit Market: Creditworthiness and Usury Laws

1. Credit for Substantively Free and Equal Persons. Our final case study involves the credit market. An accessible credit market is vital for many life projects. For many people, a good life involves a variety of credit transactions for purchasing housing and cars, covering unexpected expenses, paying tuition, or pursuing a business plan. In all of them, the credit market hinders the poor in three fundamental ways: first, poverty may lead lenders to decline loan applications; second, in approved applications, poverty may adversely affect interest charges; and third, debt collection can be devastating to the already poor as well as sink others into poverty.[75] We leave the third for another occasion.[76]

Those who identify poverty with distributive injustice may wish to resort to a public provision of fair access to credit either directly—by the government granting credit to the poor or fully guaranteeing loans obtained from private lenders—or indirectly—by subsidizing the voluntary participation of private creditors in the provision of fair access to credit. These methods relieve private creditors of the duty to accommodate the poverty of borrowers and, instead, single out the state as responsible for meeting the demands of distributive justice. These public measures, though noteworthy, are insufficient because poverty also has an irreducibly relational dimension.

Accommodating the poor in the credit market can, and should, be a matter of private responsibility as well. Private creditors are not mere vessels for the state to provide funds to the poor. Rather, fair access to credit, like fair physical access to banks and other financial institutions, should inform the determination of just terms of interaction between private creditors and would-be borrowers.

One case—obtaining a new line of credit for small businesses—will serve to illustrate the relational justice approach to accommodating the poor in the credit market.[77] We begin by noting that the inadequacy of financial resources is a primary cause of business failure—initial capitalization, survival of newly emerging businesses, economic growth, and innovation are influenced at every turn by the availability of credit.[78] The Community Reinvestment Act is a major legal attempt to provide incentives to banks and thrifts to increase the supply of credit to small businesses and home mortgages in low and medium-income communities.[79] Compliance is beneficial for lenders because regulators can take it into account when called to approve mergers and acquisitions or when facing requests to open or close bank branches.[80]

2. Accessible Credit and Relational Justice. As was true in our previous case studies, the two most common reasons used to justify the Act's incentivizing mechanism—correcting for market failures and promoting distributive justice—are controversial.[81] Concerning efficiency, it is unclear that the credit market for low-income people suffers from pervasive market failure.[82] If it does, it is unclear why banks and thrifts (as opposed to public provision of direct subsidy and other grassroots initiatives) should be singled out.[83] Concerning distributive justice, it is again unclear why private banks and thrifts, as such and when compared to other financial market participants who are not subject to this Act, should be encouraged to make potentially unprofitable and risky lending decisions.[84]

Whereas advocates of efficiency and distributive justice often fault the Community Reinvestment Act for imposing unnecessary or undesirable responsibility on the lenders it covers, relational justice views this Act as imposing too little. To begin with, the scope of the Act is limited to certain depository institutions (FDIC-insured banks and thrifts) with physical presence through branches, excluding non-banks and digital banking.[85] More critically, denying loan applications because of the applicants' poverty is permissible.[86]

By contrast, relational justice requires that, like the prohibition of the Equal Credit Opportunity Act (ECOA) on discrimination against lenders based on their traits,[87] standard creditworthiness should set poverty aside. Negatively, poverty should carry no weight in deciding whether to accept a loan application, and affirmatively, creditworthiness should be assessed solely by reference to the strength of the applicant's business plan. For instance, an application for a new line of credit for operating a food truck should be assessed according to the economic prospects of this business in the context and circumstances of its planned surroundings, regardless of the applicant's low socio-economic status. It is an "ought" grounded in (relational) justice rather than in the economics of determining creditworthiness.

Our claims relate to loan request decisions, but, in principle, they should also apply to another crucial aspect of credit transactions, namely, interest rates. Effective usury laws, rather than mere inefficient relics of ancient religious traditions,[88] can find liberal grounds in relational justice and gain appropriate legal recognition as a private law ceiling.[89]

3. *What about Creditworthiness?* At first glance, the imposition of relational justice constraints on creditworthiness standards and interest rate charges may appear as simply an extension of the anti-discrimination provisions of the ECOA.[90] Yet, unlike race, marital status, and other grounds cited in the ECOA list, a condition of poverty might prove crucial in underwriting for the small businesses' credit market. A small business requires a personal guarantee from the owner-borrower since the business is new and may be lacking in assets. Lenders will then need a creditworthiness assessment of the individual's wealth, and poverty will likely adversely affect the ability to secure a loan.[91] A legal duty to set poverty aside when determining creditworthiness and interest rates can be genuinely costly, eating away the creditors' profit and increasing the costs of borrowing to others.

Should this strong correlation between poverty and credit risk discourage accommodation in the interactions prevailing in small-businesses or similar credit transactions? We say no, since no *justice*-based reason distinguishes poverty from other traits or social conditions requiring accommodation in credit markets and elsewhere. A duty of reasonable accommodation of a physical disability is also likely to be costly to the accommodating entity and its non-disabled clients and employees. However, this fact alone does not release one from the duty. Indeed, the ambition of justice demands, relational justice demands included, is to determine whose responsibility it is to act in a certain way even, and especially, when this way can be costly.

And yet, as already noted, there is and must be an upper limit to the cost of accommodation reflecting the basic commitment of relational justice to respect the self-determination and substantive equality of the duty-ower as well. As we have reiterated, ensuring such a limit is not only compatible with relational justice but also required by it. The implication is that the duty to accommodate poverty in the credit market should apply only to lenders who are sufficiently big to bear the cost without it impinging on their self-determination.

Indeed, the Community Reinvestment Act distinguishes between large, intermediate, and small-size lenders, accordingly adjusting the demands it places on them.[92] This limit may also imply that, even regarding these lenders, the state should provide tax incentives or other publicly funded benefits to ameliorate possible hardship, perhaps stepping in by guaranteeing small businesses' loans as well as depositing more of its funds in small banks to boost their capital and thus their lending capabilities.[93] Similar refinements apply regarding accommodation duties pertaining to physical disability.[94] Implementing these and other mechanisms can support a relationally just law of credit transactions without determinations of creditworthiness and interest rates excluding loan-seekers simply because of their social condition of poverty.

15
Beyond Borders

Setting the Stage

Over twenty years ago, Pfizer sought to gain the approval of the Food and Drug Administration (FDA) for the use of a new antibiotic (Trovan) on children. Allegedly, Pfizer tested the drug on Nigerian children without securing their or their guardians' informed consent and without disclosing or explaining to them the study's experimental nature or the serious risks involved. These involuntary medical experimentations were conducted in concert with Nigerian government officials and arguably caused the death of eleven children, leaving many others blind, deaf, paralyzed, or brain damaged.[1]

These circumstances typify our increasingly globalized environment, where horizontal (interpersonal) transnational interactions play a significant role. While many of these interactions are appropriate—they are not unjust and can enhance the autonomy or well-being of all participants—others are troublesome and, at times, even morally illegitimate. Indeed, the *Pfizer* case is merely one example of a grievance against private transnational actors, a category at the focus of this chapter. Two other examples of similar types of high-stakes grievances are the sub-standard employment practices in countries like China, Bangladesh, or Indonesia and the recent land grabs in several countries, notably in Sub-Saharan Africa.

The globalization of mass production entails many valuable by-products, and boosting the economy of some developing countries is among its most significant ones. The extensive use of foreign contractors, agents, or partners by Western manufacturing companies also implies sweatshops characterized by "deplorable working conditions that include low pay and long working days, unhealthy and unsafe conditions and a regime entailing elements of force and degradation."[2] Specifically, these sweatshops do not comply with minimum labor standards regarding issues like forced labor, labor discrimination, workplace health and safety, wage minimums, hour-caps, and freedom of association.[3] Moreover, workers are often "foreclosed from seeking relief in countries where they have been trafficked or exploited," since some of those countries "have poor, corrupt judicial systems, frequently with complicit government officials."[4]

Like the globalization of manufacturing, foreign direct investment in developing countries is largely a positive, indeed crucial, component. But again, it sometimes entails pitfalls that impose substantial, unjustified harm on individuals and communities alike. Consider the recent predicament of members

Relational Justice. Hanoch Dagan and Avihay Dorfman, Oxford University Press. © Hanoch Dagan and Avihay Dorfman 2024.
DOI: 10.1093/9780191987762.003.0015

of many rural communities, especially in developing countries, whose access to land for shelter, growing food, and drawing water is threatened by transfers of lands that they improved, which are constitutive of their personal and communal identities.[5] As one report attests, in many of these large-scale land acquisitions, "those who are selling or leasing land are not the ones who are actually using it," a situation that often generates displacements.[6] Indeed, many of these large-scale land transfers are often subject to severe problems due to the capture and unrepresentativeness of local elites and/or governments "effectively unaccountable to their people."[7]

In states with weak private law institutions, corporations and other private actors are not held accountable for grave violations of fundamental private rights of persons. This is a matter of growing international concern, given the prevailing consensus that our present system faces difficulties addressing grave transnational wrongs and that remedying this plight is vital and urgent. The current efforts in this direction are hindered by the effects of bilateral investment treaties and other obstacles dealing with jurisdiction and sovereign immunity, as well as by an actual conceptual obstacle.

We begin with the two main legal strategies, respectively, in public and private international law, that apply to these concerns. Both seek to adjust the legal regime governing transnational interactions to an environment where the international human rights traditionally conceived as our rights as citizens against our states are increasingly threatened by private actors on whom we are increasingly dependent. Whereas one strategy extends state obligations under human rights law to some non-state actors, the other adapts traditional private international law doctrines, notably its public policy exception.[8]

Extending Vertical Rights to Non-State Actors?

Many human rights lawyers seeking to address grave transnational wrongs beyond the state focus on the extension of individual rights from the vertical dimension—as rights against the state—to the horizontal dimension, where they operate at the interpersonal level. These efforts often piggyback on the domestic laws of some jurisdictions that follow the model of the good citizen (discussed in Chapter 2) and conceptualize constitutional and human rights as fundamental to "the whole legal system including private law enacted by the State."[9]

Some instances of this direction are now commonplace. These aspects, dealing with war crimes like torture or genocide, emerged from the prosecution of Nazi Germany leaders in the Nuremberg trials.[10] In the contemporary context, however, where transnational interpersonal wrongs assume forms that fall outside the (rightly delimited) scope of the international criminal law framework now emerging, attempts to go further abound.

These attempts have culminated (for now) in the "Protect, Respect and Remedy" framework for business and human rights that was presented by the UN Secretary-General Special Representative John Ruggie and unanimously endorsed by the Human Rights Council. The core challenge it addresses is to "reduce or compensate for the governance gaps created by globalization," which derive from the fact that host States of transnational firms—particularly if they are developing countries—may either "lack the institutional capacity to enforce national laws" or "may feel constrained from doing so by having to compete internationally for investment." In turn, these firms' home States "may be reluctant to regulate against overseas harm by these firms . . . out of concern that those firms might lose investment opportunities or relocate their headquarters."[11] Hence, the three "core principles" of this framework are: (1) "the State duty to protect against human rights abuses by third parties, including businesses," through appropriate policies, regulation, and adjudication; (2) "the corporate responsibility to respect human rights"; and (3) "the need for more effective access to remedies," both judicial and non-judicial.[12]

We are concerned with the second principle, which means that business enterprises should act with due diligence "to avoid infringing" the "internationally recognized human rights" of others and should take "adequate measures" to prevent, mitigate, and, where appropriate, remediate "adverse human rights impacts with which they are involved."[13] This principle is further elaborated in the framework's guidelines. It has only been recognized—at least so far—in soft law instruments so that failure to meet this responsibility to respect human rights can "subject companies to the court of public opinion."[14] The framework, however, has been "endorsed or employed by individual governments, business enterprises and associations, civil society and workers' organizations, national human rights institutions, and investors."[15]

This extension of internationally recognized human rights to these corporations and, more broadly, to the horizontal dimension is normatively attractive. If human rights' "overriding aim is to protect the victim's dignity, then that victim has to be protected from everyone, state and non-state actors" alike, and it does not matter "whether the actor has public functions, is financed by the state, or is simply a private individual."[16] This intuition is particularly acute in our era, when "the interests protected by constitutional and human rights are becoming just as vulnerable to private agents as to states," given the role of these agents in social life and their "growing impact on the lives of individuals."[17]

Although the intuition of extending international human rights law to private actors is widely shared among many non-governmental organizations (NGOs) and academic writers, it is less certain "how human rights law, traditionally aimed at states, might be translated to the [horizontal] context."[18] Hugh Collins refines the "hardest and most intractable challenge" of this path as "the problem of identifying appropriate duty-bearers": "the project for the alignment of private law with fundamental rights" that has been "traditionally regarded" to apply only "to relations between the citizen and the state," "presents no obvious candidates for restrictions on who may be selected as duty-bearers."[19] This difficulty in transplanting public rights onto private law is emblematic of the good citizen model, which is inevitably limited in its ability to respond to private law's key challenge of "Why me?"

Adjusting Conflicts of Law Rules?

Private international lawyers also seek ways of addressing grave transnational wrongs, and many of the challenges they face involve jurisdiction, but our focus is on conflict of laws rules. While seemingly technical, private international law was always mindful of the concern that "blind adherence to foreign law"[20] might entail results that "violate fundamental principles of justice," and carved out to the forum's comity a public policy exception targeting such "pernicious and detestable" cases.[21] But this exception's inherent features—its focus on incompatibility with *domestic* principles, its role as a shield rather than a source for substantive norms, and its "limit of comity" foundation that implies both caution from interfering with foreign politics and an emphasis on the link between the forum and the facts of the case[22]—makes its potential use for the task at hand very limited.

The notion of *transnational* public policy is more helpful. Increasingly present in the jurisprudence of international arbitration tribunals, this notion relies on the shared values of the international community and is supposed to function as a sword, too.[23] Closely aligned to it is the gradual evolution, especially in Europe, of "'internationally mandatory rules'—rules that are deemed to be applicable in specific legal relationships" within "domains such as international labor law[,] . . . international tort law[,] or international contract law" aimed at "the protection of the weak party," irrespective of the applicable law that customarily governs the pertinent legal relationship.[24]

Alas, like public international law, private international law is not free from difficulties, two of which are particularly relevant here. *First,* transnational public policy is supposed to be shared by the "international community," but this community sometimes "seems to denote the international community of states in the public international law sense of the word, sometimes it describes legal concepts shared by different legal systems, and sometimes it refers to the values of 'international commerce.'"[25] This difficulty is not merely an epistemic problem—how to fill out the details of the law at issue—but a cue to the absence of an elaborate theory (as opposed to bare intuitions) of what this law is.

The public policy exception seemingly points—as its name suggests—mainly to the *collective* goals of a specific jurisdiction or of the world community. Thus, reliance on transnational public policy is typically denoted by reference to public international law and regarding topics like the protection of cultural goods, the sale and traffic of drugs, arms traffic between private persons, bribery, corruption, slavery, and embargoes of economic sanctions.[26] Commentators also refer to the "role of transnational public policy . . . in respect of human rights" as well as to the incorporation of a "universal notion of 'good morals' or elementary contractual morality."[27] These references echo prior use of the traditional doctrine of public policy as a means for the protection of human rights and as an anti-discrimination device[28] that, at least partly, also seems to motivate the evolution of internationally mandatory rules.[29]

Though appealing, this approach also raises a familiar difficulty: justifying (and thus guiding) the adjustment of the doctrines of private international law to extend our vertical rights to non-state actors hinges on addressing the missing link of privity. Without horizontal grounds for putative defendants' obligations, the problem of privity is bound to reemerge.

Interpersonal Human Rights

1. A Floor of Just Relationships. We hold that relational justice theory provides the key to this missing link. Transnational law scholars are likely to be skeptical about this direction. Since they often see private law as the part of law most resistant to the demands of interpersonal claims and perceive it as essentially national, private law seems particularly inapt for addressing *trans*national injustices. For them, therefore, private law is part of the problem and thus a dubious candidate for providing a solution.[30]

As should by now be clear to readers of this book, however, the conclusion that we should give up on any potential contribution from private law is both unwarranted and unfortunate. It is unwarranted because private law is neither essentially libertarian nor essentially statist, and it is unfortunate because the justice of private law—in sharp contrast to conventional wisdom—has an indispensable role to play in properly addressing transnational wrongs.

The interpersonal obligations at the core of relational justice theory are fundamentally non-statist. Therefore, it is apt to refer to their most basic instantiations as interpersonal *human* rights. Distilling a set of interpersonal human rights—the core and minimal obligations of relational justice—highlights the privity lacking in the existing frameworks. Indeed, the notion of interpersonal human rights captures a *direct* obligation rather than one we owe as subcontractors (executive agents or good citizens) acting on behalf of the polity as a whole.[31] This notion is particularly suited to our time, when so many of our private law interactions take place across, rather than within, national borders.

A discussion of private law as encapsulating interpersonal human rights may be expected to follow in the long tradition of natural lawyers who present its building blocks as the pre-political baseline of our social contract that, as such, sets the bounds of its legitimate demands.[32] Our path is different. As noted, we repudiate any attempt to naturalize private law.[33] So, we acknowledge the suspicions toward views (such as ours) that attempt to sever the allegedly conceptual link between private law and the commands issued by the sovereign state, which prescribes a particular (i.e., contingent) set of interpersonal obligations conventionally described as private law.[34] Furthermore, we do not deny the contingency of some subsets of private law.

Differences, maybe even significant ones, can exist between domestic laws—for instance, must liability for defective products be strict or fault-based? But the basic prescriptions of private law—such as the injunction not to wrong one another, to keep the promises we make to one another, or to respect each other's property rights—do not depend upon our status as members of a given political community. A risk-creator, for example, is generally required to discharge the same amount of care—or, more precisely, some minimally required amount of care—irrespective of the risk-taker's membership in a political community. Grounding this duty of care in one's civic obligations would misleadingly imply that the wrong done by its breach is fundamentally disrespecting another's privileged status of national citizenship (or residency). At least morally, the same obligation should apply if the risk-creator was acting in a stateless soil inhabited by temporary visitors.

The significance of the minimal requirements enshrined in private law does not turn on the whims of the positivist lawmaker of any state in particular. *Any* humanist polity has a compelling reason to acknowledge these obligations and the rights they vindicate.[35] The relationships private law governs are not mediated *via* the state, and their significance does not rely on their aggregate consequences. Since a significant part of private law's normative weight has nothing to do with our relationship with or through the state, the content of private law's *core* normative foundations is not tied to national legal systems and, instead, transcends the contingency of its positive instantiations. Therefore, these normative foundations that, as we argue in this book, echo (in their best version) the liberal commitment to reciprocal respect for self-determination and substantive equality, can and should take a center stage in the conceptualization of our interpersonal human rights.

2. The Role of the State. As expected, the state is the obvious locus for translating these normative commitments into legal prescriptions. Even in the present era of increasing transnational interconnectivity, the state largely remains "the most comprehensive legally-based social organization of the day."[36] Moreover, despite the normative attractions of cosmopolitanism, we still appreciate the role of sub-global units—which are currently organized geographically and known as states—as *loci* of "coercively imposed collective authority."[37]

There are two dimensions to this role. First, states enjoy significant comparative advantages—in terms of both legitimacy and competence—in performing the necessary tasks of elaborating, implementing, and enforcing interpersonal rights and obligations. This dimension is practically significant but conceptually contingent: it always depends on the calculus of the comparative advantages of the pertinent state and certain non-state institutions.[38]

The second dimension of the states' unique role is constitutive and implies that our theory of interpersonal human rights neither "targets" the state nor ousts public values or the common good from the domain of private law.[39] The commitment to individual self-determination and substantive equality that informs our theory emphatically rejects any vision of a minimal, let alone dispensable, state.

Insisting on people's rights and states' obligations should not be confused with the denigration of states. States are here to stay, which may be a good idea given the vital role they can play in upholding and enhancing people's self-determination and substantive equality. We do not claim that citizenship is only instrumental, nor do we suggest that the public-cum-political dimensions of our existence are normatively inferior to the private-cum-horizontal dimensions: citizenship may be intrinsically valuable, as may also be the pursuit of public and political roles. The robustness of citizenship is precisely why, even though vertical human rights aim in their spirit to enhance and sustain the interpersonal and civic dimensions, their form and substance are quite different from what we call interpersonal human rights. The significance of citizenship also explains the states' interest in prescribing the terms of transnational encounters that involve their citizens or residents or that affect them (or are likely to affect them) in some other way, such as encounters that happen within their boundaries.

Specifically, as noted throughout, there are various equally legitimate ways of complying with relational justice, even in its minimal rather than inspirational interpretation. Contextual considerations pertaining to a polity's legal tradition, institutional design, and economic, social, cultural, and environmental circumstances, as well as democratic choices—all count.[40] States can and should legitimately adjust their private law schemes to serve distributive justice, democratic citizenship, and well-being, in addition to the core concern of securing minimal interpersonal justice. Their choices on these fronts are likely to affect, as discussed above,[41] the proper way of implementing relational justice in private law.

Finally, the horizontal obligations that correlate with interpersonal human rights are neither meant to nor can supplant the potentially more demanding public obligations of co-citizenship. Thus, domestic private law may express civic solidarity in excess (but not in lieu) of the solidarity prescribed by the minimal cosmopolitan requirement of interpersonal human rights.[42]

3. *The Limit of States' Authority.* That said, if the worry that the concept of interpersonal human rights targets the state suggests that we think that the state's legitimate political authority must be premised on the same humanist infrastructure on which our theory of private law is founded, we plead guilty as charged. The right of collective self-determination on which states' sovereignty relies is premised on the right of self-determination of each member of these collectivities—and both

the powers and the obligations of states must serve people's self-determination and substantive equality. As Evan Fox-Decent claims, the state is an artificial legal person who is duty-bound by human rights due to its relationship to its subjects.[43]

Thus, even in their non-instrumental senses, citizenship and the public dimension of persons' lives should not be understood as competing against people's entitlements to self-determination and substantive equality. This is why, as just noted, state legitimacy depends on its compliance with our vertical human rights,[44] and it is similarly why—given the significance of our interpersonal interactions to our self-determination and substantive equality—state legitimacy also depends on its compliance with our interpersonal human rights.

Just as the traditional understanding of human rights implies that there is a limit to state authority regarding the former type of rights—some rights against the state are beyond its power to abrogate even on behalf of the common good—a humanist framework must acknowledge a core set of interpersonal human rights to which states *must* comply. When a state undermines or fails to fulfill its instrumental role in securing these rights, it can be criticized. Violating our interpersonal human rights should be censured.

Jus Gentium Privatum

1. The Missing Link of Privity. Private law's core prescriptions—our interpersonal human rights—are neither reducible to the dictates of natural law nor do they fully depend on the state for their legitimate existence. Rather, the thin skeleton of private law and its underlying commitment to reciprocal respect for self-determination and substantive equality belong to the *jus gentium*. *Jus gentium* is typified by Jeremy Waldron as a body of principles that can be extracted from the "overlap between the positive laws of particular states" using "a legal sensibility that is both lawyerly and moralized."[45]

Jus gentium, as Waldron explains, focuses on "what humans [have] constructed for themselves" rather than on "the lofty heights of philosophical speculation" but does so "in a moral mode." It "lifts us out of the positivist perspective of a particular legal system" without engaging in the "pure moral philosophy [associated] with natural law,"[46] hence both its limitations and its power. As "noninstitutionalized law," it "has no artillery of its own," but—thanks to its broad positive acceptability—it plays a relatively powerful role in our normative and critical legal thought.[47]

The types of wrongdoing that we classify as violations of interpersonal human rights transcend the particularities of existing legal traditions.[48] At least within a broadly defined humanist framework, which views other cultures and sovereignties as worthy of respect because they play a crucial role in people's lives,[49] the legal treatment of such violations should not be subject to cultural upbringing or other contingent facts about a person's culture. The core set of private law norms is inherently cosmopolitan and should thus be considered applicable to every interpersonal relation, irrespective of the political membership of the parties involved.

Conceiving interpersonal human rights in terms of *jus gentium privatum* provides the missing link of privity needed to complete the important efforts of both public and private international law surveyed above. The Ruggie framework discusses the horizontal duty to respect human rights as a duty that "means not to infringe on the rights of others—put simply, to do no harm."[50] Insofar as this maxim is supposed to rely on our vertical human rights, imposing a burden on a private actor in the name of a right that was originally conceived in vertical terms is not, as noted, an obvious step.

Our account dispenses with the detour because it insists that the obligation is indigenous to private law. Relational justice duties typify law's demands of private individuals in their interpersonal interactions and thus need not rely on the policy or collective goals of any specific jurisdiction. Relational justice theory, therefore, provides a secure baseline for evaluating such encounters in their own terms as a principled framework for the emerging category of transnational wrongs.

Jean Thomas correctly observes that "the moral intuition that something is going very wrong" in the contexts of sweatshops—or of land grabs or involuntary medical experimentations—derives from the fact that "something *is* going wrong and that that thing is much simpler than a failure of constitutional theory: one party is wronging another."[51] The tidiest way of capturing this intuition, then, is to appreciate the deviation of these episodes from the most fundamental imperatives of our private law and analyze them for what they are: infringements of interpersonal human rights. Rather than bypassing private law, transnational lawyers should explore the potential reform of securing the interpersonal justice inherent in private law based on its normative foundation of reciprocal respect for self-determination and substantive equality.[52]

2. The Post-Colonial Worry. The concept of *jus gentium* we rely on is admittedly complicated. Waldron pointedly frames the main concern it raises as "a Scylla and Charybdis situation:" refrain from including "disreputable" legal regimes so as not to reify "the lowest global common denominator" while also being wary of simply "cherry-picking one's consensus." Furthermore, Waldron adds that this "navigation" "needs to be conducted against the background worry about Eurocentrism or white, Anglo-Christian parochialism."[53]

This post-colonial worry seems to be *less* pertinent to our exercise of distilling a minimal core of private law than to a parallel exercise performed in regard to constitutional law or (vertical) human rights law. Thus, for example, given the broad global convergence of the private law injunction against the violation of bodily integrity, immunizing spousal rapes from tort liability is a clear violation of an interpersonal human right. It is hard to imagine a respectable post-colonial critique of the proposition condemning legal systems that apply such a rule.[54]

Our theory of interpersonal human rights may still be viewed as vulnerable to this critique. By marginalizing cultural differences—so the argument goes—our theory objectionably depoliticizes transnational law, leaving no adequate space for contestation. Divergences between systems reflect a reality of irresoluble conflict that neither can nor should be swept away by reference to a perceived common core and must be addressed on what are, ultimately, political grounds.[55]

We are acutely aware of the risks of relying on pseudo-universalist claims that render culturally specific choices essential.[56] It is for this reason that the requirement of space-for-contestation is—as we discuss in the next section—inherent in the architecture of interpersonal human rights. However, neither the risks of disguised parochialism nor the need for careful specification of our interpersonal human rights justifies skepticism. Let us explain.

Our starting point is similar to that of the critics. Lawyers and scholars should treat universalist claims with some suspicion due to the risk of abuse entailed by the misrepresentation of a claim as universalist, which is amply demonstrated in post-colonial scholarship. A further risk, perhaps even more prevalent, lurks in the mistaken and possibly innocent perception of cultural prescriptions as if they reflected moral injunctions. Both reify contingent hegemonic choices as if they were natural or necessary truths, and hermeneutical suspicion is thus justified.

Suspicion, however, should *not* leave us in a helpless relativism. As Isaiah Berlin famously wrote, "Forms of life differ. Ends, moral principles, are many. But not infinitely many: they must be within the human horizon."[57] We thus emphatically reject the claim that, given our conflictual reality, we must give up the "elusive" quest for a common humanist core of universal interpersonal values and, indeed, truths. The effects of political struggles on these topics, at times hotly contested, are undeniable. However, they neither do nor should preclude the political discourse our theory anticipates, one that is unapologetically normative and reason-based.

Sociological suspicion is not synonymous with philosophical skepticism about reason and normativity. Therefore, we find the approach endorsed by some critical legal scholars, characterizing reason as a disciplinary technology and normative analysis as arbitrary power, unacceptable.[58] Not only do these claims imply the dubious meta-ethical positions of relativism, skepticism, or nihilism, but by equating normative reasoning with parochial interests and idiosyncratic perspectives, they also undermine any possibility of moral justification and thus also of moral evaluation and moral criticism. Humanists can and should be open-minded, but they must resist the relativist trap, which paradoxically ends up reaffirming the status quo. The sheer fact that claims of universalism are not always true or that they are subject to substantive disagreement and open to possible abuses does not undermine our responsibility to work for what we hold to be universal rights.

This bracketing of skeptical doubts to allow for both justification and criticism also explains why we opt for a *charitable* moral reading of private law in divergent legal systems. We do not deny the many normative pitfalls of *all* human-made legal systems. As we noted at the outset, however, the idealism of our social world, even if partial and stunted, is often a crucial source of critical engagement.[59] A morally charitable reading of private law enlists the *idealized* picture that these various systems rely upon in the task of refining the minimal requirements of relational justice that all legitimate legal systems should comply with. Thus, rather than engaging in an apologetic exercise that hides prejudice and entrenches parochial practices, our theory marginalizes them and uses their underlying respectable façade, even if hypocritical, as a fruitful source of critical engagement.

Addressing Transnational Wrongs

1. Back to Pfizer. A moral reading of the basic elements of private law in various domestic systems points to a core set of private law norms that are inherently cosmopolitan and should thus be considered applicable to every interpersonal relation, irrespective of the citizenship (or residency) of the parties involved. Unlike traditional human rights, the focus of these norms is horizontal rather than vertical. Unlike traditional private law, they do not purport to set up a full-blown system of rules for interpersonal conduct and coordination. Instead, they aim to prescribe mandatory minimum standards at the global level—a floor that state laws cannot transgress even for the sake of promoting welfare or distributive justice. These interpersonal human rights can thus supply the normative foundation for claims of legal liability that current efforts to address grave transnational wrongs so urgently require.

Consider the *Pfizer* case that opened this chapter. This case was litigated under the Alien Tort Statute (ATS)[60] and resulted in a $75 million settlement after surviving a jurisdictional challenge.[61] The crux of the ATS is indeed jurisdictional and, as such, irrelevant to our topic (unfortunately, since that time, it has also been largely "chipped away" by the Supreme Court[62]). Some of the majority's reasoning in *Pfizer*, however, is still instructive. In its endeavor to comply with the prescriptions of the Supreme Court in an earlier case, the majority made a considerable effort to establish that the defendant's alleged "unspeakable" wrong (conducting nonconsensual medical experimentations on humans) belongs to the particularly "narrow class of international norms for which ATS jurisdiction applies."[63] Three moves are important for our purposes.

The *first*, which typifies every attempt (including ours) to establish a universal principle from a diverse legal record, is to insist that the inquiry should not focus on "each source of law" but assume "a more fulsome and nuanced" nature.[64] The *second* move, which echoes the strategy of extending vertical rights to non-state actors, is to bypass the traditional requirement of state action.[65] *Finally*, and most significantly here, the *Pfizer* court struggled to establish, against a particularly critical dissent,[66] that the norm at issue belongs to customary international law. In other words, the norm is not one in which states are "separately and independently interested" but rather one by which they abide "out of a sense of mutual concern" for its consequences in international affairs.[67]

This last move may have been necessary in the specific context of the ATS, given its nature as a jurisdictional statute. But in other contexts, notably in the framework of the two strategies that we focus on, the notion of interpersonal human rights emerging from the *jus gentium privatum* offers a clearer premise. Indeed, the wrongful interaction between *Pfizer* and its victims is an outright case of battery, widely understood in common law tradition as protecting human dignity.[68] This is an "easy" battery case—deceitfully procuring consent to a medical experiment on vulnerable children can hardly be compatible with respect for these children's dignity (even if doing so were desirable based on a cost–benefit analysis). The *jus gentium privatum* framework calls for holding *Pfizer* liable irrespective of the content of the applicable law, given the widespread prohibition of medical experimentation on non-consenting human subjects. Liability becomes particularly compelling given the even more prevalent and more fundamental private law injunction against the violation of bodily integrity.

There is, however, a practical concern about the substance of transnational tort law that does not show up in *Pfizer*. It arises in connection with our resistance to the reduction of a basic tort such as battery to its positivist instantiations, given that what counts as violating human dignity varies across cultures. In particular, the challenge is to show that fixing the mandatory floor for interpersonal violations of dignity in the context of a transnational tort of battery is no mere theoretical speculation.[69]

Battery gives effect to a norm against offensive and/or harmful contact with another person. The main worry is the substantial cultural variance on what counts as offensive contact. For instance, some U.S. jurisdictions tend to define offensiveness very broadly to capture mere touching unless explicitly or implicitly authorized by the victim.[70] By contrast, the culture in other countries may be less touch-sensitive, and merely touching others might appear innocent, at least when it does not carry sexual connotations or other domination-based implications. Hence, the same conduct, say horseplay, can sometimes receive opposite interpretations—offensive conduct and friendly gesture, respectively. Cultural variance of this sort seems to indicate that a transnational tort of battery must not take sides in the debate, and there is no compelling reason for imposing one cultural outlook on the entire world.[71]

Deference to cultural variance, however, must not engulf the commitment of the *jus gentium privatum* to the dignity of persons, whatever their cultural upbringing. The interpersonal human rights paradigm implies that persons possess the ultimate standing over whether and under what terms others may use their bodies, given that the notion of relating to one another as equal and self-determining agents without securing this standing makes no sense. Torture, rape, abuse, and other harsh deprivations of bodily integrity are thus clear instances of cultural variance bearing no weight (including as cultural defense). The duty against committing (transnational) battery does not owe its very existence or significance to the institutional mechanisms that deal with its violations. Just like our familiar vertical universal human rights, our interpersonal human rights know no boundaries and cannot be domestically ignored.

2. *Hard Cases and Space for Contestation.* The more difficult questions lie between core violations of dignity and more peripheral cases of (genuinely) innocent touching. Drawing the precise fault line requires extensive deliberations across different societies and discourses (academic, political, cultural et alia) in light of actual cases and changing circumstances. This way of proceeding is an asset rather than a liability for our account.

To see why, consider the obvious institutional vacuum we operate against in this chapter, which we have thus far ignored. We do know that law is institutionally instantiated (this was, recall, one of our main points in Chapter 4). Yet, we insist throughout this book that private law's core primary claim-rights and their correlative duties precede, conceptually and normatively, the institutions and procedures aimed at enforcing them. We have reiterated this issue in the domestic context—tort law, we claimed, is not reducible to the contemporary law of tort remedy, litigation, or civil recourse more generally, and the same point is widely familiar in the context of international law, including the body of law pertaining to vertical human rights.

In many contexts, it seems appropriate to begin theorizing about law with institutions and procedures and only then move on to discuss substance. But this sequence is not one of necessity or pure logic and can, therefore, be reversed.[72] Substance may precede institutions when a growing awareness of a substantive body of law pushes toward increasingly robust institutional venues and procedural paths. We need not belabor the point, well familiar to international lawyers, that extra-legal institutions, not to mention resort to hard and soft laws, may sometimes prove consequential to preventing and rectifying flagrant human rights violations. Naming transnational wrongs as interpersonal human rights violations is not an inconsequential academic maneuver.[73]

Nothing in these observations suggests that some enforcement mechanisms are not important. Indeed, they are required as the law's *fallback plan*—a derivative mechanism—in case the primary duties of respect prescribed by transnational private law have been compromised or neglected by their addressees. We do acknowledge that imagining international mechanisms for the best instantiation of interpersonal human rights—be it by extending the jurisdiction of existing fora or by forming new ones—is not easy. (As we write, the closest attempt is probably the human rights due diligence directive proposal in the European Union,[74] which may be thought of as the transnational wrongs analogous to the OSHA regime discussed in Chapter 12.[75]) But other, less ambitious, instantiations of the idea behind these mechanisms are not necessarily utopian.

This institutional conundrum brings us back to the challenge of embracing suspicion and critical thinking while rejecting relativism—the former challenge may be conducive to addressing the latter. In other words, the default institutional case of relegating to domestic courts the task of developing the universal norms of interpersonal human rights, though obviously less than optimal, may turn out to be beneficial in at least one important respect.

At its best, a process of shaping the content of the transnational tort by a range of national courts may prompt a broad and respectful dialogue among jurists seeking to distill the universal core of interpersonal human rights from their own diverse, though not chaotic, sets of domestic private law.[76] This process may help to foster a *horizontal*-rights-consciousness in the participants.[77] Translating the abstract imperatives of our interpersonal human rights into concrete cases may well benefit from a multicultural dialogue that can also serve as a crucial means for addressing legitimate concerns of parochialism.[78] It may unleash a process that "reconciles" the dichotomy of "raising and lowering a post-colonial red flag."[79]

3. Sweatshops. This process may be important even in what, here and now, seem to be easy cases. We do not aim, here or in general, to produce a comprehensive code of the norms that make up the *jus gentium privatum* of interpersonal human rights. Nor do we argue that the notion of interpersonal human rights provides a magic formula. Our account is admittedly preliminary and is offered as a call for academic and public discourse rather than a suggestion for its conclusion. Yet, it may be helpful to conclude by briefly addressing one of the other cases we mentioned at the outset—employment relations in developing countries—to demonstrate how relational justice theory can make a difference in pertinent contemporary debates.[80]

Considerations of distributive justice and welfare can sometimes counsel against foreign interference in the employment law regimes in developing countries, the idea being that having substandard employment relations is better than no employment at all (with the resulting adverse consequences of poverty, hunger, and poor health).[81] To the extent that these considerations have some merit in some (though not all) cases, the notion of relational justice provides a powerful counterforce.

Relational justice constrains how far, if at all, employment relations can be undermined for the sake of advancing distributive justice and aggregate welfare. It does so, as usual, by adding another dimension of justice to the equation: the relationship between employer and employee—as discussed in Chapters 12 and 14—can be a source of concern and value quite apart from its effects on society (or the world) as a whole. Like other (vertical) human rights, the notion of interpersonal human rights implies that the subordination of individual rights to collective concerns, however significant, has a limit.

Accordingly, the construction of the powers, rights, and duties that define the employment relationship cannot ignore considerations of interpersonal equality and autonomy.[82] This point is critical beyond the level of legal analysis in that it provides the normative foundations—the naming, as it were—that employees can draw upon in their struggle for fair terms of employment. This approach brings home the widely shared intuition that the infamous phenomenon of sweatshops amounts to a transnational wrong, that is, a *horizontal* human rights violation.

The next stage of this argument will focus on determining the threshold standard that employment relations cannot go below. Again, some cases are easily identifiable—exposing an employee to a life-threatening workplace environment is a good example. Others, such as cases involving forced labor and flagrant workplace discrimination, also fall in this category. Moving beyond the easy cases category, however, proves more challenging in both theory and practice.[83] As was true of the transnational tort of battery, setting the appropriate employment relation standard raises factual and normative questions best left to multicultural dialogue, social movements, and political forces to articulate the precise contours of our interpersonal human rights. Yet, showing that obligations of reciprocal respect for self-determination and substantive equality are endogenous to the interpersonal relationship may serve as a powerful counterargument to attempts to evade interpersonal responsibility.[84]

Part V

Conclusion

16
The Promise of Private Law

Private law is all-pervasive, and our daily life unfolds within it. Since antiquity, every society has had a set of rules explicitly or implicitly prescribing the terms of interpersonal interactions in the many settings where people encounter one another: the neighborhood, the workplace, the market, the road, the great outdoors, and more. Specifics may vary dramatically across time and space, but the fundamental question of what our rights are, which then dictates what we owe one another, remains intact. This is a question for private law to address, and it inevitably does.[1]

Different private law regimes have offered different answers to this perennial question. At times, this variety derives from necessary—and desirable—contextual and democratic inputs. In other (hopefully rare) cases, the rules of private law undermine interpersonal human rights and, as discussed above, should be handled as such. The role of private law theory, however, is not exhausted by the—important, we insist—elucidation of the rights that domestic lawmakers must respect.

Private law theory is responsible for reconstructing the language and developing the normative resources that the architects of various private laws, as well as the people meant to live by them, use when discussing what private law is or how it should be applied, interpreted, or reformed.[2] Since private law cannot be exempted from this responsibility, escaping it or sidelining its core normative commitments is not an option.

Some critics of the dominant schools of private law theory chose the escape route, and their disappointment led them to see private law as a necessary foe.[3] We share these critics' worries and, consequently, devoted many of the preceding pages to refining the failings of the dominant (both traditionalist and economic) conceptions of private law and to criticize private law rules that are indeed indefensible. Yet, it is vital to preserve the distinction between these contingent conceptions and rules and private law as a normative idea.

This book can be read as an argument against those who criticize private law by essentializing normatively unacceptable rules and conceptions, thus further reifying them. Our argument offers critics an alternative and more promising path: reforming private law by emphasizing a commitment to justice. In some measure, this commitment is already latent in private law, but the theories that govern the contemporary discourse on private law have marginalized it.

This alternative approach to private law doctrines can prove crucial for meaningful social reform. Moreover, reviving private law theory along these lines is not

Relational Justice. Hanoch Dagan and Avihay Dorfman, Oxford University Press. © Hanoch Dagan and Avihay Dorfman 2024.
DOI: 10.1093/9780191987762.003.0016

fully fungible with legal reforms oriented by public law, given the role of private law in causing or addressing unjust *pre*-distribution, namely, the structural injustices ingrained in our social and economic fabric.

Whereas these critics attempt to escape private law, some of its current American friends seeking to resuscitate it against "a backdrop of scholarly disinterest [of] nearly a century"[4] choose the other route—sidelining its core normativity. We obviously share the revitalization impetus of this "New Private Law" scholarship as well as its typical "desire to illuminate private law with theory without thereby reducing law to some other subject or discipline."[5] What we find worrisome is its tendency to stop short of appealing to normative foundations, most prominently evident in civil recourse theory.[6]

When supplemented with proper normative foundations, civil recourse and other insights of this body of literature may indeed be important, as our qualified endorsement of the value of personal rights of action demonstrates.[7] But the attempt to sideline this normativity, at times under the guise of a seemingly prosaic and normatively thin reference to coordination as the mission of private law,[8] may end up in a troublesome quietism. Coordination and similar public goals might be attained, possibly even more successfully, by new technological or other means. Taking private law seriously, by contrast, requires focusing on its core normative backbone—to wit, constructing just frameworks for interpersonal interaction.

Relational justice theory takes on this challenge, claiming that these frameworks must be shaped by the liberal commitment to reciprocal respect for the self-determination and substantive equality of the people interacting as private persons.

Relational justice theory is also responsive to some of the significant changes that private law has undergone in response to momentous shifts in our social and economic life. While industrialization and urbanization exacerbated the challenges posed by our interdependence, they also brought about new legal techniques for ensuring just interpersonal relationships, such as the worker compensation schemes and the safety and health regulations discussed in Chapter 12. In turn, the civil rights revolution implies that legally structured frameworks in the shape of contract, property, and tort laws sanctioning disrespect for people's self-determination and substantive equality are no longer acceptable.

Relational justice theory shows that the normative insight of the civil rights revolution, stating that we must "move beyond formal freedom to real-world justice,"[9] is vital not only for public law but just as crucial for private law. Relational justice theory also demonstrates that the new institutional means—notably, regulation in all its forms—can and should be seamlessly integrated into the more traditional fabric of private law once private law is properly conceptualized.

* * *

We defined our task in this book as the sympathetic reconstruction of existing private law, that is, the reconstruction of private law in a modern, industrialized society committed to human rights and personal liberties. Our starting point is unashamedly normative, and thus, we acknowledged that relational justice theory could fail in this interpretive task. When evaluating the success of a legal theory vis-à-vis its competitors, one should examine not only its ability to make sense of important aspects of the existing doctrine but also the significance and normative urgency of its recommended reforms. But reconstruction, even if radical, must have sufficient interpretive credentials. Therefore, we stated at the outset that, should relational justice theory fail at this task, we would settle for the consolation price of persuading readers to join us in endorsing it as a key source for *external* criticism of the law.

We hold that, fortunately, it has not failed—quite the contrary. The commitment of contemporary (American) law to relational justice that we demonstrated in Part III is already prominent in an increasingly large segment of existing private law. A broad set of rules across private law's most traditional doctrines that competing theories struggle with—from negligence, nuisance, and tort remedies law, through the various doctrines governing formation, performance, and breach of contract, up to mistaken payments law and other restitutionary doctrines—are directly accounted for by recourse to relational justice.

Improved understanding of the "is" of the law is intrinsically valuable. With understanding, however, comes responsibility. If we are correct in our choice of normatively fixed points that guide the extended reflective equilibrium exercise in Part III, relational justice theory should also guide the "ought" of private law. Specifically, the reform proposals we discussed in these pages, as well as others that can be gleaned from an analysis of doctrines we did not cover,[10] must be treated as *necessary* corrections of private law in its own *internal* terms. That aspect of relational justice theory renders private law both more intelligible and more appealing, providing lawyers normative resources to draw on so as to reshape private law in the light of its humanist promise.

Some implications of relational justice theory are concrete. For example, we offered legal-theoretical arguments for why the conduct of mentally disadvantaged plaintiffs, when assessed by negligence law, should be subjective, why exceptions to the nonfeasance liability rule should be expanded, and why the duress rules governing spousal agreements should be significantly reformed. Similarly, and maybe surprisingly to some, we insisted that there is a private law justification for "agency shop" contracts, thus challenging their recent prohibition by the Supreme Court.[11]

Other critical implications are broader in scope. Thus, our discussion of the crucial role of legislation and regulation in specifying, for example, employers' obligations of workplace safety (re OSHA), lenders' obligations of procedural and substantive conscionability (re the CFPB), and homeowners' obligations of proper disclosure (re states' statutory schemes prescribing the requirements of Real Estate Transfer Disclosure Statements)[12] is meant to illustrate the potential of private law's critical stance toward law-making institutions. By severing the bond between private law and common law, relational justice theory encourages private law scholars and lawmakers to expand the institutional and procedural imagination when handling the increasingly complicated challenges of our interpersonal relationships.

Just as important on this front is the lesson we hope will be drawn regarding the future course of these (and other) relational regulatory bodies of law. Insisting on their membership in the private law club implies that they must not be informed, as they increasingly are, solely by collectivist concerns. Cost–benefit analysis is clearly not irrelevant, but, as usual when the law of interpersonal relationships is at play, it must not overwhelm people's most fundamental interpersonal rights. We hope that relational justice theory will be used to entrench and elucidate the latent commitment of these critical bodies of private law to reciprocal respect for self-determination and substantive equality.

A final set of broad and indeed quite radical lessons emerged from the previous three chapters, focusing on those who may seem to be the ultimate "other" person of private law: the foreigner, the poor, and the socially marginalized. Competing private law theories have, at best, struggled to accommodate their interests through external constraints, be they from public or private international law or from domestic public law. The longstanding silence of traditional private law on these matters is unacceptable precisely because private law's most basic function is to construct terms of interpersonal interactions between self-determining and substantively equal persons. Indeed, the silence of traditionalism may explain the increasing frustration of liberal egalitarians with private law and their suspicion toward it.

Relational justice theory challenges the expulsion of these "others" from private law. Claiming that our core private law obligations do not hinge on membership in a political community implies that these obligations must apply to nonmembers just as they do to members. Similarly, by highlighting and defending the sensitivity of private law doctrines to personal differences pertaining to who we are (as opposed to those relating to our sheer preferences), relational justice theory clarifies that the same justifications that underlie, for example, the concern of private law about people's ignorance and necessity in (respectively) the contract doctrines of disclosure and duress, require it to address social marginalization and poverty. There is no principled reason for excluding social marginalization or poverty from private law's jurisdiction, and relational justice theory indeed requires situating both in its midst.

We demonstrated that there are existing and developing doctrines—such as anti-discrimination laws, minimum wage laws, or the human rights due diligence directive—that can and should be regarded as private law responses to these challenges.[13] Relational justice theory instructs us to target our societies' structural injustices at their root. It thus requires going beyond these preliminary steps, as suggested in our proposals regarding the general tort of private discrimination, the obligation of inclusionary employment of the poor, and the status of our interpersonal human rights.[14]

Since we began working on relational justice theory more than a decade ago, we repeatedly encountered the critique that it superimposes on private law commitments to self-determination and substantive equality that are "external" and "foreign" to it. We hope to have shown that this critique is misguided. We do not deny that the traditionalist view of private law as a judge-made law aimed at vindicating people's independence and formal equality still figures in private law's specific language (as we defined it on the first page of this book). We hope to have persuaded you that that language should be discarded, that the more appealing language pushes private law in a strikingly different normative direction, and that it can, and often should, transcend its traditional institutional settings. Relational justice thereby carries the transformative aspiration of opening up a new horizon of reforms toward a better, perhaps even laudable, human society.[15] That, we think, is the big promise of private law.

Notes

Chapter 1

1. *Cf.* Hanoch Dagan, *Two Genres of Interpretive Legal Theories, in* Understanding Private Law (Evan Fox Decent et al. eds., 2024).
2. Many recent political theorists tend to prefer thinner normative positions, but we find this normative modesty troublesome. Articulating our theoretical qualms goes beyond the scope of this book but we will at least point out that—as recent neo-populist and neo-theocratic revolutions around the globe demonstrate—the normative price of shying away from the more normatively robust accounts of liberalism can be (too) high and is typically paid by the weakest members of society. *See also infra* Chapter 15 text accompanying notes 56–59.
3. *Cf.* John Rawls, A Theory of Justice 396 (rev. ed. 1999). As the text implies, we take self-determination and substantive equality to be bedrock ideals and, indeed, we hold that they (should) underlie public law as well. What distinguishes private law, then, is the interpersonal setting. As we explain in Chapter 2, however, there is a principled distinction between the normative implications of these ideals for the interpersonal and public settings, so that private law *is* an important normative category.
4. *Cf.* Julie Dickson, Elucidating Law 87 (2022).
5. As the text implies—and as our discussion of "the Toronto School" in Chapter 2 (accompanying notes 21–28) clarifies—we follow the prevalent formal understanding of the term independence in current private law theory, namely, independence from the choices of others. A robust substantive conception of independence may converge with self-determination—one may say that self-determination means some measure of independence from coercive and non-coercive forms of domination, from brute bad luck, and from other forms of interference with the implementation of a self-authored life.
6. *Cf.* Michael Walzer, Interpretation and Social Criticism 1–32 (1987).
7. *See* Robin West, *The New Legal Criticism*, 117 Colum. L. Rev. Online 144 (2017).
8. *See* Rawls, *supra* note 3, at 20–21. Whether this variation is faithful to John Rawls' use of this justificatory procedure is an exegetical question we chose to set aside.
9. Strictly speaking, considered judgments need not be limited solely to particular cases. According to Rawls, considered judgments can be made at any level of generality if they seem evidently correct. *See* John Rawls, *The Independence of Moral Theory, in* Collected Papers 289 (Samuel Freeman ed., 1999).
10. We include in this list only non-technical rules or, more precisely, categories of cases suited to straightforward evaluation by appeal to our moral intuitions.
11. *See* T.M. Scanlon, Being Realistic about Reasons 85–86 (2014).
12. *See* Walzer, *supra* note 6, at 43, 46–48, 61.
13. For a recent defense of the common denominator approach in tort theory, see Paul B. Miller & Jeff Pojanowski, *Torts Against the State, in* Civil Wrongs and Justice in Private Law 323 (Paul B. Miller & John Oberdiek, eds., 2020).
14. *See further* Avihay Dorfman, Conflict between Equals: Tort Law for a Liberal Society intro. (unpublished manuscript). As the text implies, even within private law, relational justice does not claim exclusivity. For example, as one of us claims elsewhere, it is one of the three animating principles of liberal contract, alongside proactive facilitation and concern for the autonomy of the future self. *See* Hanoch Dagan & Michael Heller, *Choice Theory: A Restatement, in* Research Handbook on Private Law Theory 112 (Hanoch Dagan & Benjamin C. Zipursky eds., 2020).
15. For a discussion of property law's commitment to relational justice based on our earlier joint work, see Hanoch Dagan, A Liberal Theory of Property (2021).
16. In other words, we do not claim that, interpretively, our theory is compulsory for all specific doctrines. Indeed, we admit that regarding some of these doctrines it may only be interpretively capable, but we do argue that it is interpretively dominant vis-à-vis other "grand theories" of private law (and may even be interpretively compulsory as such).

Chapter 2

1. *See* Hanoch Dagan & Benjamin Zipursky, *The Distinction Between Private Law and Public Law*, *in* Research Handbook on Private Law Theory 1 (Hanoch Dagan & Benjamin Zipursky eds., 2020).
2. On these latter questions, see Avihay Dorfman & Alon Harel, Reclaiming the Public (2024).
3. The distinction between private and public law is important even though they interact, as an analogy to family law will clarify. Although the discussion of marriage/cohabitation cannot and should not be separated from that of parenthood, in some contexts—consider childless couples and single parents—it can be. In any event, because each dimension is significant per se, it is helpful to delve into the proper construction of each relationship separately before considering their proper combination.

   We think about the relationship between the proper governance of the social and economic realms and of the political one in similar terms. They are both intrinsically significant. In cases involving only one dimension (transnational interactions of the kind we address in Chapter 15 on the one hand, and debates, say, on gerrymandering on the other hand) and even in those involving both dimensions, where we see some overlap or reliance between them, clarifying their respective demands is helpful. *See further infra* Chapter 4, text accompanying notes 25–30 as well as our extensive discussion of poverty in Chapter 14.
4. As the text implies, like public law, private law is political in the sense that it responds to the question of how we should organize our collective lives. But private law and public law address distinctive realms of life: the former deals with our quotidian interpersonal interactions whereas the latter deals with civic life, focusing on our interactions as members of a political community.
5. *See, e.g.*, Hans-W. Micklitz, *Person, Civil Status and Private Law*, *in* New Private Law Theory: A Pluralist Approach 341, 341, 345–46, 354–57 (Stefan Grundmann et al. eds. 2021); Ernest J. Weinrib, Reciprocal Freedom: Private Law and Public Right chs. 6–7 (2022).
6. *See* Hanoch Dagan et al., *The Law of the Market*, 83 L. & Contemp. Probs. i (2020).
7. Peter Birks, *Introduction, in* English Private Law xxxvi, xliii (Peter Birks ed., 2000).
8. *See* John C.P. Goldberg & Benjamin C. Zipursky, *Torts as Wrongs*, 88 Texas L. Rev. 917, 919 (2010). *See also, e.g.*, Nathan B. Oman & Jason M. Solomon, *The Supreme Court's Theory of Private Law*, 62 Duke L. J. 1109, 1119 (2013).
9. Herman Oliphant, *A Return to Stare Decisis*, 14 A.B.A.J. 71, 73–74, 159 (1928).
10. Benjamin N. Cardozo, The Nature of The Judicial Process 179 (1921).
11. Karl L. Llewellyn, The Common Law Tradition: Deciding Appeals 37–38 (1960).
12. This description applies not only to private law but to large sections of public law as well (with the important exception of criminal law). *See* Avihay Dorfman, *Private Law Exceptionalism? Part I: A Basic Difficulty with the Arguments from Bipolarity and Civil Recourse*, 35 Law & Phil. 165, 177–85 (2016). We are not thereby suggesting that all law, or all current law, is, can, or should be structured relationally. *Compare* Zhong Xing Tan, *Rethinking Relational Architecture: Interpersonal Justice beyond Private Law*, U. Toronto L.J. 293 (2023).
13. Insofar as adjudication is concerned, private law certainly goes beyond common law, and not only in civil law jurisdictions. *See* Shyamkrishna Balganesh, *Private Law Statutory Interpretation*, 92 S. Cal. L. Rev. 949 (2019).
14. *See* John C.P. Goldberg & Benjamin C. Zipursky, Recognizing Wrongs (2020). A substantively similar position typifies corrective justice theories. *See, e.g.*, Arthur Ripstein, Private Wrongs 271–75 (2016).
15. *See, e.g.*, Deborah L. Rhode, Access to Justice 1–19 (2004). For a particularly poignant example, see Brittany Farr, *Breach by Violence: The Forgotten History of Sharecropper Litigation in the Post-Slavery South*, 69 UCLA L. Rev. 674 (2022).
16. *See, e.g.*, Emile Durkheim, The Division of Labor in Society 62–63 (W.D. Halls trans., 1984); Michael S. Moore, *The Moral Worth of Retribution*, *in* Responsibility, Character and the Emotions 179, 179–80 (Ferdinand Schoeman ed., 1987); Herbert Morris, *Persons and Punishment, in* On Guilt and Innocence 31, 33–34 (1976).
17. *See, e.g.*, Christopher Heath Wellman, Rights Forfeiture and Punishment 65, 77 (2017); Randy E. Barnett, *Restitution: A New Paradigm of Criminal Justice*, 87 Ethics 279, 287–94 (1977); John Braithwaite, *Restorative Justice and De-Professionalization*, 13(1) The Good Society 28 (2004).
18. Resemblance to regulatory schemes is only partial as criminal law involves the infliction of criminal punishment which, in turn, gives rise to a whole new set of vertical (state vis-a-vis convicted criminals) concerns. *See* Dorfman & Harel, *supra* note 2, at 115–18.

19. *Contra* Martha Albertson Fineman, *The Vulnerable Subject: Anchoring Equality in the Human Condition*, 20 YALE J.L. & FEMINISM 1 (2008).
20. The Toronto school also develops a plausible, though not the only plausible, interpretation of Immanuel Kant's political philosophy.
21. ERNEST J. WEINRIB, THE IDEA OF PRIVATE LAW 82 (1995).
22. ERNEST J. WEINRIB, CORRECTIVE JUSTICE 11 (2012).
23. IMMANUEL KANT, THE METAPHYSICS OF MORALS 63 (Mary Gregor trans., 1991). *See also* ARTHUR RIPSTEIN, FORCE AND FREEDOM: KANT'S LEGAL AND POLITICAL THEORY 35 (2009).
24. RIPSTEIN, *supra* note 23, at 4, 14–45.
25. WEINRIB, *supra* note 22, at 36.
26. *See* Hanoch Dagan & Avihay Dorfman, *Just Relationships*, 116 COLUM. L. REV. 1395, 1404–05 (2016).
27. ALAN BRUDNER, THE UNITY OF THE COMMON LAW 353 (2d ed. 2013, with Jennifer M. Nadler). Brudner supplements this view of common law with an account of equity that, on its face, is quite close to relational justice theory. As we clarify in due course, however, it is significantly different: for Brudner, real autonomy (his term) is a concern that comes into play only in the vertical dimension, specifically where equity judges interfere with the common law when exercising their duties as judges. *See infra* Chapter 4, note 22.
28. PETER BENSON, JUSTICE IN TRANSACTIONS: A THEORY OF CONTRACT LAW 188, 373, 388, 468–69 (2019). *See also id.* at 8, 24, 26–27, 186, 188, 352, 364, 367–69, 371–72, 377–78, 385, 387–88, 393–94, 396, 470.
29. *See generally* HANOCH DAGAN, A LIBERAL THEORY OF PROPERTY (2021); HANOCH DAGAN & MICHAEL HELLER, THE CHOICE THEORY OF CONTRACTS 41–47 (2017); Avihay Dorfman, Conflict between Equals: Tort Law for a Liberal Society (unpublished manuscript).
30. Put differently, accommodation stands for the inclusion of certain properties of another person into the terms of the interaction. Such properties place constraints, or impose demands, on the party owing a duty of accommodation. This course of action does not turn on how accommodation might be used by contemporary scholars of anti-discrimination law.
31. Leon Green, *Tort Law Public Law in Disguise*, 38 TEX. L. REV. 1, 1–2 (1959).
32. *See* Morton J. Horwitz, *The History of the Public/Private Distinction*, 130 U. PA. L. REV. 1423 (1982); Duncan Kennedy, *The Stages of the Decline of the Public/Private Distinction*, 130 U. PA. L. REV. 1349 (1982); Alan Freeman & Elizabeth Mensch, *The Public-Private Distinction in American Law and Life*, 36 BUFF. L. REV. 237 (1987).
33. Alon Harel, *Public and Private Law*, *in* THE OXFORD HANDBOOK OF CRIMINAL LAW 1045, 1050–51 (Markus Dubber & Tatjana Hörnle eds., 2014). For a similar approach outside the economic analysis of private law, *see, e.g.*, Larissa Katz, *Philosophy of Property Law, Three Ways*, *in* THE CAMBRIDGE PHILOSOPHY OF LAW 371 (John Tasioulas ed., 2020).
34. *See* Hanoch Dagan, *Why Markets? Welfare, Autonomy, and The Just Society*, 117 MICH. L. REV. 1289, 1295–97 (2019).
35. JOHN RAWLS, A THEORY OF JUSTICE 23–24 (rev. ed. 1999).
36. As the text implies, more modest versions of the economic analysis are not susceptible to this critique and can, and indeed should, play an important role in legal theory. *See* Hanoch Dagan & Roy Kreitner, *Economic Analysis* in *Law*, 38 YALE J. REG. 566 (2021).
37. For an example where this commitment is explicit, see Robert E. Scott, *A Joint Maximization Theory of Contract and Regulation, in* RESEARCH HANDBOOK ON PRIVATE LAW THEORY, *supra* note 1, at 22.
38. *See* Liam B. Murphy, *Institutions and the Demands of Justice*, 27 PHIL. & PUB. AFF. 251 (1998); G. A. COHEN, RESCUING JUSTICE & EQUALITY 10, 375 (2008).
39. Elizabeth S. Anderson, *What Is the Point of Equality?*, 109 ETHICS 287, 289 (1999). Another seminal piece is Samuel Scheffler, *What Is Egalitarianism?*, 31 PHIL. & PUB. AFF. 5 (2003). *See also* KASPER LIPPERT-RASMUSSEN, RELATIONAL EGALITARIANISM: LIVING AS EQUALS (2018). Scheffler's theory is somewhat ambiguous and may be read as similar to our conception of relational justice. *See* Hanoch Dagan & Avihay Dorfman, *Justice in Private: Beyond the Rawlsian Framework*, 37 L. & PHIL. 171, 181–83 & n.13 (2018).
40. Anderson, *supra* note 39, at 317.
41. *See* ELIZABETH ANDERSON, THE IMPERATIVE OF INTEGRATION 89, 94–95 (2010).
42. JÜRGEN HABERMAS, BETWEEN FACTS AND NORMS: CONTRIBUTIONS TO A DISCOURSE THEORY OF LAW AND DEMOCRACY 391, 396–97, 400–403, 405–406 (1996).
43. *Id.* at 398, 407–409, 426–28.

44. *See* Rawls, *supra* note 35, at 293–94. *Cf.* Anna Stilz, Liberal Loyalty: Freedom, Obligation, and the State (2009).
45. The republican ideal of law further demands from all members of the political community a measure of "civic virtue" or "good citizenship." The republican tradition, according to Pettit, is "primarily distinguished, not by its distinctive conception of liberty, and not by its image of the form that constitutionalism and democracy and regulation should take, but by its insistence on the need for civic virtue." Philip Pettit, Republicanism: A Theory of Freedom and Government 245 (1997). Different formulations of neo-republicanism do offer varying degrees of civic commitments, some of them less demanding than those of (the early) Pettit. But our claim applies to all of them.
46. The text should not be interpreted as degrading democratic prescriptions. Quite the contrary: it follows a happy conception of democracy that addresses people's right to justification—*Cf.* Rainer Forst, The Right to Justification: Elements of a Constructivist Theory of Justice 188–228 (Jeffrey Flynn trans., 2011)—and thus refines its specific content in the pertinent (private law) context.
47. *See* Hugh Collins, *The Challenge Presented by Fundamental Rights to Private Law*, *in* Private Law in The 21ST Century 213, 223, 234–35 (Kit Barker et al. eds., 2017).
48. *Compare* Tarunabh Khaitan, A Theory of Discrimination Law 201 (2015). For a more promising route, see Jean Thomas, Public Rights, Private Relations (2015). But the crucial step of Thomas's analysis implies that she ends up reinventing the embedded person of private law. *See* Hanoch Dagan & Avihay Dorfman, *Interpersonal Human Rights*, 51 Cornell Int'l L.J. 361, 267–68 & n.29 (2018).
49. In a liberal polity founded on people's right to self-determination and equal standing, there must be a limit to the addition of interpersonal obligations. Identifying this limit is a complex task, exceeding the scope and ambition of this book. *Cf.* Seana Valentine Shiffrin, *Paternalism, Unconscionability Doctrine, and Accommodation*, 29 Phil. & Pub. Aff. 205, 236–50 (2000).
50. Another response could argue that, in the encounters governed by private law, individuals must treat one another as citizens of the world. This formulation, however, would simply reinstate our claims in a way that might obscure the distinction between our relationships with the members of our own political community and our relationships with all other persons.
51. *See generally infra* Chapter 3, text accompanying note 27. *See also, respectively*, Chapters 15 and 14.
52. *See supra* text accompanying note 42.
53. John Gardner, *Dagan and Dorfman on the Value of Private Law*, 117 Colum. L. Rev. Online 179, 193–94, 197–98 (2017).
54. *Cf.* Thomas Christiano, Normative Conventionalism about Contracts (unpublished manuscript).
55. *Cf.* Liam Murphy, *The Artificial Morality of Private Law: The Persistence of an Illusion*, 70 U. Toronto L.J. 453 (2020). Our position is significantly different from Murphy's, as the following paragraphs imply, and as our discussions of self-determination and private law (in Chapter 3), and of the cosmopolitan features of private law (in Chapter 15) clarify. *See infra* Chapter 3, text accompanying notes 34–41, and Chapter 15, text accompanying notes 34–44.
56. H.L.A. Hart, The Concept of Law 27–28 (1961).
57. *See* Hanoch Dagan & Michael Heller, *Autonomy for Contract, Refined*, 40 L. & Phil. 213 (2021); Hanoch Dagan & Michael Heller, *Choice Theory: A Restatement*, *in* Research Handbook On Private Law Theory, *supra* note 1, at 112.
58. *See* Hanoch Dagan, *Liberal Property and the Power of Law*, 36 Can. J.L. & Jurisp. 281 (2023); Avihay Dorfman, *When, and How, Does Property Matter?*, 72 U. Toronto L.J. 81 (2022).
59. *Cf.* Seana Valentine Shiffrin, *Promising, Intimate Relationships, and Conventionalism*, 117 Phil. Rev. 481, 520 (2008). In other words, the (properly liberal) ideas of private property and freedom of contract should be included in Rawls' list of social primary goods: goods that are supposed to be desired by every human being. *Cf.* Rawls, *supra* note 35, at 92.
60. *Cf.* Elisabeth Jacobs, *Everywhere and Nowhere: Politics in Capital in the Twenty-First Century*, *in* After Piketty: The Agenda for Economics and Inequality 512, 515–18, 524–31 (Heather Boushey et al. eds., 2017).
61. *Cf.* Dorfman, *supra* note 29.
62. *Id.* at ch. 5.
63. *See respectively* John Gardner, *What Is Tort Law For? Part II: The Place of Distributive Justice*, *in* Philosophical Foundations of the Law of Torts 335, 338–39 (John Oberdiek ed., 2014) and Gardner, *supra* note 53, at 183.
64. Moral and political philosophers rarely take up the task of distilling abstract moral principles into concrete, user-friendly norms of conduct. Their primary interest is in meta-ethics, and even when

they do focus on the ethics of what we owe one another, they do not attempt to formulate rules of conduct that come anywhere near the doctrinal complexities of battery or any other tort. *See* John Gardner, Torts and Other Wrongs 78 (2019).

65. *See* Felix S. Cohen, *Transcendental Nonsense and the Functional Approach*, 35 Colum. L. Rev. 809, 811–12, 814–18, 840 (1935); Hans Kelsen, Pure Theory of Law 280–83 (Max Knight trans., 2d rev. ed. 1967); Robert W. Gordon, *New Developments in Legal Theory, in* The Politics of Law: A Progressive Critique 413, 418–21 (David Kairys ed., 2d ed. 1990); Robert W. Gordon, *Unfreezing Legal Reality: Critical Approaches to Law*, 15 Fla. St. U. L. Rev. 195, 212–14 (1987).
66. *See* Dagan, *supra* note 29; Dagan & Heller, *supra* note 57, at 112.

Chapter 3

1. As in our discussion of the public/private distinction in Chapter 2, our discussion of corrective and distributive justice is strictly confined to the contemporary articulations of these concepts.
2. *See, e.g.*, Jules L. Coleman, *The Structure of Tort Law*, 97 Yale L.J. 1233, 1248–53 (1988).
3. *See* Arthur Ripstein, Private Wrongs 288–95 (2016).
4. *See, e.g.*, Robert Nozick, Anarchy, State, and Utopia 160 (1974); Randy E. Barnett, *A Consent Theory of Contract*, 86 Colum. L. Rev. 269, 270, 302–03 (1986).
5. Ripstein, *supra* note 3, at 37, 289. *See also* Ernest J. Weinrib, Corrective Justice 263–96 (2012).
6. *See, e.g.*, Robert L. Hale, *Coercion and Distribution in a Supposedly Non-Coercive State*, 38 Pol. Sci. Q. 470 (1923); Morris R. Cohen, *Property and Sovereignty*, 13 Cornell L.Q. 8, 13 (1927).
7. *See* Hanoch Dagan, A Liberal Theory of Property 118–22 (2021).
8. Recently, even Ernest Weinrib seems to have acknowledged this, at least in the context of the workplace. *See* Ernest J. Weinrib, Reciprocal Freedom: Private Law and Public Right 107 n.23 (2022).
9. *See* Martijn W. Hesselink, Justifying Contract in Europe: Political Philosophies of European Contract Law ch. 6 (2021).
10. John Rawls, *Social Unity and Primary Goods, in* Collected Papers 371 (Samuel Freeman ed., 1999). *See further* John Rawls, Political Liberalism 268–69 (1993).
11. *Id.*
12. *See* Samuel Scheffler, Equality and Tradition: Questions of Value in Moral and Political Theory ch. 4 (2010).
13. Samuel Scheffler, *Distributive Justice, the Basic Structure and the Place of Private Law*, 35 Ox. J. Legal Stud. 226 (2015).
14. Ronald Dworkin, Law's Empire 296, 299 (1986).
15. For yet another view, see Hesselink, *supra* note 9, at 300–07.
16. *See* G.A. Cohen, Rescuing Justice & Equality 126, 375 (2008). *See also, e.g.*, Zofia Stemplowska, *On the Real World Duties Imposed on Us by Human Rights*, 40 J. Soc. Phil. 466 (2009). For an attempt to reconstruct a "micro" version of Cohen's "free-floating" commitment to distributive justice in contract law, see Zhong Xing Tan, *Where the Action Is: Macro and Micro Justice in Contract Law*, 83 Mod. L. Rev. 725 (2020).
17. G.A. Cohen, *Where the Action is: On the Site of Distributive Justice*, 26 Phil. & Pub. Aff. 3, 3 (1997).
18. *See supra* Chapter 2 text accompanying notes 31–38.
19. *See* Elizabeth S. Anderson, *What is the Point of Equality?*, 109 Ethics 287, 312 (1999).
20. *See supra* Chapter 2 text accompanying notes 39–52.
21. *See* Anderson, *supra* note 19, at 289, 317.
22. *See supra* Chapter 2 text accompanying notes 46–48.
23. We do agree that some relational egalitarians see their commitment to democracy as ultimately grounded in robust ideas of freedom and equality rather than as freestanding. Our debate with these theorists, as the text clarifies, lies elsewhere. Given that, for them, the interpersonal claims at hand are derivative from democracy, the animating worry is social or public justice. By contrast, we insist that these claims are *directly* grounded in freedom and equality and *unmediated* by democracy. Consequently, their validity is not contingent on their cumulative effects or on the parties' affiliation with the same political community. *See respectively infra* Chapters 13 & 14 and Chapter 15.
24. As the text implies, all relational views need to say more about which relations are important, but this does not collapse relational justice into distributive justice. The relevant units of interpersonal interaction are likely to vary from one society to another and prescribing their proper boundaries

may depend on the pertinent legal architecture. But neither contingency implies the lack of a principled distinction between people's status as members of a comprehensive political community and their daily interpersonal affairs.

25. In other words, relational justice does not rely on John Gardner's distinction between strictly and loosely relational duties. *See* John Gardner, *Dagan and Dorfman on the Value of Private Law*, 117 Colum. L. Rev. Online 179, 191–94 (2017).
26. *See* John Rawls, Justice as Fairness: A Restatement 10 (2001). Rawls does not subject the family to the exact same demands that figure in the case of the state. *Id.* at 164.
27. *See id.* at 162–65, 167–68. *See also, e.g.*, Iris Marion Young, *Taking the Basic Structure Seriously*, 4 Perspectives on Politics 91, 91, 93–94 (2006); Blain Neufeld, *Coercion, the Basic Structure, and the Family*, 40 J. Soc. Phil. 37, 37, 45–47 (2009).
28. *See* Iris Marion Young, Responsibility for Justice 52 (2011). *See also, e.g.*, Maeve McKeown, *Structural Injustice*, 16 (7) Philosophy Compass 1 (2021).
29. *See* Khiara M. Bridges, Critical Race Theory: A Primer 148–49 (2019).
30. Sally Haslanger, *Systemic and Structural Injustice: Is There a Difference?*, 98 Philosophy 1, 22 (2023) (our emphasis). *Cf.* Andrea Sangiovanni, *Structural Injustice and Individual Responsibility*, 49 J. Soc. Phil. 461, 461–62 (2018).
31. *Cf.* Dylan Penningroth, *Race in Contract Law*, 170 U. Pa. L. Rev. 1199, 1232–37, 1245, 1253–56, 1290 (2022); Robin Zheng, *What is My Role in Changing the System? A New Model of Responsibility for Structural Injustice*, 21 Ethical Theory & Moral Prac. 869 (2018).
32. Relational justice also provides a core answer to a question that has escaped philosophical accounts of how a social structure might be not only bad but also wrong, apart from individual moral wrongs. *See* David Estlund, What's Unjust about Structural Injustice (unpublished manuscript).
33. This discussion might seem superfluous. Private law's relational justice, one could argue, should simply follow morality, at least in its "relational interpretation," where considerations of moral rightness spring from the social relations that connect us to others "through bonds of directed duty." Relational morality, in this view, is "fundamentally a matter of what we owe *to* each other" only insofar as "they and we are both persons, equally real." This "built-in directionality," which is "characteristic of relations of interpersonal accountability," stands for "an ideal of interpersonal recognition." It thus provides "a kind of normative scaffold for the interactions between the two parties," who are "distinctively connected" through these relational moral requirements. R. Jay Wallace, The Moral Nexus, 1, 18, 57, 60, 126 (2019). Although the continuity between our account and this view of morality is clear, it is more limited in its guidance to us than might be expected, at least insofar as its most prominent versions are concerned. Thus, Thomas Scanlon's celebrated moral contractualism would advise us to opt for private law rules that "would be permitted by principles that could not reasonably be rejected, by people who were moved to find principles for the general regulation of behavior that others, similarly motivated, could not reasonably reject." T.M. Scanlon, What We Owe to Each Other 4 (1998). Indeed an appealing formulation of our task, but more an invitation to the following inquiry than a beacon of guidance. Stephen Darwall's notion of second-personal ethics, in turn, is even less informative for our task since it embraces the civil recourse conception of private law, which we reject. *See respectively* Stephen Darwall, *Civil Recourse as Mutual Accountability*, *in* Morality, Authority, & Law: Essays in Second-Personal I 179 (2013) and Chapter 2 text accompanying notes 7–15.
34. John Rawls, Justice as Fairness: A Restatement 19 (2001).
35. Joseph Raz, The Morality of Freedom 369 (1986).
36. This commitment requires us to respect every person's right to self-determination. It does not belittle the choice of an unexamined life or suggest that such respect is contingent on the accomplishment of a worthy life plan.
37. We intentionally use the adjective "meaningful" to claim that not only is adding choices not always valuable—*see, e.g.*, Hanoch Dagan & Michael Heller, The Choice Theory of Contracts 128–30 (2017)—but, as David Enoch claims, the value of choice ultimately lies in ensuring that one's life "is led by the commitments and values of the person whose life it is." David Enoch, *Autonomy as Non-Alienation, Autonomy as Sovereignty*, 30 J. Pol. Phil. 143, 150–51 (2022). Enoch refers to this ultimate value—which we call self-determination—as non-alienation, and rightly adds that one's life manifests self-determination/non-alienation "to the extent that the more central and important parts of your life-story are in line with your deep commitments and values." *Id.* at 149. The distinction between meaningful and banal choices (at times termed merely pickings) is, in a way, echoed in the core distinction we apply between ground projects and sheer preferences. *See infra* text accompanying notes 53–55.
38. *See* H.L.A. Hart, *Between Utility and Rights*, 79 Colum. L. Rev. 828, 836 (1979).

39. *See* Raz, *supra* note 35, at 372, 398. As the text below implies, our account of the role of autonomy is distinguished not only from the political liberalism of the later Rawls but also from liberal perfectionism, which is often identified with Raz. *See* Hanoch Dagan, *Liberal Property Theory*, *in* Handbook on Property Law & Theory (Chris Bevan ed., 2024).
40. As the text implies, and although our account of relational justice does not require us to take a stand in the many intricate debates regarding autonomy, we largely side with what has been broadly termed "relational autonomy." *See* Catriona Mackenzie & Natalie Stoljar, *Introduction: Autonomy Refigured*, *in* Relational Autonomy: Feminist Perspectives on Autonomy, Agency, and the Social Self 3 (Catriona Mackenzie & Natalie Stoljar eds., 2000). *See also, e.g.*, Joel Anderson & Axel Honneth, *Autonomy, Vulnerability, Recognition, and Justice*, *in* Autonomy and Challenges to Liberalism: New Essays 127 (John Christman & Joel Anderson eds., 2005).
41. *See generally* Hanoch Dagan, *Autonomy and Pluralism in Private Law*, *in* The Oxford Handbook of New Private Law 177 (Andrew Gold et al. eds., 2020), which the remainder of this subsection summarizes.
42. The term *ultra vires* is typically associated with the limited legal capacity of some legal persons, but we use it deliberately here to convey the proposition that, once we appreciate the nature of property and contract as power-conferring institutions, owners and potential promisees must be precluded from using these legal devices in discriminatory ways. (Consider, by [crude] analogy, the claim that, properly interpreted, trading in certain body parts is *ultra vires* [liberal] contract since it abuses the very normative foundation on which contract's legitimacy is founded.)
43. A related qualm is that an immutable floor entails a suspiciously normalizing effect. *See* Jürgen Habermas, Between Facts and Norms: Contributions to a Discourse Theory of Law and Democracy 413, 416 (1996). For our response, see Hanoch Dagan, *The Value of Choice and the Justice of Contract*, 10 Jurisprudence 422, 432–33 (2019).
44. *See* Alan Schwartz, *A Reexamination of Nonsubstantive Unconscionability*, 63 Va. L. Rev. 1053, 1081–82 (1977).
45. Seana Valentine Shiffrin, *Paternalism, Unconscionability Doctrine, and Accommodation*, 29 Phil. & Pub. Aff. 205, 207, 213, 215, 220, 231 (2000).
46. Shiffrin's response to the paternalism challenge seems to be based on moral sentiments external to private law. *See* Shiffrin, *supra* note 45, at 227–30, 235.
47. *Cf.* David Enoch, *Hypothetical Consent and the Value(s) of Autonomy*, 128 Ethics 6, 30–35 (2017).
48. *See, e.g.*, John Stuart Mill, On Liberty 107–44 (1863); Enoch, *supra* note 37, at 151–52.
49. Raz, *supra* note 35, at 373.
50. *See* Hart, *supra* note 38, at 834–35.
51. *Contra* Gary S. Becker, The Economic Approach to Human Behavior 7–8 (1976).
52. The text that follows offers only a sketch of a theory of autonomy accounting, but we think the numerous examples of autonomy-audits guided by this theory that we discuss below vindicate its plausibility. Here, we rely again on the reflective equilibrium theme that underlies much of our analysis.
53. *See* Avihay Dorfman, *Assumption of Risk, After All*, 15 Theoretical Inquiries L. 293, 318 (2014).
54. *See* Rawls, *supra* note 10, at 30–32; Jeremy Waldron, *Moral Autonomy and Personal Autonomy*, *in* Autonomy and Challenges to Liberalism, *supra* note 40, at 307, 316.
55. Bernard Williams, *Persons, Character and Morality*, *in* Moral Luck 1, 12 (1981).
56. Nothing in our argument hinges on Williams' psychological argument that the demands of impartial morality exert unreasonable pressure on the personal integrity of those who pursue such projects.
57. *See also* Assaf Sharon, The Limits of Authority (unpublished manuscript). *Cf.* Mark Gergen, Debt's Challenge to Autonomy Theories of Contract (unpublished manuscript), who claims that "[w]hile consumer durables often serve 'garden-variety' and 'mundane' needs (like providing electricity) often these are needs that must be satisfied before people can pursue grander projects."
58. As the text implies, these categories are linked to social structures. But, as we explained above in this chapter, relational justice does not thereby collapse into distributive justice or democratic egalitarianism.
59. *Cf.* Dagan, *supra* note 39. Relational justice theory sanctions, indeed requires, such evaluations only regarding a specific type of projects: those that deny the equal worth of others' self-determination. *See infra* text following note 71.
60. *Cf.* John Rawls, A Theory of Justice 23–24 (rev. ed. 1999). Recall that, similarly to Rawls' primary good, the frameworks that private law prescribes are largely open-ended. Furthermore, private law often sets up multiple options for people to pursue their projects of choice.

61. *See further* Avihay Dorfman, Conflict Between Equals: Tort Law for a Liberal Society ch. 8 (unpublished manuscript).
62. Contract theorists use this conformity with formal equality to support the more ambitious claim that formal equality is truly the foundational ideal of contracts, either in this context or in general. *See, e.g.*, Daniel Markovits, *Promise as an Arm's Length Relation*, *in* PROMISES AND AGREEMENTS: PHILOSOPHICAL ESSAYS 295, 316–17 (Hanoch Sheinman ed., 2011). But as the text implies—and Chapters 9 and 10 elaborate—this conclusion does not hold.
63. *See* Dorfman, *supra* note 61, at chs. 7, 9–10.
64. *Cf.* Lihi Yona, *Identity at Work*, 43 BERKELEY J. EMP. & LAB. L. 139 (2022) (discussing claims of asexuals, poor whites, and fat people).
65. For further elaboration see Dorfman, *supra* note 61, at ch. 8.
66. *See* Hanoch Dagan & Michael Heller, *Can Contract Emancipate? Contract Theory and The Law of Work*, 24 THEORETICAL INQ. L. 49 (2023); Hanoch Dagan, *Intimate Contracts and Choice Theory*, 18 EUR. REV. CONTRACT L. 104 (2022).
67. *See* Dorfman, *supra* note 61, at ch. 7.
68. ELIZABETH ANDERSON, PRIVATE GOVERNMENT: HOW EMPLOYERS RULE OUR LIVES (AND WHY WE DON'T TALK ABOUT IT) 127 (2017). *See also* Elizabeth Anderson, *How Should Egalitarians Cope with Market Risks?*, 9 THEORETICAL INQUIRIES L. 239, 263–65 (2007); Niko Kolodny, *Rule Over None II: Social Equality and the Justification of Democracy*, 42 PHIL. & PUB. AFF. 287 (2014). With Anderson and Kolodny, we do not focus on the motives and attitudes underlying the behavior of parties to egalitarian relationships. The reason behind our reluctance to integrate motives and attitudes is explained below. *See infra* main text accompanying notes 70–71.
69. *See* Shiffrin, *supra* note 45, at 207, 213, 215, 220, 224, 227–28, 231, 236, 245. Note that, contrary to our approach, Shiffrin's notion of relationality includes the state as one of the parties at the stage of contract enforcement. *Id.* at 227.
70. Another difference between our account of substantive equality and Kolodny's (and, arguably, Anderson's as well) is that the demands of substantive equality are not limited to what Kolodny calls "ongoing social relations." Kolodny, *supra* note 68, at 300. *See also* Nico Kolodny, *An Objection to Social Hierarchy Itself?*, *in* WORKING AS EQUALS: RELATIONAL EGALITARIANISM AND THE WORKPLACE 32, 37 (Julian Jonker & Grant Z. Rozeboom eds., 2023); NICO KOLODNY, THE PECKING ORDER: SOCIAL HIERARCHY AS A PHILOSOPHICAL PROBLEM 99 (2023).
71. *Cf.* Allen Buchanan, *Political Legitimacy and Democracy*, 112 ETHICS 689, 705–06 (2002).
72. *Compare* Grant J. Rozeboom, *Good Enough for Equality*, *in* WORKING AS EQUALS, *supra* note 70, at 213.
73. More generally, while the gap between giving reasons and motivating is not a conceptual truth about law, it is a normative requirement that the law governing liberal societies must adhere to. This limitation on the enforcement of motives reflects both substantive considerations—such as those pertaining to the distinction between political and personal morality of right and virtue—and instrumental ones—notably the unverifiability of persons' internal mental states. *Cf.* Hales v. Petit (1562) 75 Eng. Rep. 387, 397; 1 Plowden 253, 253.
74. *See supra* text accompanying note 12.
75. *Cf.* Tan, *supra* note 16, at 742–45.
76. *See infra* Chapter 13 text accompanying notes 72–73.
77. Prohibitive cost is a normative rather than a purely economic concept.
78. Some readers may find our focus on American law problematic given its disrespect for the private/public distinction in its traditional rendition. But Chapter 2 implies that, for us, rather than a liability, this may even be an asset. In any event, we do not think that U.S. private law is, consistently, radically different from all other common law jurisdictions.

Chapter 4

1. For a defense of the difference that law, *qua* law, makes in the moral space, see AVIHAY DORFMAN & ALON HAREL, RECLAIMING THE PUBLIC ch. 2 (2024).
2. Normatively speaking, it may even be impossible. *Id.* The same claim applies, *mutatis mutandis*, to the possibility of market forces fully incentivizing people to behave in line with the prescriptions of relational justice theory.
3. Indeed, careful analysts of areas such as corporate law and the law of finance document the trajectory of a shift *away* from the ideal of relational justice in these important areas. *See* KATHARINA PISTOR, THE CODE OF CAPITAL: HOW THE LAW CREATES WEALTH AND INEQUALITY (2019).
4. That said, we do not deny the significance of the extra-legal conditions for sustaining a conception of liberal solidarity implicit in Chapter 3. Studying the ethical, sociological, psychological,

and pedagogical aspects of this challenge goes beyond the scope of this book and, indeed, beyond the scope of legal theory. We must, however, point to the potential implications of uprooting private law's traditional way of thinking and talking about entitlements and replacing it with that endorsed by relational justice. In other words, because traditionalism in the Anglo-American world as we know it tends to entrench, as Liam Murphy notes, a disposition of "everyday libertarianism," stabilizing (in the Rawlsian meaning of this term) the relational justice conception of liberal solidarity requires an alternative legal vocabulary along the lines we hope to develop here. *Cf.* Liam Murphy, *The Artificial Morality of Private Law: The Persistence of an Illusion*, 70 U. TORONTO L.J. 453 (2020). *See also* Hanoch Dagan, Freedom of Contracts, Properly Understood (unpublished manuscript).

5. We intentionally talk here about love, rather than marriage, which does include private law implications that can, and indeed should, be legally regulated. *See* Hanoch Dagan & Carolyn J. Frantz, *Properties of Marriage*, 104 COLUM. L. REV. 75, 84 (2004).
6. The tension between legal duties and reasons for action that turn on authenticity is well captured by the Kantian distinction between *officia iuris* and *officia virtutis*. *See* IMMANUEL KANT, THE METAPHYSICS OF MORALS 31 (Mary Gregor trans., 1991).
7. *See, e.g.*, Yuval Feldman & Tom R. Tyler, *Mandated Justice: The Potential Promise and Possible Pitfalls of Mandating Procedural Justice in the Workplace*, 6 REG. & GOVERNANCE 46, 48 (2012).
8. As the text implies, evaluating the risks of alienation or of displacing authentic motivations requires particular attention to the type of relationship at hand and, specifically, its significance to people's ground projects.
9. JOHN LOCKE, THE SECOND TREATISE OF GOVERNMENT 378 (Peter Laslett ed. 1988).
10. For an elaborate discussion of these two facets of the rule of law, on which this subsection relies, see HANOCH DAGAN, A LIBERAL THEORY OF PROPERTY 159–73 (2021).
11. JOSEPH RAZ, THE MORALITY OF FREEDOM 220, 222 (1986).
12. Jeremy Waldron, *The Concept and the Rule of Law*, 43 GA. L. REV. 1, 6, 312 (2008); Jeremy Waldron, *Is the Rule of Law an Essentially Contested Concept (in Florida)?*, 21 L. & PHIL. 137, 159 (2002). As the text implies, the requirement of predictability for autonomy may be disputed in more benevolent authority settings, such as parenthood.
13. Joseph Raz, *The Law's Own Virtue*, 39 OXFORD J. LEGAL STUD. 1, 2 (2019). *See also* John Tasioulas, *The Rule of Law*, *in* THE CAMBRIDGE COMPANION TO THE PHILOSOPHY OF LAW 117, 121 (John Tasioulas ed., 2020).
14. *See* Antonin Scalia, *The Rule of Law as a Law of Rules*, 56 U. CHI. L. REV. 1175 (1989).
15. Emily Sherwin, *Rule-Oriented Realism*, 103 MICH. L. REV. 1578, 1589, 1590, 1591 (2005).
16. *See* Timothy Endicott, *The Value of Vagueness*, *in* PHILOSOPHICAL FOUNDATIONS OF LANGUAGE IN THE LAW 14, 23, 28, 30 (Andrei Marmor & Scott Soames eds., 2011); RICHARD A. POSNER, THE PROBLEMS OF JURISPRUDENCE 48 (1990).
17. *See* Jeremy Waldron, *Vagueness and the Guidance of Action*, *in* PHILOSOPHICAL FOUNDATIONS OF LANGUAGE IN THE LAW, *supra* note 16, at 58, 65–66, 69. *Cf.* Seana Valentine Shiffrin, *Inducing Moral Deliberation: On the Occasional Virtues of Fog*, 123 HARV. L. REV. 1214, 1222 (2010).
18. *See* Hanoch Dagan, *The Jurisprudence of Liberal Property*, 13 JURISPRUDENCE 668, 680–82 (2022).
19. *See* Oliver Wendell Holmes, *The Path of the Law*, *in* COLLECTED LEGAL PAPERS 167, 171 (1920).
20. *See* Hanoch Dagan, *Why Markets? Welfare, Autonomy, and The Just Society*, 117 MICH. L. REV. 1289 (2019).
21. *See* Avihay Dorfman, Conflict between Equals: Tort Law for a Liberal Society ch. 1 (unpublished manuscript).
22. Our account of relational justice may also remind readers of the Hegelian view of equity as the domain of "real autonomy" (that is, self-determination) as opposed to common law, which is strictly limited to vindicating people's "free agency" (or independence). In this Hegelian story, however, the latter commitment exhausts what private law has to tell us about our interpersonal obligations. Equity's intervention is triggered by the duty of *courts* to respect the litigants' self-determination. It governs "the relation, not between the two parties to a lawsuit, but between each litigant and the court," and is thus situated in public, rather than private, law. ALAN BRUDNER, THE UNITY OF THE COMMON LAW 34 (2d ed. 2013, with Jennifer M. Nadler); Jennifer Nadler, *What is Distinctive about the Law of Equity*, 41 OXFORD J. LEGAL STUD. 854 (2021). Much of our discussion in Chapters 2 and 3 could be read as a response to this claim since it is aimed to defend the indispensable role of an *interpersonal* responsibility for self-determination. Responding to the Hegelian perspective on equity can still be helpful in adding another way of making this point. Suppose that a law-abiding citizen approaches you with a question regarding her *legal* duties in one of the contexts at hand, insisting that she is not interested in a prediction of the judges' response but in what the Law

(whatever its institutional pedigree) prescribes. Would you not include in your answer the (many) doctrines vindicating people's self-determination covered in this book?

23. Henry E. Smith, *Equity as Meta-Law*, 130 Yale L.J. 1050, 1055–56, 1059 (2021).
24. *Cf.* Paul B. Miller, *Equity as Supplemental Law, in* Philosophical Foundations of the Law of Equity 92 (Dennis Klimchuk et al. eds., 2020).
25. *See, e.g.,* U.S. Const. art. I, § 8 ("The Congress shall have Power . . . *[t]o promote the Progress of Science* and useful Arts, by securing for limited Times to Authors and Inventors the exclusive Right to their respective Writings and Discoveries." (emphasis added)).
26. Identifying the proper transitional measures is certainly complex and controversial. *See* Dagan, *supra* note 10, at ch. 8.
27. *See* Hanoch Dagan, *Liberal Property and the Power of Law*, 36 Can. J.L. & Jurisp. 281 (2023).
28. *See* John Rawls, A Theory of Justice 542 (1971). Another controversial case relates to the proper degree of deference private law should adopt towards a robust practice of freedom of expression even when it manifests itself in complete disregard of the people's personal qualities. *See* Dorfman, *supra* note 21, at chs. 2, 5, 13.
29. *See generally* Jane Millar & Andrea Warman, Family Obligations in Europe 24 (1996); Robert I. Lerman & Elaine Sorensen, *Child Support: Interactions Between Private and Public Transfers, in* Means-Tested Transfer Programs in the United States 587 (Robert A. Moffitt ed., 2003). *Cf.* Anne L. Alstott, No Exit: What Parents Owe Their Children and What Society Owes Parents ch. 4 (2004).
30. *Cf.* Duncan Kennedy, *The Stakes of Law, or Hale and Foucault, in* Sexy Dressing Etc. 83, 98–99 (1993). Likewise, the indeterminacy addressed in the text also carries important implications for the scope of public responsibility and, specifically, for our responsibility as members of a political community. *See* Dorfman & Harel, *supra* note 1, at ch. 5.
31. This distinction was made familiar by David Hume and, more recently, by Rawls (who, in turn, follows H.L.A. Hart). *See* Rawls, *supra* note 28, at 109–12.
32. *See* John Rawls, *Kantian Constructivism in Moral Theory*, 77 J. Phil. 515, 536 (1980). Note that Rawls emphasizes a different "subjective" circumstance, namely, the fact that people hold divergent conceptions of the good life.
33. In Chapter 3, we noted how this contextual variance affects the scope of relational justice's duties of accommodation. *See* Chapter 3 text following note 74.
34. *See* Hanoch Dagan & Elizabeth S. Scott, *Reinterpreting the Status-Contract Divide: The Case of Fiduciaries, in* Contract, Status, and Fiduciary 51, 58–59, 62–66 (Paul B. Miller & Andrew S. Gold, eds., 2016).
35. For a discussion of some of these contexts, see Hanoch Dagan, *Intimate Contracts and Choice Theory*, 18 Eur. Rev. Contract L. 104, 121–25 (2022); Hanoch Dagan, *Autonomy, Relational Justice, and Restitution, in* Research Handbook on Unjust Enrichment and Restitution 219, 230–35 (Elise Bant et al. eds., 2020); Hanoch Dagan & Michael Heller, *Can Contract Emancipate? Contract Theory and The Law of Work*, 24 Theoretical Inq. L. 49 (2023).
36. *See supra* Chapter 3 text accompanying note 72.
37. *See supra* Chapter 3 text accompanying notes 28–32.
38. *See infra* Chapter 7 text accompanying note 29.
39. *See infra* Chapter 13 text accompanying note 44–45.
40. *See supra* Chapter 2 text accompanying notes 14–15.
41. Legal personality and its impact on private law and theory raise further complications. Some incorporated entities may not fit either category (consider research universities as we know them). This uncharted territory will be left for another occasion.
42. Democratic prescriptions in this context do not necessarily refer to the political community as a whole. At times, both democracy and relational justice require the pertinent legal subjects to participate in lawmaking. In this book, we only address one (relatively easy) example of such convergence—*see infra* Chapter 12 text accompanying note 36—recognizing the complexity of the connection between the democratizing effects of an inclusive process and the substantive demands of relational justice.
43. The input of administrative determinations on the interpersonal regime of tort law via the doctrine of negligence per se clearly illustrates this. *See* Restatement (Third) of Torts: Liab. Phys. & Emot. Harm § 14 cmt. d (2010). *See also, e.g.,* Dan B. Dobbs et al., Hornbook on Torts 253 (2d ed. 2016); John C. P. Goldberg & Benjamin C. Zipursky, The Oxford Introductions to US Law: Torts 155–56 (2010). The regulatory compliance defense and the federal preemption doctrine may also be related, but they point to further complexities exceeding the scope of this book. *See, e.g.,* Mark A. Geistfeld, *Tort Law in the Age of Statutes*, 99 Iowa L. Rev. 957, 996 (2014);

Catherine M. Sharkey, *Products Liability Preemption: An Institutional Approach*, 76 Geo. Wash. L. Rev. 449 (2008).

44. *See, e.g.*, George L. Priest, *Private Litigants and the Court Congestion Problem*, 69 B.U. L. Rev. 527, 527, 529–30, 557–58 (1989); Kevin M. Clermont & Theodore Eisenberg, *Litigation Realities*, 88 Cornell L. Rev. 119, 129, 131 (2002).
45. *See, e.g.*, Deborah L. Rhode, Access to Justice 3–5 (2004); Marc Galanter, *Why the "Haves" Come Out Ahead: Speculations on the Limits of Legal Change*, 9 Law & Soc. Rev. 95, 98, 103–04, 121–22 (1974).
46. *See* Hanoch Dagan & Roy Kreitner, 52 *The Other Half of Regulatory Theory*, 52 Conn. L. Rev. 605, 609–10, 622–23 (2020), on which this and the following paragraph rely. *See also* William J. Novak, The People's Welfare (1996); Joseph William Singer, No Freedom Without Regulation: The Hidden Lesson of the Subprime Crisis 58–95 (2015); William Forbath, *Politics, State-Building, and the Courts, 1870–1920*, *in* 2 The Cambridge History of Law in America 643 (Michael Grossberg & Christopher Tomlins eds., 2008); Catherine M. Sharkey, *The Administrative State and the Common Law: Regulatory Substitutes or Complements?*, 65 Emory L.J. 1705, 1706–1707, 1710, 1734, 1739 (2016); Edward L. Glaeser & Anderi Shleifer, *The Rise of the Regulatory State*, 41 J. Econ. Lit. 401, 401–03 (2003).
47. *See* Avihay Dorfman & Alon Harel, *The Necessity of Institutional Pluralism*, 43 Oxford J. Legal Stud. 753 (2023); Dorfman & Harel, *supra* note 1, at ch. 3.
48. *See supra* Chapter 2 text accompanying notes 14–15.

Chapter 5

1. *See* John C.P. Goldberg & Benjamin C. Zipursky, Recognizing Wrongs (2020).
2. *See* Avihay Dorfman, Conflict between Equals: Tort Law for a Liberal Society (unpublished manuscript).
3. *See further id.* at chs. 10–11.
4. *See, e.g.*, G. Edward White, *The Unexpected Persistence of Negligence, 1980–2000*, 54 Vand. L. Rev. 1337, 1346 (2001).
5. *See further* Gregory C. Keating, *Is Tort Law "Private"?*, *in* Civil Wrongs and Justice in Private Law 351, 357, 359, 371 (Paul B. Miller and John Oberdiek eds., 2020); *cf.* Catherine M. Sharkey, *Modern Tort Law: Preventing Harms, Not Recognizing Wrongs*, 134 Harv. L. Rev. 1423, 1444–54 (2021) (book review).
6. The locus classicus is Oliver Wendell Holmes, Jr., *Lecture III, Torts: Trespass and Negligence*, *in* The Common Law 71–117 (Dover Publ'ns 1991) (1881).
7. 338 P.2d 743, 744 (Wash. 1959).
8. *See, e.g.*, Robert Stevens, *Should Contributory Fault Be Analogue or Digital?*, *in* Defenses in Tort 247, 253 (Andrew Dyson et al. eds., 2015); Gregory C. Keating, *Reasonableness and Rationality in Negligence Theory*, 48 Stan. L. Rev. 311, 371 (1996); Gary T. Schwartz, *Contributory and Comparative Negligence: A Reappraisal*, 87 Yale L.J. 697, 722–23 (1978).
9. *See* Avihay Dorfman, *Negligence and Accommodation*, 22 Legal Theory 77, 90–92, 119–21 (2016).
10. On the former exception, *see id.* at 90 n.41. Concerning the second, see Dorfman, *supra* note 2, ch. 6.
11. *See* Vaughan v. Menlove, 132 Eng. Rep. 490 (Ct. Com. Pl. 1837).
12. *Fletcher*, 338 P.2d at 746. Note that the plaintiff's standard of care immediately and necessarily implicates the level of defendant care and (or) the scope of defendant's negligence liability.
13. *See* Restatement (Third) of Torts: Liab. Phys. & Emot. Harm § 11 cmt. e (2010).
14. This trend can be split into two classes. First, most states exonerate plaintiffs suffering from outright insanity or incompetence from being held contributorily or comparatively negligent. *See* Young v. State Dept. of Social Services, 92 Misc. 2d 795, 796 (N.Y. Ct. Cl. 1978). Second, with respect to plaintiffs suffering from diminished capacity short of outright insanity, it was observed half a century ago that "many" states deploy a subjective assessment of contributory or comparative negligence. *See* Snider v. Callahan, 250 F. Supp. 1022, 1023 (W.D. Mo. 1966) (Missouri Law); Noel v. McCaig, 258 P.2d 234, 240–41 (Kan. 1953); Feldman v. Howard, 214 N.E.2d 235 (Ohio App. 1966), *judgment reversed on other grounds*, Feldman v. Howard, 226 N.E.2d 564 (1967). A comparative study reports that most states follow this trend. W.C. Crais III, Comment Note, *Contributory Negligence of Mentally Incompetent or Mentally or Emotionally Disturbed Person*, 91 A.L.R.2d 392 §§ 2[a], 4[a] (1963). *See also* Johnson v. Primm, 396 P.2d 426, 430 (N.M. 1964);

Campbell v. Cluster Hous. Dev. Fund Co., 668 N.Y.S.2d 634, 635 (App. Div. 1998); Stacy v. Jedco Constr., Inc., 457 S.E.2d 875, 879 (N.C. Ct. App. 1995).

15. As the text implies, respectful regard for potential victims can manifest itself at two points in time. First, accommodating the victim's disability can occur ex post, as when the court is called to divide the costs of the victim's injury between the defendant and the plaintiff based on their respective—primary and comparative—fault. There, the asymmetric assessment of fault implies that the defendant had been expected to display due regard for the plaintiff's disabilities. Second, the respect conveyed in taking extra care can also be established ex ante, as when potential tortfeasors are expected to moderate their activity in compliance with the duty of care. There, the foreseeable presence of victims with physical disability within the danger zone partly determines the level of care that would properly count as "reasonable."
16. *See, e.g.*, AMARTYA SEN, INEQUALITY REEXAMINED 44–45 (1995).
17. In some exceptional cases, the proper response must go even further and endorse the strict defendant liability famously associated with the doctrine of ultrahazardous activities. *See* Dorfman, *supra* note 9, at 117–19.
18. By contrast, as noted, when the risk-creator is a physically or mentally disadvantaged person, no accommodation is justified. A subjective assessment of defendant care in this type of case necessarily undermines the privileged normative status of life and limb.
19. Balcom v. City of Independence, 160 N.W. 305, 308 (Iowa 1916). *See also, e.g.*, Weinstein v. Wheeler, 271 P. 733, 735 (Or. 1928).
20. For other normative claims where negligence law (and the reasonable care standard in particular) upholds the lexical priority of bodily integrity, *see, e.g.*, Richard W. Wright, *Justice and Reasonable Care in Negligence Law*, 47 AM. J. JURIS. 143, 170–94 (2003); Gregory C. Keating, *The Priority of Respect over Repair*, 18 LEGAL THEORY 293, 344 (2012); Mark Geistfeld, *Reconciling Cost-Benefit Analysis with the Principle that Safety Matters More than Money*, 76 N.Y.U. L. REV. 114, 122–28 (2001).
21. *See supra* Chapter 3 text accompanying notes 74–77.
22. For familiar examples, *see, e.g.*, *Vaughan*, 132 Eng. Rep. at 492 (noting that prudence varies with the faculties of men); Holmes, *supra* note 6, at 99 (describing the person who was "born hasty and awkward"); W. PAGE KEETON ET AL., PROSSER AND KEETON ON TORTS § 32, at 176 (5th ed. 1984) (describing the person suffering from "weaknesses of old age"); Richard A. Posner, *A Theory of Negligence*, 1 J. LEGAL STUD. 29, 31 (1972) (describing the person who is "clumsier than average").
23. *See further* Dorfman, supra note 2, at chs. 2–3.
24. Haley v. London Elec. Bd. [1965] AC 778 (HL) 805 (appeal taken from Eng.). The requirement of reasonable foreseeability may explain why it was easier for courts to prescribe duties of accommodation toward physically than toward mentally disadvantaged victims, given that physical disabilities are typically clearly manifest—consider a person in a wheelchair or a person with a complete loss of sight using a stick.
25. *See supra* Chapter 4 text accompanying notes 9–17.
26. *See* Toth v. Cmty. Hosp. at Glen Cove, 239 N.E.2d 368, 372–73 (1968).
27. *See, e.g.*, LaVine v. Clear Creek Skiing Corp., 557 F.2d 730, 734 (10th Cir., 1977) (Col. Law).
28. The reason for the qualified prescription is that all else is not always equal. Some defendants *fully control* the acquisition of their skills, so that the expected amount of care might implicate the defendant's choice concerning skills acquisition.
29. Note that the standard of usability and enjoyability cannot be specified without making some assumptions about the potential victim's condition or vulnerability.
30. *See, e.g.*, Langan v. Bellinger, 611 N.Y.S.2d 59, 59–60 (App. Div. 1994) (requiring "objective evidence" of nuisance); PROSSER AND KEETON, *supra* note 22, at § 88, p. 628.
31. Bie v. Ingersoll, 135 N.W.2d 250, 252 (Wis. 1965). *See also* Goeke v. National Farms, Inc., 512 N.W.2d 626, 632 (Neb. 1994); Rogers v. Elliot, 15 N.E. 768 (Mass. 1888).
32. For more on private nuisance and its fitting response to the different kinds of conflicts between neighbors, *see* Dorfman, *supra* note 2, ch. 4.
33. Not all theories belong in one of these two categories. Moreover, executive agent theories also include views where tort law is, or should be, responsive to distributive justice above all so as to ensure the fair allocation of the costs of accidents. *See* Keating, *supra* note 20, at 319. *See also, e.g.*, TSACHI KEREN-PAZ, TORTS, EGALITARIANISM AND DISTRIBUTIVE JUSTICE (2007); Guido Calabresi, *Some Thoughts on Risk Distribution and the Law of Torts*, 70 YALE L.J. 499, 502, 532–33 (1961). *Cf.* John Gardner, *What Is Tort Law For? Part II: The Place of Distributive Justice*, *in* PHILOSOPHICAL FOUNDATIONS OF THE LAW OF TORTS 335 (John Oberdiek ed., 2014).
34. *See, e.g.*, WILLIAM M. LANDES & RICHARD A. POSNER, THE ECONOMIC STRUCTURE OF TORT LAW 124–28 (1987).

35. *See* Omri Ben-Shahar & Ariel Porat, *Personalizing Negligence Law*, 91 N.Y.U. L. Rev. 627 (2016).
36. Landes & Posner, *supra* note 34, at 124, 126.
37. Matthew D. Adler & Eric A. Posner, New Foundations of Cost-Benefit Analysis 178 (2006).
38. *See generally* Robert Cooter & Ariel Porat, *Disgorgement Damages for Accidents*, 44 J. legal Stud. 249, 256, 261 (2015).
39. *See* Lewis A. Kornhauser, *The Domain of Preference*, 151 U. Pa. L. Rev. 717 (2003); Eyal Zamir & Barak Medina, Law, Economics, and Morality 20 (2010).
40. *See* Alon Harel & Ariel Porat, *Commensurability and Agency: Two Yet-to-Be-Met Challenges for Law and Economics*, 96 Cornell L. Rev. 749, 751–67 (2011). The difficulty with strict economic analysis in these contexts goes even deeper, as it makes the value of life dependent on people's willingness to pay, a view that, normatively, is clearly unacceptable. *See* Daniel A. Farber, *Inequality and Regulation: Designing Rules to Address Race, Poverty, and Environmental Justice*, 3 Am. J.L. & Equality 2 (2023).
41. This is not the only correction that the economic treatment of preferences requires. *See infra* Chapter 9 text accompanying notes 37–38.
42. Ernest J. Weinrib, The Idea of Private Law 82 (2012). *See also, e.g.*, Jules Coleman & Arthur Ripstein, *Mischief and Misfortune*, 41 McGill L.J. 91, 109, 112 (1995); Martin Stone, *The Significance of Doing and Suffering*, *in* Philosophy and the Law of Torts, 131, 156–57 (Gerald J. Postema ed., 2001).
43. Arthur Ripstein, Force and Freedom: Kant's Legal and Political Theory 171 (2009); Weinrib, *supra* note 42, at 147–52, 177–78; Jules Coleman, *Tort Law and Tort Theory: Preliminary Reflections on Method*, *in* Philosophy and the Law of Torts *supra* note 42, at 183, 205.
44. Arthur Ripstein, *Civil Recourse and Separation of Wrongs and Remedies*, 39 Fla. St. U. L. Rev. 163, 181 (2011). *See also* Weinrib, *supra* note 42, at 169 n.53, 183 n.22.
45. Even libertarians seem to subscribe to this position. *See* Robert Nozick, Anarchy, State, and Utopia 78–79, 82–83, 87, 115 (1974).
46. *See* Arthur Ripstein, *Justice and Responsibility*, 17 Can. J.L. & Juris. 361, 372 (2004); Weinrib, *supra* note 42, at 183 n.22.
47. *See* Arthur Ripstein, Equality, Responsibility, and the Law 111–13 (1999).
48. *See id.* at 112 (discussing the case of voluntary intoxication).
49. *See, e.g.*, Peter Davis et al., *Compensation for Medical Injury in New Zealand: Does "No-Fault" Increase the Level of Claims Making and Reduce Social and Clinical Selectivity?*, 27 J. Health Pol. Pol'y & L. 833, 835–36, 851–52 (2002).
50. *See, e.g.*, *id.* at 851–52. *See also* Craig Brown, *Deterrence in Tort and No-Fault: The New Zealand Experience*, 73 Calif. L. Rev. 976, 1002 (1985).
51. *See, e.g.*, Alan Brudner, The Unity of the Common Law 270 (2d ed. 2013, with Jennifer M. Nadler); Robert Stevens, Torts and Rights 324 (2007); Coleman & Ripstein, *supra* note 42, at 128 n.56.
52. *Cf.* Guido Calabresi, *A Broader View of the Cathedral: The Significance of the Liability Rule, Correcting a Misapprehension*, 77 Law & Contemp. Probs., no. 2, 2014, at 1, 2.
53. *Contra* David Enoch, *Tort Liability and Taking Responsibility*, *in* Philosophical Foundations of the Law of Torts, *supra* note 33, at 250.
54. *See supra* Chapter 2 text accompanying notes 14–15.
55. *See* Susan Couch v. Attorney Gen. [2010] NZSC 27, [2010] 3 NZLR 149 at [2].

Chapter 6

1. Alan Brudner, The Unity of the Common Law 278 (2d ed. 2013, with Jennifer M. Nadler).
2. Peter Benson, *Misfeasance as an Organizing Normative Idea in Private Law*, 60 U. Toronto L.J. 731, 733, 788 (2010).
3. *See* Ernest J. Weinrib, The Idea of Private Law 10 (1995).
4. Arthur Ripstein, *The Division of Responsibility and the Law of Tort*, 72 Fordham L. Rev. 1811, 1823–25 (2004). *See also* Arthur Ripstein, Private Wrongs 53–80, 288–95 (2016); Arthur Ripstein, *Three Duties to Rescue: Moral, Civil, Criminal*, 19 Law & Phil. 751, 764–65, 767–68 (2000).
5. *See, e.g.*, Riedel v. ICI Ams. Inc., 968 A.2d 17, 22–23 (Del. 2009).
6. For other insightful articulations of the institutional constraints on imposing tort liability for nonfeasance *see* Mark A. Geistfeld, Tort Law: The Essentials 155 (2008); Saul Levmore, *Waiting for Rescue: An Essay on the Evolution and Incentive Structure of the Law of Affirmative Obligations*,

72 VA. L. REV. 879 (1986); James A. Henderson, Jr., *Process Constraints in Tort*, 67 CORNELL L. REV. 901, 928–41 (1982).

7. *See* RIPSTEIN, *supra* note 4, at 54; Benson, *supra* note 2.
8. *See* RESTATEMENT (THIRD) OF TORTS: LIAB. PHYS. & EMOT. HARM § 37 (2012) (nonfeasance concerns "[a]n actor whose conduct has not created a risk of physical or emotional harm to another").
9. Ramsey v. Georgia S. Univ. Advanced Dev. Ctr., 189 A.3d 1255, 1284 (Del. 2018).
10. Estates of Morgan v. Fairfield Family Counseling Ctr., 673 N.E.2d 1311, 1319 n.2 (Oh. 1997).
11. *See, e.g.*, Hill v. Osterlind, 160 N.E. 301, 302 (Mass. 1928); Handiboe v. McCarthy, 151 S.E.2d 905, 907 (Ga. Ct. App. 1966).
12. *See, e.g.*, Richard A. Epstein, *A Theory of Strict Liability*, 2 J. LEGAL STUD. 151, 198–99 (1973).
13. RIPSTEIN, *supra* note 4, at 12.
14. *Id.* at 64.
15. *Id.* at 57.
16. As the text implies, we do not think that a virtue-based obligation of rescue (or, for that matter, a public right to be rescued) can offer a satisfactory response to this challenge.
17. *But see* Liam Murphy, *Beneficence, Law, and Liberty: The Case of Required Rescue*, 89 GEO. L.J. 605, 649 (2001).
18. *See supra* Chapter 3 text accompanying notes 74–77.
19. *Cf.* Robert L. Hale, *Prima Facie Torts, Combination, and Non-Feasance*, 46 COLUM. L. REV. 196, 214 (1946).
20. In this characterization, cases of pure economic loss or certain types of nuisance (such as interfering with the free flow of light onto the plaintiff's land) do not fall in the category of nonfeasance. It is a separate question whether a no-duty rule should apply in these cases.
21. *See* Ernest J. Weinrib, *The Case for a Duty to Rescue*, 90 Yale L.J. 247, 251, 262, 293 (1980). It should by now be clear that Weinrib has since retreated from this argument.
22. This identification difficulty in the nonfeasance context differs from the typical difficulty of tortfeasor identification in misfeasance cases: whereas the latter asks who caused the injury, the former asks why only me. Imposing a joint-and-several-liability regime may only replicate the why-only-me problem if the class of potential nonfeasors is large enough (so now the question would be why only us).
23. *See supra* Chapter 4 text accompanying notes 9–17.
24. Tarasoff v. The Regents of the Univ. of Cal., 551 P.2d 334, 343, 345, 347 (Cal. 1976). The court observes that "[o]ur current crowded and computerized society compels the interdependence of its members." *Id.* at 347.
25. RESTATEMENT (THIRD) OF TORTS: LIAB. PHYS. & EMOT. HARM § 41 cmn. g (2012).
26. *See, e.g.*, Boynton v. Burglass, 590 So. 2d 446, 449 (Fla. Dist. Ct. App. 1991); Thapar v. Zezulka, 994 S.W.2d 635, 638 (Tex. 1999).
27. *See* RESTATEMENT (THIRD) OF TORTS: LIAB. PHYS. & EMOT. HARM §§ 39–44 (2012). A fourth exception, statutory imposition of an affirmative duty, is just another form of special relationship. *Id.* § 38.
28. We say *to some extent* because some types of special relationship cannot possibly be re-described in terms of undertaking or some other voluntary assumption of responsibility.
29. RESTATEMENT (THIRD) OF TORTS: LIAB. PHYS. & EMOT. HARM § 39 (2012).
30. Palsgraf v. Long Island R.R. Co., 162 N.E. 99, 99 (N.Y. 1928). On the duty-based explanation of *Palsgraf*, see Avihay Dorfman, *Foreseeability as Re-Cognition*, 59 AM. J. JURIS. 163 (2014).
31. *See* RESTATEMENT (THIRD) OF TORTS: LIAB. PHYS. & EMOT. HARM § 39 cmts. e & g (2012).
32. *See* DAN B. DOBBS ET AL., THE LAW OF TORTS 619 (2d ed. 2016).
33. South v. Nat'l R. R. Passenger Corp. (AMTRAK), 290 N.W.2d 819, 837 (N.D. 1980).
34. Private necessity applies not only to cases where the person of the defendant is at risk but also when only her property is imperiled. *See respectively* Vincent v. Lake Erie Transp. Co., 124 N.W. 221 (Minn. 1910); Ploof v. Putnam, 71 A. 188 (Vt. 1908).
35. *See* ARTHUR RIPSTEIN, FORCE AND FREEDOM: KANT'S LEGAL AND POLITICAL THEORY 274–75, 277 (2009).
36. *See supra* Chapter 3 text accompanying note 62.
37. *See* HANOCH DAGAN, UNJUST ENRICHMENT: A STUDY OF PRIVATE LAW AND PUBLIC VALUES 81–82 (1997); Avihay Dorfman, *Private Law Exceptionalism? Part II: A Basic Difficulty with the Argument from Formal Equality*, 31 CAN. J.L. & JURIS. 5, 30–31 (2018).
38. The leading authority on this point is *Ploof*, 71 A. at 189.
39. See Francis H. Bohlen, *Incomplete Privilege to Inflict Intentional Invasions of Interest of Property and Personality*, 39 HARV. L. REV. 307, 313 (1926).

40. *See, e.g.*, Thomas W. Merrill, *Property as Modularity*, 125 Harv. L. Rev. F. 151, 157 (2012).
41. *See, e.g.*, Robert Stevens, Torts and Rights 205–06 (2007).
42. *See, e.g.*, Hanoch Dagan, Property: Values and Institutions 18–26 (2011); Avihay Dorfman & Assaf Jacob, *The Fault of Trespass*, 65 U. Toronto L.J. 48, 75 (2015).
43. *See* Adam J. MacLeod, Trespass and Intention: Three Forms (unpublished manuscript).
44. *See* Hanoch Dagan & Irit Samet, *Express Trust: The Dark Horse of the Liberal Property Regime, in* Philosophical Foundations of Trust Law 139, 161–63 (Simone Degeling et al. eds., 2023).
45. *See supra* text accompanying note 10.
46. Damien Schiff, *Samaritans: Good, Bad, and Ugly: A Comparative Law Analysis*, 11 Roger Williams U. L. Rev. 77, 79 (2005). For a discussion of the French and German approaches to nonfeasance liability, see Jeroen Kortmann, Altruism in Private Law: Liability for Nonfeasance and Negotiorum Gestio 29–50 (2005). For traditionalists' attempts to set aside or face this comparative challenge and our critique thereof, see Hanoch Dagan & Avihay Dorfman, *Just Relationships*, 116 Colum. L. Rev. 1395, 1453–54 nn. 246–47 (2005).
47. *See generally* Dan B. Dobbs et al., The Law of Torts § 424 (2d ed. 2021).
48. Commercial sellers are often subject to dram shop laws. These laws (at least in their modern instantiation) are designed to protect third-party victims of drunk drivers from intoxicated patrons of commercial sellers of alcoholic beverages. Some jurisdictions, however, have extended dram shop liability to social hosts. *See* Main Liquor Liability Act, Title 28-A, Ch. 100, § 2505(2).
49. The leading Canadian case of Childs v. Desormeaux, [2006] 1 S.C.R. 643 applies the traditional common law rule of no liability for social hosts, but its express reasoning seems to support the prescriptions of relational justice analysis. Thus, the Court notes that "[i]t might be argued that a host who continues to serve alcohol to a visibly inebriated person knowing that he or she will be driving home has become implicated in the creation or enhancement of a risk sufficient to give rise to a *prima facie* duty of care to third parties, which would be subject to contrary policy considerations at the second stage of the *Anns* test." *Id.* at para. 44.

Chapter 7

1. 257 N.E.2d 870 (1970).
2. Daniel A. Farber, *The Story of* Boomer*: Pollution and the Common Law*, 32 Ecology L.Q. 113, 113 (2005).
3. *See* Guido Calabresi & A. Douglas Melamed, *Property Rules, Liability Rules, and Inalienability: One View of the Cathedral*, 85 Harv. L. Rev. 1089, 1106 n.34, 1116 n.55 (1972).
4. *Boomer*, 257 N.E.2d at 872–73.
5. *See, e.g.*, Adkins v. Thomas Solvent Co., 487 N.W.2d 715, 719 (Mich. 1992).
6. *Boomer*, 257 N.E.2d at 871.
7. *See* Richard A. Posner, Economic Analysis of Law 69–72 (7th ed. 2007); A. Mitchell Polinsky, *Resolving Nuisance Disputes: The Simple Economics of Injunctive and Damage Remedies*, 32 Stan. L. Rev. 1075 (1980). Other lawyer-economists, who emphasize institutional concerns, reach other conclusions. *See* Henry E. Smith, *Exclusion and Property Rules in the Law of Nuisance*, 90 Va. L. Rev. 965, 1040–45 (2004); Yair Listokin, Law and Macroeconomics: Legal Remedies to Recessions 196–97 (2019).
8. *See* Ernest J. Weinrib, The Idea of Private Law 195 (1995); Ernest J. Weinrib, Corrective Justice 104 n.53 (2012); Arthur Ripstein, Private Wrongs 126 n.9 (2016); Richard A. Epstein, *Defenses and Subsequent Pleas in a System of Strict Liability*, 3 J. Legal Stud. 165, 200 (1974).
9. *Boomer*, 257 N.E.2d 870, 871, 873.
10. *See* Douglas Laycock, *The Neglected Defense of Undue Hardship (and the Doctrinal Train Wreck in Boomer v. Atlantic Cement)*, 4(3) J. Tort L. 1 (2012); John C.P. Goldberg & Benjamin C. Zipursky, Torts 244 (2010).
11. *Boomer*, 257 N.E.2d at 872–73.
12. Samuel L. Bray, *Remedies, Meet Economics; Economics, Meet Remedies*, 38 Oxford J. Legal Stud. 71, 85 (2018). *See also, e.g.*, Ripstein, *supra* note 8, at 251.
13. Weinrib, The Idea of Private Law, *supra* note 8, at 192.
14. *See* Calabresi & Melamed, *supra* note 3, at 1090, 1902.
15. *See, e.g.*, Robert D. Cooter & Ariel Porat, Getting Incentives Right 12 (2014).
16. *See* Stephen A. Smith, *Duties, Liabilities, and Damages*, 125 Harv. L. Rev. 1727 (2012); John C. P. Goldberg, *Two Conceptions of Tort Damages: Fair v. Full Compensation*, 55 DePaul L. Rev. 435 (2006); Benjamin C. Zipursky, *Civil Recourse, Not Corrective Justice*, 91 Geo. L.J. 695 (2003).

17. *See* Scott Hershovitz, *Corrective Justice for Civil Recourse Theorists*, 39 Fla. St. U. L. Rev. 107 (2011).
18. *See* Smith, *supra* note 16; Stephen A. Smith, Rights, Wrongs, and Injustices: The Structure of Remedial Law 202 (2019). The pre-payment rule that Smith relies upon cannot vindicate his radical conclusion since it is better viewed as a means for precluding disagreements.
19. *See* Weinrib, Corrective Justice, *supra* note 8, at 98, 102, 106–08.
20. *See also* Jules L. Coleman & Jody Kraus, *Rethinking the Theory of Legal Rights*, 95 Yale L.J. 1335, 1339–40, 1342–43, 1345, 1369–71 (1986); John Gardner, *What is Tort Law For? Part I: The Place of Corrective Justice*, 30 L. & Phil. 1 (2011).
21. *See further* Erik Encarnacion, *Making Whole, Making Better, and Accommodating Resilience*, 108 Minn. L. Rev. 1335 (2024).
22. *See* Stephen A. Smith, *Rights and Remedies: A Complex Relationship*, *in* Taking Remedies Seriously 31 (Kent Roach & Robert Sharpe eds. 2010). *See also* Wesley Newcomb Hohfeld, *Fundamental Legal Conceptions as Applied in Judicial Reasoning*, 26 Yale L.J. 710, 753–57, 763 (1917); Seana Valentine Shiffrin, *Remedial Clauses: The Overprivatization of Private Law*, 67 Hastings L.J. 407, 433, 436 (2016). Using the concept of systematicity, Kantians can accommodate institutional limitations on the make-whole aspirations of remedies in private law. *Cf.* Ernest J. Weinrib, *Private Law and Public Right*, 61 U. Toronto L.J. 191, 196 (2011); Ripstein, *supra* note 8, at 238, 251–52.
23. *See, e.g.*, Weinrib, Corrective Justice, *supra* note 8, at 61, 117; Ripstein, *supra* note 8, at 245–61.
24. Arthur Ripstein observes that the traditionalist account of making the plaintiff whole is not about restoring "the condition of either [party] in relation to their own previous condition," but about reversing a wrongful transaction so as to restore "how things stand between the parties." Arthur Ripstein, *Corrective Justice*, *in* Research Handbook on Private Law Theory 255, 258 (Hanoch Dagan & Benjamin Zipursky eds., 2020). But characterizing it as reversing a transaction does not change the fact that nothing in the defendant's post-wrong condition could make a difference in the legal analysis recommended by this approach.
25. Due to rule of law considerations of finality of adjudication, judgment, and law more generally, our account of substantive remedies begins and ends with *second*-looking even if remedies law *could* implement a principle of third-, fourth-, or n*th*-looking.
26. *See* Hanoch Dagan, *The Liberal Promise of Contract*, *in* Private Law and Practical Reason 315, 328–29 (Haris Psarras & Sandy Steel eds., 2022). *See also* Hanoch Dagan & Michael Heller, *Specific Performance: On Freedom and Commitment in Contract Law*, 98 Notre Dame L. Rev. 1323, 1364 (2023) (criticizing unjustified limitations on parties' ability to adjust contractual remedies).
27. *See also* Daniel Markovits & Alan Schwartz, Rights and Remedies in Private Law (unpublished manuscript). Markovits and Schwartz argue that remedies *always* reflect the nature of the rights they enforce so that, for instance, a compensatory damages remedy reflects a primary right to the value of the thing rather than to the thing itself. They cannot be right, however. While the default remedy for conversion is damages measured by the thing's value, to suppose that one could get away with deliberately taking a generic chattel and paying its market value up front to the right-holder is false. *See respectively* Armstrong v. Bromley Quarry & Asphalt, Inc., 378 P.3d 1090, 1096 (Kan. 2016); Nacol v. Metallic Dev. Corp., 614 S.W.2d 172, 175 (Tex. Civ. App. 1980). Moreover, as we note in the text below, a great deal of tort law resists this: a deliberate attempt to unilaterally convert a duty of care (or any other duty whose violation triggers compensatory damages) into a liability rule typically gives rise to super-compensatory damages.
28. *See* Pickett v. Crook, 20 Wis. 358, 359 (1866).
29. *See, e.g.*, Cashin v. Northern Pac. Ry. Co., 28 P.2d 862 (Mont. 1934).
30. For an earlier development of this theme, see Avihay Dorfman, *What is the Point of the Tort Remedy*, 55 Am. J. Juris. 105, 153–62 (2010). *See also* Mark Geistfeld, *The Tort Entitlement to Physical Security as the Distributive Basis for Environmental, Health, and Safety Regulations*, 15 Theoretical Inq. L. 387, 400 (2014).
31. Marc Galanter & David Luban, *Poetic Justice: Punitive Damages and Legal Pluralism*, 42 Am. U. L. Rev. 1393, 1430 (1993).
32. However, concern about the defendant's financial collapse due to the imposition of punitive damages may place outer limits on the looking-back pursuit, though not necessarily when intended for second looking. *See, e.g.*, Dillard Dept. Stores v. Beckwith, 989 P.2d 889, 887–88 (Nev. 1999); Sherman v. McDermott, 329 A.2d 195, 197 (R.I. 1974).
33. *See supra* Chapter 4 text accompanying notes 9–13.

34. *See, e.g.*, EMILY SHERWIN & SAMUEL L. BRAY, AMES, CHAFEE, AND RE ON REMEDIES: CASES AND MATERIALS 4 (2d ed. 2018); Emily Sherwin, *Compensation and Revenge*, 40 SAN DIEGO L. REV. 1387, 1389–96 (2003). *Cf.* Felipe Jiménez, *Rethinking Contract Remedies*, 53 ARIZ. ST. L.J. 1153 (2021).
35. *See supra* Chapter 4 text accompanying notes 14–17.
36. In other cases, feasibility may be impinged because most schemes of liability insurance come unbundled: they apply to a particular context, such as homeowner liability insurance, or take up a particular activity, such as car insurance and professional malpractice liability insurance. There are exceptions, such as umbrella insurance, which provides liability insurance for claims not covered by other policies, but its coverage is peripheral rather than residual.
37. *See respectively* Robins Dry Dock & Repair Co v. Flint, 275 U.S. 303, 309 (1927); RESTATEMENT (THIRD) OF TORTS: LIAB. PHYS. & EMOT. HARM § 7 (2010); and RESTATEMENT, *id.* § 48 cmnt. a.
38. *Compare* Stephen R. Perry, *Protected Interests and Undertakings in the Law of Negligence*, 42 U. TORONTO L.J. 247, 263 (1992) *with* Ultramares Corp. v. Touche, 174 N.E. 441, 444 (N.Y. 1931).
39. *See, e.g.*, A. Mitchell Polinsky & Steven Shavell, *The Uneasy Case for Products Liability*, 123 HARV. L. REV. 1438, 1459–60 (2009).
40. *See supra* Chapter 4 text following note 24.
41. *See, e.g.*, Eisenhauer v. Burger, 431 F.2d 833, 837 (6th Cir. 1970) (Oh. law); Dawson v. Shannon, 9 S.W.2d 998, 999 (Ky. 1928). Nordic law offers interesting counterexamples. *See* THOMAS WILHELMSSON, CRITICAL STUDIES IN PRIVATE LAW: A TREATISE ON NEED-RATIONAL PRINCIPLES IN MODERN LAW 111–13, 151–52 (1992).
42. *See, e.g.*, Jeremy Waldron, *Moments of Carelessness and Massive Loss*, *in* PHILOSOPHICAL FOUNDATIONS OF TORT LAW 387, 387–88 (David G. Owen ed., 1995); Jules Coleman, *The Structure of Tort Law*, 97 YALE L.J. 1233, 1248 (1988); KENNETH S. ABRAHAM, THE LIABILITY CENTURY 214 (2008).
43. *See* Stephen G. Gilles, *The Judgment-Proof Society*, 63 WASH. & LEE L. REV. 603 (2006).
44. *See* Tom Baker, *Blood Money, and the Moral Economy of Tort Law in Action*, 35 L. & SOC'Y REV. 275 (2001).
45. *See* ABRAHAM, *supra* note 42.
46. *See* DAN B. DOBBS, THE LAW OF TORTS 1059 (2000).
47. *See* JENNIFER K. ROBBENNOLT & VALERIE P. HANS, THE PSYCHOLOGY OF TORT LAW 131 (2016).
48. *See, e.g.*, Va. Code. Ann. § 8.01-581.15.
49. *But see* Gregory C. Keating, *Nuisance as a Strict Liability Tort*, 4(3) J. TORT L., article 2, at 6 (2012). On the general idea of an excuse, see J. L. Austin, *A Plea for Excuses*, 57 PROCEED. ARISTOTELIAN SOC'Y 1, 2 (1956–57).
50. A no-duty explanation has been defended on economic and non-economic grounds, to no avail. *See* Hanoch Dagan & Avihay Dorfman, *Substantive Remedies*, 96 NOTRE DAME L. REV. 513, 547–48 (2020). For a critique of a public-regarding rationale, *see id.* at 549–50.
51. *Ultramares v. Touche*, 174 N.E. 441, 444 (N.Y. 1931).
52. *See* Credit Alliance Corp. v. Arthur Andersen & co., 483 N.E.2d 110 (N.Y. 1985); *see generally* Walpert, Sumullian & Bluthental, P.A. v. Katz, 762 A.2d 582, 586–87 (Md. 2000).
53. *Ultramares*, 174 N.E. at 447.
54. *See supra* text accompanying notes 28–31.
55. *Ultramares*, 174 N.E. at 445.
56. *See, e.g.*, Union Oil Company v. Oppen, 501 F.2d 558, 563–69 (9th Cir. 1974) (Cal. law).
57. *See, e.g.*, Martinez v. Milburn Enters., 233 P.3d 205, 208 (Kan. 2010).
58. DOBBS, *supra* note 46, at 1059.
59. Harding v. Town of Townshend, 43 Vt. 536, 539 (1871).
60. The distinction between accidental and deliberate wrongdoers is implicitly reflected in those statutory schemes that limit the abrogation of the collateral source rule to medical malpractice. *See, e.g.*, 231 MASS. GEN. ANN. § 60G. But some statutory schemes make no such distinction, either implicit or explicit. *See, e.g.*, N.J. STAT. ANN. 2A:15–97.
61. The collateral source rule could be unnecessary even here due to the availability of bankruptcy and other legal protections. But bankruptcy protections render non-collectable certain all-purpose assets (viz., exempt income and homestead) that are linked to the basic ingredients of subsistence necessary for all people to experience a decent life. *See* Gilles, *supra* note 43, at 624, 632. By contrast, the notion of ground projects informing our reconstruction of the collateral source rule focuses on pursuing a meaningful life.
62. *See also* Bynum v. Magno, 101 P.3d 1149, 1167 (Ha. 2004) (dissenting opinion).

63. *See* Roger C. Henderson, *Designing a Responsible Periodic Payment System for Tort Awards: Arizona Enacts a Prototype*, 32 ARIZ. L. REV. 21, 27–29 (1990).
64. *See, e.g.*, Henry E. Smith, *Structured Settlements as Structures of Rights*, 88 VA. L. REV. 1953, 1955 (2002).
65. We focus on the case of infants and their loss of earning capacity but our analysis applies to related questions, such as calculating a victim's expected lifespan (which, in turn, affects the size of the medical expenses as well as the victim's lifelong pain and suffering). *See generally* MARTHA CHAMALLAS & JENNIFER B. WRIGGINS, THE MEASURE OF INJURY: RACE, GENDER, AND TORT LAW (2010).
66. Martha Chamallas, *Civil Rights in Ordinary Tort Cases: Race, Gender, and the Calculation of Economic Loss*, 38 Loy. L.A. L. Rev. 1435, 1440 (2005).
67. *See* Jennifer B. Wriggins, *Damages in Tort Litigation: Thoughts on Race and Remedies, 1865–2007*, 27 REV. LITIG. 37, 61 (2007).
68. *See, e.g.*, Ronen Avraham & Kimberly Yuracko, *Torts and Discrimination*, 78 OHIO ST. L.J. 661, 677 (2017); Ariel Porat, *Misalignments in Tort Law*, 121 YALE L.J. 82, 97–105 (2011); Martha Chamallas, *Questioning the Use of Race-Specific and Gender-Specific Economic Data in Tort Litigation: A Constitutional Argument*, 63 FORDHAM L. REV. 73, 75 (1994).
69. *See* McMillan v. City of New York, 253 F.R.D. 247, 249–51 (E.D.N.Y. 2008); Wheeler Tarpeh-Doe. v. United States, 771 F. Supp. 427, 455 (D.C.C. 1991), *rev'd on other grounds* Wheeler Tarpeh-Doe. v. United States, 28 F.3d 120 (D.C. Cir. 1994).
70. *See* McMillan, 253 F.R.D. at 255–56; G.M.M. v. Kimpson, 116 F. Supp.3d 126, 140 (E.D.N.Y. 2015). *See also* United States v. Bedonie, 317 F. Supp.2d. 1285, 1319 (D. Utah 2004); Chamallas, *supra* note 66, at 1441.
71. *See supra* Chapter 3 text accompanying notes 28–32.
72. *See supra* Chapter 2 text accompanying notes 46–51.
73. *See, e.g.*, Vosburg v. Putney, 50 N.W. 403, 404 (Wis. 1891).
74. *See* Avihay Dorfman, *Can Tort Law be Moral?*, 23 RATIO JURIS 205, 225–26 (2010).
75. For a non-relational defense of the thin-skull rule based on fairness considerations across the entire victim class, see Mark A. Geistfeld, *Proximate Cause Untangled*, 80 MD. L. REV. 420, 453–54 (2021).
76. *See, e.g.*, Ragsdale v. Jones, 117 S.E.2d 114 (Va. 1960); Bryan v. City of New Orleans, 737 So.2d 696, 698 (La. 1999).
77. RESTATEMENT (THIRD) OF TORTS: LIAB. PHYS. & EMOT. HARM § 31 cmt. D (2010).
78. *See, e.g.*, *Id.* ; Richard W. Wright, *The Grounds and Extent of Legal Responsibility*, 40 SAN DIEGO L. REV. 1425, 1491 (2003).
79. *See similarly supra* Chapter 5 text accompanying and following notes 30–31. A further refinement of the doctrine may subdivide the category of property so as to afford rigorous protection to holdings that play a constitutive role in people's self-determination. *Cf.* HANOCH DAGAN, A LIBERAL THEORY OF PROPERTY 50–51, 69–70 (2021).

Chapter 8

1. *See* William L. Prosser, *Private Action for Public Nuisance*, 52 VA. L. REV. 997, 1005 (1966).
2. J. W. Neyers, *Reconceptualizing the Tort of Public Nuisance*, 76 CAMBRIDGE L.J. 87, 93 (2017).
3. *See* Thomas W. Merrill, *Is Public Nuisance a Tort?*, J. TORT L. Vol. 4 (2011), Iss. 2, Art. 4, at 7–8.
4. Ganim v. Smith & Wesson Corp., 780 A.2d 98, 131 (Conn. 2001); *see also* State v. Lead Industries Association, *Inc.*, 951 A.2d 428, 446–47 (R.I. 2008).
5. *See respectively* RESTATEMENT (SECOND) OF TORT § 812B 1 (1979); W. PAGE KEETON ET AL., PROSSER AND KEETON ON TORTS 643 (5th ed. 1984).
6. Victor E. Schwartz & Phil Goldberg, *The Law of Public Nuisance: Maintaining Rational Boundaries on a Rational Tort*, 45 WASHBURN L.J. 541, 552 (2006).
7. Merrill, *supra* note 3, at 4.
8. Catherine M. Sharkey, *Public Nuisance as Modern Business Tort: A New Unified Framework for Liability for Economic Harms*, 70 DEPAUL L. REV. 431, 431 (2021).
9. People v. Lim, 118 P.2d 472, 473 (Cal. 1941).
10. Benetatos v. City of Los Angeles, 186 Cal. Rptr. 3d 46 (Ct. App. 2015).
11. People v. Rubenfeld, 172 N.E. 485 (N.Y. 1930); Gardner v. International Shoe Co., 49 N.E.2d 328 (1943).
12. *See* Schwartz & Goldberg, *supra* note 6, at 557–61.
13. Master Settlement Agreement, Nov. 14, 1998 (tobacco settlement) https://publichealthlawcenter.org/sites/default/files/resources/master-settlement-agreement.pdf; State of Tennessee v. Pursue Pharma, 2019 WL 2331282 (Tenn. Cir. Ct. 2019).

14. *See* Kate Markey, *Comment: Air Pollution as Public Nuisance: Comparing Modern-Day Greenhouse Gas Abatement with Nineteenth-Century Smoke Abatement*, 120 MICH. L. REV. 1535 (2022).
15. On the two main challenges to it, dealing with standing and the economic loss conundrum, see Hanoch Dagan & Avihay Dorfman, *Public Nuisance for Private Persons*, 74 U. TORONTO L.J. 198, 217–22 (2024), where we also discuss and criticize the two most influential accounts of public nuisance in contemporary legal scholarship.
16. *See* Professor Richard Epstein's (and others') *Amicus Curiae* Brief of Competitive Enterprise Institute, Oklahoma v. Johnson & Johnson, Appeal no. 118,474 (Okla. Oct. 22, 2020) at https://cei.org/wp-content/uploads/2020/11/CEI_Brief_-_OK_Opiods_Case_-_Supreme_Court_of_Oklahoma_-_final_v2.pdf.
17. Merrill, *supra* note 3, at 54.
18. Kate Fritz, *Public Pollution/Public Solution: A Framework for City-Led Toxic Tort Litigation*, 28 N.Y.U. ENVTL. L.J. 319, 326 (2020).
19. *See* Arthur Ripstein, Public and Private in the Tort of Public Nuisance (unpublished manuscript, May 2022); Neyers, *supra* note 2. This critical difference is evident, for example, in Ripstein's core claim, where the wrong of public nuisance can be characterized in terms of privatization. *Id.* at 25, 33. We reject this view because many instances of public nuisance involve no plan to either wield political authority or de facto gain control (even if temporarily) over public resources. Instead, they represent *accidental* interference with the right to use and enjoy the public sphere (as when a truck driver accidentally drops flour bags and thus, inadvertently and unaware of it, blocks a public road).

    As will become clear below, these different normative explications of the wrong of public nuisance generate differing doctrinal implications and, thus, quite divergent practical consequences.
20. This is not to deny that members of the political community may have entitlements that non-members do not. As our discussion in Chapter 2 implies, there are at least two different layers of right: a thinner layer of relational justice and a thicker one of democratic equality. Being a member of the political community is the admission ticket to the latter while being a person is the admission ticket to the former. Additionally, the thicker layer of rights must not negate the thinner one (for instance, granting free admission to a public museum only to citizens can only be permissible if non-members are allowed in for a reasonable fare).
21. It also suggests that public nuisance—like private nuisance and privacy—belongs to the class of torts whose rights exist only within a particular sphere. No overlap is possible, then, between private and public nuisance since the former can only protect the right to use private premises. On the historical connections between public and private nuisance, *see* Richard A. Epstein, *The Private Law Connections to Public Nuisance: Some Realism about Today's Intellectual Nominalism*, 17 J. L. ECON. & POL'Y 282, 284, 288–89 (2022). Another implication of our account is that public nuisance may not be invoked to tackle risks to life and limb occurring within private spaces, such as lead paint in private homes. Other causes of action, including products liability and negligence, provide a better fit.
22. It is hard to predict what virtual public spaces will be formed (in the metaverse or in some other virtual format). We use this conceptual point to make a normative claim, namely, that there is no reason to define the scope of public nuisance by reference to historical instances.
23. *See* ARTHUR RIPSTEIN, FORCE AND FREEDOM ch.8 (2009).
24. In that, public nuisance resembles the reliance of the tort of negligence, in the form of negligence per se, on statutory safety norms to determine what counts as negligence (i.e., breach of duty of care). *See* RESTATEMENT (SECOND) OF TORTS § 821B(2)(b) (1979).
25. The example draws on Union Oil Company v. Oppen, 501 F.2d 558 (1974) (9th Cir.) (Cal. Law).
26. *See, e.g.*, City of Chicago v. Beretta U.S.A. Corp., 821 N.E.2d 1099, 1116 (Ill. 2004); N. J. MCBRIDE & R. BAGSHAW, TORT LAW 659 (5th ed. 2015); Prosser, *supra* note 1, at 999.
27. *See* Tate & Lyle Food & Distribution Ltd. v G.L.C. [1983] 2 A.C. 509, 531 (H.L.).
28. *Id.* at 537.
29. *Id.*
30. Further, as in the case of private property rights, public rights may (and often should) also give rise to control rather than merely use rights. *See* Avihay Dorfman, *Public Ownership*, L. & PHIL. (forthcoming 2024).
31. *See, e.g.*, R v Rimmington [2005] UKHL 63, [2006] 1 AC 459 at 470 and 484; CA 128/2020 Smith v. Fonterra Co-Operative Group Limited [2021] NZCA 552, para. 42. *See also* R. v. Cross (1812) 170 E.R. 1362, 1363 (*per* Ellenborough L.); 4 WILLIAM BLACKSTONE, COMMENTARIES ON THE LAW OF ENGLAND *166 (1765–69).
32. That is, membership in the relevant political community is either a ground or a condition for having primary rights to use and enjoy the public space, secondary rights of repair, and tertiary

rights of action. *See* J.W. Neyers, *Divergence and Convergence in the Tort of Public Nuisance, in* Divergences in Private Law 69, 77 (Andrew Robertson & Michael Tilbury eds., 2015). *See also* Ripstein, *supra* note 23, at 262; David Bullock, *Public Nuisance and Climate Change: The Common Law's Solutions to the Plaintiff, Defendant and Causation Problems*, 85 Modern L. Rev. 1136, 1142 (2022).

33. *Compare* Carol Rose, *The Comedy of the Commons: Custom, Commerce, and Inherently Public Property*, 53 U. Chi. L. Rev. 711 (1986); Katy Wells, *Crucial Options: Dagan on Self-determination and Structural Pluralism*, 33 King's L.J. 53, 59–60 (2022).
34. *See supra* Chapter 2 text accompanying notes 39–51.
35. Ripstein, *supra* note 23, at 246, 248, 251, 252, 256–57; Christopher Essert, Yours and Mine: Property Law in the Society of Equals (2024).
36. *See also* Hanoch Dagan, A Liberal Theory of Property ch. 5 (2021).
37. *See* Avihay Dorfman, *When, and How, Does Property Matter?*, 72 U. Toronto L.J. 81, 89–93 (2022).
38. We set aside the question of whether "seeing to it" requires public provision in particular or can allow for private provision. For more on the considerations underlying this choice, see Avihay Dorfman & Alon Harel, Reclaiming the Public chs. 5–6 (2024); Dorfman, *supra* note 30.
39. On double-parking as an instance of public nuisance, see Salsbury v. United Parcel Service, 203 Misc. 1008, 120 N.Y.S.2d 33 (N.Y. Municipal Ct. 1953).
40. Markey, *supra* note 14, at 1540–41.
41. David A. Dana, *The Mismatch between Public Nuisance and Global Warming*, 18 Sup. Ct. Econ. Rev. 9, 9–10 (2010).
42. There are any number of legal reasons, procedural and substantive, for this state of affairs. *See, e.g.*, Smith v. Fonterra Co-Operative Group Ltd. [2021] NZCA 552, para. [87]; Am. Elec. Power Co. v. Connecticut, 564 U.S. 410, 418–20 (2011); City of Oakland v. BP PLC, 960 F.3d 570, 575–76 (9th Cir. 2020). *See also* Markey, *supra* note 14, at 1537; Sabrin McCormick et al., *Science in Litigation, the Third Branch of U.S. Climate Policy*, 357 Science 979, 980 (2017).
43. *See* Joshua Ulan Galperin & Douglas A. Kysar, *Uncommon Law: Judging in the Anthropocene, in* Climate Change Litigation in the Asia Pacific 15, 22 (Jolene Line & Douglas Kysar eds., 2020) and Dana, *supra* note 41, at 12, 21, 38–41, respectively.
44. *See, e.g.*, Bullock, *supra* note 32; and Markey, *supra* note 14, respectively.
45. Background justice is defined in terms of the *state*'s duty to provide the basic "conditions of full membership in society." Arthur Ripstein, Private Wrongs 291 (2016). A universal version of background justice will support the extension of this duty beyond the special case of the state (or of a particular society).
46. Bullock, *supra* note 32, at 1145. *See also id.* at 17. *Cf.* Juliana v. United States, 947 F.3d 1159, 1169 (9th Cir. 2020).
47. For instance, the plaintiff in *Lliuya v. RWE AG*, a pending climate change lawsuit brought by a Peruvian farmer against a German utility company in a German regional court, seeks to redress an injury to his right to use his land. On our account, this complaint does not state a case for *public* nuisance. For details, see http://climatecasechart.com/non-us-case/lliuya-v-rwe-ag/.
48. It is also under-inclusive if, by protecting the ability to use the atmosphere, the revised tort fails to capture instances of obstructing use of public spaces that fall short of environmental harm (such as double-parking other vehicles).
49. *See* Avihay Dorfman, *The Work of Tort Law: Why Non-Consensual Access to the Workplace Matters?*, 24 Theoretical Inq. L. 74 (2023).
50. *See supra* Chapter 2 text accompanying notes 7–15.
51. Avihay Dorfman, Conflict between Equals: Tort Law for a Liberal Society [Introduction] (unpublished manuscript).
52. *See respectively, e.g.,* Dan B. Dobbs, The Law of Torts § 467 at 1335 (2000); Lower Commerce Ins. Inc. v. Halliday, 636 So.2d 430, 431 (Ala. 1994). *See also* Dagan & Dorfman, supra note 15, at 218.
53. *See* David Grossman, *Warming Up to a Not-So-Radical Idea: Tort-Based Climate Change Litigation*, 28 Colum. J. Envtl. L. 1, 53054 (2003).
54. Our approach, therefore, shows that the net of liability cast by public nuisance is sufficiently broad to capture future consequences of greenhouse gas emission. *Compare* Caroline E. Foster, *Novel Climate Tort? The New Zealand Court of Appeal Decision in Smith v. Fonterra Co-operative Group Limited and Others*, 24 Env. L. Rev. 224, 227, 233 (2022).
55. We use seawalls as an example without necessarily commending this measure.
56. The *locus classicus* is Martin v. Herzog, 126 N.E. 814 (N.Y. 1920).

57. *See, e.g.*, Emily Boyd et al., *Loss and Damage from Climate Change: A New Climate Justice Agenda*, 4 One Earth 1365, 1365 (2021).
58. *See, e.g.*, Rachel James et al., *Characterizing Loss and Damage from Climate Change*, 4 Nature Climate Change 938, 939 (2014).
59. *See, e.g.*, Friederike E. L. Otto et al., *Causality and the fate of Climate Change Litigation: The Role of the Social Superstructure Narrative*, Public Pol'y 1, 7 (2022).
60. *See* Leah Aronowsky, *The Limits of Climate Change Litigation*, N.Y. Rev. Books (Nov. 3 2021) available at https://www.nybooks.com/daily/2021/11/03/the-limits-of-climate-change-litigation/.
61. Otto, *supra* note 59, at 7.
62. *Id. See further* Sjoukje Philip et al., *A Protocol for Probabilistic Extreme Event Attribution Analyses*, 6 Adv. Stat. Clim. Meteorol. Oceanogr. 177 (2020).
63. *See* Benjamin Franta, *Early Oil Industry Disinformation on Global Warming*, 31 Environmental Pol. 663 (2021).
64. *See, e.g.*, Brenda Ekwurzel et al., *The Rise in Global Atmospheric CO2, Surface Temperature, and Sea Level from Emissions Traced to Major Carbon Producers*, 144 Climate Change 579 (2017).
65. *See* Richard Heede, *Tracing Anthropogenic Carbon Dioxide and Methane Emissions to Fossil Fuel and Cement Producers, 1854–2010*, 122 Climate Change 229 (2014).
66. *Id.* at 229, 233, 234.
67. *See, e.g.*, Lambton v Mellish [1894] 3 Ch.D 163. The but-for cause test looks for a necessary connection between the breach of duty by the defendant and the injury to the plaintiff so that the latter could not have occurred without the former.
68. As, for example, the tort of misrepresentation, and especially deceit, and the tort of battery. *See respectively* Standard Chartered Bank v. Pakistan National Shipping Corp. (Nos 2 & 4) [2002] UKHL 43; In re White, 18 B.R. 246 (Bankr. E.D. Va. 1982) (relying on the doctrine of transferred intent to hold a tortfeasor liable in battery even when his intentional physical contact ended up harming a person other than the intended target).
69. Blair v. Deakin (1887) 57 LT 522, 526 (per Justice Kay). *See also* Bullock, *supra* note 32, at 1156–65.
70. CA 128/2020 Smith v. Fonterra Co-Operative Group Limited [2021] NZCA 552, para. 90. The New Zealand court did not endorse this standard; rather, it only restated what might be the standard of causation in the English law of nuisance.
71. *See* Sindell v. Abbott Laboratories, 607 P.2d 924 (Cal. 1980).
72. *See* Restatement (Third) of Torts: Liab. Phys. & Emot. Harm § 27 cmn. f (2010). *See also* Eagle-Picher Indus. Inc. v. Balbos, 604 A.2d 445, 459 (Md. 1992).
73. It is beyond the scope of this Chapter to determine whether courts would need a new type of injunction for the purpose of tackling global warming.

Chapter 9

1. *See, e.g.*, Stees v. Leonard, 20 Minn. 494 (1874). *Cf.* Nick Sage, *Contractual Liability and the Theory of Contract Law*, 30 King's L.J. 459 (2019).
2. Restatement (Second) of Contracts § 344(a) (1981).
3. *See* Hanoch Dagan & Michael Heller, *Autonomy for Contract, Refined*, 40 L. & Phil. 213 (2021).
4. *Cf.* Peter Benson, *Abstract Right and the Possibility of a Nondistributive Conception of Contract: Hegel and Contemporary Contract Theory*, 10 Cardozo L. Rev. 1077, 1100, 1111–16 (1989); Peter Benson, *Contract as Transfer of Ownership*, 48 Wm. & Mary L. Rev. 1673, 1682–83 (2007). Benson argues that such a breach amounts to a wrongful *dispossession* of the promisee, but the transfer theory that this claim is premised on is indefensible. *See* Hanoch Dagan & Michael Heller, The Choice Theory of Contracts 33–40 (2017); Dagan & Heller, *supra* note 3; Hanoch Dagan, *Two Visions of Contract*, 119 Mich. L. Rev. 1247 (2021).
5. *See* Dagan & Heller, *supra* note 3, at 38–39; Dagan & Heller, *supra* note 3; Hanoch Dagan & Michael Heller, *Why Autonomy Must Be Contract's Ultimate Value*, 20 Jerusalem Rev. Legal Stud. 148, 158–64 (2019).
6. *See* Dagan & Heller, *supra* note 3; Dagan & Heller, *supra* note 5, at 152.
7. As the text implies, formal equality is still relevant in contractual settings where the parties are roughly equally situated since, in these circumstances, it properly functions as the best proxy for substantive equality, which can explain why the legal treatment of commercial contracts (say, between traders) largely conforms to formal equality. *See supra* Chapter 3 note 62 and accompanying text.
8. The scope of this requirement is broader, including developments preceding, or leading to, the conclusion of the contract, such as advertising. *See* Szymon Osmola, Reflective Choices: A Liberal Theory of Consumer Law (PhD thesis, European University Institute, Florence 2022).

9. *See supra* Chapter 3 text accompanying notes 69–73.
10. *See, e.g.*, Richard A. Epstein, *Unconscionability: A Critical Appraisal*, 18 J.L. & Econ. 293, 293–301 (1975).
11. The term laissez-faire is misleading since, like any other economic system, it necessarily relies on a robust legal infrastructure. *See* Hanoch Dagan et al., *The Law of the Market*, 83 L. & Contemp. Probs. i (2020).
12. P.S. Atiyah, The Rise and Fall of Freedom of Contract 479 (1979).
13. This is our interpretation of Chief Justice Marshall's opinion in the classic laissez-faire case of Laidlaw v. Organ, 15 U.S. (2 Wheat.) 178 (1817), which focuses on the difficulty of delineating a doctrine compliant with the rule of law that implements relational justice in the precontractual context. *See* Hanoch Dagan & Avihay Dorfman, *Precontractual Justice*, 28 Legal Theory 89, 109–11 (2022).
14. *See supra* Chapter 4 text accompanying notes 43–48.
15. Melvin A. Eisenberg, *The Duty to Rescue in Contract Law*, 71 Fordham L. Rev. 647, 647, 654 (2002).
16. *See* Arthur Ripstein, *The Contracting Theory of Choices*, 40 Law & Phil. 185 (2021).
17. James Gordley, *Equality in Exchange*, 69 Calif. L. Rev. 1587, 1612, 1616–19, 1624 (1981).
18. *Id.* at 1604, 1616.
19. *See generally* Hanoch Dagan, The Law and Ethics of Restitution 11–36 (2004).
20. *See* Robert C. Hockett & Roy Kreitner, *Just Prices*, Cornell J.L. & Pub. Pol'y 771, 782 (2018). *See also* David Singh Grewal, *The Laws of Capitalism*, 128 Harv. L. Rev. 626, 658–60 (2014).
21. *See* David Singh Grewal & Jedediah Britton-Purdy, Liberalism, Property, and the Means of Production, *available at*: https://lpeproject.org/blog/liberalism-property-and-the-means-of-production/.
22. In this respect, Bagchi follows Anthony T. Kronman, *Contract Law and Distributive Justice*, 89 Yale L.J. 472 (1980). Kronman's familiar account, which focuses on the just distribution of the "forms of advantage-taking possible in exchange relations," relies on the controversial view that "the notion of individual liberty . . . offers no guidance in determining which of the many forms of advantage-taking possible in exchange relations render an agreement involuntary." *Id.* at 474.
23. Aditi Bagchi, *Distributive Injustice and Private Law*, 60 Hastings L.J. 105, 128, 135 (2008).
24. *See* Aditi Bagchi, *Distributive Justice and Contracts, in* Philosophical Foundations of Contract 193, 197 (Gregory Klass et al. eds., 2014); Bagchi, *supra* note 23, at 125.
25. *See* Bagchi, *supra* note 24, at 193–94, 199.
26. *See* Bagchi, *supra* note 23, at 136.
27. *See supra* Chapter 3 text accompanying notes 28–32.
28. *See supra* Chapter 4 text accompanying note 19.
29. *See* Richard Craswell, *Passing on the Costs of Legal Rules: Efficiency and Distribution in Buyer-Seller Relationships*, 43 Stan. L. Rev. 361, 376–77 (1991); Daniel Shaviro, *The Minimum Wage, the Earned Income Tax Credit, and Optimal Subsidy Policy*, 64 U. Chi. L. Rev. 405 (1997(; David A. Super, *The Rise and Fall of the Implied Warranty of Habitability*, 99 Cal. L. Rev. 389, 461 (2011).
30. *See infra* Chapter 14 note 45.
31. *See supra* Chapter 4 text accompanying note 28.
32. *See supra* Chapter 4 text accompanying note 19.
33. *See supra* Chapter 4 text accompanying note 20.
34. Liam Murphy, *The Practice of Promise and Contract, in* Philosophical Foundations of Contract, *supra* note 24, at 151, 168.
35. *Cf.* Yair Listokin & Peter Bassine, Efficient Legal Rules in a Cyclical Economy (unpublished manuscript).
36. *See supra* Chapter 3 text accompanying notes 51–57.
37. Joseph Raz, Ethics in the Public Domain 112 (1994). *See also* Christine Korsgaard, The Sources of Normativity 47, 49, 113 (1996).
38. Raz, *supra* note 37, at 112.
39. *See* Gregory Klass, *The Law of Deception: A Research Agenda*, 89 U. Colo. L. Rev. 707, 715 (2018). *See also, e.g.*, Stewart v. The Wyoming Cattle Ranche Co., 128 U.S. 383, 388 (1888).
40. *See, e.g.*, W. Page Keeton, *Fraud—Concealment and Non-Disclosure*, 15 Texas L. Rev. 1, 5 (1937).
41. Restatement (Second) of Contracts § 161(b) (1981).
42. *See, e.g.*, Stambovsky v. Ackley, 169 A.D.2d 254, 257 (N.Y. 1991).
43. *See, e.g.*, Obde v. Schlemeyer, 353 P.2d 672, 674–75 (Wash. 1960); Weintraub v. Krobatsch, 317 A.2d 68, 71–75 (N.J. 1974); Reed v. King, 145 Cal. App. 3d. 261, 265 (1983).
44. Barnard v. Kellogg, 77 U.S. 383, 388 (1871).

45. *See* Restatement (Second) of Contracts § 153 (1981).
46. *See* Robert M. Washburn, *Residential Real Estate Condition Disclosure Legislation*, 44 DePaul L. Rev. 381, 390 (1995).
47. *See* Eric H. Franklin, *Mandating Precontractual Disclosure*, 67 U. Miami L. Rev. 553, 583–84 (2013).
48. George Lefcoe, *Property Condition Disclosure Forms: How the Real Estate Industry Eased the Transition from* Caveat Emptor *to "Seller Tell All"*, 39 Real Prop. Prob. & Tr. J. 193, 226 (2004).
49. *See* Alex M. Johnson, *An Economic Analysis of the Duty to Disclose Information: Lessons Learned. From the* Caveat Emptor *Doctrine*, 45 San Diego L. Rev. 79, 114 (2008).
50. *What We Do*, U.S. Securities and Exchange Commission, https://www.sec.gov/Article/whatwedo.html.
51. *See, e.g.*, Omri Ben-Shahar & Carl E. Schneider, More Than You Wanted to Know: The Failure of Mandated Disclosure (2014).
52. Furthermore, in certain contexts—notably that of consumer contracts—disclosure may well be insufficient. As Szymon Osmola argues, nothing short of withdrawal rights, along the lines of the European pertinent regulation, can ensure consumers' reflective choices. *See* Osmola, *supra* note 8.
53. *See* Anthony T. Kronman, *Mistake, Disclosure, Information, and the Law of Contracts*, 7 J. Legal Stud. 1, 12–18 (1978). *See also, e.g.*, Michael J. Trebilcock, The Limits of Freedom of Contract 108, 112, 117–18 (1993).
54. Kim Lane Scheppele, Legal Secrets: Equality and Efficiency in the Common Law 77–78, 120 (1988).
55. Kimberly D. Krawiec & Kathryn Zeiler, *Common Law Disclosure Duties and the Sin of Omission: Testing the Meta-Theories*, 91 Va. L. Rev. 1795, 1800 (2005). Krawiec & Zeiler also show that "courts actually have become *less* likely over time to impose duties to disclose." *Id.* But as they acknowledge, "other factors, such as the codification of certain areas of fraudulent silence law through statutes that mandate particular disclosures, [might have] altered the type of case that survives to litigation under the common law." *Id.* at 1881.
56. *Id.* at 1800, 1815, 1853–55, 1864.
57. *See, e.g.*, 13 Williston on Contracts 704 § 1617 (3d ed. 1970).
58. Union Pac. R. v. Public Serv. Com'n, 248 U.S. 67, 70 (1918).
59. *See, e.g.*, Mitchell N. Berman, *The Normative Functions of Coercion Claims*, 8 Legal Theory 45, 53–54 (2002).
60. Restatement (Second) of Contracts § 175(1) (1981).
61. *See* John P. Dawson, *Economic Duress—An Essay in Perspective*, 45 Mich. L. Rev. 253, 253–56 (1947).
62. Restatement (Second) of Contracts § 175 cmt a (1981).
63. *Id.* at § 176 & cmt a.
64. Dawson, *supra* note 61, at 255.
65. Restatement (Second) of Contracts § 175 cmt c (1981).
66. Grace M. Giesel, *A Realistic Proposal for the Contract Duress Doctrine*, 107 W. Va. L. Rev. 443, 444, 446 (2005). There are some relatively easy cases, notably where "the threatened act would harm the recipient and would not significantly benefit the party making the threat." Restatement (Second) of Contracts § 176(2)(a) & cmt a (1981).
67. *See* Joseph M. Perillo, Contracts 292 (7th ed. 2014). *But see, e.g.*, Rodziewicz v. Waffco Heavy Duty Towing, 763 N.E. 2d 491, 493 (Ind. Ct. App. 2002).
68. *See, e.g.*, Dawson, *supra* note 61, at 2587–88.
69. *See* Alan Wertheimer, Coercion 40–41 (1987); Jonathan Wolff, *Structures of Exploitation, in* Philosophical Foundations of Labour Law 175 (Hugh Collins et al. eds., 2018). *Cf.* Charles Fried, Contract as Promise 110–11 (rev. ed. 2015).
70. *See, e.g.*, Cabot Corp. v. AVX Corp., 448 Mass. 629, 638 (2007); Starr Int'l Co. v. United States, 106 Fed. Cl. 50, 77 (2012). Among the few notable exceptions, *see* Justice Frankfurter's dissent in United States v. Bethlehem Steel Corp., 315 U.S. 289, 326, 330–31 (1942).
71. *See* Wertheimer, *supra* note 69, at 226; Jeffrie G. Murphy, *Consent, Coercion, and Hard Choices*, 67 Va. L. Rev. 79, 87–89 (1981).
72. *See supra* Chapter 4 text accompanying note 19.
73. Oren Bar-Gill & Omri Ben-Shahar, *Credible Coercion*, 83 Tex. L. Rev. 717, 718–19, 724, 728–29 (2005).
74. *Id.* at 720, 730–36, 779.
75. *Cf.* Robert L. Hale, *Bargaining, Duress, and Economic Liberty*, 43 Colum. L. Rev. 603, 625 (1943).

76. *See* https://worldpopulationreview.com/state-rankings/usury-laws-by-state.
77. WERTHEIMER, *supra* note 69, at 238–39. *See also, e.g.*, Winnick v. Aetna Acceptance Co., 275 Ill. App. 438, 443–44 (Ill. App. Ct. 1934).
78. Nicolas Cornell & Sarah E. Light, *Wrongful Benefit and Arctic Drilling*, 50 U.C.D. L. REV. 1845, 1864–65 (2017).
79. Post v. Jones, 60 U.S. (19 How.) 150, 160 (1857).
80. *See* Bar-Gill & Ben-Shahar, *supra* note 73, at 777–78. In many other categories of cases, ex post price modification may not generate happy consequences.
81. *See, e.g.*, Orit Gan, *Contractual Duress and Relations of Power*, 36 HARV. J.L. & GENDER 171 (2013).
82. AMERICAN LAW INSTITUTE, PRINCIPLES OF THE LAW OF FAMILY DISSOLUTION: ANALYSIS AND RECOMMENDATIONS (2000) [hereinafter ALI PRINCIPLES].
83. For its rules for separation agreements, *see id.* at § 7.09. For the rules governing marital agreements and agreements between domestic partners, which are very similar to those governing premarital ones, *see id.* at § 7.04(4) & cmt. d.
84. *Id.* at § 7.04(2) & cmt. b. This position regarding the burden of proof thus far reflects the law of only a few states. Most states place the burden of proof on the party challenging the agreement. *See* UNIFORM PREMARITAL AND MARITAL AGREEMENTS ACT Pref. Note (2012) [hereinafter UPMAA].
85. *See* ALI PRINCIPLES, *supra* note 82, at § 7.04(3) & cmts. b, d, & e. *See* also UPMAA, *supra* note 84, at § 5 cmt. & § 9(b).
86. For a heroic attempt to reconcile unconscionability and interpersonal independence, *see* Peter Benson, *The Unity of Contract Law*, *in* THE THEORY OF CONTRACT LAW: NEW ESSAYS 118, 185–98 (Peter Benson ed., 2001); PETER BENSON, JUSTICE IN TRANSACTIONS: A THEORY OF CONTRACT LAW 167–91 (2019). For critiques of it, *see, respectively*, Avihay Dorfman, *Private Law Exceptionalism? Part II: A Basic Difficulty with the Argument from Formal Equality*, 31 CAN. J.L. & JURIS. 5, 29–30 n.88 (2018); Dagan, *supra* note 3, at 1259–63.
87. Williams v. Walker-Thomas Furniture Co., 350 F.2d 445, 449 (D.C. Cir. 1965).
88. Arthur Allen Leff, *Unconscionability and the Code-Emperor's New Clause*, 115 U. PA. L. REV. 485, 487 (1967).
89. This understanding of exploitation draws on—but does not simply duplicate—Robert Goodin's and Ruth Sample's accounts. *See, respectively*, Robert E. Goodin, *Exploiting a Situation and Exploiting a Person*, *in* MODERN THEORIES OF EXPLOITATION 166, 166–67, 185–89 (Andrew Reeve ed., 1987); RUTH J. SAMPLE, EXPLOITATION: WHAT IT IS AND WHY IT'S WRONG 57, 81 (2003).
90. RESTATEMENT (SECOND) OF CONTRACTS § 208 cmt d (1981).
91. *See* Russell Korobkin, *Bounded Rationality, Standard Form Contracts, and Unconscionability*, 70 U. CHI. L. REV. 1203, 1266–68 (2003).
92. *See supra* Chapter 3 text accompanying notes 61–69.
93. *See* Epstein, *supra* note 10, at 306–308.
94. *See* Russell Korobkin, *A "Traditional" and "Behavioral" Law-and Economics Analysis of* Williams v. Walker-Thomas Furniture Company, 26 U. HAWAI'I L. REV. 441, 458–65 (2004); Korobkin, *supra* note 91, at 1206, 1222–44.
95. Anne Fleming, *The Rise and Fall of Unconscionability as the "Law of the Poor"*, 102 GEO. L.J. 1383, 1388–89, 91 (2014).
96. *See supra* Chapter 3 text accompanying notes 28–32.
97. *See* NATIONAL CONSUMER LAW CENTER, CONSUMER PROTECTION IN THE STATES: A 50-STATE EVALUATION OF UNFAIR AND DECEPTIVE ACTS AND PRACTICES LAWS appendix C (2018).
98. *See* DEE PRIDGEN & RICHARD M. ALDERMAN, CONSUMER PROTECTION AND THE LAW §§ 7:1, 7:28 (2014 ed.).
99. *See id.* at §§ 11:1, 9:10, 10:1, 9:11; J. Howard Beales, III, *Advertising to Kids and the FTC: A Regulatory Retrospective That Advises the Present*, 12 GEO. MASON L. REV. 873 (2004).
100. *See* Dodd-Frank Wall Street Reform and Consumer Protection Act (Dodd-Frank Act), P.L. 111–203, 12 U.S.C. Ch. 53 §§ 5481–5603.
101. David H. Carpenter, The Consumer Financial Protection Bureau (CFPB): A Legal Analysis 1 (U.S. Congressional Research Service R42572; Jan. 14, 2014), available at: https://www.fas.org/sgp/crs/misc/R42572.pdf.
102. Adam J. Levitin, *The Consumer Financial Protection Bureau: An Introduction*, 32 REV. BANKING & FIN. L. 321, 344 (2013).
103. Dodd-Frank Act § 1031(d), 12 U.S.C. § 5531(d). *See also* Hanoch Dagan & Roy Kreitner, 52 *The Other Half of Regulatory Theory*, 52 CONN. L. REV. 605, 637–41 (2020).

104. Korobkin, *supra* note 94, at 467.
105. *See supra* Chapter 3 text accompanying notes 51–57.
106. *See, respectively,* Seabrook v. Commuter Hous. Co., 338 N.Y.S.2d 67 (Civ. Ct. 1972); Armendariz v. Found. Health Psychcare Servs. Inc., 6 P.3d 669 (Cal. 2000).
107. U.C.C. § 2-719(3).
108. *See* Greenman v. Yuba Power Prods., Inc. 377 P.2d 897, 901 (Cal. 1963).
109. *See* Sabine Tsuruda, *Resistance and Recognition in Contract,* 60 Harv. C.R.-C.L. Rev. (2024).

Chapter 10

1. Jacob & Youngs, Inc. v. Kent, 129 N.E 889 (N.Y. 1921).
2. Sales contracts are governed by the perfect tender rule. *See* U.C.C. § 2-601. Its absolutist appearance notwithstanding, this rule too is accompanied by an anti-opportunistic device, in the form of the seller's right to cure the defect. *See* U.C.C. § 2–508.
3. 129 N.E at 890, 892.
4. *Id.* at 890–91.
5. *Id.* at 891.
6. Ian Ayres justifies sticky defaults on efficiency grounds: minimizing the costs of party error or judicial error and channeling contractors' efforts towards means that better control externalities. *See* Ian Ayres, *Regulating Opt Outs: An Economic Analysis of Altering Rules,* 121 Yale L.J. 2032, 2097 (2012). We hold that sticky defaults are at least as important for relational justice.
7. 129 N.E at 891.
8. *See* Alan Schwartz & Robert E. Scott, *Contract Theory and the Limits of Contract Law,* 113 Yale L.J. 541, 615–16 (2003).
9. *See* Ayres, *supra* note 6, at 2049, 2056–58, 2082–83, 2095.
10. Altering rules are rules that regulate "how contractors can opt out of the default legal consequences." They are, in other words, "the necessary and sufficient conditions for displacing a default legal treatment with some particular other legal treatment." Ayres, *id.* at 2036.
11. As the text implies, there is another possible reading of *Jacob & Youngs*, focusing on the ex post effects of economic waste. *Cf.* Charles J. Goetz & Robert E. Scott, *The Mitigation Principle: Toward a General Theory of Contractual Obligation,* 69 Va. L. Rev. 967, 1009–11 (1983); Alan Schwartz & Robert E. Scott, *Market Damages, Efficient Contracting, and The Economic Waste Fallacy,* 108 Colum. L. Rev. 1610, 1656 (2008). We distance ourselves from this reading of the case for the same reason that we distance ourselves from other readings of justice-based doctrines of private law as equity-based sources of discretionary power. *See supra* Chapter 3 text accompanying notes 22–24. Our general critique is particularly relevant regarding contract, given its core role as a planning device. *Cf.* Jody S. Kraus & Robert E. Scott, *The Case Against Equity in American Contract Law,* 93 S. Cal. L. Rev. 1323 (2020).
12. *See supra* Chapter 4 text following note 35.
13. Schwartz & Scott, *supra* note 8, at 559–60, 565.
14. G. Richard Shell, *Opportunism and Trust in the Negotiation of Commercial Contracts: Toward a New Cause of Action,* 44 Vand. L. Rev. 221, 222, 230 (1991).
15. *See* Charles J. Goetz & Robert E. Scott, *Principles of Relational Contracts,* 67 Va. L. Rev. 1089 (1981).
16. *See* Goetz & Scott, *supra* note 11, at 1002; Shell, *supra* note 14, at 223.
17. Richard A. Posner, Economic Analysis of Law § 4.1, at 102 (5th ed. 1998).
18. The *locus classicus* here is Lisa Bernstein, *Merchant Law in a Merchant Court: Rethinking the Codes Search for Immanent Business Norms,* 144 U. Pa. L. Rev. 1765 (1996). *See also, e.g.,* Lisa Bernstein, *Private Commercial Law in the Cotton Industry: Creating Cooperation through Rules, Norms, and Institutions,* 99 Mich. L. Rev. 1724 (2001).
19. In some contexts, the contract-related vulnerability that leads to opportunism arises in the *pre*-contractual stage as well, blurring to some extent the line between precontractual and contractual justice. *See* Alan Schwartz & Robert E. Scott, *Precontractual Liability and Preliminary Agreements,* 120 Harv. L. Rev. 661 (2007); Shell, *supra* note 14; Albert H. Choi & George Triantis, *Designing and Enforcing Preliminary Agreements,* 98 Tex. L. Rev. 439 (2020).
20. *See generally* Kevin Werbach & Nicholas Cornell, *Contracts* Ex Machina, 67 Duke. L. J. 313 (2017).
21. *See generally* Hanoch Dagan, *Two Visions of Contract,* 119 Mich. L. Rev. 1247 (2021).
22. *See supra* Chapter 9 text accompanying notes 1–6.

23. *See* Hanoch Dagan & Michael Heller, *Choice Theory: A Restatement, in* Research Handbook on Private Law Theory 112, 129 (Hanoch Dagan & Benjamin Zipursky eds., 2020).
24. *See* Hanoch Dagan, *The Liberal Promise of Contract, in* Private Law and Practical Reason 315 (Haris Psarras & Sandy Steel eds., 2022).
25. In that, our account of normative defaults is reminiscent of the "exemplary role" (*Leitbildfunktion*) attributed to default rules in European contract law. *See* Martijn W. Hesselink, Justifying Contract in Europe: Political Philosophies of European Contract Law 395–97 (2021).
26. The other subset of contract's normative defaults is guided by the concern for the parties' future self. *See* Hanoch Dagan & Ohad Somech, *When Contract's Basic Assumptions Fail*, 34 Can. J.L. & Juris. 297 (2021).
27. To reemphasize, rules pertaining to the life of ongoing contracts that address clear relational injustices must be mandatory rather than defaults.
28. *See* Ronald J. Gilson, Charles F. Sabel & Robert E. Scott, *Braiding: The Interaction of Formal and Informal Contracting in Theory, Practice, and Doctrine*, 110 Colum. L. Rev. 1137 (2010). *See also, e.g.*, Lisa Bernstein, *Beyond Relational Contracts: Social Capital and Network Governance in Procurement Contracts*, 7 J. Legal Analysis 561 (2015).
29. The notion of normative default is no stranger to some aspects of precontractual justice, notably the law of disclosure, as attested by the validity and enforceability of "As Is" clauses. *See, e.g.*, U.C.C. § 2–316(3)(a).
30. 129 N.E at 891.
31. *See supra* Chapter 4 text accompanying note 20.
32. *See, e.g.*, Robert E. Scott, *A Joint Maximization Theory of Contract and Regulation, in* Research Handbook on Private Law Theory, *supra* note 23, at 22.
33. *See* Alan Schwartz, *The Default Rule Paradigm and the Limits of Contract Law*, 3 S. Cal. Interdisc. L.J. 389, 402–03 (1993).
34. *See* Hanoch Dagan & Michael Heller, *Why Autonomy Must Be Contract's Ultimate Value*, 20 Jerusalem Rev. Legal Stud. 148, 158–60 (2019).
35. *See, e.g.*, Alan Schwartz & Robert E. Scott, *The Common Law of Contract and the Default Rule Project*, 102 Va. L. Rev. 1523 (2016).
36. *See* Robert E. Scott, *A Relational Theory of Default Rules for Commercial Contracts*, 19 J. Legal Stud. 597, 602 (1990).
37. *See* Daniel Markovits, *Contract and Collaboration*, 113 Yale L.J. 1417 (2004).
38. Daniel Markovits, *Good Faith as Contract's Core Value, in* Philosophical Foundations of Contract 272, 272, 280, 285, 287–88, 290, 292–93 (Gregory Klass et al. eds., 2014). For a similar account, see Peter Benson, Justice in Transactions: A Theory of Contract Law 256–64 (2019).
39. Markovits, *supra* note 38, at 276–77, 280, 282, 284, 287, 291.
40. *Id.* at 282–83, 287–88.
41. *Id.* at 278–80, 284, 290–91.
42. *See also supra* Chapter 3 text accompanying notes 43–46.
43. *See supra* Chapter 3 text accompanying note 74.
44. Markovits' critique of utopian violations of freedom of contract may indeed shatter theories that do not sufficiently appreciate the foundational role of the parties' voluntary choices for the legitimacy of contract. In this context, the veteran theory of just exchange, which we criticized in Chapter 9, may be the main culprit.
45. *Cf.* Alan Schwartz & Robert E. Scott, *Contract Interpretation Redux*, 119 Yale L.J. 926 (2010).
46. Markovits, *supra* note 38, at 287 n.62.
47. *See* Hanoch Dagan, *Types of Contracts and Law's Autonomy-Enhancing Role,* European Contract Law and The Creation of Norms 109 (Stefan Grundmann & Mateusz Grochowski eds., 2021).
48. *Cf.* George K. Gardner, *An Inquiry into the Principles of the Law of Contracts*, 46 Harv. L. Rev. 1, 20–22 (1932). For a somewhat similar approach to contract interpretation, see Todd D. Rakoff, *The Five Justices of Contract Law*, 2016 Wisc. L. Rev. 733, 745, 756–64; Aditi Bagchi, *Interpreting Contracts in a Regulatory State*, 54 U.S.F. L. Rev. 35 (2019).
49. *Cf.* Arthur Corbin, *Conditions in the Law of Contract*, 28 Yale L.J. 739, 744 (1919).
50. Restatement (Second) of Contracts § 245 cmt. a (1981).
51. E. Allan Farnsworth, Farnsworth on Contracts 528 (4th ed. 2004).
52. *Id. See also, e.g.*, N.L.R.B. v. Local 554, Graphic Commc'ns Int'l Union, AFL-CIO, 991 F.2d 1302, 1306–1308 (7th Cir. 1993).

53. *Cf.* JOHN D. CALAMARY & JOSEPH M. PERILLO, THE LAW OF CONTRACTS 486 (3d ed. 1987).
54. FARNSWORTH, *supra* note 51, at 528. *See also* Tabatabai v. W. Coast Life Ins. Co., 664 F.3d 663, 666–67 (7th Cir. 2011); Edwin W. Patterson, *Constructive Conditions in Contracts*, 43 COLUM. L. REV. 903, 937–38 (1942).
55. RESTATEMENT (SECOND) OF CONTRACTS § 245 cmt. a (1981).
56. *See* RESTATEMENT (SECOND) OF CONTRACTS § 227(1) (1981).
57. RESTATEMENT (SECOND) OF CONTRACTS § 229 cmts. a & c (1981).
58. Scott & Kraus, *supra* note 11, at 1329, 1361, 1377. For a more elaborate discussion, see Jody S. Kraus & Robert E. Scott, *Contract Design and the Structure of Contractual Intent*, 84 N.Y.U. L. REV. 1023, 1081–84 (2009).
59. Scott & Kraus, *supra* note 11, at 1376.
60. *See, e.g.*, Sy Jack Realty Co. v. Pergament Syosset Corp., 267 N.E.2d 462, 463–64 (1971); Burger King Corp. v. Family Dining, Inc., 426 F. Supp. 485, 492, 494–95 (E.D. Pa.), aff'd, 566 F.2d 1168 (3d Cir. 1977); Elliott v. Snyder, 143 S.E.2d 374, 375–76 (1965).
61. *See, e.g.*, Franklin E. Penny Co. v. United States, 524 F.2d 668, 677 (Ct. Cl. 1975); Williamson v. Wanlass, 545 P.2d 1145, 1148 (Utah 1976); Hegeberg v. New England Fish Co., 110 P.2d 182, 187–89 (1941).
62. Scott & Kraus, *supra* note 11, at 1376.
63. *See, respectively, e.g.*, Williamson v. Wanlass, 545 P.2d 1145, 1147–48 (Utah 1976); Janssen Bros. v. Northbrook Tr. & Sav. Bank, 299 N.E.2d 431, 434–35 (1973); Delaware Steel Co. v. Calmar S. S. Corp., 378 F.2d 386, 388–89 (3d Cir. 1967).
64. 129 N.E at 891. *See also, e.g.*, Naftalin v. John Wood Co., 116 N.W.2d 91, 100 (Minn. 1962).
65. Kenneth S. Abraham, *Insurance, in* THE OXFORD HANDBOOK OF THE NEW PRIVATE LAW 432 (Andrew Gold et al. eds., 2020).
66. *See* U.C.C. § 1–304.
67. RESTATEMENT (SECOND) OF CONTRACTS § 205 (1981). *See also, e.g.*, Northwest, Inc. v. Ginsberg, 572 U.S. 273, 285 (2014); 511 W. 232nd Owners Corp. v. Jennifer Realty Co., 773 N.E.2d 496, 500 (N.Y. 2002); Brown v. Superior Court in & for Los Angeles County., 212 P.2d 878, 881 (Cal. 1949). Texas law, by contrast, "does not impose a generalized contractual duty of good faith and fair dealing and, in fact, rejects it in almost all circumstances." Hux v. S. Methodist Univ., 819 F.3d 776, 781 (5th Cir. 2016).
68. Mkt. St. Assocs. Ltd. P'ship v. Frey, 941 F.2d 588, 595–96 (7th Cir. 1991).
69. AMPAT/Midwest, Inc. v. Illinois Tool Works, Inc., 896 F.2d 1035, 1041 (7th Cir. 1990).
70. Nw., Inc. v. Ginsberg, 572 U.S. 273, 286 (2014).
71. This is also how good faith is understood in German law. *See* Simon Wittaker & Reinhard Zimmermann, *Good Faith in European Contract Law: Surveying the Legal Landscape, in* GOOD FAITH IN EUROPEAN CONTRACT LAW 7, 24–25 (Mauro Bussani et al. eds., 2000).
72. Markovits, *supra* note 38, at 275. *See also, e.g.,* Brassil v. Maryland Cas. Co., 104 N.E. 622 (N.Y. 1914); Abraham, *supra* note 65.
73. *See* ROBERT E. SCOTT & JODY S. KRAUS, CONTRACT LAW AND THEORY 334–35 (5th ed. 2013).
74. *See* U.C.C. § 2–306(1).
75. Another such "moment" comes up when "an obligee reasonably believes that the obligor will commit a breach by non-performance," and is thereby entitled to "demand adequate assurance of due performance" and even suspend her performance until such an assurance is properly received. *See* RESTATEMENT (SECOND) OF CONTRACTS § 251 & cmt. a (1981). *See also* U.C.C. § 2–609.
76. Markovits, *supra* note 38, at 273 (citing U.C.C. § 2–311 cmt. 1).
77. *Id.* (citing U.C.C. § 2–309 cmts. 5 & 8). *See also, e.g.*, K.M.C. Co. v. Irving Tr. Co., 757 F.2d 752, 759 (6th Cir. 1985).
78. *See* U.C.C. § 2–209 cmt. 2.
79. *Id. See also* RESTATEMENT (SECOND) OF CONTRACTS § 205 cmt. e (1981); King v. Duluth, M. & N. Railway, 63 N.W. 1105, 1107 (Minn. 1895); *Lowey v. Watt*, 684 F.2d 957, 969 (D.C. Cir. 1982); Einer Elhauge, *Contrived Threats versus Uncontrived Warnings: A General Solution to the Puzzles of Contractual Duress, Unconstitutional Conditions, and Blackmail*, 83 U. CHI. L. REV. 503, 511 (2016); Christine Jolls, *Contracts as Bilateral Commitments: A New Perspective on Contract Modifications*, 26 J. LEGAL STUD. 203, 208, 219–20 (1997).
80. RESTATEMENT (SECOND) OF CONTRACTS § 205 cmt. d (1981).
81. *Id.* at cmt. e.
82. *See, respectively,* Hugh Collins, *Implied Duty to Give Information During Performance of Contracts*, 55 MOD. L. REV. 556 (1992); Melvin A. Eisenberg, *The Duty to Rescue in Contract Law*, 71 FORDHAM L. REV. 647, 674 (2002).

83. *Cf.* Robert E. Scott, *In (Partial) Defense of Strict Liability in Contract*, 107 MICH. L. REV. 1381, 1390–92 (2009).
84. *See* Mkt. St. Assocs. Ltd. P'ship, 941 F.2d at 594–96; Metro. Ventures, LLC v. GEA Assocs., 717 N.W.2d 58, 69 (Wis. 2006).
85. *See* Markovits, *supra* note 38, at 276.
86. Daniel Friedmann, *Good Faith and Remedies for Breach of Contract*, *in* GOOD FAITH AND FAULT IN CONTRACT LAW 399, 400 (Jack Beatson & Daniel Friedmann eds., 1995).
87. FARNSWORTH, *supra* note 51, at 361–62.
88. *See, respectively*, *e.g.*, Brunswick Hills Racquet Club, Inc. v. Route 18 Shopping Ctr. Assocs., 864 A.2d 387, 399 (N.J. 2005); Cenac v. Murry, 609 So. 2d 1257, 1272 (Miss. 1992).
89. *See* ARTHUR L. CORBIN, CORBIN ON CONTRACTS § 654A(B) (2d ed. 1993). *See also*, *e.g.*, Idaho Power Co. v. Cogeneration, Inc., 9 P.3d 204, 1216 (2000).
90. U.C.C. § 1-302(b). *See also*, *e.g.*, PPG Indus., Inc. v. Shell Oil Co., 919 F.2d 17, 19 (5th Cir. 1990).
91. Carma Developers (Cal.), Inc. v. Marathon Dev. California, Inc., 826 P.2d 710, 728 (Cal. 1992). *See also*, *e.g.*, Farris v. Hutchinson, 338, 838 P.2d 374, 377 (Mont. 1992); Am. Tower, L.P. v. Local TV Iowa, L.L.C., 809 N.W.2d 546, 551 (Iowa Ct. App. 2011); Keene Corp. v. Bogan, No. 88 CIV. 0217 (MBM), 1990 WL 1864, at *14 (S.D.N.Y. Jan. 11, 1990).
92. *See* Fireman v. News Am. Mktg. In-Store, Inc., No. C.A. 05-11740-MLW, 2009 WL 3080716, at *9 (D. Mass. Sept. 26, 2009); P.A. Bergner & Co. v. Martinez, 823 F. Supp. 151, 158–60 (S.D.N.Y. 1993); Tymshare, Inc. v. Covell, 727 F.2d 1145, 1153–54 (D.C. Cir. 1984).
93. This does not imply that the continuity of contract's rights–remedies is uncontroversial. Champions of contract's transfer theory, who view a breach as tantamount to conversion, assume a categorical difference between terms and remedies. *See* BENSON, *supra* note 38, at 207–209, 212–13, 255, 261–62, 313. For a critique, see Dagan, *supra* note 21.
94. *See* U.C.C. §§ 1-302(a) & 2-715. *See also supra* Chapter 8 text accompanying notes 26–27.
95. RESTATEMENT (SECOND) OF CONTRACTS § 350 & cmt. b (1981) (the emphasis is ours).
96. Seana Valentine Shiffrin, *The Divergence of Contract and Promise*, 120 HARV. L. REV. 708, 725 (2007). Shiffrin's harsh verdict relies on her equation of breach of contract with conversion, which is in turn dubious. *See* HANOCH DAGAN & MICHAEL HELLER, THE CHOICE THEORY OF CONTRACT 25–40 (2017); Dagan, *supra* note 24, at 328–29. Even in its best light, it presents, as the text implies, an entailment of an interpersonal independence view of contractual justice, which is indefensible.
97. Goetz & Scott, *supra* note 11, at 971, 973–74.
98. *Id.* at 972.
99. *Id.* at 975, 992.
100. RESTATEMENT (SECOND) OF CONTRACTS § 350 (1981). *See also id.* at cmt. g.
101. Frederick Raff Co. v. Murphy, 147 A. 709, 712 (Conn. 1929). *See also, e.g.*, O'Brien v. Black, 648 A.2d 1374, 1377 (Vt. 1994); Southhaven Assocs., LLC v. McMerlin, LLC, 122 A.3d 670, 674 (Conn. App. 2015).
102. *See* George Lestas & Prince Saprai, *Mitigation, Fairness, and Contract Law*, *in* PHILOSOPHICAL FOUNDATIONS OF CONTRACT, *supra* note 38, at 319, 331–32.
103. Sommer v. Kridel, 378 A.2d 767, 772–73 (N.J. 1977). *See also*, *e.g.*, Rubin v. Dondysh, 555 N.Y.S.2d 1004, 1007 (Civ. Ct. 1990); Ringwood Assocs., Ltd. v. Jack's of Route 23, Inc., 379 A.2d 508, 515 (N.J. Law. Div. 1977), aff'd, 398 A.2d 1315 (N.J. App. Div. 1979); Drutman Realty Co. P'ship v. Jindo Corp., 865 F. Supp. 1093, 1100 (S.D.N.Y. 1994); Manglona v. Gov't of the Commonwealth of the N. Mariana Islands, No. 04-012-GA, 2005 WL 3771373, at *12–14 (N. Mar. I. Oct. 4, 2005).
104. Cruise Connections Charter Mgmt. 1, LP v. Attorney Gen. of Canada, 55 F. Supp. 3d 156, 175 (D.D.C. 2014). *See also*, *e.g.*, Paragon Indus., Inc. v. Williams, 473 N.Y.S.2d 92, 93 (App. Term 1983).
105. FARNSWORTH, *supra* note 51, at 781.
106. George Lastas and Prince Saprai justify such an expectation by reconstructing it in Rawlsian terms. *See* Lastas & Saprai, *supra* note 102, at 325–30. But their reconstruction is both unnecessary and inadequate. *See* Hanoch Dagan & Avihay Dorfman, *Justice in Contracts*, 67 AM. J. JURIS. 1, 30 n.37 (2022).
107. Charles Fried, *The Convergence of Contract and Promise*, 120 HARV. L. REV. F. 1, 8 (2007).
108. *See* Charles Fried, *The Ambitions of Contract as Promise*, *in* PHILOSOPHICAL FOUNDATIONS OF CONTRACT, *supra* note 38, at 17, 29.
109. Goetz & Scott, *supra* note 11, at 975.
110. RESTATEMENT (SECOND) OF CONTRACTS § 350 cmt. g (1981). *See also* Levin v. Standard Fashion Co., 11 N.Y.S. 706, 708–09 (Com. Pl. 1890); Price v. Davis, 173 S.W. 64, 68 (Mo. Ct. App 1915);

Voorhees v. Guyan Mach. Co., 446 S.E.2d 672, 679 (W. Va. 1994); Small v. Springs Indus., Inc., 388 S.E.2d 808, 811 (S.C. 1990); Brewster v. Martin Marietta Aluminum Sales, Inc., 378 N.W.2d 558, 567 (Mich. App. 1985).

111. *See* Ariel Porat, *A Comparative Fault Defense in Contract Law*, 107 MICH. L. REV. 1397 (2009). Israeli law recognizes such a defense. *See* C.A. 3912/90 Eximin SA v. Itel Style Ferarri, available at https://versa.cardozo.yu.edu/opinions/eximin-sa-v-itel-style-ferarri.
112. *See* Scott, *supra* note 83.
113. In addition to mitigation, the doctrine of foreseeability can also be read as a normative default grounded in contractual justice. *See* Roy Kreitner, *Multiplicity in Contract Remedies, in* COMPARATIVE REMEDIES FOR BREACH OF CONTRACT 19, 39–41 (Nili Cohen & Ewan McKendrick eds., 2005).
114. *See* Charles Szladits, *The Concept of Specific Performance in Civil Law*, 4 AM. J. COMP. L. 208, 215–17, 221 (1955).
115. *See* RESTATEMENT (SECOND) OF CONTRACTS §§ 359–60 (1981); U.C.C. § 2–716. As the text implies, relational justice is not the sole justification for this. For another (and wider) key justification, premised on contract's concern for the parties' future self, see Hanoch Dagan & Michael Heller, *Specific Performance: On Freedom and Commitment in Contract Law,* 98 NOTRE DAME L. REV. 1323 (2023).
116. *See* Shiffrin, *supra* note 96, at 722–24.
117. SCOTT & KRAUS, *supra* note 73, at 114–15.

Chapter 11

1. RESTATEMENT (THIRD) OF RESTITUTION & UNJUST ENRICHMENT § 1 & cmts. a & h (2011).
2. *See* HANOCH DAGAN, THE LAW AND ETHICS OF RESTITUTION 11–25 (2004).
3. For a discussion of a third set of restitutionary rules dealing with an array of interpersonal interactions, from money management up to intimacy, whose value is also a source of severe vulnerability, see Hanoch Dagan, *Autonomy, Relational Justice, and Restitution, in* RESEARCH HANDBOOK ON UNJUST ENRICHMENT AND RESTITUTION 219, 230–35 (Elise Bant et al. eds., 2020).
4. PETER BIRKS, UNJUST ENRICHMENT 3 (2d ed. 2005).
5. RESTATEMENT (THIRD) OF RESTITUTION & UNJUST ENRICHMENT § 5 (2011).
6. J.E. Penner, *We all Make Mistakes: A 'Duty of Virtue' Theory of Restitutionary Liability for Mistaken Payments*, 81 MODERN L. REV. 222, 225 (2018).
7. ALAN BRUDNER, THE UNITY OF THE COMMON LAW 242–43 (2d ed. 2013, with Jennifer M. Nadler).
8. *See* Penner, *supra* note 6, at 233, 244.
9. *See* Frederick Wilmot-Smith, *Should the Payee Pay?*, 37 OXFORD J. LEGAL STUD. 844, 855–61 (2017). *See also* Dennis Klimchuk, *Unjust Enrichment and the Forms of Justice, in* RESEARCH HANDBOOK ON UNJUST ENRICHMENT AND RESTITUTION, *supra* note 3, at 186.
10. *See* BRUDNER, *supra* note 7, at 247, 252–53.
11. *See* Penner, *supra* note 6, at 223, 243, 246.
12. BRUDNER, *supra* note 7, at 253–55.
13. *See* DAGAN, *supra* note 2, at 43–44.
14. *See id.* at 43, 47, 49.
15. *See* John P. Dawson, *Restitution Without Enrichment*, 61 B.U. L. REV. 563, 568 (1981).
16. *See* DAGAN, *supra* note 2, at 45–46. *See also* CHARLIE WEBB, REASON AND RESTITUTION: A THEORY OF UNJUST ENRICHMENT 223 (2016); Tatiana Cutts, *Unjust Enrichment: What We Owe to Each Other*, 41 OXFORD J. LEGAL STUD. 114 (2021); Ross Grantham, *Change of Position-Based Defences, in* RESEARCH HANDBOOK ON UNJUST ENRICHMENT AND RESTITUTION, *supra* note 3, at 418.
17. RESTATEMENT (THIRD) OF RESTITUTION & UNJUST ENRICHMENT § 65 (2011).
18. *See* DAGAN, *supra* note 2, at 68–70.
19. *See supra* Chapter 4 text accompanying note 41.
20. *Cf.* DAGAN, *supra* note 2, at 60–63, 51–52.
21. *Cf. id.* at 47–49, 63.
22. *See* ROBERT NOZICK, ANARCHY, STATE, AND UTOPIA 95 (1974); *see also* JULES L. COLEMAN, RISKS AND WRONGS 166–69 (1992).
23. *See* RESTATEMENT (THIRD) OF RESTITUTION & UNJUST ENRICHMENT §§ 23, 26 (2011).
24. The following discussion draws on DAGAN, *supra* note 2, at 123–63.

25. *See generally* Russell Hardin, Collective Action 9–10 (1982); Mancur Olson, The Logic of Collective Action: Public Goods and the Theory of Groups 2, 8, 10–11, 21, 51, 60–61 (2d ed. 1971); Michael Taylor, The Possibility of Cooperation 3 (1987).
26. *See* Olson, *supra*, at 41.
27. For more detailed analyses, on which the next two paragraphs draw, see Hanoch Dagan & Michael Heller, The Choice Theory of Contracts 72–76 (2017).
28. *Cf.* Peter Benson, Justice in Transactions: A Theory of Contract Law 23, 123–24, 132–34, 142 (2019). In theory, they could alternatively argue that the private law doctrines that address strategic behavior in the context of joint projects and common endeavors embody a norm against abuse of rights, particularly the right to independence. But such an argument, we suspect, would inevitably involve stretching the norm against abuse of rights beyond its appropriate scope as a *limiting* principle.
29. *See* Dagan, *supra* note 2, at 135.
30. Brudner, *supra* note 7, at 250.
31. *See* Ariel Porat, *Private Production of Public Goods: Liability for Unrequested Benefits*, 108 Mich. L. Rev. 189, 206 (2009).
32. Graham Virgo, The Principles of the Law of Restitution 81 (2d ed. 2006). *See also* Mitchell McInnes, *Enrichment, in* Research Handbook on Unjust Enrichment and Restitution, *supra* note 3, at 238.
33. *Compare* Lord Goff of Chieveley & Gareth Jones, The Law of Restitution 25 (Gareth Jones ed., 6th ed. 2002) *with* Peter Birks, *supra* note 4, at 121–24.
34. *See supra* Chapter 4 text accompanying note 20.
35. *See* Hanoch Dagan & Michael A. Heller, *The Liberal Commons*, 110 Yale L.J. 549, 611–13 (2001). Although the line between improvement and preservation is often blurry, a defendant's objection to investing in an improvement is more likely to express her genuine valuation rather than be a strategic holdout.
36. *See* Janus v. Am. Fed'n of State, Cty., & Mun. Emps., Council 31, 138 S. Ct. 2448 (2018).
37. *See, e.g.*, Joseph Fishkin & William E. Forbath, The Anti-Oligarchy Constitution: Reconstructing The Economic Foundations of American Democracy 441–47 (2022).

Chapter 12

1. *See supra* Chapter 2 text accompanying notes 3–6.
2. *See* Joseph W. Singer, No Freedom Without Regulation: The Hidden Lesson of the Subprime Crisis 74, 125 (2015).
3. *See supra* Chapter 5 text accompanying notes 49–55.
4. *See* John Fabian Witt, The Accidental Republic 202, 206 (2004). For a somewhat parallel observation made by tort theorists, *see* Alan Brudner, The Unity of the Common Law 315 (2d ed. 2013 with Jennifer M. Nadler); John C. P. Goldberg & Benjamin C. Zipursky, Torts 267, 394–95 (2010); Ernest J. Weinrib, The Idea of Private Law 210 (1995).
5. *See, e.g.*, Iowa Code § 85.20 (2016).
6. *See, e.g.*, Delgado v. Phelps Dodge Chino, Inc., 34 P.3d 1148, 1156 (N.M. 2001).
7. *See, e.g.*, Smith v. W. Elec. Co., 643 S.W.2d 10, 12–13 (Mo. Ct. App. 1982).
8. *See, e.g.*, La. R.S. 23:1032(B); *see also* Johns-Manville Prod. Corp. v. Contra Costa Superior Court, 612 P.2d 948, 956 (Cal. 1980).
9. *See* Avihay Dorfman, *What is the Point of the Tort Remedy*, 55 Am. J. Juris. 105, 153–62 (2010).
10. *See* Avihay Dorfman, *Assumption of Risk, After All*, 15 Theoretical Inq. L. 293 (2014) on which the remainder of this section relies.
11. 152 E.R. 402 (1842).
12. *See* Hanoch Dagan & Roy Kreitner, 52 *The Other Half of Regulatory Theory*, 52 Conn. L. Rev. 605 (2020), on which both this and the next section heavily draw.
13. *See* OSHA's Field Operations Manual 6–1 (2015), available at: https://www.osha.gov/OshDoc/Directive_pdf/CPL_02-00-159.pdf; Nicholas A. Ashford & Charles C. Caldart, Technology, Law, and the Working Environment 458 (rev. ed. 1996).
14. The qualified language of the text reflects that a comparative institutional analysis may show that an ex post workers' compensation (or tort) approach is in fact more effective in securing employees' fundamental right to safety and health.
15. *See* Charles Noble, Liberalism at Work: The Rise and Fall of OSHA 68, 94 (1986).
16. In fact, its safety provisions reinforce the traditional common law adjudication system via the doctrine of negligence per se. According to his doctrine, the plaintiff can prove breach of duty simply by proving the defendant's breach of safety regulation.

17. This does not imply that OSHA works perfectly. Like other complex bureaucracies, it suffers from delays and distortions due to the influence of interest groups. *See*, *respectively*, Multiple Challenges Lengthen OSHA's Standard Setting, GAO-12-330 (2012), available at: http://www.gao.gov/assets/590/589825.pdf; Noble, *supra* note 15, at 205.
18. 29 U.S.C. § 655(b)(5). Aggregative concerns also affect OSHA's regime as, for example, when it incorporates concerns about the economic burden on small businesses. *See* https://www.osha.gov/dcsp/smallbusiness/sbrefa.html.
19. Gregory C. Keating, *Is Cost-Benefit Analysis the Only Game in Town?*, 91 S. Cal. L. Rev. 195, 231 (2018).
20. *Id.*
21. *See* Jonathan S. Masur & Eric A. Posner, *Against Feasibility Analysis*, 77 U. Chi. L. Rev. 657, 707, 709 (2010).
22. Cass R. Sunstein, *Is OSHA Unconstitutional?*, 94 Va. L. Rev. 1407, 1410 (2008).
23. This principled asymmetry may also explain—and possibly justify—OSHA's reluctance to impose the burden of protection on employees. *Cf.* Note, *OSHA's Feasibility Policy: The Implications of the "Infeasibility" of Respirators*, 129 Harv. L. Rev. 2235 (2016).
24. Keating, *supra* note 19, at 248.
25. Dov A. Waisman, *Reasonable Precaution for the Individual*, 88 St. John's L. Rev. 653, 670 (2014).
26. All About OSHA (2015), available at: https://www.osha.gov/publications/all_about_osha.pdf. *See* Whirlpool Corporation v. Marshall, 445 U.S. 1 (1980).
27. *See* Nicholas A. Ashford & Charles C. Caldart, Technology, Law, and the Working Environment 425–26, 441 (rev. ed. 1996).
28. All About OSHA, *supra* note 26.
29. Ashford & Caldart, *supra* note 27, at 184.
30. *Id.* at 92. *See also* Paul A. Erickson, Practical Guide to Occupational Health and Safety 3 (1994).
31. 29 U.S.C. § 654(a)(1).
32. *See* All About OSHA, *supra* note 26.
33. *See* The Administrative Procedure Act (APA), Pub.L. 79–404, 60 Stat. 237 § 4 (codified at 5 U.S.C. § 553).
34. *See* All About OSHA, *supra* note 26.
35. *See id.*
36. *See* https://www.osha.gov/dop/nacosh/nacosh.html.
37. OSHA's Field Operations Manual, *supra* note 13, at 2–3. Inspections are based on the following priorities: imminent danger, catastrophes, worker complaints and referrals, and follow-up inspections. *See* OSHA Inspections (2002), available at: https://www.osha.gov/Publications/osha2098.pdf.
38. *See* Ashford & Caldart, *supra* note 27, at 96.
39. *See supra* Chapter 3 text accompanying notes 28–32.
40. *See* All About OSHA, *supra* note 26. Unfortunately, given OSHA's limited resources and its lack of an independent regulatory agenda, immigrant (and other non-unionized) workers are still disadvantaged vis-à-vis unionized workers. *See* Jayesh Rathod, *Immigrant Labor and the Occupational Safety & Health Regime; Part I: A New Vision for Workplace Regulation*, 38 N.Y.U Rev. L. & Soc. Change 480, 515–16 (2009).
41. Letter of Arrangement between OSHA and The Department of Foreign Affairs of The Philippines Concerning Workplace Safety and Health Protections Applicable to Filipino Workers in The United States (2012), available at: https://www.osha.gov/international/docs/loa_philippines.pdf. OSHA signed similar agreements with Mexico, Costa Rica, Nicaragua, The Dominican Republic, El Salvador, Guatemala, Honduras, Peru, Ecuador, Brazil, The Philippines, and China. *See* https://www.osha.gov/international/index.html. These agreements contain no commitments from these countries regarding American workers. They thus lack any statist rationale, and can best be explained as a manifestation of the foreign workers' interpersonal human rights. *See infra* Chapter 15.
42. *See* Dagan & Kreitner, *supra* note 12.
43. *See, e.g.*, Robert Baldwin et al., Understanding Regulation: Theory, Strategy, and Practice 15–22 (2d ed. 2012); Cass R. Sunstein, After the Rights Revolution: Reconceiving the Regulatory State 55–63 (1990).
44. A recent White House draft of the pertinent Guidelines seeks to address the distributive aspects of this concern. *See Memorandum for Heads of Executive Departments and Establishments: Guidelines and Discount Rates for Benefit-Cost Analysis of Federal Programs* § 10, https://www.

whitehouse.gov/wp-content/uploads/2023/04/CircularA94.pdf (April 2022). *See also* Jeremy K. Kessler & David E. Pozen, *Working Themselves Impure: A Life Cycle Theory of Legal Theories.* 83 U. Chi. L. Rev. 1819, 1866–68 (2016).
45. About the EEOC: Overview, U.S. Equal Emp. Opportunity Commission, https://www.eeoc.gov/eeoc/index.cfm.
46. *Id.*
47. About FHEO, U.S. Dep't Housing & Urb. Dev., http://portal.hud.gov/hudportal/HUD?src=/program_offices/fair_housing_equal_opp/aboutfheo.

Chapter 13

1. *See* Martin v. Herzog, 126 N.E. 814 (N.Y. 1920).
2. It is not the only one. A horizontal right to free speech is another fundamental right that has not received proper recognition in the law of torts. *See* Avihay Dorfman, Conflict between Equals: Tort Law for a Liberal Society ch. 14 (unpublished manuscript).
3. The reference to third parties must not be interpreted as an attempt to smuggle in the public concerns dominating the existing scholarship on anti-discrimination discussed below, but as a necessary means for determining what counts as just terms of interaction between the pertinent parties. Thus, while traditionalists hold that a seller needs to respect only a buyer's capacity for choice, relational justice theory requires addressing the buyer's traits and ground projects. Eliminating wrongful discrimination, then, implies comparing this seller's treatment of this buyer to her treatment of other (existing and potential) buyers.
4. *Cf.* Andrei Marmor, Foundations of Institutional Reality 137, 149 (2023).
5. *See* 42 U.S.C. § 2000e-2 (employment); 42 U.S.C. § 3604 (housing); 42 U.S.C. § 2000a (public accommodations); 20 U.S.C. § 1681 (discrimination based on sex in federally funded educational institutions), respectively.
6. *See, e.g.*, 42 U.S.C. § 2000e-2. Even the vastly underenforced 42 U.S.C. § 1981 has a "retailish" character, as it prohibits discrimination on the basis of race.
7. *See, e.g.*, Jalal v. Columbia Univ., 4 F. Supp. 2d. 224, 241 (S.D.N.Y. 1998).
8. *See infra* text accompanying note 33.
9. *See* Paula England et al., *Progress toward Gender Equality in the United States Has Slowed or Stalled*, 117 Proc. Nat. Acad'y Sci. 6990, 6995 (2020).
10. *See, e.g.*, Anderson v. Macy's Inc., 2012 WL 3155717 (W.D. Pa., 2012).
11. For more on the non-instrumental value of judge-made law (as opposed to statutory law) of nondiscrimination, see Avihay Dorfman & Alon Harel, Reclaiming the Public 84–91 (2024).
12. As is often the case, this is most clearly evident in the modern Kantian (Toronto) account of private law. For other, libertarian and welfarist accounts, *see, e.g.*, Robert Bork, *Civil Rights—A Challenge*, New Republic (Aug. 31, 1963) at 22; Richard A. Epstein, *Public Accommodations under the Human Rights Act of 1964: Why Freedom of Association Counts as a Human Right*, 66 Stan. L. Rev. 1241, 1260–61 (2014).
13. *See supra* Chapter 8 text accompanying note 23.
14. Joseph William Singer, *Property and Sovereignty Imbricated: Why Religion is not an Excuse to Discriminate in Public Accommodations*, 18 Theoretical Inq. L. 519, 542 (2017). *See also* Creative LLC v. Elenis, 600 U.S. 570, 604-05 (2023) (Sotomayor J., dissenting).
15. *Cf.* Jody Freeman, *Extending Public Law Norms through Privatization*, 116 Harv. L. Rev. 1285 (2003).
16. The Civil Rights Cases, 109 U.S. 3, 37–39 (1883).
17. Packingham v. North Carolina, 137 S. Ct. 1730, 1737 (2017); Robins v. PruneYard Shopping Ctr., 592 P.2d 341 (1979) *aff'd.* 447 U.S. 74 (1980).
18. *See* Richard A. Epstein, *Takings, Exclusivity, and Speech: The Legacy of* PruneYard v. Robins, 64 U. Chi. L. Rev. 21, 39 (1997); Aravind Ganesh, *Wirtbarkeit: Cosmopolitan Right and Innkeeping*, 24 Legal Theory 159, 166–69 (2018).
19. Other possible accounts encounter parallel difficulties. *See* Hanoch Dagan, *Liberal Property: Clarifications and Refinements*, 33 King's L.J. 3, 17–18 (2022).
20. This relationship of entailment can be resisted by adopting a non-absolutist conception of independence. *See generally* Anna Stilz, Territorial Sovereignty: Philosophical Exploration 112, 116 (2019).
21. *See* 3 Bruce Ackerman, We the People: The Civil Rights Revolution 154, 211, 215 (2014).
22. *See, e.g.*, Ontario Human Rights Code, R.S.O. 1990, ch.19.
23. *But see* Martijn W. Hesselink, *Reconstituting the Code of Capital: Could a Progressive European Code of Private Law Help Us Reduce Inequality and Regain Democratic Control?*, 1 Eur. L. Open 316, 337–38 (2022).

24. *See* Tarunabh Khaitan, A Theory of Discrimination Law 201 (2015); Johan van der Walt, The Horizontal Effect Revolution and the Question of Sovereignty 22 (2014).
25. *See, e.g.*, Elizabeth Anderson, The Imperative of Integration chs. 6–7 (2010); Judith N. Shklar, American Citizenship: The Quest for Inclusion 79–88 (1991).
26. *See further* Anthony Sangiuliano, *Against Moralism in Antidiscrimination Law*, 73 U. Toronto L.J. 467 (2023).
27. *See* Tarunabh Khaitan & Sandy Steel, *Wrongs, Group Disadvantage and the Legitimacy of Indirect Discrimination Law*, *in* Foundations of Indirect Discrimination Law 197, 199 (Hugh Collins & Tarunabh Khaitan eds. 2018).
28. For an account of the value (in terms of relational equality) of being duty-bound to respect others as opposed to voluntarily respecting them, see Dorfman, *supra* note 2, at ch. 9.
29. *Contra* Erik Encarnacion, *Discrimination, Mandatory Arbitration, and Courts*, 108 Geo. L.J. 855, 865 (2020).
30. *See* Joseph William Singer, *No Right to Exclude: Public Accommodations and Private Property*, 90 Nw. U. L. Rev. 1283, 1288–93 (1996).
31. *See* Suja A. Thomas, *The Consumer Caste: Lawful Discrimination by Public Businesses*, 109 Cal. L. Rev. 141, 206 (2021). For the prevalence of such "consumer redlining," see Andrea Cann Chandrasekher, The "Good" Starbucks: Consumer Redlining in Large American Chain Stores (unpublished manuscript).
32. *See* Singer, *supra* note 30, at 1290–91.
33. *See respectively* Manisha Padi, *Contractual Inequality*, 120 Mich. L. Rev. 825 (2022); Nancy Leong & Aaron Belzer, *The New Public Accommodations: Race Discrimination in the Platform Economy*, 105 Geo. L.J. 1271, 1276, 1297–98 (2017).
34. *See also* Joseph William Singer, *We Don't Serve Your Kind Here: Public Accommodations and the Mark of Sodom*, 95 B.U. L. Rev. 929 (2015).
35. Political views are absent from major employment discrimination laws such as U.S.'s Title VII and U.K.'s Equality Act 2010.
36. *See, e.g.*, Naomi Chan et al., *Discrimination by Design?*, 51 Ariz. St. L Rev. 1, 54–55 (2019).
37. *Cf.* George Rutherglen, *Concrete or Abstract Conceptions of Discrimination?*, *in* Philosophical Foundations of Discrimination Law 115 (Deborah Hellman & Sophia Moreau eds. 2013).
38. *See, e.g.*, Sophia Moreau, Faces of Inequality: A Theory of Wrongful Discrimination 50–51, 59, 62 (2020).
39. Relatedly, even if (or when) the public ills of current discriminatory practices against marginalized groups are eliminated—say, when residential segregation is fully overcome—discrimination would still be wrongful and must be treated as such. *See* Hanoch Dagan & Roy Kreitner, *The Other Half of Regulatory Theory*, 52 Conn. L. Rev. 605, 649 (2020).
40. *See* Moreau, *supra* note 38, at 191, 227.
41. *See supra* Chapter 3 text accompanying notes 51–57.
42. There is some overlap between our account and Frankfurt's account of the wrong of disrespect as "deal[ing] with [a person] as though he is not what he actually is." Harry Frankfurt, *Equality and Respect*, 64 Soc. Research 3, 12 (1997). That said, we do not share his narrow understanding (and critique) of what is egalitarianism. Moreover, unlike Frankfurt, we deny that wrongful discrimination (disrespect in his case) hinges on the discriminator's intention. *Id.* at 8.
43. *Contra* Kasper Lippert-Rasmussen, *The Badness of Discrimination*, 9 Ethical Theory & Moral Practice 167, 169 (2006).
44. *Contra* John Gardner, *Discrimination: The Good, the Bad, and the Wrongful*, 118 Proc. Aristotelian Soc'y 55, 57–58 (2018); Benjamin Eidelson, Discrimination and Disrespect 17 (2015).
45. Based, in part, on a true story. *See* Claudia Goldin & Cecilia Rouse, *Orchestrating Impartiality: The Impact of "Blind" Auditions on Female Musicians*, 90 Am. Econ. Rev. 715 (2000).
46. Deborah Hellman, When is Discrimination Wrong? (2008).
47. Sophia Moreau, *What Is Discrimination?*, 38 Phil. & Pub. Aff. 143, 147–53 (2010).
48. John Gardner, *Liberals and Unlawful Discrimination*, 9 Oxford J. L. Stud. 1, 18–19, 21 (1989).
49. *Contra* Kasper Lippert-Rasmussen, Born Free and Equal: A Philosophical Inquiry into the Nature of Discrimination 157, 161, 173–74 (2014).
50. As will become clear, we do not discuss the true case of *Masterpiece Cakeshop v. Colorado Civil Rights Commission*, 138 S. Ct. 1719 (2018), but a substantively modified one.
51. For a different discussion of the idea of harmless discrimination, see Adam Slavny & Tom Parr, *Harmless Discrimination*, 21 Legal Theory 100 (2015).
52. Deborah Hellman, *Discrimination and Social Meaning*, *in* The Routledge Handbook of the Ethics of Discrimination 97, 102 (Lippert-Rasmussen ed. 2018).

53. *See* MOREAU, *supra* note 38, at 50–51, 59, 62.
54. *Cf.* CHRISTOPHER L. EISGRUBER & LAWRENCE G. SAGER, RELIGIOUS FREEDOM AND THE CONSTITUTION 52, 59 (2007).
55. *See further* Ontario Human Rights Commission v. Brockie, 222 DLR (4th) 174 (Ont. Div. Ct., 2002) at para. 20, in which a Canadian Court defined the matter in terms of a "conflict of dignities."
56. Moreau, *supra* note 47, at 149.
57. MOREAU, *supra* note 38, at 191. *See also id.* at 83, 84, 85, 91, 94, 105, 109. Moreau argues that being forced to take one's conception of marriage and family life should be seen "as costs." In that light, it is reasonable to claim that these costs (like costs generally) are relative. The cost of being discriminated by one out of two available service providers is entirely different from a case featuring one discriminator out of one-hundred providers—to wit, the latter is virtually costless and, accordingly, nearly harmless.
58. Gardner, *supra* note 48, at 21.
59. *See* Mohr v. Williams, 104 N.W. 12 (Minn. 1905). Note that battery is an intentional tort. As we argue below, the tort of discrimination should go beyond intentional wrongdoing to capture unintentional acts of discrimination.
60. *See generally* Kenneth Arrow, *The Theory of Discrimination* (Princeton Univ. Indus. Rel. Working Paper, No. 30A, 1971); Michelle J. Budig & Paula England, *The Wage Penalty for Motherhood*, 66 AM. SOCIO. REV. 204, 208–10 (2001).
61. A decision is made "on the basis" of specific data if, in the case of refusing to hire the person, such data is a but-for cause for disqualifying the candidate.
62. Algorithmic decision-making raises further challenges, which we cannot address here.
63. *See* Dorfman, *supra* note 2, at ch. 6.
64. Some readers may object to the analogy between discrimination and negligence, given the former's deep embeddedness in broader public circumstances. Insofar as this objection denies the free-standing significance of discrimination's interpersonal wrongness, we of course disagree. We also dispute the other possible reading of this objection, in which negligence is immune from such embeddedness. As we clarify in Chapter 4, private law—even in its narrow, traditionalist domain—is always embedded in the background regime and thus inevitably affected by its features.
65. The defense of undue hardship provides an instantiation of the standard of reasonable accommodation. For more on this instantiation, in the context of employers' Title VII duty of reasonable accommodation, see Groff v. DeJoy, 600 U.S. 447, 468–70 (2023).
66. *See supra* Chapter 3 text following note 71.
67. *See supra* Chapter 4 text accompanying note 18.
68. *Contra* 303 Creative LLC v. Elenis, 600 U.S. 570, 587, 595 (2023).
69. The discussion in this paragraph draws on Avihay Dorfman, *When, and How, Does Property Matter?*, 72 U. TORONTO L.J. 81, 111–12 (2022).
70. *See, e.g.*, Mrs. Murphy's exemption in the Fair Housing Act (42 U.S.C. § 3603(b)(2)). Note that the example in the main text below delineates a narrower basis for exemption than the one articulated in this Act.
71. *Cf.* Fair Housing Council of San Fernando Valley v. Roommate.com, 666 F.3d 1216 (9th Cir. 2012).
72. Two caveats are in order. The excellence quality of a particular practice should be defined narrowly to include its core aspects only. Thus, professional ballet dancers may be required (by the internal demands of the practice) to a certain dress code while on stage; however, they may not be subject to discrimination for their dress-related choices elsewhere. Moreover, some excellence-striving practices may be (and perhaps have always been) corrupt or seriously deficient, in which case our argument for excellence-based exemption does not apply.
73. We leave for another occasion the question of whether religious and other expressive associations are part of the first or the second type of practices that we identify in the text (or somewhere in between).
74. The cautious language of the text is intentional: if—but only if—the *sole* reason for rejecting an otherwise perfectly qualified candidate is the need to increase the representation of members from disenfranchised groups, this candidate has a prima facie complaint for relational injustice. This claim then needs to be considered against the distributive justice premises of the pertinent affirmative action program, along the lines of the main text following this footnote.
75. *Contra* Students for Fair Admission, Inc. v. President and Fellows of Harvard College, 600 U.S. 181 (2023).
76. *See, e.g.*, International Brotherhood of Teamsters v. United States, 431 U.S. 324, 335 n.15 (1977); KHAITAN, *supra* note 24, at 151–52.

77. *See* David Benjamin Oppenheimer, *Negligent Discrimination*, 141 U. PENN. L. REV. 899, 919 (1993).
78. *See, e.g.*, Deborah Hellman, *Indirect Discrimination and the Duty to Avoid Compound Injustice*, *in* PHILOSOPHICAL FOUNDATIONS, *supra* note 37, at 105; EIDELSON, *supra* note 44, at 19; MATT CAVANAGH, AGAINST EQUALITY OF OPPORTUNITY 199 (2002); IRIS YOUNG, JUSTICE AND THE POLITICS OF DIFFERENCE 196 (1990).
79. The connection between wrongful discrimination and negligence is not new. *See* Oppenheimer, *supra* note 77, at 933; Richard Thompson Ford, *Rethinking Rights After the Second Reconstruction*, 123 YALE L.J. 2942, 2945 (2014). *See also* MOREAU, *supra* note 38, at 205. As the main text mentions and the discussion of the injury element clarifies, however, our account also draws an important distinction between the (proposed) tort of discrimination and that of negligence.
80. Note, moreover, that this characterization also captures discrimination based on proxies—for instance, denying service or charging higher prices relying on zip code addresses is often an indirect way to segregate people according to race or socio-economic condition.
81. *See* text accompanying *infra* notes 88–89.
82. Cheryl Pritlove et al., *The Good, the Bad, and the Ugly of Implicit Bias*, 393 LANCET 502, 502 (2019).
83. *See* Anthony G. Greenwald & Linda Hamilton Krieger, *Implicit Bias: Scientific Foundations*, 94 CAL. L. REV. 945 (2006).
84. *See supra* Chapter 2 text accompanying notes 56–57.
85. *See* Avihay Dorfman, *The Limited Case for Discrimination's Legality*, 83 L. & CONTEMP. PROB. 175 (2020), on which this paragraph draws.
86. *See further id.* at 189–91.
87. *See* IAN AYRES, PRIVATE PREJUDICE? UNCONVENTIONAL EVIDENCE ON RACE AND GENDER DISCRIMINATION 127–36 (2001). *See also* Lee Anne Fennel, *Searching for Fair Housing*, 97 B.U.L. REV. 349 (2017); Saul Levmore, *Title VII to Tinder: Law's Antidiscrimination Asymmetry and Occasional Market Superiority*, 68 ALA. L. REV. 877 (2017); Katherine T. Bartlett & Mitu Gulati, *Discrimination by Customers*, 102 IOWA L. REV. 223 (2016).
88. Foreseeability is most famously associated with the duty and proximate cause elements of the prima facie case of negligence, but can also inform the analysis of the breach element. The *locus classicus* is *Adams v. Bullock*, 128 N.E. 93 (N.Y. 1919).
89. *Cf.* Lihi Yona, *Identity at Work*, 43 BERKELEY J. EMP. & LAB. L. 139 (2022) (discussing claims raised by asexuals, poor whites, and fat people).
90. *See* EYAL ZAMIR & BARAK MEDINA, LAW, ECONOMICS, AND MORALITY 255 (2010).
91. *See* Dagan & Kreitner, *supra* note 39, at 648.
92. *See supra* Chapter 7 text accompanying note 29–30.
93. Causation in anti-discrimination law has developed its own standards of proof and, most significantly, rules on burden allocation with respect to causation (i.e., shifting the burden of persuasion in "mix-motive" cases of employment discrimination). *See* Price Waterhouse v. Hopkins, 490 U.S. 228 (1989).
94. We do not argue that this or the other doctrine does not require some revisions, and we certainly do not agree with the Supreme Court's restrictive understanding of the common law doctrine of causation in tort law. *See further* Sandra F. Sperino, *The Causation Canon*, 108 IOWA L. REV. 703 (2023); Sandra F. Sperino, *Discrimination Law: The New Franken-Tort*, 65 DEPAUL L. REV. 721 (2016); Dorfman, *supra* note 2, at ch. 13. Rather, we argue that this doctrine, properly conceived, offers a sensible starting platform.
95. *See further* John C. P. Goldberg & Benjamin C. Zipursky, *The Moral of* MacPherson, 146 U. PA. L. REV. 1733 (1998).

Chapter 14

1. *See supra* Chapter 9 text accompanying notes 22–26.
2. JOHN RAWLS, A THEORY OF JUSTICE 277 (1971).
3. According to Ernest Weinrib's reconstruction of Kant, the alleviation of poverty is a task of the state in its public law function since, if it is left to the voluntary choice of individuals, the poor will necessarily remain unfree. *See* ERNEST J. WEINRIB, CORRECTIVE JUSTICE 263–96 (2012). This argument suggests that, regarding poverty, it is either public law or charity. We reject this either/or view and defend, instead, the place of private law in establishing private responsibility for poverty alleviation.
4. *See* Sustainable Development Goals, Goal 1: End poverty in all its forms everywhere, available at https://www.un.org/sustainabledevelopment/poverty/. This definition of poverty is used by the

U.S. Federal Government to determine financial eligibility for government programs (for details, see https://aspe.hhs.gov/topics/poverty-economic-mobility/poverty-guidelines/prior-hhs-poverty-guidelines-federal-register-references/2021-poverty-guidelines), as well as by the World Bank and other organizations tasked with alleviating poverty in developing countries.

5. Adam Smith, Inquiry into the Nature and Causes of the Wealth of Nations, Bk. 5, Ch. II, Part II, Art. IV p. 522 (2017). Ongoing debates involving policy makers and economists have focused on the right way of translating Smith's qualitative baseline into a quantitative measure. *See* Martin Ravallion & Shaohua Chen, *Weakly Relative Poverty*, 93(4) Rev. Econ. & Stat. 1251, 1251 (2011).
6. *See* Smith, *supra*.
7. Smith articulated his account of poverty more than a century before Thorstein Veblen developed his theory of conspicuous consumption. *See* Thorstein Veblen, The Theory of the Leisure Class (1899). We do not take up the normative question re the permissibility of Veblen goods.
8. This reading fits the views of democratic egalitarians who claim that, rather than distributive justice, we should (publicly) pursue relational equality. *See supra* Chapter 2 text accompanying notes 39–42.
9. Our endorsement of the relational conception is normative rather than exegetical. We do not claim that it necessarily reflects Smith's actual view.
10. On law's irreducible role in constructing the market, see Hanoch Dagan et al., *The Law of the Market*, 83 L. & Contemp. Probs. i (2020).
11. *But cf.* G. A. Cohen, On the Currency of Egalitarian Justice, and other Essays in Political Philosophy 174 (2011) (arguing that poverty is different from other conditions of disadvantage and that while insufficient "intelligence or strength" restricts the ability to use one's freedom, poverty "induces the lack of freedom" itself).
12. *See supra* Chapter 4 text accompanying note 31.
13. *Cf.* Jedediah Britton-Purdy et al., *Building a Law-And-Political-Economy Framework: Beyond The Twentieth-Century Synthesis*, 129 Yale L.J. 1784 (2020).
14. *Cf.* Seana Valentine Shiffrin, *Egalitarianism, Choice-Sensitivity, and Accommodation, in* Reason and Value: Themes from the Moral Philosophy of Joseph Raz 270 (R. Jay Wallace et al. eds., 2004).
15. G.A. Cohen has further argued that poverty is not merely a limitation on freedom (and, by implication, on self-determination), but rather a lack of freedom-from-interference itself. Cohen, *supra* note 11, at 175–76. However, Cohen's argument for identifying poverty with the very absence of freedom relies on his view, which we (and many others) do not share, stating that the institution of private property distributes "rights of interference." *Id.* at 176.
16. *See supra* Chapter 3 text accompanying notes 73–77.
17. *Cf.* Elizabeth S. Anderson, *What is the Point of Equality*, 109 Ethics 287, 314 (1999).
18. It is unclear whether Artificial Intelligence and other sophisticated technologies of information gathering and processing could eliminate these effects and at what moral and other costs. Considering the operational challenges of accommodating the poor in an AI age, therefore, is beyond the scope of our argument.
19. *See* Stefano DellaVigna & Matthew Gentzkow, *Uniform Pricing in US Retail Chains*, 134 Q. J. Econ. 2011 (2019). Non-uniform pricing is certainly on display at the *sector* level—consider discount grocery chains in poor areas versus luxury groceries in high income areas.
20. On the historical practice of redlining, see Kristen B. Crossney & David W. Bartelt, *The Legacy of the Home Owners' Loan Corporation*, 16 House Pol'y Debate 547, 552–56 (2005).
21. Reverse redlining is the related practice of subjecting people living in redlined areas to stringent requirements, say, by enacting predatory lending procedures.
22. *Cf.* Consumer Financial Protection Bureau et al. v. Hudson City Savings Bank, F. S. B., 2:15-CV-07056 (D.N.J.).
23. *Cf.* Fair Housing Act, 42 U.S.C. §§ 3610–11; Equal Credit Opportunity Act, 15 U.S.C. §§ 1691C.
24. Our argument assumes, quite reasonably we believe, that higher education is not a luxurious good as it is valuable, and highly consequential, to being a self-determining and substantively equal person in our world.
25. *See* Rupert Wilkinson, Aiding Students, Buying Students 18–24 (2005).
26. *See* American with Disabilities Act, 42 U.S.C. § 12182(a) (1990).
27. *Id.* at § 12181 (7)(J).
28. Religious schools are entitled by the First Amendment and by certain statutes to some measure of preferential treatment, typically in the form of exemptions from generally applicable laws. *See, e.g.*, *id.* at § 121827 (1990). This approach appears to be inconsistent with the demands of relational

justice regarding physical disability and, by extension, poverty. Considering the pertinence of the free exercise of religion exceeds the scope of our current argument.

29. *See* Juliet Brodie et al., Poverty Law, Policy, and Practice 413–14, 425–31 (2d ed. 2020); Paula A. Franzese & Stephanie J. Beach, *Promises Still to Keep: Fair Housing Act Fifty Years Later*, 40 Cardozo L. Rev. 1207, 1225–35 (2019); Stewart E. Sterk, *Incentivizing Fair Housing*, 101 B.U. L. Rev. 1607 (2021).
30. *See* S. Burlington Cty. NAACP v. Twp. of Mount Laurel, 336 A.2d 713, 743–44 (N.J. 1975), *app. dis. and cert. den.*, 423 U.S. 808 (1975).
31. The New Jersey Fair Housing Act, N.J. Rev. Stat. 52:27D-311 (2013). *See also* Laura M. Padilla, *Reflections on Inclusionary Housing and a Renewed Look at its Vitality*, 23 Hofstra L. Rev. 539, 568 (1995).
32. *See* Robert C. Ellickson, *The Irony of "Inclusionary Zoning,"* 54 S. Cal. L. Rev. 1167, 1170 (1981).
33. *See* Latham & Watkins LLP, A Survey of Pro Bono Practices and Opportunities in 84 Jurisdictions 687 (2016) available at https://www.lw.com/admin/Upload/Documents/Global%20Pro%20Bono%20Survey/A-Survey-of-Pro-Bono-Practices-and-Opportunities.pdf.
34. Cynthia Adcock, *Shaped by Educational, Professional, and Social Crises: The History of Law Student Pro Bono Service*, *in* Private Lawyers & The Public Good 25, 30 (Robert Granfield et al. eds., 2009).
35. *See* ABA Opinion 191 (1939) cited in ABA Compendium of Professional Responsibility Rules and Standards 232 n.42 (2008).
36. *See* Model Rules for Professional Conduct 6.1 (2020) available at https://www.americanbar.org/groups/professional_responsibility/publications/model_rules_of_professional_conduct/rule_6_1_voluntary_pro_bono_publico_service/. *See also* NY's Lawyer Code of Professional Responsibility EC 2–34 (formerly 2-25) (2007).
37. *See* Deborah L. Rhode, *Rethinking the Public in Lawyers' Public Service: Strategic Philanthropy and the Bottom Line*, 77 Fordham L. Rev. 1435, 1445 (2009).
38. *See* Latham & Watkins LLP, *supra* note 33, at 690. *See also* Steven A. Boutcher, *The Institutionalization of Pro Bono in Large Law Firms*, *in* Private Lawyers & The Public Good, *supra* note 34, at 135, 136–40.
39. Inclusionary employment along the lines mentioned in the text—namely, professional training—is a familiar idea in some federal and state legislation, but appears in both as a public law technique of incentivizing the private sector through grants or tax incentives. For federal law, see respectively Workforce Innovation and Opportunity Act, 29 U.S.C. §§ 3101–3361 & I.R.C. § 51. For examples of state law, see, e.g., Iowa Admin. Code r. 701–502.11(422); La. Stat. Ann. § 47:297.13; Md. Educ. Code Ann. § 21–309 (West).
40. *See* The Federal Emergency Medical Treatment and Labor Act, 42 U.S.C.A. §§ 1395dd & 1395cc.
41. Not all structural strategies help to promote relational justice. Consider the case of rent control, which is *not* a corollary of price control but rather a scheme for regulating such aspects as tenant eviction, lease termination, and rent-stabilization (as opposed to rent-setting). Housing is a basic good in our view and, therefore, warrants specific accommodation. One scheme noted above is affordable housing programs, and another could come in the form of imposing a *pied-à-terre* tax on dwellings used by their owners only infrequently (say, for the occasional vacation). Yet another is rent control. There are different ways of implementing a rent control scheme for dwellings, and the variance between housing markets across cities and even states only complicates the assessment of its success and failure even further. However, *if* it turns out that not only does this scheme usually decrease dwellings supply, thus substantially increasing rents for everyone (*see, e.g.*, Rebecca Diamond et al., *The Effects of Rent Control Expansion on Tenants, Landlords, and Inequality: Evidence from San Francisco*, 109 Am. Econ. Rev. 3365 (2019)), but that it also undermines relational justice by unintendedly protecting well-to-do tenants from their landlords, the case for insisting on this form of accommodation is weakened. Its failure justifies abandoning rent control as we know it.
42. *See Adkins v. Children's Hospital*, 261 U.S. 525, 545 (1923).
43. *See* Jerold L. Waltman, Minimum Wage Policy in Great Britain and the United States 8–11 (2009); David Neumark & William Wascher, *Minimum Wages and Low-Wage Workers: How Well Does Reality Match the Rhetoric?*, 92 Minn. L. Rev. 1296, 1302–03 (2008).
44. *See* Fair Labor Standards Act of 1938, 29 U.S.C. § 206; West Coast Hotel v. Parrish, 300 U.S. 379 (1937).
45. For an early, and classic, critique, see George J. Stigler, *The Economics of Minimum Wage Legislation*, 36 Am. Econ. Rev. 358 (1946). A celebrated empirical study found that a relatively modest increase in minimum wage need not reduce employment. *See* David Card & Alan B.

Krueger, *Minimum Wage and Employment: A Case Study of the Fast Food Industry in New Jersey and Pennsylvania*, 84 AM. ECON. REV. 772 (1994). *See also* Arindrajit Dube, *Minimum Wages and the Distribution of Family Incomes*, 11 AM. ECON. J. 268 (2019). The opportunity cost of cutting low-skilled jobs may decline still further with the growing availability of jobs automation. *See* Grace Lordan & David Neumark, *People versus Machines: The Impact of Minimum Wages on Automatable Jobs*, 52 LABOUR ECON. 40, 44–45 (2018).

46. *See, e.g.*, Daniel Shaviro, *The Minimum Wage, the Earned Income Tax Credit, and Optional Subsidy Policy*, 64 U. CHIC. L. REV. 405 (1997).
47. RAWLS, *supra* note 2, at 277. *See also* Anne L. Alstott, *Work vs. Freedom: A Liberal Challenge to Employment Subsidies*, 108 YALE L.J. 967 (1999).
48. *See* Noah D. Zatz, *The Minimum Wage as a Civil Rights Protection: An Alternative to Antipoverty Arguments?*, 2009 U. CHI. LEGAL F. 1 (2009).
49. *See* Anderson, *supra* note 17, at 325. *See also* Brishen Rogers, *Justice at Work: Minimum Wage Laws and Social Equality*, 92 TEXAS L. REV. 1543, 1565 (2014). Rogers' understanding of "social equality" can also be interpreted in a way that ties it to our account of relational justice. *See id.* at 1562, 1594.
50. *See* G.A. Res. 217 (III) A, Universal Declaration of Human Rights, art. 23(3) (Dec. 10, 1948).
51. Are unpaid internships and other forms of volunteering permissible? We leave this question for another occasion. The category of internship or of volunteering comprises many cases and raises substantive questions not only about the nature of employment but also about the meaning of work itself.
52. RAWLS, *supra* note 2, at 277.
53. *See further* BRODIE ET AL., *supra* note 29, at 360–61, 264–66.
54. An analogous case in point is the doctrine of undue hardship in the American with Disabilities Act. *See* 42 U.S.C. § 12111(10)(B) (2018); 29 C.F.R. § 1630.2(p)(2)(v) (2018); EEOC, Enforcement Guidance: Reasonable Accommodation and Undue Hardship Under the Americans with Disabilities Act (2002), https://www.eeoc.gov/laws/guidance/enforcement-guidance-reasonable-accommodation-and-undue-hardship-under-ada.
55. *See Javins v. First Nat. Realty Corp.*, 428 F.2d 1071, 1074 (D.C. Cir. 1970).
56. *See* Jonathan M. Purver, Annotation, *Modern Status of Rules as to Existence of Implied Warranty of Habitability or Fitness for Use of Leased Premises*, 40 A.L.R.3d 646 § 5a (2018).
57. For more on the law's characterization of these inequalities, see *Javins*, 428 F.2d at 1079; Green v. Superior Court, 10 Cal.3d 616, 625 (1974).
58. *See, e.g.*, Cass R. Sunstein, *Paradoxes of the Regulatory State*, 57 U. CHI. L. REV. 407, 422–23 (1990); Richard Craswell, *Passing on the Costs of Legal Rules: Efficiency and Distribution in Buyer-Seller Relationships*, 43 STAN. L. REV. 361, 376–77 (1991). For a recent assessment of the doctrine in action, see Paula A. Franzese et al., *The Implied Warranty of Habitability Lives: Making Real the Promise of Landlord-Tenant Reform*, 69 RUTGERS U.L. REV. 1, 5, 23, 30 (2016). For the distributive justice case for the implied warranty of habitability, see Bruce Ackerman, *Regulating Slum Housing Markets on Behalf of the Poor: On Housing Codes, Housing Subsidies and Income Redistribution Policy*, 80 YALE L.J. 1093, 1195 (1971); Anthony T. Kronman, *Paternalism and the Law of Contracts*, 92 YALE L.J. 763, 774 (1983); GREGORY S. ALEXANDER & EDUARDO M. PEÑALVER, AN INTRODUCTION TO PROPERTY THEORY 126–27 (2012).
59. *See* Neil K. Komesar, *Return to Slumville: A Critique of the Ackerman Analysis of Housing Code Enforcement and the Poor*, 82 YALE L.J. 1175 (1973); David A. Super, *The Rise and Fall of the Implied Warranty of Habitability*, 99 CAL. L. REV. 389, 461 (2011).
60. *See* JOSEPH W. SINGER, PROPERTY LAW: RULES, POLICES, AND PRACTICES 754 (1993). *See also* Gregory A. Alexander, *Property, Dignity, and Human Flourishing*, 104 CORNELL L. REV. 101, 135–38 (2019). *Cf.* Nadav Shoked, *American Courts' Image of a Tenant*, 117 NW. U.L. REV. 251 (2022).
61. Hilder v. St. Peter, 478 A.2d 202, 208 (Vt. 1984).
62. *See, e.g.*, David Colander, *Galbraith and the Theory of Price Control*, 7 J. POST KAYNESIAN ECON. 30, 38 (1984); Milton Friedman, *From Galbraith to Economic Freedom*, 49 OCCASIONAL PAPERS 12 (1977).
63. *See* JOHN KENNETH GALBRAITH, A THEORY OF PRICE CONTROL: THE CLASSIC ACCOUNT (1980).
64. *See, e.g.*, JEAN TIROLE, THE THEORY OF INDUSTRIAL ORGANIZATION 9 (1988).
65. SMITH, *supra* note 5, at 522–23.
66. Price control also invites strategic behavior from the regulated actors. *See* Paul L. Joskow, *Incentive Regulation in Theory and Practice: Electricity Distribution and Transmission Networks*, *in* ECONOMIC REGULATION AND ITS REFORM: WHAT HAVE WE LEARNED? 291, 295 (Nancy L. Rose ed., 2014).

67. *See* PHILIPPE VAN PARIJS & YANNICK VANDERBORGHT, BASIC INCOME: A RADICAL PROPOSAL FOR A FREE SOCIETY AND A SANE ECONOMY (2017); GUY STANDING, BASIC INCOME AND HOW WE CAN MAKE IT HAPPEN (2017).
68. *See* https://www.fns.usda.gov/pd/overview.
69. National Health Services Act of 2006 § 260.
70. *See* Jordan A. Huffman, *Cause and Effect: A Comparative Analysis on How Allowing Medicare Pharmaceutical Price Negotiations Could Impact Research and the Greater Pharmaceutical Industry*, 34 ARIZ. J. INT'L & COMP. L. 227, 236–40 (2017).
71. *See* The Inflation Reduction Act 2022 (H.R. 5376) §§ 1191–1192. For discussion of non-market methods of determining drug prices see Peter J. Neumann et al., *Drug-Pricing Debate Redux—Should Cost-Effectiveness Analysis Be Used Now to Price Pharmaceuticals?*, 385 N. ENG. J. MED. 1923 (2021).
72. This scheme is largely managed by the Ministry of Economy and Industry. Further details, and up-to-date prices, are available at http://economy.gov.il/English/trade/PriceControl/Pages/Prices.aspx.
73. *See* Yossi Spiegel, *Antitrust Enforcement of the Prohibition of Excessive Prices: The Israeli Experience*, *in* EXCESSIVE PRICING AND COMPETITION LAW ENFORCEMENT 127, 150–51 (Yannis Katsoulacos & Frédéric Jenny eds. 2018).
74. On the special case of rent control, *see supra* note 41.
75. Indeed, although accessible credit is necessary in the relational justice account of poverty alleviation, it is not sufficient: with credit comes debt. Therefore, any comprehensive attempt to accommodate the poor in the laws governing the credit market must also address the potential problem of increasing their debt. *See* Abbye Atkinson, *Borrowing Equality*, 120 COLUM. L. REV. 1403, 1406, 1410, 1446–57 (2020).
76. *Cf.* Mark Gergen, Debt's Challenge to Autonomy Theories of Contract (unpublished manuscript); Dan Largman, Two Visions of Mortgage Law Pt. IV.1 (LL.M. Thesis, Tel Aviv University, 2019).
77. We use the example of opening a small business as opposed to cases of borrowing for purposes of present consumption to preempt the critique that, under some circumstances, accessible credit might have regressive implications for the poor because it involves shifting "an individual's future capital to facilitate present consumption." *See* Abbye Atkinson, *Rethinking Credit as Social Provision*, 71 STAN. L. REV. 1093, 1098 (2019). Although the claim that that "credit of any quality and at any price is of limited benefit to low-income Americans" (*id.* at 1148) is too sweeping, some types of credit transaction (such as payday loans) do tend to undermine the self-determination and equal standing of the poor.
78. *See* Gaylen N. Chandler & Steven H. Hanks, *An Examination of the Substitutability of Founders of Human and Financial Capital in Emerging Business Ventures*, 13 J. BUS. VENTURING 353 (1998); Patrick Musso & Stefano Schiavo, *The Impact of Financial Constraints on Firm Survival and Growth*, 18 J. EVOLUTIONARY ECON. 135 (2008); Robert E. Carpenter & Bruce C. Petersen, *Is the Growth of Small Firms Constrained by Internal Finance?*, 84 REV. ECON. & STAT. 298 (2002); Ari Hyytinen & Otto Toivanen, *Do Financial Constraints Hold Back Innovation and Growth? Evidence on the Role of Public Policy*, 34 RESEARCH POL'Y 1385 (2005), respectively.
79. 12 U.S.C. §§ 2901–2908 (2000). *See also* BRODIE ET AL., *supra* note 29, at 759–60.
80. 12 U.S.C. § 2901(b) (2000).
81. *But see* Michael S. Barr, *Credit Where it Counts: The Community Reinvestment Act and Its Critics*, 80 N.Y.U. L. REV. 513 (2005). For an empirical assessment, see Paul Kaboth, *History and Overview of the Community Reinvestment Act*, 26 J. AFFORDABLE HOUS. & CMT'Y DEV. L. 391 (2017) (collecting data showing that access to both the mortgage lending and small business credit markets has been enhanced by financial institution lending subject to the CRA).
82. *See, e.g.*, Jeffrey M. Lacker, *Neighborhoods and Banking*, 81 ECON. Q. 13, 15–24 (1995).
83. *See* Jonathan R. Macey & Geoffrey P. Miller, *The Community Reinvestment Act: An Economic Analysis*, 79 VA. L. REV. 291, 296 (1993).
84. *Id.* at 296, 312–13, 340.
85. 12 U.S.C. § 2902(2) (2000); 12 U.S.C. § 1813(2) (2010). *See also* Michael Barr, *Concluding Observations on CRA Reform*, 30 HOUSING POL'Y DEBATE 116, 117 (2020).
86. 12 U.S.C. § 2901(b) (2000).
87. 15 U.S.C. § 1691(a)(1).
88. *See* Peter Temin & Hans-Joachim Voth, *Interest Rate Restrictions in a Natural Experiment: Loan Allocation and the Change in the Usury Law in 1714*, 118 ECON. J. 743 (2008). *But see* Eric A. Posner, *Contract Law in the Welfare State: A Defense of the Unconscionability Doctrine, Usury Laws, and Related Limitations on the Freedom to Contract*, 24 J. LEGAL STUD. 283 (1995); Robert Mayer, *When and Why Usury Should be Prohibited*, 116 J. BUS. ETHICS 513 (2013).

89. *See supra* Chapter 9 text accompanying notes 76–77.
90. 15 U.S. Code § 1691(a)(1).
91. The five creditworthiness criteria that bankers commonly consider when making lending decisions are character, capacity, capital, conditions, and collateral. Low-income borrowers often score low on the third. *See* Dev Strischek, *The 5 Cs of Credit*, 91(8) Risk Management Ass'n J 34 (2009).
92. *See* Community Reinvestment Act (CRA) and Interstate Deposit Production Regulations, 12 C.F.R. Subpart B., pt. 25.12 (2001).
93. *Cf.* The Minority Bank Deposit Program, available at https://fiscal.treasury.gov/mbdp/about.html.
94. *See* Americans with Disabilities Act of 1990, 42 U.S.C. § 12112(b)(5)(A) (2012). Another, perhaps even better, solution (available in other jurisdictions) is to use direct subsidies. See Eyal Zamir & Barak Medina, Law, Economics, and Morality 255 (2010).

Chapter 15

1. *See* Abdullahi v. Pfizer, Inc., 562 F.3d 163, 169 (2d Cir. 2009).
2. Lyn K.L. Tjon Soei Len, Minimum Contract Justice: A Capabilities Perspective on Sweatshops and Consumer Contracts 23 (2017).
3. *See* Alexandra Rose Caleca, *The Effects of Globalization on Bangladesh's Ready-Made Garment Industry*, 40 Brook. J. Int'l L. 279, 279 (2014).
4. Naomi Jiyoung Bang, *Unmasking the Charade of the Global Supply Contract*, 35 Hous. J. Int'l L. 255, 271 (2013).
5. *See generally* Smita Narula, *The Global Land Rush: Markets, Rights, and the Politics of Food*, 49 Stan. J. Int'l L. 101 (2013).
6. *See* Ward Anseeuw et al., Transnational Land Deals for Agriculture in the Global South 39, 41 (2012).
7. Olivier DeSchutter, *The Green Rush: The Global Race for Farmland and the Rights of Land Users*, 52 Harv. Int'l L.J. 504, 528 (2011).
8. Other routes have also been pursued or suggested, such as seeking the enforcement of corporate social responsibility codes or the invalidation of consumer contracts, which implicate transnational wrongs. *See, e.g.*, Anna Beckers, Enforcing Corporate Social Responsibility Codes—On Global Self-Regulation and National Private Law (2015); Len, *supra* note 2.
9. Gunther Teubner, *The Anonymous Matrix: Human Rights Violations by "Private" Transnational Actors* 69 Mod. L. Rev. 327, 329 (2006); *see also, e.g.*, Aharon Barak, *Constitutional Human Rights and Private Law*, 3 Rev. Const. Stud. 218, 221 (1996).
10. *See International Military Tribunal (Nuremberg), Judgment and Sentences*, 41 Am. J. Int'l L. 173 (1947).
11. Special Representative of the Secretary-General, *Protect, Respect and Remedy: a Framework for Business and Human Rights*, U.N. Doc. A/HRC/8/5 (2008), at 5–6 ("The Framework").
12. *Id.* at 4.
13. Special Representative of the Secretary-General, *Guiding Principles on Business and Human Rights: Implementing the United Nations "Protect, Respect and Remedy" Framework*, U.N. Doc. A/HRC/17/31 (2011), at 13, 16 ("The U.N. Guiding Principles").
14. The Framework, *supra* note 11, at 8, 16.
15. The U.N. Guiding Principles, *supra* note 13, at 4. *See also* John Gerard Ruggie et al., *Ten Years After: From UN Guiding Principles to Multi-Fiduciary Obligations*, 6 Bus. & Hum. Rights J. 181, 192–93 (2021).
16. Andrew Clapham, Human Rights Obligations of Non-State Actors 546 (2006).
17. Jean Thomas, Public Rights, Private Relations 8 (2015).
18. Jennifer A. Zerk, Multinational and Corporate Social Responsibility 28 (2006).
19. Hugh Collins, *The Challenge Presented by Fundamental Rights to Private Law*, *in* Private Law in The 21st Century 213, 223, 234–35 (Kit Barker et al. eds., 2017).
20. David McClean et al., Morris: The Conflict of Laws 47 (8th ed. 2012).
21. Monard G. Paulsen & Michael I. Sovern, *"Public Policy" in the Conflict of Laws*, 56 Colum. L. Rev. 969, 969 (1956).
22. *See respectively* David Clifford Burger, *Transnational Public Policy as a Factor in Choice of Law Analysis*, 5 N.Y.L. Sch. J. Int'l & Comp. L. 367, 369, 376 (1984); Martin Wolff, Private International Law 182–83 (2d ed. 1950); Arthur Nussbaum, *Public Policy and the Political*

Crisis in the Conflict of Laws, 49 YALE L.J. 1027, 1037, 1048 (1940); Paulsen & Sovern, *supra* note 21, at 981.

23. *See* Moritz Renner, *Towards a Hierarchy of Norms in Transnational Law*, 26 J. INT'L ARB. 533, 543 (2009); Moritz Renner, *Private Justice, Public Policy: The Constitutionalization of International Commercial Arbitration, in* INTERNATIONAL ARBITRATION & GLOBAL GOVERNANCE 117, 123–24, 130–33 (Walter Mattli & Thomas Dietz eds., 2014).
24. Veerle Van Den Eeckhout, *Promoting Human Rights within the Union: The Role of European Private International Law*, 14 EUR. L.J. 105, 109–10, 113, 119 (2008).
25. Renner, *Private Justice*, *supra* note 23, at 131.
26. *See* Pierre Lalive, *Transnational (or Truly International) Public Policy and International Arbitration, in* COMPARATIVE ARBITRATION PRACTICE AND PUBLIC POLICY IN ARBITRATION 257, 282, 293 (Pieter Sanders ed., 1987).
27. *Id.* at 306–07.
28. *See* Paul Lagarde, *Public Policy*, in 3 INT'L ENCYCLOPEDIA OF COMPARATIVE LAW: PRIVATE INTERNATIONAL LAW 25, 48–50, 53–54 (Kurt Lipstein ed., 1994).
29. *See* Van Den Eeckhout, *supra* note 24, at 112.
30. *See* Horatia Muir Watt, *The Relevance of Private International Law to the Global Governance Debate, in* PRIVATE INTERNATIONAL LAW AND GLOBAL GOVERNANCE 1, 2 (Horatia Muir Watt & Diego P. Fernández Arroyo eds., 2014); Daniela Caruso, *Private Law and State Making in the Age of Globalization*, 39 N.Y.U. J. INT'L L. & POL. 1, 7–8 (2006); Nathan J. Miller, *Human Rights Abuses as Tort Harms: Losses in Translation*, 46 SETON HALL L. REV. 505, 514, 540–43 (2016).
31. *Cf.* Martijn W. Hesselink, *Reconstituting the Code of Capital: Could a Progressive European Code of Private Law Help Us Reduce Inequality and Regain Democratic Control?*, 1 EUR. L. OPEN 316, 337–38 (2022).
32. *See, e.g.*, ROBERT NOZICK, ANARCHY, STATE, AND UTOPIA (1974).
33. *See supra* Chapter 2 text accompanying notes 52–56 and Chapter 3 note 33.
34. *See* JEREMY BENTHAM, THE THEORY OF LEGISLATION 113 (R. Hildreth trans., 2d ed. 1914); JOHN AUSTIN, THE PROVINCE OF JURISPRUDENCE DETERMINED 15, 18 (London, Richard Taylor 1832).
35. *Cf.* Seana Valentine Shiffrin, *Promising, Intimate Relationships, and Conventionalism*, 117 PHIL. REV. 481, 520 (2008).
36. Joseph Raz, *Why the State?, in* IN PURSUIT OF PLURALIST JURISPRUDENCE 136, 137 (Nicole Roughan & Andrew Halpin, eds. 2017).
37. Thomas Nagel, *The Problem of Global Justice*, 33 PHIL. & PUB. AFF. 114, 140 (2005).
38. We emphasize *certain* non-state institutions to rule out most (perhaps all) private institutions. The distinction between state and non-state institutions does not overlap the one between public and private institutions but rather between different public institutions (a statist and a non-statist one).
39. These concerns were raised by Mitchel Lasser, *Purging Private Law of the State*, 51 CORNELL INT'L L.J. ONLINE 119 (2018).
40. The text also explains why the new role we ascribe to private law in this chapter—as a source of interpersonal human rights—is not meant to replace the rules of public and private international law discussed above. We do not advocate the universal harmonization of private law or the creation of a uniform body of transnational private law. In this respect, our account departs from the (otherwise similar) individual-centered internationalist perspective of private international law, which was most powerfully advanced by Josephus Jitta at the end of the nineteenth and beginning of the twentieth century. *See* Hanoch Dagan & Avihay Dorfman, *Interpersonal Human Rights*, 51 CORNELL INT'L L.J. 361, 381 n.87 (2018). For more on the relationship between our theory and earlier instantiations of *ius gentium*, see Hanoch Dagan & Avihay Dorfman, *Justice, Politics, and Interpersonal Human Rights*, 51 CORNELL INT'L L.J. ONLINE 139, 141–45 (2018).
41. *See supra* Chapter 4 text accompanying notes 25–32.
42. This possibility raises intricate questions re the degree of additional citizen-based interpersonal obligations, which are legitimate in a liberal polity. *Cf.* Seana Valentine Shiffrin, *Paternalism, Unconscionability Doctrine, and Accommodation*, 29 PHIL. & PUB. AFF. 205, 236–50 (2000).
43. Evan Fox-Decent, *Dagan and Dorfman's* Jus Gentium Privatum, 51 CORNELL INT'L L.J. ONLINE 112, 116–18 (2018).
44. This is, arguably, the animating spirit behind some of the arguments developed in JOHN RAWLS, A THEORY OF JUSTICE (1971).
45. JEREMY WALDRON, "PARTLY COMMON TO ALL MANKIND": FOREIGN LAW IN AMERICAN COURTS 28, 35–36 (2012). On its face, *jus gentium's* reliance on domestic legal systems may imply a backdoor return to statism. Notice, however, that the reference here is not to the *authority* of any municipal

system but to these systems as *epistemically* valuable sources for identifying what deserves to be treated as universal principles of (in our case relational) justice.

46. *Id.* at 38–40.
47. *Id.* at 56, 59.
48. *See, e.g.*, Abdul Basir bin Mohamad, *Islamic Tort Law, in* COMPARATIVE TORT LAW: GLOBAL PERSPECTIVES 441 (Mauro Bussani & Anthony J. Sebok eds., 2015).
49. On the humanist foundations of the significance of culture see, e.g., CHAIM GANS, THE LIMITS OF NATIONALISM (2003); on sovereignty, see the sources discussed in Eyal Benvenisti, *Sovereigns as Trustees of Humanity: On the Accountability of States to Foreign Stakeholders*, 107 AM. J. INT'L L. 295, 302–05 (2013).
50. The Framework, *supra* note 11, at 9.
51. THOMAS, *supra* note 17, at 14.
52. *Cf.* Karen Knop, *Citizenship, Public and Private*, 71 L. & CONTEMP. PROBS. 309, 312 (2008).
53. WALDRON, *supra* note 45, at 193.
54. *Cf.* Stacy-Ann Elvy, *A Postcolonial Theory of Spousal Rape: The Caribbean and Beyond*, 22 MICH. J. GENDER & L. 89 (2015).
55. These concerns were raised by Horatia Muir Watt, *On the Moral Commitments of Private Law and the Curbing of Global Corporate Power*, 51 CORNELL INT'L L.J. ONLINE 133 (2018); Ralf Michaels, *The New, Old,* Ius Gentium Privatum, 51 CORNELL INT'L L.J. ONLINE 125 (2018).
56. We do agree that basic concepts of private law—notably property—have been abused. *See, e.g.*, Martii Koskenniemi, *Empire and International Law: The Real Spanish Contribution,* 61 U. TORONTO L.J. 1 (2011). Abuses, however, should be treated as products of a "distorted and selective application" of an ideal. Arthur Ripstein, *Distinctions of Power and the Power of Distinctions: A Response to Professor Koskenniemi*, 61 U. TORONTO L.J. 37, 39, 41 (2011). For an account of the value of property, *see* Hanoch Dagan & Avihay Dorfman, *The Human Right to Private Property,* 18 THEORETICAL INQ. L. 391 (2017). *See also* HANOCH DAGAN, A LIBERAL THEORY OF PROPERTY (2021).
57. ISAIAH BERLIN, *The Pursuit of the Ideal, in* THE CROOKED TIMBER OF HUMANITY: CHAPTERS IN THE HISTORY OF IDEAS 1, 11 (Henry Hardy ed., 1991).
58. *See* DUNCAN KENNEDY, A CRITIQUE OF ADJUDICATION 109–13, 147–48, 155 (1997); Gary Peller, *Reason and the Mob: The Politics of Representation*, 2 TIKKUN 28, 92 (1987); Gary Peller, *The Metaphysics of American Law*, 73 CAL. L. REV. 1151, 1152, 1155 (1985).
59. *See supra* Chapter 1 text accompanying note 12.
60. 28 U.S.C. § 1350 (2012).
61. *See* BEN GOLDACRE, BAD PHARMA: HOW DRUG COMPANIES MISLEAD DOCTORS AND HARM PATIENTS 118 (2012).
62. Oona A. Hathaway et al., *Has the Alien Tort Statute Made a Difference: A Historical, Empirical, and Normative Assessment*, 107 CORNELL L. REV. 1205, 1208 (2022).
63. *Pfizer*, 562 F.3d 163, 213.
64. *Id.* at 176.
65. *See id.* at 213.
66. *Id.* at 194–95.
67. *Id.* at 176, 185.
68. Although civil law tradition employs a different set of legal concepts, it recognizes a duty against committing battery and imposes liability for failing to meet that duty. *See, e.g.*, BÜRGERLICHES GESETZBUCH ("B.G.B.") [German Civil Code] § 823.
69. We hold that the question discussed in the main text poses the most crucial challenge to the elaboration of a transnational tort of battery. But other questions (concerning the burden of proof, the meaning of intent, affirmative defenses, and so forth) may also arise. Although we cannot do justice to all these questions in this chapter, one concern—dealing with the somewhat complex structural makeup and market dynamism of defendant-corporations—justifies a few comments here. The first worry is that the legal organization of the modern economic firm can sometimes take the form of several divided subsidiaries, incorporated along different jurisdictions. The second worry (of market dynamism) arises in connection with the growing practices of mergers and acquisitions. Both pose a similar threat of liability evasion. A practice of redressing transnational wrongs may face the hurdle of attributing responsibility to a corporation that, formally speaking, is far removed from the actual tortfeasor (the one that pulled the proverbial trigger, as it were). To address this difficulty, we begin by positing the rather uncontroversial proposition that corporations should be held accountable to (at least) the same standards as natural persons. Furthermore, there is no reason to let a corporation off the liability hook just because it has a complex structure. As the case

of tort law's products liability law in the U.S. demonstrates, private law can develop the doctrinal resources to address this issue. To begin with, liability for defective products spans the entire range of actors involved in production and sale, including manufacturers, distributors, and retailers. *See* RESTATEMENT (THIRD) OF TORTS: PRODUCTS LIABILITY § 1 (1998). Moreover, products liability law sets aside the formal discontinuity between the predecessor manufacturer and the successor manufacturer of a defective product; it recognizes the liability of the successor manufacturer for harm caused by defective products sold commercially by its predecessor. *See id.* at § 12. Incorporating these doctrines into transnational private law would require some modifications (to reflect the fact that not all transnational wrongs are product-related). That said, products liability is one of the many doctrinal manifestations of principles and insights in contemporary private law that courts, scholars, policymakers, and NGOs could draw on to develop the practice of transnational private law.

70. *See* Cole v. Hibberd, No. CA94-01-015, 1994 WL 424103, at *2 (Ohio App. 1994)*; but see* Spivey v. Battaglia, 258 So. 2d 815, 817 (Fla. 1972).
71. *See generally* Mauro Bussani & Marta Infantino, *Tort Law and Legal Cultures*, 63 AM. J. COMP. L. 77 (2015).
72. Even H.L.A. Hart, whose celebrated account—in H.L.A. HART, THE CONCEPT OF LAW (1961)—of what law is pays particular attention to secondary rules, makes ample conceptual space for primary rules (especially in his critique of Holmes, Austin, and Kelsen, and in connection with the discussion of international law as law).
73. *Cf.* William L.F. Felstiner et al., *The Emergence and Transformation of Disputes: Naming, Blaming, Claiming*, 15 L. & SOC'Y REV. 631 (1980).
74. *See Commission Proposal for a Directive of the European Parliament and of the Council on Corporate Sustainability Due Diligence and amending Directive (EU) 2019/1937*, COM (2022) 71 final (Feb. 23, 2022), https://eurlex.europa.eu/resource.html?uri=cellar:bc4dcea4-9584-11ec-b4e4-01aa75ed71a1.0001.02/DOC_1&format=PDF. As Oona Hathaway and co-authors note, the directive is "still in flux, but it will likely require all Member States to enact a legal duty to 'ensure that companies conduct human rights and environmental due diligence' in their value chain, including the operations of their subcontractors." Hathaway, *supra* note 62, at 1297.
75. As Debadatta Bose notes, "The process of human rights due diligence is inherently *proactive* rather than *reactive*, so it concerns, at its core, ex ante prevention and mitigation of harm rather than ex post remediation." *See* Debadatta Bose, Human Rights Due Diligence as a Process: Just relationships at its Core (unpublished manuscript).
76. *Cf.* Christopher McCrudden, *A Common Law on Human Rights? Transnational Judicial Conversations on Constitutional Rights*, 20 OXFORD J. LEGAL STUD. 499 (2000); Anne-Marie Slaughter, *A Typology of Transjudicial Communication*, 29 U. RICH. L. REV. 99 (1994); Michael Kirby, *Transnational Judicial Dialogue, Internationalization of Law, and Australian Judges*, 9 MELB. J. INT'L L. 171 (2008); Monica Claes & Maartje de Visser, *Are You Networked Yet? On Dialogues in European Judicial Networks*, 8 UTRECHT L. REV. 100 (2012).
77. *Cf.* Jeremy Waldron, *Human Rights: Universalism or the Integrity of a Common Enterprise?*, 17 (N.Y.U. PUB. LAW & LEGAL THEORY Res. Paper Ser. No. 16-48) (2016) (discussing the "immeasurable educational, psychological, and cultural" importance of giving people "recognized legal terms" in which they can "put their grievances and their outrage").
78. *Cf.* Robert Wai, *Transnational Private Law and Private Ordering in a Contested Global Society*, 46 HARV. INT'L L.J. 471, 482–83 (2005).
79. Roxana Banu, *From The Law of Nations to the Private Law of Mankind*, 51 CORNELL INT'L L.J. ONLINE 101, 105–06 (2018). For a related proposition, where process is crucial for the determination of the pertinent parameters of human rights due diligence, see Bose, *supra* note 75.
80. For our preliminary account regarding the theory's implications on the land grab cases, *see* Dagan & Dorfman, *Interpersonal Human Rights*, *supra* note 40, at 413–15. *See also* Hanoch Dagan, *Property Theory, Essential Resources, and the Global Land Rush*, *in* GOVERNING ACCESS TO ESSENTIAL RESOURCES 81 (Olivier DeSchutter & Katharina Pistor eds., 2015). For some support in the emerging international soft law on these issues, *see* FOOD & AGRIC. ORG. OF THE UNITED NATIONS, *Voluntary Guidelines on the Responsible Governance of Tenure of Land, Fisheries and Forests in the Context of National Food Security* §§ 7.1, 7.3, 10.1, 16.1, 16.2, 16.8, 16.9 (2012). For a preliminary discussion of the highly contested question of whether female circumcision is a violation of bodily integrity or the exercise of a religious practice, see Dagan & Dorfman, *Justice, Politics*, *supra* note 40, at 148–49.
81. *See, e.g.*, Nicholas D. Kristof & Sheryl WuDunn, *Two Cheers for Sweatshops*, N.Y. TIMES, Sept. 2000, http://www.nytimes.com/2000/09/24/magazine/two-cheers-for-sweatshops.html.

82. *See* Hanoch Dagan & Michael Heller, *Can Contract Emancipate? Contract Theory and the Law of Work*, 24 Theoretical Inq. L. 49 (2023).
83. *Cf.* Debra Cohen Maryanov, *Sweatshop Liability: Corporate Codes of Conduct and the Governance of Labor Standards in the International Supply Chain*, 14 Lewis & Clark L. Rev. 397 (2010); Marisa Anne Pagnattaro, *Enforcing International Labor Standards: The Potential of the Alien Tort Claims Act*, 37 Vand. J. Transnat'l L. 203 (2004).
84. Similarly, it may help to fend off the welfarist critique of human rights' due diligence. *See, e.g.*, Gerhard Wagner, *Tort Law and Human Rights, in* Transnational Legal Activism in Global Value Chains 209 (M. Saage-Maaß et al. eds., 2021).

Chapter 16

1. *Cf.* Hanoch Dagan, *The Distributive Foundation of Corrective Justice*, 98 Mich. L. Rev. 138 (1999).
2. As the text implies, we think that claims for democratizing some aspects of private law are largely orthogonal to substantive private law theories, such as ours. *Contra* Arie Rosen, *The Role of Democracy in Private Law*, 2 Oxford Stud. Private L. 211 (2023). At their best, these claims rely on a conception of the person as a justificatory equal, which must presuppose the basic rights to individual self-determination and substantive equality assumed by relational justice. *Cf.* Martijn W. Hesselink, *Private Law Subjects in Citizens' Assemblies: On the Dialects of Private and Public Autonomy in the EU, in* The Future of The Person (Hans-Wolfgang Micklitz & Giuseppe Vettori eds., 2024).
3. *See, e.g.*, Joseph Fishkin & William E. Forbath, The Anti-Oligarchy Constitution: Reconstructing The Economic Foundations of American Democracy 454, 462–63 (2022). *Cf.* Cynthia Estlund, *Is Labor Law Internal or External to Private Law? The View from* Cedar Point, 24 Theoretical Inq. L. 124 (2023).
4. Paul B. Miller, *The New Formalism in Private Law*, 66 Am. J. Jurisp. 175, 175–76 (2022).
5. Andrew Gold et al. eds., *Introduction, in* The Oxford Handbook of New Private Law xiii, xiii (Andrew Gold et al. eds., 2020). *See* Hanoch Dagan & Roy Kreitner, *The Character of Legal Theory*, 96 Cornell L. Rev. 671 (2011).
6. *See* John C.P. Goldberg & Benjamin C. Zipursky, Recognizing Wrongs (2020). *See also* Miller, *supra* note 4.
7. *See supra* Chapter 2 text accompanying notes 14–15. For more detail, see Hanoch Dagan & Avihay Dorfman, *From Civil Recourse to Class Actions: Comments on John Goldberg & Benjamin Zipursky's* Recognizing Wrongs, 27 Jerusalem Rev. Legal Stud. 57 (2023).
8. *See, e.g.*, Miller, *supra* note 4, at 178.
9. 3 Bruce Ackerman, We The People: The Civil Rights Revolution 211 (2014).
10. As well as adjustments that may be needed, as we already acknowledged, in adapting the theory's prescriptions to cases involving corporations on both sides of the interaction and cases involving duties that natural persons owe corporations. Further challenges may come from the increasing significance of AI and big data in social life.
11. *See respectively* Chapter 5 text accompanying notes 12–25, Chapter 6 text accompanying notes 46–49, Chapter 9 text accompanying notes 81–85, and Chapter 11 text accompanying notes 36–37.
12. *See respectively* Chapter 12 text accompanying notes 12–41, Chapter 9 text accompanying notes 100–03, and text accompanying notes 47–49.
13. *See respectively* Chapter 13, Chapter 14 text accompanying notes 42–54, and Chapter 15 text accompanying note 74.
14. *See respectively* Chapter 13, Chapter 14 text accompanying note 39, and Chapter 15 text accompanying notes 30–59.
15. We hope that this book is a significant step forward in the development of the language of relational justice. Many more are called for, however, and we indeed hope that some of the book's readers will be moved to take on this challenge. Some of these steps may bring relational justice theory to bear on doctrines (or areas) we have not covered here. Yet a second category—and maybe there are more—would develop accounts of the various types of relational injustices that private law can (or should, or already does) address. For example, we offered a relatively precise account of discrimination as a form of relational injustice but we do acknowledge that our treatment of exploitation and subordination was more intuitive and that we did not address other forms of relational injustice, such as commodification.

Index

For the benefit of digital users, indexed terms that span two pages (e.g., 52–53) may, on occasion, appear on only one of those pages.

The manufacturer's authorised representative in the EU for product safety is Oxford University Press España S.A. of el Parque Empresarial San Fernando de Henares, Avenida de Castilla, 2 – 28830 Madrid (www.oup.es/en or product.safety@oup.com). OUP España S.A. also acts as importer into Spain of products made by the manufacturer.

www.ingramcontent.com/pod-product-compliance
Ingram Content Group UK Ltd.
Pitfield, Milton Keynes, MK11 3LW, UK
UKHW022114180926
475726UK00014B/161
* 9 7 8 0 1 9 7 9 2 1 4 2 5 *